Chinua Achebe and the Igbo-African World

Chinua Achebe and the Igbo-African World

Between Fiction, Fact, and Historical Representation

Edited by Chima J. Korieh and
Ijeoma C. Nwajiaku

LEXINGTON BOOKS
Lanham • Boulder • New York • London

Published by Lexington Books
An imprint of The Rowman & Littlefield Publishing Group, Inc.
4501 Forbes Boulevard, Suite 200, Lanham, Maryland 20706
www.rowman.com

86-90 Paul Street, London EC2A 4NE

Copyright © 2022 by The Rowman & Littlefield Publishing Group, Inc.

All rights reserved. No part of this book may be reproduced in any form or by any electronic or mechanical means, including information storage and retrieval systems, without written permission from the publisher, except by a reviewer who may quote passages in a review.

British Library Cataloguing in Publication Information Available

Library of Congress Cataloging-in-Publication Data

Library of Congress Control Number: 2021945116
ISBN: 978-1-7936-5269-0 (cloth)
ISBN: 978-1-7936-5271-3 (pbk.)
ISBN: 978-1-7936-5270-6 (electronic)

Contents

Introduction: Chinua Achebe, Writing Culture, and the Politics of
   Representation   1
   Chima J. Korieh and Ijeoma C. Nwajiaku

**PART I: CHINUA ACHEBE AND IGBO-AFRICAN
   REALITIES**   17

Chapter 1: Causality in Selected Cultural Novels by Chinua
   Achebe: Perspectives in Igbo Metaphysics   19
   B. E. Nwigwe

Chapter 2: (Re)Discovering the Igbo Oral Tradition in Chinua
   Achebe's *Things Fall Apart* and Anthills of the Savannah   37
   Alassane Abdoulaye Dia

Chapter 3: Symbols and Imageries in Chinua Achebe's *Things Fall
   Apart*   57
   Nureni Oyewole Fadare

Chapter 4: Igbo Communal Ethos: A Reading of Chinua Achebe's
   Things Fall Apart and Arrow of God   73
   Ijeoma Nwajiaku

Chapter 5: *Things Fall Apart* and Igbo Leadership: Learning and
   Unlearning the Lessons of Okonkwo's Life   91
   N. Tony Nwaezeigwe

Chapter 6: Achebe and the Pedagogy of Indigenous Knowledge
   Systems: Gleanings from *Arrow of God*   111
   Ijeoma C. Nwajiaku

PART II: CHINUA ACHEBE AND POLITICS OF REPRESENTATION — 131

Chapter 7: Chinua Achebe's "'Chi' in Igbo Cosmology": Revisiting a Classic — 133
Chijioke Azuawusiefe

Chapter 8: Discourse, Imagination, and Models of Resistance: Rereading *Arrow of God* — 153
Ifi Amaduime

Chapter 9: The Collision of Asymmetric Civilizations: A Reading of *Things Fall Apart* — 179
Ihechukwu C. Madubuike

Chapter 10: (Re)Memorising Igbo Traditions in Achebe's *Arrow of God*: A Psychoanalytical Study — 205
Linda Jummai Mustafa

PART III: ACHEBE, HISTORY, AND THE NATIONAL QUESTION — 223

Chapter 11: Telling Africa's Story: Chinua Achebe and the Power of Narratives — 225
Chijioke Azuawusiefe

Chapter 12: Narrativizing History: Chinua Achebe and the Politics of Interpretation — 243
Anwesha Das

Chapter 13: Achebeism and the Nigerian Leadership Problem — 253
Ada Uzoamaka Azodo

Chapter 14: Chinua Achebe as a Voice of Reason on the Nigerian Crisis: A Historical Look at the Larger Picture — 269
Odigwe A. Nwaokocha

Chapter 15: Chinua Achebe and the National Question — 289
Bernard Steiner Ifekwe

Index — 305

About the Contributors — 309

Introduction

Chinua Achebe, Writing Culture, and the Politics of Representation

Chima J. Korieh and Ijeoma C. Nwajiaku

Modern African literature gained significant recognition following the publication of Chinua Achebe's *Things Fall Apart* and other classics as Ngugi wa Thiongo's *Weep Not Child*, among many others. Yet none has been more influential in the emergence of African literature than Achebe's works. Chinua Achebe, who has been described as the father of African literature in the English language, was "undoubtedly one of the most important writers of the second half of the twentieth century."[1] This is no exaggeration, considering that his most famous novel, *Things Fall Apart,* has been translated into several languages and is the most widely read book by an African writer. Achebe was pivotal in giving agency to African voices at a time when, as Clement Okafor rightly observed, "there was nothing in the tradition of the English novel that portrayed an even vaguely authentic image of his fatherland."[2] The influence of his works has been profound and powerful in post-colonial literature and in challenging western representations of Africa. As Boluwatife Akinro and Joshua Segun Lean affirm, "Achebe had a keen grasp of how language demonstrated power, how power determined what was considered knowledge, and how this knowledge could become truth."[3] On a broader level, Achebe challenged the image of Africa portrayed in Western ethnographies and works of fiction. Indeed, Achebe acknowledged:

> I was quite certain that I was going to try my hand at writing, and one of the things that set me thinking was Joyce Carey's novel set in Nigeria, Mr. Johnson, which was praised so much, and it was clear to me that this was a most superficial picture—not only of the country but even of the Nigerian character and so I thought if this was famous, then perhaps someone ought to try and look at this from the inside.[4]

The prevalent image of Africa as portrayed in the Tarzan movies or in the farcical novels of Rider Haggard, or Joyce Carey's novel, Mr. Johnson, praised at the time as "an authentic portrait of Nigeria and her people," provoked a strong rebuttal in Achebe's *Things Fall Apart*.[5] Such fictional representation of the African world traversed the boundaries between the fictional and the political world and their intersection with Western encounters. Achebe gave an Afrocentric meaning to that world through his writing by demystifying deterministic views of race and cultural ethnocentrism.

Achebe brought the Igbo-African culture to the attention of the literary world when perspective on African was dominated by western ethnocentric views. His creative genius drew from the Igbo orature and worldview[6] and scholars in other fields such as history and anthropology which have often referenced Achebe's portrayal of Igbo culture as a source for reconstructing the past. While his books and commentaries have been very influential in shaping a unique but multifaceted view and perspective on the African World, scholars have also challenged Achebe's representations of historical reality.

This collection focuses on Chinua Achebe's works and their intersection with historical and cultural facts, focusing mainly on the Igbo, and on Nigeria as the larger context within which his literary works and commentaries are anchored. The writer creates and establishes what Simon Gikandi described as networks of connections between reader, writers, and context.[7] Here texts are acknowledged as crucial to modes of knowledge about subjects and objects and the image we "associate with certain localities and institutions."[8] Achebe, like many other African writers of his generation, wrote what can be described as protest literature. Such literature emerged as a reaction and response to colonialism and western representations of African cultures. At the same time, African literature served as a medium through which African writers explored and represented African indigenous culture as "different but equal," while portraying the devastating impact of Europe's impact on African societies and cultures. Through literature, African writers reflected the realities of Africa and the changes and transformations that have occurred.

Achebe, like many Africanist scholars, was influenced by the environment and the worldview of the society he represented in his works. Achebe's achievement in this regard "lie in his presenting his readers with an array of cultural-social-historical-political settings in his writing."[9] As Clement Okafor rightly points out, Chinua Achebe's writings reflected an acute awareness of his environment and the fact that he "belongs to two traditions: the first is the Igbo oral narrative tradition into which he was born, while the second is the English tradition of the novel which he has adopted."[10] Such attention to the social and cultural context in which a writer like Achebe created his works, calls for a critical evaluation of the intersection of fiction, fact, and what Anya O. Anya called "operative conditions" necessary to explain African and Igbo realities.[11]

There is a political dimension in the author's representations. Clement Abiaziem Okafor argues that "several critics of African literature have pointed out that one of the major reasons Chinua Achebe was inspired to become a writer was his desire to counter the demeaning image of Africa that was portrayed in the English tradition of the novel.'"[12] And Simon Gikandi explains in "Chinua Achebe and the Invention of African Culture" that reading *Things Fall Apart*

> brought me to the sudden realization that fiction was not merely about a set of texts which one studied for the Cambridge Overseas exam; . . . on the contrary, literature was about real and familiar worlds, of culture and human experience, of politics and economies, now re-routed through a language and structure that seemed at odds with the history or geography books we were reading at the time.[13]

Like many others who wrote and were published under Heinemann's African Writers Series, Achebe's writings had a strong identification with "a broad politico-cultural movement that asserted African political independence and cultural autonomy."[14] African intellectuals like Achebe drew from and infused indigenous ideologies in their formulation of an African-centered epistemology. And as Merun Nasser notes, social scientists have "extensively utilize African novels in and out of their classrooms as highly valued sources of information on African societies."[15]

The representation of the Igbo world on the eve of the nineteenth century and as they encountered European hegemonic imposition of a foreign culture was a central point of interest in Achebe's first and most influential novel, *Things Fall Apart*. Achebe's articulation of the Igbo experience paralleled those of other African societies as they encountered European missionary and colonial hegemony. Achebe masterfully penned what has continued to compete with works in history, anthropology, and other humanistic disciplines in explaining the Igbo world on the eve of European colonialism. On a broader level, Achebe and other Afrocentric writers challenged the established canon of European literature and Eurocentric representation of Africa. Indeed, African voices in the tradition of Achebe, challenged the canonical orthodoxy and the perceived supremacy of western literature with an audacity that reflects common human experiences. His essays on Joseph Conrad's Heart of Darkness were a bold step in rewriting the Western imagination of Africa. He spoke for many Africans when he concluded " *Heart of Darkness* projects the image of Africa as "the other world," the antithesis of Europe and therefore of civilization, a place where man's vaunted intelligence and refinement are finally mocked by triumphant bestiality."[16]

Achebe's other novels, *No Longer at Ease* and *Arrow of God* are reflections of the changes that confronted Nigeria and Africa as European rule took hold as well as the postcolonial conditions and the monumental crisis that followed independence from colonial rule. Ellah Wakatama Allfrey captures the genius of Achebe's intellectual and literary contribution in these words: "With prose that takes the English language and infuses it with inflections and a history that is uniquely Igbo, discernibly Nigerian and unmistakably African, Achebe's is a realism that ensures the enduring relevance of his fiction."[17]

Critics have challenged Chinua Achebe's literary works, focusing on how he communicated the Igbo-African World to the reader. What interpretations did he impose on the Igbo and African culture through his texts? In what ways has his work interrogated critical issues as they relate to fiction and historical representation, gender relations and representations, indigenous political institution, and power structures. Feminist scholars, in particular, have challenged the gender presentations in some of Achebe's most influential works, including *Things Fall Apart*. In a 2010 essay, "Patriarchy in *Things Fall Apart*: A Study of Gender Discrimination," Datta Sawant evaluated whether or not Chinua Achebe was a sexist writer with a limited gendered vision. In his evaluation, Sawant noted that not only were women in *Things Fall Apart* generally nameless and therefore lacking all claims to individuality, but also even the crimes that were perpetrated in the story were gender-coded by the Umuofia society."[18] Evident in Achebe's *Things Fall Apart* is what Ben-Iheanacho described as "the cultural contestation of patriarchy as a social power dynamic," which succeeds because it "denies women recognition and a platform for expression and agency within the shared communal space." Ben-Iheanacho notes that as ideology, "patriarchy strictly constrains the role of the woman as the diametrical opposite of the male."[19]

This collection consists of fifteen essays which are divided into three parts: "Chinua Achebe and Igbo-African Realities," "Chinua Achebe and Politics of Representation and "Achebe, History, and the National Question." The rationale behind this division is that, although some aspects of the Igbo experience can be addressed in their relationship to African and Nigerian culture, unique contextual circumstances warrant such division.

ACHEBE AND THE IGBO WORLD

In part I, "Chinua Achebe and Igbo-African Realities," the authors consider the Igbo World and its representations from Achebe's most celebrated literary works. The focus on the Igbo in this volume is deliberate. Achebe is Igbo and one with a clear ethnographic understanding of the culture and the historical experiences that emerged from their encounter with colonialism and the sociopolitical dynamics that resulted from the incorporation of Igboland into what became British colonial Nigeria. G. D. Killam, in "Chinua Achebe's Novels," argues that *Things Fall Apart* is a "vision of what life was like in Iboland between 1850 and 1900. Achebe makes a serious attempt to capture realistically the strains and tensions of the experiences of Ibo people under the impact of colonialism." He maintains that

> It is not wholly true, however, to say that the novel is written consistently from their point of view. Achebe is a twentieth-century Ibo man, and recognizes the gulf which exists between his present-day society and that of Ibo villagers sixty years ago, sixty years which have seen remarkable changes in the texture and structure of Ibo society. Achebe is able to view objectively the forces which resistibly and inevitably destroyed traditional Ibo social ties and with them the quality of Ibo life. His success proceeds not from his interest in the history of his people and their folklore and legend in an academic sense, but from his ability to create a sense of real-life and real issues in the book and to see his subject from a point of view which is neither idealistic nor dishonest.[20]

The Igbo experiences under colonialism and in the post-colonial period are treated as part of the human experience in a changing and transforming society. The changing power relations, changing identity, ethnicity, dispute over control of power and struggle over state institutions and structures are the context from which Achebe's trilogy *Things Fall Apart* (1958), *No Longer at Ease* (1960), and *Arrow of God* (1964) can be understood. Yet the complexity of the changing dynamics of Igbo society and African societies in general as they encountered colonialism and westernization and as they transition to the nation-states of the post-colonial period call for continued interrogation as they relate to realities and representations.

While Achebe has been praised for masterfully portraying the Igbo world and challenging the framework from which viewed African culture as a foil through which it affirmed her perceived moral superiority, Achebe has also had his critics. He has been challenged for his representation of aspects of the dynamics of Igbo society. While such literary criticism is warranted, the historian, philosopher, anthropolinguist, or linguist might read the text differently and find value within these disciplinary boundaries. In interpreting *Things Fall Apart*, for example, Jude Okpala notes:

> I recognize in the critical history of *Things Fall Apart* three forms of hermeneutics. The first group reads the novel from a linguistic paradigm and argues for the illegitimacy of any anthropological interpretation of the text. For this group, what is important is the symbolic nature of such a novel, which "continually restructures a variety of subtexts: cultural, political, historical and at times even biographical (Quayson 123)."

The second group, particularly A.G. Stock, sees a rapport between Achebe's Igboland and Yeats's England. The third group, comprised of Obiechina, Chinweizu, et al., Robert Wren, and Nnolim, explores the historical and cultural contexts of the novel.[21]

The chapters in this book address some of these themes as they relate to Achebe's representation of the Igbo World. Achebe's *Things Fall Apart* has been praised for its representation of Igbo value systems. Achebe profoundly captures a hierarchy of values that are uniquely Igbo, which all well-adjusted moral agents possess. He demonstrated the uniqueness of Igbo value systems and how the imposition of Western value systems became a source of conflict in Igbo and African societies as they encountered Europeans. Chinua Achebe tells the story of the Igbos in *Things Fall Apart* (1958) and *Arrow of God* (1964). Although both texts are creative works of literature, they are essentially historical in scope and content. One recreates the story of the Igbos from the precolonial to the colonial era, and the other dwells squarely on the colonial period. They depict the Igbo indigenous sociopolitical structure, traditional cosmology, religion, norms, and values before her subjugation and eventual disintegration of her culture via British imperialism. Achebe demonstrates that the Igbo past indeed "was not one long night of savagery."[22]

Yet, some of the contributions in this volume affirm the ambivalences in the representation of the Igbo world. B. E. Nwigwe's contribution draws attention to perspectives in Igbo metaphysics in Achebe's novels. He argues that the works of Igbo novelists and chroniclers writing in English or Igbo, especially the works of those who set their narratives in the older provincial environment, provide useful details and information on the history and traditional belief systems of the African people. In this respect, Achebe's works, especially *Things Fall Apart* provide useful insight into the special relationships between humans, and the environment, the external world, and the world beyond. Besides, in traditional Igbo society, literature was always generally a purposeful affair. In order words, it was not meant merely to satisfy some aesthetic craving or to engender intellectual appeal. As reflected in Achebe's reconstruction of the Igbo world, the purpose ranged from the performance of rituals through demonstration of accepted values to simple moral or ethical education. In these dimensions, the emphasis was consistently placed on the relationship between man and man, which if it was healthy becomes instrumental to the growth of a harmonious society.

In making these claims, Achebe draws from Igbo traditions of orality. Alassane Abdoulaye Dia in (Re)Discovering the Igbo Oral Tradition in Chinua Achebe's *Things Fall Apart* and *Anthills of the Savannah* affirms that the literary aesthetics reflected in these novels draw strongly upon orature particularly Igbo culture as a source of inspiration, which hooks the attention of both categories of readers, implied and unimplied ones. The *hallmarks* of these novels lie mostly in the recurrent use of cultural elements such as myths, folktales, and proverbs recapturing a typical "Igbo-African world" of imagery. Achebe succeeds in doing so using "cosmogonic narration" and "magical realism," which prompts a great deal of interest of readers to get in touch with his cultural roots as well as familiarize with the socio-cultural environment of his characters. He builds the storytelling upon a "local color writing style" borrowing from African oral genres in order to produce sophisticated literary works that account for "ethno-texts." Dia concludes that reading Achebe's novels is a twofold journey of discovering and rediscovering the "Igbo-African world."

Nureni Oyewole Fadare, "Symbols and Imageries in Chinua Achebe's *Things Fall Apart*," extends the discourse on Chinua Achebe's reliance on Igbo culture to frame his narrative. Fadare rightly claims that Achebe had contributed largely to the projection of Igbo cultures, and by extension, African cultures through his literary productions. Fadare examines Achebe's deployment of proverbs, imageries, symbols, and Igbo cultural totems to project Igbo cultures and traditions in *Things Fall Apart*. Drawing on Postcolonial theory while emphasizing Achebe's preoccupation of foregrounding Igbo's cultures using symbols and totems, Fadare argues that Achebe is a cultural activist who speaks through *Things Fall Apart* to challenge the previously held opinion that Africans have no culture. Through his use of proverbs and metaphoric expressions, Achebe has also helped to advance the argument that the people of Africa, especially the Igbo people, are highly organized people with their religion, occupation, a well-articulated judicial system, and family life before the advent of colonialism. The work also projects the communal life of the Igbo people and their worldview. It is also evident in the novel that the European incursion in Igbo land destroyed the cultural life of the people and caused divisions among the once united and strong society. The chapter concludes on the note that Achebe's proficiency and mastery of Igbos culture as evident in his use of proverbs encapsulated in imageries and symbols adds glamour to his work.

Diana Akers Rhoads has noted that what is remarkable about Achebe's Igbos "is the degree to which they have achieved the foundations of what most people seek today—democratic institutions, tolerance of other cultures, a balance of male and female principles, capacity to change for the better or to meet new circumstances, a means of redistributing wealth, a viable system of morality, support for industriousness, an effective system of justice, striking and memorable poetry and art."[23] She continued, "Achebe appears to have tested Igbo culture against the goals of modern liberal democracy and to have set out to show how the Igbo meet those standards."[24] As reflected in Achebe's representation of the Igbo, like many African societies, the Igbo are guided by a communal ethical philosophy. This finds expression in all aspects of Igbo life and their attitude towards others, the recognition that community is supreme, and the value of humanity towards others.[25] In the "Communal, the Supreme," Ijeoma Nwajiaku uses the Igbo notion of Ohaka, signifying the supremacy of the community over the individual as one that has strong historical roots. There is much evidence in precolonial Igbo society to portray a system that was and still is, "*oha* centered." Her chapter examines how the dual concepts of *oha* and *ohaka* assume relevance as indigenous Igbo sociopolitical viewpoints in two texts by Chinua Achebe—*Things Fall Apart* and *Arrow of God*. In particular, she explores the consequence of an individual's will in conflict with that of *oha*. The concept, she argues, is integral for formulating an ideological stance that informs part of the value system of the Igbo as reflected in Achebe's works. *Oha*, as an assembly of the free-born adult male population of the community, becomes representative of the unanimous "Voice" of the people. With the homogeneity of its status so enshrined in the culture and tradition of the Igbo, an individual who attempts to struggle with *oha*, positions himself for a herculean task. There are epistemological issues raised in several of Achebe's works. These provide a window into the Igbo and African world as they relate to knowledge production in the face of Western epistemological hegemony. N. Tony Nwaezeigwe's *Things Fall Apart* and *Igbo Leadership: Learning and Unlearning the Lessons of Okonkwo's Life* to interrogate the nature and structure of Igbo leadership vis-à-vis, the democratic principles of its indigenous structures. How does that structure fit into a modern state structure in which the Igbo are only a constituent part? Nwaezeigwe undertakes a critical look at the "current problem of contemporary Igbo political leadership through the literary historiography of Achebe's *Things Fall Apart*. The novel, being a classic literary replay of precolonial political dynamics of the Igbo society is thus an important lever for the understanding of the problems of contemporary Igbo leadership in the context of Nigerian national politics. The chapter draws attention to the challenges of Igbo leadership within a contemporary setting where indigenous principles and political frames of reference still shape people's lives.

Ijeoma Nwajiaku's chapter, "Achebe and the Pedagogy of Indigenous Knowledge Systems: Gleanings from *Arrow of God*," draws attention to the concept of indigenous knowledge and uncovers Chinua Achebe's liberal utilization of the indigenous knowledge system in *Arrow of God*. She argues that a re-engagement with the invaluable treasures embedded in this body of knowledge would yield indispensable insights in the establishment and fostering of an ideological stance, required by the African in contemporary society.

CHINUA ACHEBE AND POLITICS OF REPRESENTATION

In part II, "Chinua Achebe and Politics of Representation," the authors consider the relationship between society, historical, and artistic representation by examining the challenges and possibilities in specific contexts of the Igbo and Africa World. Rooted in Igbo worldview is the concept of *chi* which Achebe draws upon in his representation of the Igbo World in *Things Fall Apart*. In "Chi" in Igbo cosmology, Chijioke Azuawusiefe revisits Achebe's representation of *chi* and Chukwu in Igbo religious thought in the light of the prevailing scholarship on Igbo cosmology as well as on African Traditional Religions. Azuawusiefe questions Achebe's assumption that the ascendancy of the Supreme God "is well known in Igbo cosmology" and expanding the scope of his reading of chi and Chukwu. He argues that Achebe's uncritical examination of the place and position of the Supreme God in Igbo religious thought led to his assumption—in the mode of the colonial African nationalists, who asserted the existence and monotheism of the Supreme God among Africans in reaction to its denial by Western scholarship. Linda Jummai Mustafa in (Re)Memorising the Idealised Self in Chinua Achebe's Man of the People and Girls at War approaches Achebe's fictional work, Arrow of God using Trauma-Memory, a sub theory embedded in Freud's psychoanalysis. The discourse combines trauma and rememory as an epistemology put forward to advance a proper understanding of trauma experienced by Africans and in this case, Achebe's concerns on the didactic traumatic experiences of the Igbos as they slowly lose their culture to British traditions. In so doing, the adoption of Trauma-Memory brings to the fore Achebe's narcissist resolve to decipher the dilemma of his characters who are caught in a struggle to keep their customs as they battle colonialist invasion through the enforcement of Christianity, a religion alien to the worship of the sacred python god. Mustafa interrogates whether Achebe embraces an intellectual ambivalence of rememorizing trauma in order to assert a definite Igbo identity that cannot be fragmented by colonialist exploitative ideals.

Ifi Amadiume's "Discourse, Imagination and Models of Resistance: Re-reading *Arrow of God*," examines what we learn about Achebe's life experiences toward a better understanding of his imagination, the unraveling of the characters of this novel, and the outcome of events. The climax to unravel in Chinua Achebe's novel *Arrow of God* involves several intersecting conflicts and characters that reveal ideas about the colonial encounter, survival instincts, strategies and models of resistance, and social justice consciousness. Most important is the analysis of these issues from indigenous thought processes and realities on the eve of colonization, since there is yet no other reality other than indigenous Igbo traditions as fictionalized in the novel. Amadiume probes deeper into and analyses models of resistance through an understanding of points of rupture and the setting of a new paradigm. It is a perspective that works from within to understand and give voice to local dynamics in the encounter with change. It raises concerns with narrative voices and actions by all social groups, including that of the writer through the novel and his autobiography.

Ihechukwu C. Madubuike's contribution to the book, "The Collision of Asymmetric Civilizations—A Reading of *Things Fall Apart* reveals how Achebe uses art as a celebration of life, not of death. Igbo culture abhors the theory of a return to nothingness when our brief existence here on earth is over. His vision of life is one of hope and of determination, of struggles and conquests. Achebe's own life exemplified this. Despite his physical disability caused by a near-fatal motor accident, he continued to lead a productive life churning out essays, lectures, and books that challenged some accepted orthodoxies, activated debates in intellectual and political milieus, and added value to universal episteme. Achebe, Madubuike argues, essentialized the Igbo spirit of "Onye kwe chi ya ekwe." That spirit is what has kept the Igbo on the upbeat of a life of continuous struggle and competition, of triumph and celebrations, of not standing at one place to watch the masquerade. It is no wonder that in his first novel, Achebe recreates and captures the essential values embedded in the Igbo Weltanschauung to demystify the source of imperialism. *Things Fall Apart* is a novel of change, and it is only apposite to show how that novel literally "changed" the world when a pristine Igbo society came into contact with western alien culture to spawn a countervailing ideology of values, cultures, and civilizations.

ACHEBE, HISTORY, AND THE NATIONAL QUESTION

Part III addresses Achebe's commentaries on history, leadership and the national question in Nigeria. In "Writing Africa's History: Chinua Achebe and the Power of Narratives" Chijioke Azuawusiefe draws on Chinua Achebe's writings to grapple with the questions of where, why, and when the Other began to seize the initiative to tell Africa's stories. These questions inform Achebe's commitment to exploring a new order of knowledge that decenters the colonial discourse and evokes an alternative space for representation. Like the African proverb says: Until lions learn to write their history, the tale of the hunt will always glorify the hunter. Storytelling, hence, possesses for Achebe, a fundamental, "deeper meaning" of asserting Africa's history and culture before its encounter with Europe. This deeper pedagogical value, Achebe insists, engages the storyteller to radically reorientate contemporary cultural discourse, to re-position the mind on the realities and truths it has been conditioned to ignore. The writer, as a storyteller, becomes implicated in the deconstruction and reconstruction of culture and cultural mindset. In seeking, then, to write a new African identity, Achebe interrogates the colonial ideologies, historical claims as well as theories of Africa. He engages his task in earnest, examining not only the conditions under which African knowledge could be produced but also the problematics of such knowledge. This chapter uses critical discourse analysis to investigate a selection of Achebe's oeuvre and argues that Achebe's central position in the history of African literature derives from his ability to mobilize storytelling as a novel tool for reorganizing African cultures for the post-independence transition as well as repositioning them for the subsequent relations of power.

Anwesha Das in "Narrativizing History: Chinua Achebe and the Politics of Interpretation" examines Hayden White's notions of historical interpretation and narrative in reading Chinua Achebe. How does the politics of interpretation address Achebe's narrativization of colonial history in his novels? The question of Achebe's narrative and politics of interpreting historical pasts uphold the main argument of the chapter. In addressing the question of narrative and White's analysis of historical theory, Das focuses on the question that marks the end of White's "The Question of Narrative in Contemporary Historical Theory": "Is it not possible that the question of narrative in any discussion of historical theory is always finally about the function of imagination in the production of a specifically human truth?"

Chinua Achebe's public intellectualism beamed a searchlight on the national question in Nigeria. From his *Trouble With Nigeria* to numerous other works that incudes *There was a Country*, Achebe's commentaries on Nigeria, the question of nation-building and ethnicity have drawn both praise and criticism. Ada Uzoamaka Azodo's chapter, "Achebeism and the Nigerian Leadership Problem" advances new ideas and visions on leadership by personal example and public responsibility. Employing Chinua Achebe's parlance in his 1984 pamphlet *The Trouble with Nigeria*, she addresses the issue of leadership failure and the inability and unwillingness of Nigerian leaders to govern responsibly or be good role models of leadership for future generations. Whereas current views blame past colonial history and contemporary endemic corruption and nepotism, this chapter interrogates the quality of great leaders, the place of language, worldview, beliefs, moods, and emotions in leadership, and the benefits of such self-awareness at the inceptive and transformative stages of leadership. The goal is to foster the foundation for leadership authenticity while increasing the ability, capacity, and competence of present and future leaders.

In "Chinua Achebe as a Voice of Reason on the Nigerian Crisis: A Historical Look at the Larger Picture," Odigwe A. Nwaokocha argues that Chinua Achebe while emerged as one that Africa's greatest literary icons, his contribution to African studies and knowledge generally goes beyond the field of literature. Nwaokocha highlights his works on the Nigerian crisis that is looking increasingly intractable. He argues that Achebe's comments on the Nigerian crises both in his fictional pieces and pseudo-historical writings highlighted epochal issues and place his works within the historical epochs in which they are situated particularly as they related to the larger understanding of the Nigerian crisis. Nwaokocha concludes that the iconic Chinua Achebe and his works can never be fully understood and appreciated without his breathtaking writings outside the literary field, particularly those dealing with the Nigerian crisis.

Bernard Steiner Ifekwe's chapter, "Chinua Achebe and the National Question," continues the probe into Achebe's contributions to the debate on Nigeria and Nigerian nationhood. Ifekwe examines Chinua Achebe's perspectives on the national question in Nigeria through the prism of his fictional works. And perennial conflicts in Nigeria prompting a prominent imaginative writer such as Chinua Achebe to explore these problems in his novels, poems, and essays. Achebe thus submits that the leadership question since 1960 compromised and created a nation in perpetual conflict against itself. Consequently, this essay has deepened our understanding of the interplay between fact and fiction in historical narrations.

According to Clement Abiaziem Okafor, "Several critics of African literature have pointed out that one of the major reasons Chinua Achebe was inspired to become a writer was his desire to counter the demeaning image of Africa that was portrayed in the English tradition of the novel."[26] Yet, "Achebe's novel portrays a society that cannot be described as one of primordial chaos. On the contrary, it shows a society in which there are clearly defined parameters of right conduct on both personal and communal levels."[27] Thus, Achebe's stature as an author, intellectual, and spokesman for his people and Africa will endure. His commentaries on African personhood, the national question, and as a public intellectual will continue to draw the attention of scholars for a long time to come. This book demonstrates and agrees with Merun Nasser, who argues that "African novelists truly represent their respective societies and the social concerns expressed within them" and have " reduced the gap between literature and social science by paying heed to societal concerns."[28] As the chapters in this book demonstrate, Achebe was not just a writer, he was an educator and an Afrocentric voice who sought to demonstrate the viability of African epistemology and worldview. His work on the Igbo, especially his most famous novel, *Things Fall Apart*, has followed the tradition of other Igbo intellectuals like Olaudah Equiano in demonstrating the existence of an indigenous African society with a well-developed republican and democratic tradition before the contact with Western cultures.

Yet, some criticisms are leveled against Achebe for his portrayal of gender and women in his most celebrated work. Most of the criticism has bordered on his perspectives on women. For Merun Nasser, a critical question remains:

If indeed Achebe must act as an anthropologist, an artist, and a historian, then why has he chosen to disregard women and their contributions during the various periods in his major works? Is it by mere accident that Achebe does not give the full picture of the women's contributions, or is it that the women were passive and subservient and made no outstanding contributions to the society?[29]

NOTES

1. Caryl Phillips. On this claim, see also Clement A. Okafor, "Chinua Achebe: His Novels and the Environment." *CLA Journal* 32, no. 4 (1989): 433.

2. Clement A. Okafor, "Chinua Achebe: His Novels and the Environment." *CLA Journal* 32, no. 4 (1989): 433.

3. Boluwatife Akinro and Joshua Segun Lean, *The Prophetic Vision of Chinua Achebe: Reclaiming Africa's Past, Writing Its Present and Shaping Its Future* by The Republic, 13 January 2020, December 19/January 20, Vol 4, No. 1 https://republic.com.ng/december-19-january-20/prophetic-vision-of-chinua-achebe/

4. Okafor, "Chinua Achebe: His Novels and the Environment," 434.

5. Okafor, "Chinua Achebe: His Novels and the Environment," 433.

6. Simon Gikandi, "Chinua Achebe and the Invention of African Culture," *Research in African Literatures* 32, no. 3 (2001): 3–8.

7. Gikandi, "Chinua Achebe and the Invention of African Culture," 3.

8. Ibid.

9. Merun Nasser, "Achebe and His Women: A Social Science Perspective," *Africa Today*, Vol. 27, No. 3, African Literature and Literature about Africa (3rd Qtr., 1980), 25.

10. Okafor, "Chinua Achebe: His Novels and the Environment," 433.

11. Anya O. Anya, *The Environment of Isolation: 1982 Ahiajoku Lecture* (Owerri: Ministry of Information, Culture, Youth and Sports, 1982), 13.

12. Clement Abiaziem Okafor, "Joseph Conrad and Chinua Achebe: Two Antipodal Portraits of Africa Author(s)," *Journal of Black Studies*, Vol. 19, No. 1 (Sept. 1988), 17.

13. Gikandi, Simon. "Chinua Achebe and the Invention of African Culture." *Research in African Literatures* 32, no. 3 (2001): 3.

14. Barnett, Clive, "Disseminating Africa: Burdens of representation and the African Writers Series," *New Formations* 57 (Winter 2006): 74–94. http://oro.open.ac.uk/7140/1/New_Formations2.pdf

15. Merun Nasser, "Achebe and His Women: A Social Science Perspective Africa Today, Vol. 27, No. 3," *African Literature and Literature about Africa* (3rd Qtr., 1980), 21.

16. Achebe, Chinua. "An Image of Africa: Racism in Conrad's 'Heart of Darkness'" Massachusetts Review. 18. 1977. Rpt. in *Heart of Darkness, An Authoritative Text, Background and Sources Criticism*. 1961. 3rd ed. Ed. Robert Kimbrough, London: W. W. Norton and Co., 1988, 251–261 https://polonistyka.amu.edu.pl/__data/assets/pdf_file/0007/259954/Chinua-Achebe,-An-Image-of-Africa.-Racism-in-Conrads-Heart-of-Darkness.pdf. see also Curtler, Hugh Mercer. "Achebe on Conrad: Racism and Greatness in "Heat of Darkness," *Conradiana* 29, no. 1 (1997): 30–40. www.jstor.org/stable/24634988.

17. Ellah Wakatama Allfrey, "The great Chinua Achebe was the man who gave Africa a voice," https://www.theguardian.com/commentisfree/2013/mar/24/chinua-achebe-african-literature 11/27/19.

18. Elizabeth O. Ben-Iheanacho, "Achebe's Women: A Feminist Reading of Things Fall Apart and Anthills of the Savannah," *The Republic*, January 20, 2020, December 19/January 20, Vol. 4, No. 1 https://republic.com.ng/december-19-january-20/feminist-reading-achebes-women/

19. Ben-Iheanacho, "Achebe's Women: A Feminist Reading of Things Fall Apart and Anthills of the Savannah."

20. G. D. Killam, "Chinua Achebe's Novels," *The Sewanee Review*, Vol. 79, No. 4 (Autumn 1971), 515–520.

21. Jude Chudi Okpala, "Igbo Metaphysics in Chinua Achebe's "Things Fall Apart," *Callaloo* 25, no. 2 (2002): 559–66.

22. The novelist as teacher, 45. http://mrhuman.weebly.com/uploads/2/1/5/1/21516316/thenovelistasteacher.pdf. First published in the *New Statesman*, London, January 29, 1965; subsequently in *Morning Yet on Creation Day*, Doubleday Anchor Books, 1975.

23. Diana Akers Rhoads, "Culture in Chinua Achebe's *Things Fall Apart*," *African Studies Review*, Vol. 36, No. 2 (Sep. 1993), 61.

24. Akers Rhoads, "Culture in Chinua Achebe's *Things Fall Apart*."

25. This is in line with the Nguni Bantu term "Ubuntu" meaning "humanity," and often translated as "I am because we are," or "humanity towards others." See, for example, Christian B. N. Gade, "The Historical Development of the Written Discourses on Ubuntu," *South African Journal of Philosophy*. 30 (3): 303–329.

26. Clement Abiaziem Okafor, "Joseph Conrad and Chinua Achebe: Two Antipodal Portraits of Africa," *Journal of Black Studies*, Vol. 19, No. 1 (Sept., 1988), 17.

27. Okafor, "Joseph Conrad and Chinua Achebe," 22.
28. Merun Nasser, "Achebe and His Women: A Social Science Perspective," *Africa Today*, Vol. 27, No. 3, *African Literature and Literature about Africa* (3rd Qtr., 1980), 21
29. Nasser, "Achebe and His Women."

BIBLIOGRAPHY

Achebe, Chinua. *Things Fall Apart*. New York: Penguin Books, 1994.
Gikandi, Simon. "Chinua Achebe and the Invention of African Culture." *Research in African Literatures* 32, no. 3 (2001): 3–8.
Lindfors, Bernth. "A Checklist of Works by Chinua Achebe." *Obsidian (1975–1982)* 4, no. 1 (1978): 103–17.
Okafor, Clement A. "Chinua Achebe: His Novels and the Environment." *CLA Journal* 32, no. 4 (1989): 433–42.
Okafor, Clement Abiaziem. "Joseph Conrad and Chinua Achebe: Two Antipodal Portraits of Africa." *Journal of Black Studies*, Vol. 19, No. 1 (September 1988): 17–28.
Okpala, Jude Chudi. "Igbo Metaphysics in Chinua Achebe's "Things Fall Apart." *Callaloo* 25, no. 2 (2002): 559–66.
Rhoads, Diana Akers. "Culture in Chinua Achebe's *Things Fall Apart*." *African Studies Review*, Vol. 36, No. 2 (Sept. 1993): 61–72.
Gade, Christian B. N. "The Historical Development of the Written Discourses on Ubuntu." *South African Journal of Philosophy*. 30 (3): 303–329.
Nasser, Merun. "Achebe and His Women: A Social Science Perspective," *Africa Today*. *African Literature and Literature about Africa* Vol. 27, No. 3, (3rd Qtr., 1980), 21.

PART I

Chinua Achebe and Igbo-African Realities

Chapter 1

Causality in Selected Cultural Novels by Chinua Achebe
Perspectives in Igbo Metaphysics

B. E. Nwigwe

The works of Igbo novelists and chroniclers writing in English or Igbo, especially the works of those who set their narratives in the older provincial environment, provide useful details and information on the history and traditional belief systems of the African people. They provide useful insight into the special relationships between humans, humans and environment, the external world and the world beyond. Besides, in traditional Igbo Society, literature was always generally a purposeful affair. In order words, it was not meant merely to satisfy some aesthetic craving or to engender intellectual appeal. The purpose ranged from the performance of rituals through demonstration of accepted values to simple moral or ethical education. In these dimensions of the purpose, emphasis was consistently placed on the relationship between man and man, which if it was healthy becomes instrumental to the growth of a harmonious society.

Published in 1958 and 1964, *Things Fall Apart* and *Arrow of God*,[1] respectively, on which this reflection is based, are Igbo cultural novels of great significance, in the sense that they provide aspects of the history, worldview, ethical views and belief system of the people. Igbo culture is a culture with lofty values: respect for human life and the liberty of man, love of truth (*ezi okwu bu ndu*—truth is life), social justice (*egbe bere ugo bere*—let the kite and the eagle coexist with each other) the people cherish equality of opportunity, parental authority, filial loyalty, domestic solidarity and responsibility, hospitality, respect for elders, integrity in the administration of public trust, belief in retribution and reward in life after death, and so on. It is the existence of such vital value elements in the novels that makes them significant factors in the social life of the people and thus qualify them as useful elements for philosophical reflection—after all part of the job of philosophy is the investigation of reality, values and value judgments, knowledge and value reasoning.[2] As a great source of such vital philosophical elements, the novels serve as classics of moral lessons, history, and chronicles of Igbo people, presenting the areas of agreement and conflict between African traditional beliefs and practices and Western European civilization.

Chinua Achebe's viewpoints in the two novels *Things Fall Apart* and *Arrow of God* present to some extent a middle ground between Western Civilization and African cultural heritage. Such heritage includes intellectual, aesthetic, and artistic deposits of past generations of African peoples. Such legacies are documented as stories, proverbs, riddles, myths, and legends—some are records of actual events, others are imagined. It is some of these that have come to shape their cultures, social life, political organizations, and economic activities—forging, so to speak, for them, some specific mark of identity as Africans. Having sketched a problem with him on the possible sources of the ingredients for the discussion of the problem, we now gradually put into focus the main strands of this reflection.

PUTTING THE QUESTION INTO FOCUS

No matter how seemingly divergent worldviews and belief systems may be among the various cultures of the world, there are important common grounds among them. About the most basic of such questions is, are there only material entities or only mental entities or are there both material and mental entities? This is a basic question in Metaphysics and in traditional western Metaphysics, it is considered under the headings Materialism, Idealism and Dualism respectively. Besides this, there are other very important metaphysical questions that cut across all cultures. There are, for instance, questions whether there is a necessary connection between events such that one event is the necessary cause of the other. This has in the history of ideas been discussed under the major heading fatalism, determinism, and so on.

Allied basic philosophical questions include among others the problem of God's existence, the issue of the immortality of the soul, human freewill, and so on. There are other basic philosophical issues whose status as metaphysical questions is not generally accepted. These include the question of whether supernatural or occult phenomena such as ghosts and telekinesis exist. In Igbo belief system, these feature very prominently. For this, a would-be critic schooled in Western European philosophy would dismiss as fetish and occultic—a theoretical frame work involving gods, ghosts, and all forms of telekinesis. Those who deny phenomena such as these do so often merely on grounds that such beliefs are ordinary popular beliefs that lack any form of philosophical or scientific backing. To reason this way would not be totally right, because even Aristotle himself included such issues in the subject matter of metaphysics in the area of his metaphysical consideration on being qua being.[3] For Aristotle, the immediate aim of the inquiry in metaphysics is to arrive at a general understanding of the causes and principles of perceptible substances an understanding which should also enable us to explain non-substantial being by reference to substantial being and show the manner in which the Ousia of a non-substantial being explains why it is a being. Aristotle's subscription of status to non-substantial being opens up to my mind a great window to the study of African metaphysical thought.

What motivated this reflection was primarily the consideration that every account of knowledge of reality presents a limited perspective of what reality entails. This is evident in the various theories of knowledge, especially in their spatial and temporal dimensions in their very inner constitutions and linguistic expression. For this reason, it is plausible to imagine that there could be indefinite ways of looking at the same issues. In more modern terms, this could be said to be the idea informing what philosophers now refer to as "possible worlds."[4] Relating this to our issue of consideration, namely, causation we identify several understandings of the concept.

VARYING CONCEPTIONS OF THE WORD CAUSATION

Taken generally, causation denotes the relation that exists between cause and effect. In this sense it is equivalent to the expression "to produce," "bring about" or serves as exploration for the coming to be of an effect, like a sculptor bringing about a work of art.[5] The next conception of causality is that of "causal-chain." This has to do with a sequence of causally connected events—for example, my turning on the light caused the room to be lit, in this, there is an analytic or essential relation between cause and effect. This is a justified way in which a predicate can be part of the subject term. A good example is a bachelor is an unmarried man.

The central issue in discussions involving causation is, what is usually referred to as event-causation. This is the notion of causality that is usually associated with David Hume and John Stuart Mill, among others.[6] Four perspectives of event-causation have been identified; its central notion, however, is that causally connected events must instantiate a general regularity between like kinds of events such as fire and burning effect or fire and smoke effect.[7] For David Hume, there is no nomological necessity and no causal law involved between "event cause" and "event effect." Hume's contention is that a stronghold on such nomological necessity would have great difficulty in explaining the central issue in the problem of induction. Hume is formidable critique against inductive knowledge. I say formidable reasoning against inductive argument because if cause is taken in terms of laws it runs into serious difficulty. Reason for this is that all inductive reasoning remains inconclusive, since there is no way of exhausting in time all possible singular instances of the cause event relation.

Some philosophers now think that a cause may not necessarily be explained in terms of a law.[8] In what they refer to as counterfactual causation, there is no dependence between the cause-event and the effect-event. For instance, in the sentences "If my mother had not died, my father would not have become a widower," and "If I had not raised my hand, I would not have signaled," the cause-event and the effect-event do not stay in a relation of law, but in terms of explanation.

In a discussion involving causation, there does not seem to be any unitary conception of this subject matter that can be captured in an enlightening philosophical analysis. But causation in terms of counterfactual analysis reduces, to my mind the problem of looking at causation in terms of invariable regularity as is the case in physical laws. Taken as mere law, causation would qualify, in the words of contemporary philosophers as a "primitive concept,"[9] that is, one that does not require further analysis. It is on ground of this, and in order to avoid whipping a dead horse, I wish to tailor this discussion of causation in terms of counterfactual analysis (explanation).[10] I say this because it is the peoples' belief in the way events happen that serves as the sustaining causes of the events happening the way they happen.

In this discussion, therefore, I want to maintain that causality does not necessarily involve analytic proposition. It does not embody essential necessity in the sense of a predicate being already in the subject term. I want to look at causality as involving a synthetic—a prior[11] analysis—that is, as involving the principle of sufficient reason. Even though Hume has a strong objection against inductive knowledge, there seems to be a basic misconception in his understanding of causation. This involves confusing the specific category of causation with the generic category of determination. But discussions involving causation unlike discussions in certain variants of determination must not always be tied to necessity, because the same cause may produce the same effect only if the conditions necessary for this are there present. For instance, unlike in some instances of causation involving metaphysical determinism, there are other shades of determinism, like is the case in the Marxian historical determinism, in which a man's consciousness is determined by the social and material conditions of his time.

In the case of metaphysical determinism, the destinies of individuals seem to have been predetermined before their births, a situation which poses great problems for moral responsibility. In the case of historical determinism, the individual's moral responsibility is not denied him by the constrains of the social and material conditions of his time. This double aspect conception of determinism in which at one time every event seems predetermined and there is no room for human freewill and another sense in which there is room for human responsibility seems to pervade the Igbo worldview on this subject matter. In this culture, the category determination is seen as involving two mutually, independent but essentially coextensive concepts, namely determination as productivity or explanation and determination as lawfulness.[12] The first involves the genetic principle that nothing comes out of nothing. This is to say that events in the world require some explanations for their coming to be. The second namely determination as involving lawfulness is based on the consideration that nothing happens in an unconditional and an altogether irregular way. In Igbo understanding, whatever happens is an aspect of an organic reality, which on account of the limitations of the language we use and the concepts we arbitrarily impose on the world result in our cutting up reality into bits and parts in order to try to comprehend it. We shall see the Igbo conception of reality later in this discussion.

Meanwhile there are philosophers, for instance Immanuel Kant, who would object to our approach of looking at our subject matter from the perspective of the principle of sufficient reason. His reason would be that cause-effect statements like:

i. There is no effect without a cause.
ii. Everything which has a beginning has also a cause cannot be tautologically correct in the first case (i) and in the second on ground that the temporal beginning of the world cannot in anyway be convincingly provable.

We have so far examined the topic of our consideration from various dimensions within the western European philosophical tradition. In what follows we examine it from Igbo cultural perspective. We present an overview of the elements of Igbo Metaphysics that apply to our subject matter.

ELEMENTS OF IGBO METAPHYSICS

Igbo Metaphysics as is the case in general metaphysics recognizes the phenomenon of causality in nature. This is based on the principle of sufficient reason, namely that whatever exists must have justification for its existence.[13] This has to do with the issue of teleology, namely that even what are often regarded as accidents belong to an eventual grand design put in place by some great intelligence. Teleological considerations have also led to speculations about the meaning and nature of the universe, especially questions that involve what lies after or beyond the physical world of sensory experience.

In the Igbo worldview, there are several levels of beings: *Chukwu (Chi)*[14] the great creator of all things: the earth deity (*ala*) which serves as the custodian of moral conscience and as protector and provider of human society, the *alusi*—are invisible supernatural forces that serve all forms of functions some good some bad; the *Ikenga*[15] relates to a man's right or left arm, depending on which he uses more or better. It stands for a man's talent, strength, enterprise and achievement. There are the ancestors (*Ndichie*) and the invisible spirits of the living dead.[16] Belonging also to the hierarchy of beings are human beings, the environment—including animals, trees and the other constituent aspects of the overall physical or material sphere. For their importance and relevance to our subject matter, we shall briefly discuss three of these: the Chi, the Ikenga, and the Earth goddess.

Chi

Chi (Chukwu) or *Okike* denotes the highest form of existence and is seen as the source of all created reality. The concept *Chi* is in Igbo worldview of very fundamental importance. It has given rise to a lot of controversy[17] regarding its actual denotation: does it stand for personal god, guardian spirit, spirit-double, spirit-being, soul, transcendental self, or is it the designation for the highest being? This issue has been seriously debated in contemporary African Traditional Religion (ATR), and in many literary debates in the last few years. But the actual impulse came, as a reaction against certain European ethnologists, especially Levi Bruhl. R. F. Burton, according to whom the African was not capable of rational thinking, especially regarding such transcendental issues, as the possible nature and attributes of God.[18] This erroneous wishful imaginative thinking was actually responsible for the various references tagged on African Traditional Religion—as animism, fetishism, idol worship, and so on. Problems and levels of reasoning of this nature have been overtaken by more serious and up-to-date writings and researches in the field. What is at stake in African Traditional Religion at the moment are issues like the right nomenclature in God talk, the problem of whether African Traditional Religion is monotheistic or polytheistic, and so on. These problems are typified in the debate regarding the right, designation for the highest being. Some scholars think that the names Chukwu, Chi, and Chineke mean the same thing as names for the Supreme Being."[19] Others maintain that the right Igbo name for the highest being is Chi and not Chukwu,[20] whichever of the two positions is right it is quite obvious that the idea of the highest being was nothing strange to the Igbo cosmology as is evident in their proverb, prayer patterns, and wise sayings.[21] However, it is necessary to remark that it is a matter of empty debate except for its advantage of setting the records right[22] to waste so much time and energy on the issue of nomenclature, because names given to God are no proper names, but are mere descriptive designations for the highest being. For this, we shall apply the name Chi, Chukwu, Chineke, interchangeably in this work.

Ikenga

Ikenga is another vital Igbo Cult, which relates to a man's right or left arm depending on which he uses more or better. In essence, it symbolizes a man's talent and strength, enterprise and achievement. Generally speaking, the concept is that a man's *Chi* bestows on him peculiar talents and skill, and the man's Ikenga, through the exploits of his right or left arm, supports and protects him in forging and creating his way to achievement and success in life. It is expected of a man for continued success in life, that he maintains good relationship with both his *Chi* and his Ikenga. Since the Ikenga represents a man's ancestors, and the ancestors are custodians of the moral and social order he must constantly offer daily sacrifice to them and show readiness and interest in keeping the laws and customs of the land, without which neither his life nor well-being would be assured. The power and importance of the Ikenga is easily illustrated in an unfortunate incident in Chinua Achebe's Cultural Novel—*Things Fall Apart*. It was perceived as a great insult on Ebo, when an overbearing but light headed Akukalia took up Ebo's Ikenga and smashed it to pieces before his eyes. Ebo reacted to this outrage by murdering Akukalia. This unfortunate murder was rightly regrettable but understood by the two families involved (Ebo's and Akukalia's). Akukalia has done an unforgivable thing.[23] It was analogous to cutting someone off from his roots and in his case cutting off from his ancestors.

The Earth Goddess

In the hierarchy of deities, the Earth goddess occupies a very important position. There is a relationship of covenance between her and the people. She is not just a mythicised entity, but a real object and she is taken as staying in close communion with the community's dead ancestors. The Earth goddess provides life nourishment and protection and acts as the arch custodian of all laws, including the moral laws for the assurance of peace and harmony among the people. As is the case with the other divinities, the function of the earth goddess stems from the very needs of man: health, wealth, protection, children, and so on, acquisition of all these or any of them depends on the "purity of the members that constitute the community. Transgression of the customs of the community by any member of the land could attract heavy punishment for all (*otu aka ruta nmanu ozuo oha onu*) if one finger touches oil, it smears the other fingers too).

In case of an abomination against her, her chief priest performs certain ritual sacrifice to appease her wrath.[24] Such abomination against the deity are shedding of innocent blood, incest, killing of sacred totemic animals and trees, stealing of crops especially yams, suicide, violation of oaths, etc. Misconduct of this nature was always considered to be crime against the land or as a general pollution of the maternal earth. In the cultural novel *Things Fall Apart*, Okonkwo kills Ikemefuna—a young boy entrusted to his care—a boy who called him "Father." Referring to Okonkwo's misdeed, Achebe writes "It is the kind of action for which the goddess wipes out whole families.[25] When offended, the earth goddess manifested her displeasure through allowing catastrophe, sickness, appearance of strange phenomena, and so on.

In several parts of Igbo land, the week preceding the planting season is declared a sacred week or a week of peace. According to P. A. Talbot, "during this period no war or battle sound was heard the world around, the idle spear and shield were high up hung."[26] This absolute peace in Igbo thought pattern was seen as necessary in order to maintain the cosmic balance and the ontological equilibrium necessary for the survival of the people. The people observed the rites very scrupulously, because as Talbot notes:

> should the peace of the earth-mother be broken she would permit the ground to bring forth but scanty harvest, whereas did but universal goodwill reign at such a time, crops would spring forth with luxuriance, flocks yield great increase and multitude of strong and healthy babies be sent to gladden happy hearts.[27]

A classic example of such violation is repotted by Chinua Achebe in the novel *Things Fall Apart* where Okonkwo beats up his wife during the week of peace. He gets a reprimand from the Ezeani (priest of the goddess) "you are not a stranger in Umuofia. You have committed a great evil. The evil you have done can ruin the whole clan. The earth goddess who you have insulted may refuse to give us her increase and we shall all perish."[28] As we can see, there was need to maintain cosmic equilibrium through the conscious effort of the individual and the community to maintain the customs and traditions of the people, without which nothing was bound to go well.

Having attempted a presentation of these three levels of deities; Ikenga, Chi, and the Earth goddess, we see in what follows how they interrelate with each other. As is already somewhat evident there is a very close relation among these three levels of deities. If one's Chi is awake or active and one keeps oneself unpolluted from abominations one gets on well in life; but if one's Chi is replaced by Agwu-a trickster spirit, there is bound to be misfortunes and failures. However, to ensure that things go on well, constant libation must be made to the ancestors, who then intervene to ensure wellbeing. According to Onwuejiogwu,

> if one's Chi is active one's energy and actions are well directed and so one's Ikenga becomes effective. When one's Ikenga is effective, through hard work, one makes social and economic progress as can be seen in the acquisition of knowledge, and wealth. Wealth and knowledge have to be transferred into social status and prestige by the social titles (*Echichi*).[29]

It is evident that in Igbo worldview, there are three basic factors that determine the success or failure, good luck or bad luck regarding the events that happen in an individual's life, namely—the benevolence of one's Chi, one's own individual effort symbolized by the Ikenga and one's conscious effort to maintain the laws and customs of the community. These three factors are represented in sayings like.

  i. Onye kwe chi ya ekwe (when one says yes to life, one's personal god (chi) says yes too. In other words, one must cooperate with the benevolence of one's personal god in order to achieve success in life.
  ii. Ma aka emeghi aja onaghi eweta onu manumanu (if the hand is not soiled, it never brings about a mouth that is smeared with oil). This is to say that it is personal effort that guarantees satisfaction etc.

In these saying and beliefs, individual freedom and responsibility can be guaranteed since the individual's success or failure depends on the degree of his cooperation with nature's endowments. A good example of this is the case of Unoka in *Things Fall Apart*. He was a very lazy man even though he erroneously believed that he worked as hard as everyone else. Paradoxically, he went to the gods to ascertain the cause of his failure in life. The oracle said to him, "When your neighbours go out with their axe to cut down virgin forests, you sow your yams on exhausted farms that take no labour to clear. They cross seven rivers to make their farms, you stay at home and offer sacrifice to a reluctant soil. Go home and work like a man."[30]

This aspect of Igbo thought reminds me of the Marxian economic determinism in the sense that it holds the world is marred or made through the state of the physical economy at any stage of the world's history. This depends also on the level of awareness of the people to liberate themselves from oppressive economic circumstances and turn to a new order of consciousness, which brings them well-being.

Parallel to the belief that guarantees individual cooperation and involvement in determining one's own destiny, there is a contrary parallel view.

According to this other view, an individual's destiny can be determined to be good or evil even before the individual's birth. In other words, a man can be of good destiny (*onye uwa oma*) or of bad destiny (*onye uwa ojoo*). There are vivid sayings to show this in Igbo language. *Onye uwa oma jiri ekete kuru mmiri* (a man of good destiny can even fetch water with a basket) on the contrary do everything he may, a man of bad destiny is doomed to failure: *Onye uwa ojoo gara nku na uguru mmiri ama ya* (a man of bad destiny goes in the dry reason to fetch firewood and gets beaten by the rain). This reminds me of what western philosophy refers to as metaphysical determinism. According to this, there is only one possible history of the world which began from some definite source, and is going and is being directed to some definite end.[31] In this case, there is scarcely room for human freewill and responsibility. Cases of this shade of determinism abound in our projected cultural novels. For instance in *Things Fall Apart*, Chinua Achebe presents the hero of the narrative Okonkwo's life as dominated by fear of the ghost of his father. Rather than rely on his own will and energy to forge a livelihood for himself, as was the case with his peers, he was guided and hunted by the fear of ever becoming like his father who was a worthless lazy man, who later died in a state of penury.

What further seemed to confirm his belief that he was destined for failure was the fact that in spite of his stringent effort to achieve success, he went from one tragedy to the other. The first tragedy that stood beyond his control was the killing by accident of the sixteen-year-old son of Ezeudu and the killing of the child Ikemefuna under circumstances in which he would not have acted differently.[32] There is also the unfortunate incident of the killing of the messenger and Okonkwo's eventual taking of his own life. Events around his life seem to suggest that he was destined to failure in spite of his own efforts to the contrary. In line with this, Achebe writes regarding Okonkwo: "He could not rise beyond the destiny of his Chi. He was a man whose Chi said no, in spite of his own affirmation."[33]

In the *Arrow of God*, this view of metaphysical determinism is set forth. In this novel, Ezeulu is a chief priest mediating between the deity (Ulu) and the people of Umuaro, his people, but unknown to Ezeulu, the deity is the type that leads his priest to ruin himself.[34] For reasons that would militate against established customs of the land, Ezeulu refuses to call the New Yam Festival, but he and his family are grievously punished by the very deity whose cause the chief priest was pursuing. "But why he asked himself again and again, why had Ulu chosen to deal thus with him, to strike him down and then cover him with mud?[35]

In his other novels, similar thoughts feature. In the *Anthills of the Savannah* for instance the death by accident of a philanthropist in the hands of a reckless policeman and the other attendant events in the victim's life lead another character in the novel to wonder if "Chris and Ikem were not in fact trailed travelers whose journeys from start to finish had carefully programmed in advance by an alienated history."[36] In all these instances, the destinies of the individuals do not seem to depend on their own self effort, but on impersonal forces that are beyond their control.

There are others who are destined to greatness, even if they make very little personal effort on their own. They are those, according to Chinua Achebe "Whose palm kernel had been cracked for them by a benevolent spirit.[37] To sustain this and to show how the gods can gratuitously favour anyone of their choice, Achebe writes, the deity Eru, when he likes a man wealth, flows like water into his house, his yams grow as big as human beings, his goats produce three and his hen hatch nine.[38]

We have in the course of this discussion identified three main Igbo conception of determinism: the first is the type in which one can through one's own freewill and energy and with the cooperation of one's personal god achieve success and well-being in life. The second understanding is that in which one's destiny seems to be predetermined to the effect that do what he may, the individual ends up in failure. The third is the version in which the individual's life is perceived as predetermined to success, even when the one in question does not expend much effort of his own.

Seen merely from these perspectives alone, the Igbo conception of causality or determination would not be much different from its western European counterpart. In the European metaphysical theories, reality is contrived either as totally materialistic (materialism) or as purely mental (idealism) or as a dualistic combination of both mind and body. Such conceptions as those lead to different levels of difficulties.

i. They do not pay sufficient attention to the limitations of language, a fact which is becoming increasingly appreciated in contemporary philosophy especially among philosophers of the various strands of analytic philosophy and the philosophy of language.[39]
ii. Those who want to put all reality into the perspective of a theory fail to realize that what we refer to as reality is simply a function of the language we speak. We impose meaning and concepts on reality as ways of communication among ourselves and with the objects we encounter in real life. However, the question remains as to whether the way we perceive reality is the way it actually is.

When we look at events in life, from which perspective do we do so? Is it from our own wishful imaginations or our own psychological disposition or habitual dispositions? These questions constitute great problems for the theoreticians of any of the above-mentioned affiliations. This is, however, not the case in Igbo traditional worldview.

IGBO CONCEPTION OF REALITY

The Igbo conception of reality is ambivalent in the sense that everything coexists with its opposite, in fact body and spirit are coextensive with each other, so do suffering—joy, pain-pleasure, life—death, good—evil, and so on. They all constitute part of the existential issues that belong to life itself. This is why very stringent initiation rites accompany the advent of manhood and womanhood to prepare the initiates for the unavoidable odds of life. As Achebe puts it, "reality is like a masquerade which cannot be comprehended by watching it from one side alone."[40]

In Igbo understanding, being is seen as dual, not in the sense of sharp distinction into separate principles of mind and matter, physics, and metaphysics, but in the sense of a co-extensiveness of these with one another. This is evident in the usual practice of ascribing mental or spiritual qualities to physical objects and vice versa. For instance, a kind person is said to be *onye obi oma* or *onye afo oma* (i.e., a person of good heart or a person of good stomach) *obi* (heart) and *afo* (stomach) are physical organs of the body whereas kindness is a mental concept. This dual perception of reality is behind the practice of revering certain animals, trees, cultic objects, and in fact every aspect of nature as being endowed with mythic powers. They are seen as manifestations of a powerful but invisible reality.

The universe is perceived as highly ordered in the sense that there are well established physical and moral laws in it. Through such laws positive customs and institutions are derived. Such moral order helps in the working out and knowledge of what is permitted or forbidden, good or evil, right or wrong, truthful or false, beautiful or ugly. A person's fortune or misfortune depends on the degree of his perception of and cooperation with the demands of such moral order expressed through the customs and institutions of the society. For this reason, though he did not find life a very smooth affair, Okonkwo facilitated his own failure due to his own personal character. For instance, due to his achievement of some measure of economic and social success, he became overbearing to the extent that he was ready to challenge established customs and traditions of his people, and even also his own personal god. As Achebe tells us in *Things Fall Apart*, "Okonkwo was like the little bird nza who so far forgot himself after a heavy meal that he challenged his Chi."[41] In the Igbo worldview, therefore, what is referred to as misfortune, fortune, good, evil, taken singly on their own is like looking at events of life from one perspective alone. A person, who is perceived as unsuccessful in certain aspects of life, may be very successful if an overall picture of his life is taken. It is also possible that much of the misfortunes we encounter in the course of our lives may be due to our own fault or due to some issues that inexorably are connected with our lives. Belief in divination, prayers, and sacrifices show that events in life could be reversed even when things seem invariable.

CONCLUSION

We have in the course of this discussion operated somewhat at the level of what might be referred to as mythical thinking. What we have considered has had to do with mythical thinking, expressed through beliefs, proverbs, saying and practices. At this level of thinking, as we have seen, the world is conceived as being made up of a galaxy of deities in a hierarchy. For the western mind or anybody trained in the western category of thinking some such beliefs and practices as expressed here would not have much intellectual merit. But to reason this way would be erroneous. Every level of reasoning, whether mythical, logical or scientific, has its own inner lawfulness. This is so because even at the mythical level of reasoning, the beliefs and practices therein serve very useful needs at the time in which they feature, in ensuring social, moral and religious order and control. They help the people at their level to master their world, create and establish harmony between themselves and their gods and among themselves. As the saying goes: "It is the firewood that is found in a land that its people use for cooking their food."

Even the French philosopher, Lucien Levy-Bruhl, who championed the view that primitive man was at that stage at the level of "prelogical thinking," expressed his thought on this issue differently in his later works. According to him, the mythical forms in which the primitives expressed themselves did not prevent them from possessing those elements of rationality which are to be found in every human intelligence[42] and according to Jacque Chevelier.

> whether primitive or civilized, reason is governed by the same principles and constitutes the rationality of nature. It postulates order, or it insists that there is no such thing as chance, that everything has a purpose, and that everything is linked to a cause or a reason which determines its existence and value, even when such cause or reason eludes or outstrips our understanding.[43]

What Chevelier has said has a lot of merit. Even at the level of the so-called mythical thinking, there is a lot of value judgment in the sense that such belief systems lead to moral reasoning as to the goodness or badness of a human action. For this, they constitute valid materials for philosophical reflection. This is the justification that motivated this discussion in the first place. If this discussion has achieved anything, it is the suggestion that philosophical issues must not be treated in isolation outside the scope of reality as a coordinated unity of various aspects. The problem of philosophical theories: rationalism, idealism, empiricism, and so on, consists in the fact that their way of reasoning is spurious. Their analysis of reality in terms of things and processes, permanent and transitory aspects, objects and actions do not precede language as a substratum of given fact, but that language itself is what initiates such articulation and develops them in its sphere. Words serve as function of what we refer to as reality. Words also help us to divide the world, but words do not create reality. The Igbo worldview is that the various events in life are various perspectives of one common whole.

NOTES

1. Chinua Achebe, *Things Fall Apart* (London: Heinemann Educational Book, 1958); and his book *Arrow of God* (London: Heinemann Educational Books, 1964).

2. One of the jobs of philosophy is examination of value, reasoning and judgement. This is proper since its job is conceptual analysis.

3. Aristotle, *Metaphysics,* 1041a 6–7; Z16, 1040619–2L

4. This designation "possible worlds" has played important role both in Leibniz's philosophical theology and in the development of modal logic. Leibniz used it in his account of creation. For him God's mind contains the ideas of infinitely many worlds. In our time it has played important role in modal logic, especially through the effects of Saul Kripke and others.

5. To cause something is to bring it about or to produce it.

6. D. Hume and St. Mill are both in association with what I prefer to call regularity analysis of causality, the heart of this regularity (or nomological) analysis, is the idea that causally connected events must instantiate a general regularity between of what will happen in the future. According to him nothing in the future can be logically guaranteed for us by our knowledge of what has been observed to happen in the past. David Hume, Enquiry into Human Understanding, 12: Section IV, Part 11.

7. David Hume argues as follows: in vain do you pretend to have learned the nature of bodies from past experience. Their secret nature, and consequently all their effects and influences may change, without any change in their sensible qualities. This happens sometimes, and with regard to some objects; why may it not happen always and with regard to all objects? What logic, what process of argument secures you against this supposition?" David Hume, Enquiry into Human Understanding 12: Section IV Part II).

8. Some philosophers are of the view that a cause may not necessarily be explained in terms of a law, arguing that the way a cause relates to an effect does not involve logical necessity in the way a predicate term may be implied in the subject term of a sentence.

9. "Primitive concept" is one that has been so analyzed in the course of the history of philosophical discussion, that it can no longer be further analyzed. Causality is one of such terms.

10. Causation involves explanation, that is, could be understood in terms of explanation to the effect that everything that happens must have some sufficient reason why it happens.

11. "Synthetic apriori"—Kant introduces in the Critique of Pure Reason, the distinction between analytic and synthetic judgments see (Critique of Pure Reason B 3–4).

12. Included in Igbo culture is an area delimitable by an imaginary like running outside the settlements of Agbor, Kwale, Obiaruku, Ebu (West Niger Igbo area) Ahoada, Diobu, Umuagbayi, Port Harcourt area, Arochukwu, Afikpo, Ndinioafu, Isiogo Abakaliki area and Enugu Ezike (Nsukka area) and Nzarn.

13. Aristotle puts it thus: Whatever moves is moved by something else—this is metaphysical causality. Cfr. Aristotle Metaphysics, Book 12. 1071bff.

14. The concept Chi is in Igbo worldview of very fundamental importance. It has given rise to a lot of controversy. This controversy revolves around the question: does it stand for the highest being, or is used merely to designate someone's personal god, guardian angel, spirit-double, spirit-being, soul, transcendental self-etc. Many authors have written stimulatingly about it, for example, Chinua Achebe, article "Chi in Igbo Cosmology," reproduced in his *Morning Yet on Creation Day*, Essays (Ibadan: Heinemann) 1975. We shall see other writers on this issue as we go on.

15. Ikenga is a deity-usually represented in the form of carved short wood. Its numerous representations symbolize a man's talent and strength, enterprise and achievement.

16. The living-dead are the ancestors, who though dead are spiritual beings, whose influence constitute guidance and protection for the community.

17. A good summary of the issues involved and the contributions made by scholars to this ongoing debate,—see for example F.O.C. Njoku's, article 'A Phenomenological Critique of the Igbo God-talk, in: *Essays in African Philosophy, Thought and Theology*, (Enugu: Snaap Press Ltd. 2002), 142 ff.

18. L. Levy-Bruhl, Les Fonctions mentales dans les societies inferioures (1910) and La Mentalite primitive (1922), 40 ff.

19. Ikenga E. Metuh, "The Nature of African Theism, Analysis of two Nigerian Models," in: *Nigerian Cultural Heritage*, ed., Ikenga E. Metuh and Olowo Ojade (Nigeria: IMCO Publishing Co. 1990), 108ff.

20. D. I. Nwoga, *The Supreme God as Stranger in Igbo Religion* (Owerri: Hawk Press, 1984), 33ff.

21. Not names alone but other practices and expressions could give some representation of the idea of a supreme being in a culture. In Igbo culture, the Supreme Being is also called: Eze bi n'igwe ogodo ya na-akpu n'ala—The King who lives in the sky and his robes touch and roll on the ground.

22. D. I. Nwoga claims that the Igbo name for the Supreme Being is Chi not Chukwu. Chukwu was the deity of a community in Igbo land—the Arochukwus. Historically speaking Nwoga claims have merit, but he is not saying the same thing as

those who deny the Igbos knowledge of the idea of the Supreme Being. Such baseless claims have been adequately and variously refuted.

23. Achebe, *Arrow of God*, 25.

24. In Arrow of God, the festival of pumpkin was a ritual exercise to cleanse the people and the land from ritual impurities.

25. Achebe, *Things Fall Apart*, 45. In Plato's dialogue Euthypro, a death brings on the man or family who caused or condoned it a contagious defilement. Euthypro tries to avert this by prosecuting his father, who was the actual culprit in the matter.

26. P. A. Talbot, *The Tribes of the Lower Niger* (London: Frank Cass, 1932), 45.

27. Talbot, *The Tribes of the Lower Niger*, 45.

28. Achebe, *Things Fall Apart*, 22.

29. The Word *Echichi* is very significant in Igbo Culture. People assume or are accorded certain levels of social recognitions through giving them social titles. Such titles, of course, go with very serious moral and economic responsibility towards the society that confers them.

30. Achebe, *Things Fall Apart*, 13.

31. Metaphysical determinism could be represented in the words of Aristotle by: whatever moves, is moved by something else. It does not give room for human free with and responsibility.

32. In *Things Fall Apart*, the gods ordered the killing of Ikemefuna and Okonkwo acted according to the instruction, but it later turned out that his obedience was a trap set up against him.

33. A case of metaphysical determinism is Okonkwo, who said yes to life, when his personal Chi said no, that is, was not for it that Okonkwo succeeded.

34. Achebe, *Arrow of God*, 219.

35. Ibid., 229.

36. Chinua Achebe, *Anthills of the Savannah*. Ibadan: Heinemann Educational Books (Nigeria) PLC, 1988, 21.

37. Achebe, *Arrow of God*, 9.

38. Ibid.

39. By the various strands of analytic philosophy we mean the ordinary language school, the artificial language school or the school that pays much attention to the logical syntax of language, and so on.

40. The saying: You don't watch a masquerade by staying at one point alone—says much about epistemology regarding the various perspective from which reality can be known.

41. Achebe, *Things Fall Apart*, 22.

42. Lucian Levy-Bruhl, Les Fonctions Mentales dans les societies inferiors (1910) and La Mortalite primitive (1922), 12ff.

43. J. Chevelier, *Histoire de la Pensee*, 1, 2.

BIBLIOGRAPHY

Achebe, Chinua. *Anthills of the Savannah.* Ibadan: Heinemann Educational Books (Nigeria) PLC, 1988.
Achebe, Chinua. *Arrow of God.* London: Heinemann Educational Books, 1964.
Achebe, Chinua. *Morning Yet on Creation Day, Essays.* Ibadan: Heinemann, 1975.
Achebe, Chinua. *Things Fall Apart.* London: Heinemann Educational Book, 1958.
Achebe, Chinua. *Arrow of God.* London: Heinemann Educational Books, 1964.
Hume, David. *Enquiry into Human Understanding* 12: Section IV Part II.
Levy-Bruhl, L. Les Fonctions mentales dans les societes inferioures, 1910.
Metuh, Ikenga E. "The Nature of African Theism, Analysis of two Nigerian Models," in: *Nigerian Cultural Heritage*, ed., Ikenga E. Metuh and Olowo Ojade. Nigeria: IMCO Publishing Co. 1990.
Njoku, F. O. C. *Essays in African Philosophy Thought and Theology.* Enugu: Snaap Press Ltd. 2002.
Nwoga, D. I. *The Supreme God as Stranger in Igbo Religion.* Owerri: Hawk Press, 1984.
Talbot, P. A. *The Tribes of the Lower Niger.* London: Frank Cass, 1932.

Chapter 2

(Re)Discovering the Igbo Oral Tradition in Chinua Achebe's *Things Fall Apart* and *Anthills of the Savannah*

Alassane Abdoulaye Dia

The African oral tradition has strongly influenced the literary productions of many writers such as Chinua Achebe, Wole Soyinka, and Aminata Sow Fall to name but a few among them. Of these prominent African literary icons, Achebe mostly engerders interest in the interplay of orality and literacy in the African novel. He introduces his readers to the Igbo world in an artistic way that shows aesthetically the values of such cultural heritage. Indeed, his techniques of writing build upon a sophisticated "cosmogonic narration" that aims not only to revalorize African culture in general but also to give to his novels a "cultural stamp" characterizing them as "ethno-texts." As such, many writers across Africa engage into this form of writing. Ruth Rowe and Douglass Killam sustain the idea in this statement:

> Writers as diverse as Uganda's Okotp'Bitek, Ghana's Ama Ata Aidoo, Kenya's Ngugi WaThiongo, and Nigeria's Wole Soyinka incorporate in their texts the diverse forms of their orature, with its grounding in performance and the sound of language spoken, chanted or sung. As importantly, the writers and many others are attempting to recapture the multiple social purposes of orature to recreate the important aesthetic, political, religious, and psychological links it forces between artists and their communities and African communities and their histories.[1]

Rowe and Killam's analysis as literary critics also contends that Achebe plays the role of a "literary griot" inasmuch as he recaptures the Igbo oral tradition in his novels not only to provide them with a solid and didactic material in terms of content but also to aesthetically magnify his artistic ideology of "local color writing." For these critics, "Achebe's interest in orature goes beyond African novelists' conventional opposition of traditional to western education."[2] Thus, "writing contemporizes the oral *raconteur*'s function of conserving, interpreting, and transmitting communal history."[3]

Keith Booker postulates the same idea defending that "African writers such as Achebe "have employed a number of strategies to give back a sense of history to African societies and thereby to recover a past that can support valuable and viable cultural identities in the present."[4] A telling example of this fact is Achebe's first and latest novels, which introduce the literary world to the arts of the "Igbo-African" oral tradition.

Chinua Achebe belongs to the first generation of African writers whose early literary productions had been harshly criticized, but have regained consideration over the years. Today, Achebe's literary adventure is acclaimed as a revalorization of African folklore and the redefinition of the literariness of African arts.[5] He is regarded as a literary icon and one of the pioneers of African literature who has left the younger generation of writers with particular literary aesthetics of which he is the founding father.[6]

Such reality proven in the preceding paragraphs and widely shared by critics gives currency to the relevance of this study and the choice drawn upon Achebe's *Things Fall Apart* and *Anthills of the Savannah*. There is a period of almost three decades between their publications, respectively 1958 and 1987. Thus, Achebe's style is striking in these two novels in which his literary talent, his cultural background, and his "verbal craftsmanship" are unravelled through the use of language by means of narrative techniques.

Things Fall Apart is set in pre-colonial and colonial Africa. It aesthetically depicts the Igbo oral tradition and African folklore in general. Later on in 1987, *Anthills of the Savannah* was published as a political satire, but critics' concern and focus on it lie also in the style, which is impregnated with the same cultural reality. Rowe and Killam confirm it in the following terms: "The language and expository devices reflect this development along orality-literacy continuum as Achebe moves from peasant former protagonist to intellectual political leaders."[7]

This chapter studies the reflection of the Igbo oral tradition in Achebe's *Things Fall Apart* and *Anthills of the Savannah*. It shows, through a stylistic and thematic analysis, how the writer uses his works as archaeological instruments to teach his community their past and present. It also highlights Achebe's main narrative strategy to abide by his philosophy, "the *novelist as teacher*," thus, use Igbo culture as a *microcosm* in order to depict African culture as a *macrocosm*.

THE REPRESENTATION OF MYTHS AND LEGENDS

African writers take most of their sources from mythology which foregrounds the oral tradition and the traditional African religious universe. Then, myths or mythology are found in many African societies depending on their cultural realities.[8] The most recurrent ones are the Yoruba myth—Abiku—similar to the Igbo myth—Obanje—the Mammy Water of the Ghanaian people, the Dogon myth—Kaidara—and others found in Senegalese societies. Many of these myths have been transcribed and translated into different languages, which enables their access and their incorporation into literary works. According to *Dictionnaire des mythes africains*:

> The works of ethnologists and Africanists underscore the importance of the myth in traditional Negro-African societies through a very close connection of social and sacred facts. The myth defines origins; it is the foreground of beliefs and it explains and legitimates the social institutions. In Black African societies, especially with the oral tradition, a set of mystical things of speech and knowledge has developed within itself the myth that belongs to the esoteric world reserved to ritual ceremonies and meetings for initiation.[9]

This assertion justifies the presence of such cultural reality in Achebe's works. The purpose of this from of writing is for the author a way of producing an "ethno-text" through a "cosmogonic narration."[10] The elements that I have mentioned as aspects of the "ethno-text" are found in *Things Fall Apart* and *Anthills of the Savannah* (hereafter referred to respectively as *TFA* and *AOS*[11]). In both novels, the mythology lies in the myth of the "Oracle of the Hills and Caves" through Chielo—in *TFA*—and that of Idemili in *AOS* through the myth of the Sun "Pillar of Fire" and the "Pillar of Water" through Beatrice. As one notes, Africans are religious people who take much from their traditional beliefs, which mystifies the supernatural world. Achebe explains this reality:

> Every people has a body of myths or sacred tales received from its antiquity. There are supernatural stories which man recreated to explain the problems and mysteries of life and death—his attempt to make sense of the bewildering complexity of existence.[12]

In this regard, *TFA* expounds Igbo rituals through the myth of Chielo the Priestess of Agabala, "Oracle of the Hills and Caves." This ritual is usually evoked on some occasions mainly in times of war. It manifests itself through the character of Chielo, a female and the Priestess of Agbala. This mythological allusion first appears in chapter two of *TFA* when the narrator says: "And so the neighbouring clans who naturally knew of these things feared

Umuofia, and would not go to war against it without first trying a peaceful settlement. If the clan had disobeyed the Oracle they would surely have been beaten, because their dreaded *agadi-nwayi* would never fight what the Igbo call *a fight of blame* (*TFA*, 9)." Through this, Achebe highlights the power of the supernatural world, the spirit, which regulates the Igbo traditional and religious universe to some extent. The Oracle remains a legend of the Igbo people, which prefigures their spiritual force and predicts the prospects of the future. By means of this narration called "cosmogonic," Achebe tells the story of the "Igbo-African" supernatural world.

As Jacques Chevrier puts it, "The myth belongs to the serious speech which is the object of belief."[13] The sacred word of the myth is taken into account in the Igbo society. The latter pays much attention to the message of the Oracle whether it gives them a good or bad omen. In *TFA*, the narrator reminds it pointing that if the clan disobeys the Oracle, they will certainly lose a war as their dreaded *agadi-nwayi* will never fight against what the Ibo call *a fight of blame*.

The implication of such cultural reality in Igbo land within Achebe's narration provides *TFA* with verisimilitude because these aspects are typical prototypes of the pre-colonial African society he describes in the novel. The era which he alludes to, dates back to the period between the late nineteenth century and the mid twentieth century. Through this evocation of the past, the reader is introduced to what Eurocentrists call "primitive societies." This stereotypical judgement of the African society, albeit unfair, testifies to the hard times of tribal wars in which killing human beings was a mark for raising one's honor or title. This was also the time of "human sacrifices." This is probably why the myth of the "Oracle of the Hills and Caves" depicted through Chielo is present in the novel, which also tells about the Igbo society's past.

Through the character of Chielo who is a real human being, Achebe activates both a mythical and supernatural world upon which depends the actual physical one in which individuals live. The narrator introduces the reader to this unknown world of Igbo people in chapter 11: "She broke off because at that very moment a loud and high-pitched voice broke the outer silence of the night. It was Chielo, the Priestess of Agbala, prophesying./ . . ./ The folk stopped.'Agbalad-o-o-! Agbala! ekeneo-oo-oo' came the voice like a sharp knife cutting through the night" (*TFA*, 70).

From this narration, the author disconnects his reader from the physical world to metaphysically familiarize him with another one that is rather magical. The production of such narration can be understood through the idea raised in the quotation below:

It is always with a certain nostalgia that contemporary African writers, as well in the transcription of the ancient legends (Birago Diop or Bernard Dadié for example), as in the interior modern ones (Sony LabouTansi for example) refer to the mythical time of the genesis of the world.[14]

This argument sustained by Francophone novels applies also to Achebe'sworks, which perpetuates it in the African Anglophone novel's tradition. As a matter of fact, this type of narration imbued with magical realism is found in Amos Tutuola's novels which build heavily upon the Yoruba myth. Tutuola's *The Palmwine Drinkard* highlights it thus: "As I was Father of gods who could do anything in this world, when it was at night I sacrificed to my juju with a goat."[15]

Next to the myth of Chielo attributed to the ancient Igbo society, as it is described in *TFA*, Achebe textualizes this cultural reality in his latest novel, *AOS* in which the context has changed totally from tribal war to political chaos—with a sophisticated adaptation of myths to the realities. In *AOS,* the concern is political issues and leadership crisis in which the imbalance of power rampage is figuratively exposed through the two myths: "the Hymn of the Sun" also postulated as the "Pillar of Fire" as opposed to that of the "Pillar of Water."

These myths are technically drawn from what Chika Nwanko calls "traditional imagery."[16] Indeed, analyzing the myth of the sun also referred to as "the Pillar of Fire" and that of the Pillar of Water is tantamount to studying imagery and figurative language by means of which the reader decodes the novel and understands the message. In fact, these two myths are technically used as a dichotomy between "the Pillar of Fire" and the "Pillar of Water." The former symbolizes Sam the dictator and the latter epitomizes Beatrice the savior.

As far as the "Hymn of the Sun" is concerned, Ikem the poet uses it as a myth to put in light the destructive nature of the sun corroborated with the excessive disaster that the drought has caused to Abazonian people of which representation is a personification of power through Sam Okoli the dictator. The narrator focalizes it in the following lines:

> In the beginning Power rampaged through our world, naked. So the almighty, looking at his creation through the round undying eye of the Sun, saw and pondered and finally decided to send his daughter, Idemili, to bear witness to the moral nature of authority by wrapping around Power's rude waist a loincloth of place and modesty (*AOS*, 102).

In this passage, Achebe takes the reader back to the past to disclose the myth of Idemili and the significance of the supernatural fact. When describing the effects of the sun, he puts the reader in touch with the dictator's moral and political deceits. Indrasena K. Reddy makes the point in these lines:

> The novelist uses the myth of the sun (symbolized in Sam) whose power scorching heat destroys everything around. The destructive nature of the sun creates a terrible drought in Abazon, forcing its leadership to visit H.E for the redressal of their problem caused by the drought.[17]

This phenomenon can be sustained by the significance of the title of *AOS*, which Achebe uses as both a metaphor and a code that derives from the myth of the sun, "the Pillar of Fire." Ikem prefigures it sophisticatedly in this passage: "The trees had become hydra-headed bronze statues so ancient that only residual features remained on their faces, like anthills surviving to tell the new grass of the savannah about last year's bush fires" (*AOS*, 31).

The title of the novel is a key to decode the myth that Achebe displays within the image of the sun through the "Pillar of Fire" as Indrasena K. Reddy puts it:

> The title *Anthills of the Savannah* strikes the keynote of the novel's theme. The anthills are the living witness to unfold the recurring cycle of the destruction and regeneration of the savannah "surviving to tell the new grass of the savannah about last year's brush fires." The story, thus, outlives the event and the writer by narrating the cataclysismic changes in human history leaves it to us to draw the right lessons.[18]

Through the myth of the sun, Sam is prefigured as a destructor of society whose remedy should be sought in its "so-called" mythical concept, the "Pillar of Water." This is the reason why I deem it necessary to study both myths together. In fact, they are related to each other to the extent that one of them—the Pillar of Water—is the opposite as well as the remedy to the other—"the Pillar of Fire." In this regard, Indrasena K. Reddy defends that these myths are "twin myths" highlighted in Idemili's supernatural character: "The twin myths of the Sun and the "Pillar of Water reinforce" Idemili's content for man's unquenchable thirst to sit in authority on his fellow."[19]

As demonstrated in Reddy's statement, the two myths are related. The first one—the Sun—destroys whereas the other, the "Pillar of Water" makes it die out and turns out to be its remedy. Reddy argues:

> The second most powerful myth is related to the Pillar of water (Beatrice in the context of the novel) which seeks to put out the fire of the Sun and also quench the thirst of the parched lands of (Abazon).[20]

In combining both myths as twins, the narrator acquaints the reader with Idemili, who is a daughter of God and a savior. Idemili epitomizes Beatrice, who, despite the political and social hindrances, tries her best to prove to be a "celestial power" in the mind of the Abazonian people and her presence thereby is considered by Omar Sougou to be a hypogram. Sougou defends:

> The other noteworthy component of the intertextual construction occurs in the first part of chapter Eight "Idemili". It is kindred in tone and with "hymn of the sun" [. . .] The figure "Pillar of water" exists in the legend of Idemili, a hypogram yoked with the narrative. The goddess Idemili was sent by her father the Almighty to bridle power that was ramping through the world. Idemili descends from the sky to the earth in the "resplendent" Pillar of Water."[21]

From this perspective, the implication of Idemili in setting political justice in *AOS* is quite similar to the role that Chielo plays in *TFA*. Even if the issues are not the same, Idemili sometimes identifies herself with Chielo, thanks to the role they play in the Igbo world of spirits. Idemili reveals it when she says that she "feels like Chielo in the novel." (*AOS*, 114).

THE REPRESENTATION OF FOLKTALES

Folktales are oral features that abound in the writings of Achebe. They culturally mark the "Igbo-African" folklore and are of great depth in the stories recounted in the novels under study. Thanks to their philosophical content, they contribute significantly to the richness of the African oral tradition. Cora Agatucci asserts in this regard:

> Traditionally, Africans have reserved good stories and storytellers, as have most past and present people around the world who are rooted in oral cultures and traditions [. . .] every human culture in the world seems to create stories (narratives) as a way of making sense of the world. Some particular features of the folktales common kind of story around the world, for example, can be discerned in Tortoise and the Birds, an Igbo folktale recounted in chapter 11 of Chinua Achebe's acclaimed 1958 novel, *Things Fall Apart*.[22]

Achebe's novels are imbued with cultural *hallmarks* such as folktales. Indeed, the presence of these elements is common in many cultures. Baydallaye Kane evokes this old tradition in the novel in general:

> The use of animal imagery as an artistic device is an old and universal tradition. For ages, many folklores throughout the world –through fables, tales, songs, etc.—have resorted to the animal world to build metaphors and/ or characters

for stories. In West Africa, the main protagonists in most tales are Leuk the hare and Bouki the Hyena: those tales recount—usually in funny tones, sometimes with a dose of cynism.[23]

Thus, folklore is meaningful in human history. As a result, there is a range of fictional works in both western and African literatures that build upon it to carry out a didactic text like Achebe's "ethno-text." Among these, one can mention George Owell's *Animal Farm*, Jean de La Fontaine's *The Fables*, etc.

In former times in the African oral tradition, folktales had a significant role which consisted in teaching wisdom. This kind of teaching was done around the fireplace. This was a typical African traditional school which was most of the time devoted to "rocking" and awakening children and giving them mood by telling them stories. This form of teaching is of great significance. As Jacques Chevrier puts it,

African wisdom finds its best from the tale; an oral mode of expression of the major thought of an ethnic group. The tale has indeed as a function to transmit to a human community the thought of the gods or ancestors. Thus, it turns out to be a translation, interpretation of a reality which is higher than Man.[. . .] The universe of the tale is an ambiguous universe where without contradiction the real and the unreal cohabit in the world of humans and that of animals.[24]

Ancestors too, regarded folktales as one of their classics and a rich heritage of their antiquity, thanks to the moral lessons they give to people. Ernest Emenyonu sustains the importance of this practice:

Folktales are rich and authentic sources of raw African values in traditional societies. They are used for purposes of acculturation and were therefore, necessarily didactic and morality-laden. Children generally grew up under the tutelage of their mothers who at chosen times during the formative years, told them folktales in which enshrined community values were explicitly extolled. Such occasion served as pastimes and to sustain the interest and curiosity of the children, the raconteur must make the story real and entertaining and then experience worthwhile.[25]

Before the contact with western culture, African people used to give lessons about their traditional values by means of this storytelling found in folktales. Most of the time, these lessons were delivered on ceremonial occasions like the harvest, the naming ceremony, cultural activities, and so on. Next to these ones, there is another tradition which consists in telling stories at night around the fireplace or on the mat in the middle of the house while watching the night. Of these values, folktales are one of the most reflective in terms of cultural reality. These events are illustrated through time and space in *TFA* particularly in Okonkwo's household through this scene: "Ekwefi and her daughter, Ezinma, sat on a mat on the floor. It was Ekwefi's turn to tell a story" (*TFA*, 67–68).

For the sake of verisimilitude, Achebe has craftily respected the techniques of this oral genre which he incorporates in his novels to describe people of the countryside. He evokes the first two fundamental elements of the form of this genre: time and space. It happens in the night, and takes place in the rural area. Its setting as an unreal one is also specific. Agatucci explains it:

> These stories are examples of the Ibo folktale that explain how animals got their physical characteristics—a genre common in many cultures around the world. They have many variations and abound in the oral traditions of Africa and the African Diaspora. Achebe himself explains that "a story does many things; it entertains, it informs, it instructs" [. . .] The storyteller works out what is right and what is wrong, what is courageous and what is coward, and they translate this into stories.[26]

In fact, Achebe's main technique here is to produce an "ethno-text," which helps educate his people by means of animal imagery as Agatucci points:

> Every human culture seems to create stories (narrated as a way of making sense of the world. Some familiar features of the folktales, a common kind of story around the world, for example, can be discerned in Tortoise and Birds, an Igbo folktale recounted in chapter 11 of Chinua Achebe's acclaimed 1958 novel *Things Fall Apart*.[27]

Agatucci evokes in the above quotation the connection between the real and the unreal world. Achebe, therefore, by means of fiction depicts the unrealistic world through animal imagery to highlight the realistic world. This technique is then to educate his community through a didactic "ethno-text." His task is like that of Jean De La Fontaine: "to educate human beings by means of animal imagery."[28] This point is also sustained by Agatucci's statement:

> Achebe himself explains that a story does many things. It entertains, it informs, it instructs [. . .]. The storyteller works out what is right and what is wrong, what is courageous [. . .] and they translate this into stories.[29]

The interpretation given above justifies that the main function of folktales is to teach didacticism. Therefore, after learning or reading a story, the reader needs to decode the tale, understand, and interpret it. It is after a deep analysis that one can realize that folktales and fables are close to myths to some extent. However, the slight difference between these two genres is that the myth hides the sacred and mystical aspect of the real world whereas folktales are well-discerned between the unrealistic and the realistic world and demystify each of them. Jacques Chevrier affirms in the sense:

> The transition between the myth and the tale is sometimes fuzzy, but what one can say with certainty is that the myth begins desacralizing itself, to slacken its bonds with the supernatural world; thus in this sense that one delves into the issue of the tale. ¶In the myth the natural still occupied a major role, in the tale the division between real and the unreal tends to be balanced.[30]

Through the story of Tortoise and the Birds, in *TFA* (67–69), Achebe demonstrates what Jacques Chevrier explains in his afore-mentioned statement: To better understand the tale, one needs to familiarize with the world of animals which Achebe uses in the place of human beings and the second step is to take into account the depth of wisdom that the tale implies within its didacticism. This is tantamount to discovering how animals are personified in an unreal world to educate people of the real world. The core of this tale lies in its high level of imagination and thinking that has been given to animals both to react and think like human beings. Annie Gagiano comments on the core of the tale in the following lines:

> By foregrounding the tale of Tortoise and the Birds (70–71), the fascinating "Political" story of manipulative "cunning" (69) and the cooperative, cunning resistance to it, Achebe indicates how much more complex and reflective such stories are—and how necessary to situations where the nearly unthinking taking up of inappropriate and outdated weapons (Okonkwo's 'tall feather head-gear and his shield"—(143) is inadequate. The detail of Tortoise's "sweet tongue" (69) links him decisively with the "sweet-tongued" messenger of the British District Commissioner (138), the DC. Who will broadcast his story of the events in Igboland as an admirable account of venturesome European civilisation?[31]

In addition to Gagiano's comment, Agatucci gives in details the reason why Tortoise is found in most Igbo folktales as is the case of Hare in many West African folktales:

> Chinua Achebe explains that the tricker Tortoise is a favourite in Igbo children stories, for "he is a character that children can relate to. He is a rogue, but he is a nice kind of rogue. I think children don't trust him but they like to hear that he is round, because they know that he is going to do something unexpected and generally he will be punished too." This is the moral side of it. He is not allowed to get away with murder. [. . .] Tortoise is wicked but he is not irredeemably so.[32]

Above all, one can maintain that Tortoise plays in Igbo folktales the role that Hare plays in most common African stories even if people are more familiar with the former in Igbo culture. However, in Senegal or other areas of the

same region, Tortoise can be understood in the light of Hare. Indeed, in West African folktales, Hare and Tortoise are regarded as the favorites of children. Both animals are known as the most cunning and fascinating. Achebe justifies his choice in children's storytelling: "Nwoye / . . ./ preferred the stories that his mother used to tell him and which she no doubt still tells to her younger children—stories of the Tortoise and the birds" (*TFA*, 38).
Agatucci also supports this idea:

> Oral African storytelling is essentially a communal experience. Everyone in most traditional African societies participates in formal and informal storytelling as interactive oral performance—such participation is an essential part of traditional African communal life, and basic training in a particular culture's oral arts and skills is an essential part of children's traditional indigenous education on their way to initiation into humanness.[33]

The same reality is found in *AOS*, but in other circumstances. In this novel, it is a villager again—even if the scene takes place in a town, Kangan—who recounts the story of Tortoise and the Leopard as an allegory to denounce the socio-political injustices that prevail in their country. In this story, Achebe draws the attention of the reader to the content of the tale particularly to its didacticism. The question of time and space is not a concern in the fabric of the story of Tortoise and the Leopard told in *AOS*. A telling example of this fact is that the story is told in daylight. It does not abide by the tradition I evoked previously, which usually requires telling stories at night.

In the context of *AOS*, the author shows animal imagery within folktales exceptionally told in daylight for other purposes. This is strategically to underscore the imbalance of power and to encourage the oppressed to struggle against the injustice they are suffering from. Thus, the tale is recounted in this way:

> Once upon a time the leopard who had been trying for a long time to catch the tortoise finally chanced upon him on a solitary road. *Aha*, he said; *at long last! Prepare to die.* And the tortoise said: *can I ask you a favour before you kill me?* [. . .] But instead of standing still as the leopard had expected the tortoise went into the strange action of the road, scratching with hands and feet and throwing sand furiously in all directions. *Why are you doing that?* asked the puzzled leopard. The tortoise replied: *Because even if after I am dead I would want anyone passing by this spot to say, yes, a fellow and his match struggled here* (*AOS*, 128).

This story is adapted as a parable to the situation that Abazonians face under the rule of a ruthless dictator. Once again, the tale shows out the significance of its didacticism. It raises the views of struggle that the Abazonians have to adopt to hold a revolution for the sake of justice. What is also highlighted by the story is the sense of honor and dignity. The rationale behind the recounting of the tale in daylight is to sensitize the dominated about their sense of responsibility. Thus, the old man concludes the folktale with a significant message: "My people, that is all we are doing now. Struggling. Perhaps to no purpose except that those who come after us will be able to say: true, our fathers were defected but they tried" (*AOS*, 128).

From the old man's explanation, the story is a lesson to be learned by heart because it recalls the experience of the glorious past. This story whose essence lies in animal imagery is relevant to the "views of struggle" that the Abazonian people should have. It is also interesting in terms of style because in case Tortoise speaks, its speech is put in italics. This form of writing is called graphology.

The purpose of this form of writing is to emphasize the power of the story particularly on the actions of the "cunning animal." This is a way of personifying Tortoise in the tale. It also helps to identify the focus of the story. The reader pays attention to the actions of the animal who is the hero and whose deeds are put in emphasis by means of italics. Omar Sougou underscores the purpose of this style: "The writer graphically marks the narrator's voice with italics so as to emphasise the speaker."[34]

Throughout the story, the few sentences written in this style can help the reader grasp the content of the fable. Graphology, then, as a technique is the study of distinctive units (graphemes) that make up written language, that is, letters, punctuation, capitalization, use of italics, letters in bold, and so on, it is about the process of uniting itself as well as the language of observation.

In a word, folktales are embedded narratives that account for material sources that teach and entertain readers, thanks to the didactic and humoristic form they give to the novels.

PROVERBIAL PATTERNS

Proverbs are maxims stated in few words to tell about the attitudes and the behavioral codes adapted to the circumstances of life. They depict general, universal truths and practices which order the common experience in the everyday life and they represent a set of social and legal codes.[35]

Proverbial patterns are of paramount significance in the study of the Igbo oral tradition in Achebe's novels. Indeed, they are used in order to valorize the African folklore. These patterns comprise proverbs, enigmas, and sayings as well. All these aspects are fundamental elements in the power of speech in the African palaver. Achebe's famous statement is illustrative of this point,

"Among the Igbo art of conversation is regarded very highly, and proverbs are the palm-oil with which words are eaten" (*TFA*, 3).

In other words, proverbs, as Achebe puts it, are the rhetoric of culture. As shown above through the two novels and other African ones, African folklore is well represented with abundance in the patterns. Many instances are found in *TFA* and *AOS* with significance. Agatucci delves into the importance of proverbs in the following words: "African proverbs and stories draw upon the collective of oral peoples, express their "structures of meaning, feeling, thought, and expression" wisdom and thus serve important social and ethical purposes."[36]

The following enigma unravels this aspect: "If a child washed his hands he could eat with kings" (*TFA*, 6). Mwamba Cabakulu analyzes that proverbs contain human wisdom which they emphasize. They cover broad semantic fields including other forms of the word: sayings, maxims, and aphorisms.[37] The above enigma taken from *TFA* underscores the value of wisdom, dignity and responsibility that Man has to embody within society so as to have respect from elders. In addition, Man has to endeavor to gain all these necessary qualities: respect and honor or titles which his society requires. The old man uses this enigma to show his people that Okonkwo has followed the same itinerary. The narrator gives details of this enigma in the passage below:

> To crown it all he had taken and had drawn incredible prowess in two inter-tribal wars. And so although Okonkwo was already young, he was still one of the greatest men of his time. Age was respected among his people, but achievement was revered. As the elders said, if a child washed his hands he could eat with kings. Okonkwo had clearly washed his hands he could eat with kings and elders (*TFA*, 6).

In the same regard, enigmas are used in *AOS*. The Abazonian old man evokes it: "The cock that crows in the morning belongs to the household but his voice is a property of the neighbourhood (*AOS*, 122). Such cultural representation reveals the richness of the Igbo-African oral tradition. This phenomenon is particularly shown in the speech of the Abazonian old man whose rhetoric draws upon proverbial patterns: "If you want to get at the root of murder, they said, you have to look at the blacksmith who made the machete" (*AOS*, 159).

Proverbs are what Bernth Lindfors calls "the grammar of values."[38] They embellish the speech and give them more flavor to be perceived. Phanuel Egejuru qualifies this type of local color writing as an attribute of the Mbari artist, which she postulates stylistically as *Achebeism*:

> Through the novels of Chinua Achebe, the literary world has learned a great deal about the art of conversation and fine speech among the Igbos of Nigeria. It is

Achebe's exploration of Igbo patterns of speech that has created a distinctive feature which can be appropriately called Achebeism in literature. The most outstanding Igbo oral aesthetics in his novels is what Achebe identifies as oratory.[39]

The old man justifies it in his speech: "Wonderful, proverb isn't it? But it was only intended to enlarge the scope of thinking not to guide policeman to investigating an actual crime." (*AOS*, 159). He highlights that the relevance of this proverb is not to guide policemen to charge the blacksmith any time there is a crime, but rather to widen the thought and make it alive so as to use it in allegorical instances. As the old man puts it, the significance of enigmas or proverbs is to be found in their implication. Simon Gikandi puts it in the following terms:

> Proverbs are figures of thought which comment on the logic of the culture and its discourse; they provide censure and guidance, but they also provide a cultural text from which the individual can read the rules that govern society and the conditions in which such rules are established.[40]

Gikandi's analysis is in accordance with that of Alioune Tine who proffers that the recurrence of proverbs and the other aspects of the "Igbo-African" folklore in the novels is to provide an "ethno-text." They are not the only ones who have observed this phenomenon. A. Rutherford and Kirsten confirm:

> African proverbs have been described as repositories of communal wisdom, mnemonic devices for effective communication, and educational tools. Because they have their origin in specific communal experiences and are reproduced by a memory; their epistemological basis may give us insight into the (male) African appreciative mode. [. . .] the use of proverbs in Chinua Achebe's native—culture –based novels—*Things Fall Apart* and *Arrow of God* (1964)—had often been considered as an embellishment or a stamp of authenticity and it was only in the early seventies that critics became aware of their functional significance.[41]

One can infer that the "stamp of authenticity" asserted by Rutherford and Kirsten qualifies Achebe's works as "ethno-texts." In addition to the characteristics of proverbs as *hallmarks* in his creation of such texts, one can focus on the stylistic features of his novels, which is striking through its entertaining folklore. The abundance of proverbs which is a marker of local color too is examined by Chantal Zabus as a "textual glottophagia." Zabus comments on this fact:

> My own recent findings bear witness to a form of glottophagia or even neo-glottophagia in West African European literature. We shall call it "textual glottophagia," an extension of linguistic glottophagia. Such a phenomenon is

most apparent in the case of "indigenization," that is, when the writer attempts to convey African concepts, thought patterns and linguistic features via the European medium. [. . .] When extended to the Igbo-informed novel and more specifically, to the Igbo gnomic or proverbial discourse in the Nigerian novel of English expression, glottophagia becomes discursive.[42]

A telling example is the Igbo saying: "I cannot live on the bank of the river and wash my hands with spittle" (*TFA*, 117). This saying is of great significance in the Igbo culture because of its repetitive use in several instances. The same saying is used in *No Longer at Ease*: "I cannot live on the bank of the river and wash my hands with spittle."[43] Chantal Zabus denotes this stylistic feature as a *hallmark* in Achebe's texts: "Another *hallmark* of Achebe's style is the use of proverbs, which often illustrates the values of the rural Igbo tradition. He sprinkles them throughout the narratives, repeating points made in conversation."[44] Thus, the recurrence of proverbs and sayings in speech is a marker of embellishment first and that of the "local color," because these elements are basic items of speech in the African oral tradition. So, the "stamp of authenticity" given to the speech reflects the personality of the speaker.

The Abazonian old man and Obierika are typical examples of this kind. They are proud of the practice of proverbs which is for them the "rhetoric of culture," which Lindfords also calls "the grammar of values." This literary critic also delves into a deep analysis of this practice of proverbs in Achebe's novels:

> It is my contention that Achebe, a skilful style, achieves an appropriate language for each of his novels largely through the use of proverbs. Indeed, Achebe's use of proverbs can serve as keys to an understanding of his novels because he uses them not merely to add touches of local colour but to sound reiterate themes.[45]

There is no denying that the abundance of proverbial patterns in Achebe's texts marks his local color writing. Thus, this form of writing is his attribute as an Mbari artist. Phanuel Egejuru postulates this stylistic marker of his writing as *Achebeism* thanks to "the verbal craftsmanship" found in the style; which is also aesthetically handled through the narrative techniques.

CONCLUSION

It is remarkable that Chinua Achebe's works help readers (re) discover the "Igbo-African" oral tradition. Hence, the recurrence of cultural elements such as myths, legends, folktales, and proverbs built upon a creative African world of imagery. All these elements are relevantly shown in the corpus through an artistic combination of orature and literacy.

By means of the cosmogonic narration, one realizes that reading Achebe's novels is a twofold journey of discovering and rediscovering the "Igbo-African world." This implies that such reading accounts for a discovery of the Igbo world for unimplied readers and its rediscovery for implied ones. Achebe succeeds in doing so by means of "cosmogonic narration" and "magical realism," which prompts a great deal of interest of readers to get in touch with his cultural roots as well as familiarize with the socio-cultural environment of his characters. He also builds the storytelling upon a "local color writing style" borrowing from African oral genres in order to produce sophisticated literary works that account for "ethno-texts."

NOTES

1. Ruth Rowe and Douglass Killam, eds. *The Companion to African Literature* (Oxford: James Currey, 2000), 204.
2. Ibid., 2.
3. Ibid.
4. Keith Booker, *The African Novel in English: An Introduction* (Oxford: James Currey, 1998), 5.
5. Cf. Alassane Abdoulaye Dia, "*Achebeism*: Verbal Artistry and Style in the Writings of Chinua Achebe" in *AFRREV: LALIGENS: Journal of Language, Literature and Gender Studies*: Ethiopia, vol 3 n° 1, February 2014, 56–75.
6. Alassane Abdoulaye Dia, *The Voice of the Tradition in the African Novel: Chinua Achebe's Artistic Use of Orature in Things Fall Apart and Anthills of the Savannah*, New Jersey: Goldline and Jacobs Publishing, 2015), 3.
7. Ruth Rowe and Douglass Killam, *Op, cit.,* 81.
8. Cf. *Dictionnaire des mythes littéraires*, ed. Jean-Paul Bertrand (Paris: Editions du Rocher, 1988), 44. "Each ethnic group has cosmogonic accounts reporting the various stages of the creation of the universe and Man by God and his geniuses. These accounts constitute the foreground of the education conceived like a progressive revelation of the mysteries of creation. Referring to the time of origins, the myth binds to the initiated person like an essential knowledge a sum total of the first untenable truths whose knowledge is essential to the happy integration of any member of the community" (my translation).
9. Ibid., 44. (My translation).

(Les travaux des ethnologues et Africanistes soulignent l'importance du mythe dans les sociétés négro-africaines traditionnelles par une liaison très étroite du social et du sacré. Le mythe définit les origines, fonde la croyance, explique et légitime les institutions sociales [. . .]. Dans les sociétés d'Afrique noire à tradition exclusivement orale, s'est développé toute une mystique de la parole et de la connaissance au sein de laquelle le mythe appartient au domaine ésotérique réservé aux rituels et aux séances d'initiation.)

10. Ibid., 44–5.

"The cosmogonic narration explains, clarifies, and orders the secrecies of life, death, evil. It reveals symbols, and discloses the bonds established between the human and the supernatural order. In so-doing, it answers to the existential anguish; it puts the human being's mind at ease by situating him/ her in the universe" (my translation).

11. Chinua Achebe, *Anthills of the Savannah* (Ibadan: Heinemann Educational Books, 1988). Hereafter, the acronyms *TFA* will be used for *Things Fall Apart* and *AOS* for *Anthills of the Savannah* and subsequent references to them will be incorporated in the main text.

12. Chinua Achebe, *Hopes and Impediments* (London: Anchor Books, 1988), 134.

13. Jacques Chevrier, *Littérature africaine: Histoire et grands thèmes*(Paris: Hatier. 1985), 197. (my translation). (Le mythe fait partie de la parole sérieuse qui est l'objet de croyance.)

14. Cf. *Dictionnaire des mythes africains, Op. cit.*, 45. (My translation). "C'est toujours avec une certaine nostalgie que les écrivains africains contemporains, tant dans la transcription des légendes anciennes(Birago Diop ou Bernard Dadié par exemple), qu'à l'intérieur de modernes (Sony Labou Tansi par exemple) font référence au temps mythique de la genèse du monde.

15. Amos Tutuola, *The Palmwine Drinkard* (London: Faber and Faber Limited, 1961), 23.

16. Chika Nwankwo, in *The Growth of African Literature* (Twenty-*Five Years After Dakar and Fourah Bay*), *Op.cit.*, 35.

17. Indrasena K. Reddy, "Preface" *The Novels of Achebe and Ngugi: A Study in the Dialectics of Commitment* (New Delhi: Prestige Books, 1994).

Ruth Rowe and Douglass Killam, *Op cit.,*116.

18. Ibid., 123.

19. Ibid., 117.

20. Ibid., 176–78.

21. Omar Sougou, "Language Foregrounding and Intertextuality in *Anthills of the Savannah*" in *Critical Approaches to Anthills of the Savannah*," Ed. Holger G. Ehling (Matatu n° 8) (Atlanta and Amsterdam: Rodopi, 1991), 48.

22. Cora Agatucci, African Storytelling: An Introduction In: http://ueb.cocc.edu/cagatucci/afrstory/htlm (accessed on 05/ 08/ 08).

23. Baydallaye Kane, "From the Tick to the Brontosaurus: Animal Imagery in Alex La Guma's Novels" in *GELL (Revue de Langues et Littératures)* n°7, (Saint-Louis: XAMAL, Janvier. 2003), 120.

24. Jacques Chevrier, *Op. cit.,* 202. (My translation). "La sagesse africaine trouve son meilleur dans le conte; mode oral d'expression de la pensée profonde d'un groupe ethnique, le conte a en effet pour fonction de transmettre à une communauté humaine la pensée des dieux ou des ancêtres. Il se veut donc traduction, interptétaion d'une réalité supérieure à l'homme. [. . .] L'univers du conte est un univers ambiguë où

se côtoient sans contradiction le réel et l'irréel, le monde des hommes et le monde des animaux."

25. Ernest Emenyonu, "Selection and Validation of Oral Materials for Children's Literature; Artistic Resources in Chinua Achebe's Fiction for Children"in: *Emerging Perspectives on Chinua Achebe OMENKA: The Master Artist*, Vol. 1, Eds, Ernest N. Emenyonou (Trenton-Asmara: Africa World Press, 2004), 147.

26. Cora Agatucci, *Op. cit.*, In: http://ueb.cocc.edu/cagatucci/afrstory/htlm (accessed on 05/ 08/ 08).

27. Ibid.

28. Jean De La Fontaine, Postface *Les Fables* (Editions Gallimard, Paris: 1980).

29. Cora Agatucci, *Op. cit.*, In: http://ueb.cocc.edu/cagatucci/afrstory/htlm (accessed on 05/ 08/ 08).

30. Jacques Chevrier, *Op. cit.*, p. 197. (My translation). (La zone de transition entre le mythe et le conte est parfois floue, mais ce que l'on peut dire avec certitude c'est que le mythe commence à se désacraliser, à relâcher ses liens avec le monde surnaturel, nous abordons aux rives du conte. Dans le mythe le naturel occupait encore une place prépondérante, dans le conte le partage entre le réel et l'irréel tend à s'équilibrer.)

31. Annie Gagiano, *Achebe, Head, Marechera on Power and Change in Africa* (London: Lynne Rienner Publishers, 2000), 72.

32. Cora Agatucci, *Op. cit.*, In: http://ueb.cocc.edu/cagatucci/afrstory/htlm. (accessed on 05/ 08/ 08).

33. Ibid.

34. Omar Sougou, "Didactic Aesthetics: Achebe the Griot and the Mbari Artist" in *GELL (Revue de Langues et Littératures)* n° 2 (Saint-Louis: XAMAL, mars 1998), 43.

35. Mwamba Cabakulu, *Dictionnaire des proverbes africains* (Paris: L'Harmattan-ACIVA, 1992), 11 (my translation).

(Les proverbes constituent des maximes énoncés en peu de mots, pour instruire sur les attitudes et les règles de conduite adaptées aux circonstances de la vie. Ils dépeignent des vérités générales, universelles et des habitudes que commande l'expérience commune devant la réalité et la vie quotidienne ils représentent tous un code social et juridique.)

36. Cora Agatucci, *Op. cit.*, http://ueb.cocc.edu/cagatucci/afrstory/htlm (accessed on 5/8/8).

37. Cf. Mwamba Cabakulu, *Op. cit.*, 11 (my translation).

(Les proverbes contiennent donc la sagesse humaine qu'ils mettent en valeur. Ils couvrent un vaste champ sémantique comprenant d'autres formes de la parole; dicton, maximes, sentence, aphorisme.)

38. Cf. Bernth Lindfords, "The Palm Oil with Which Achebe's Words are Eaten" In: *African Literature Today: A Journal of Explanatory Criticism, N° 1-2-3-4*ed, Eldred D. Jones (London: Heinemann, 1972).

39. Egejuru, *Op. cit.*, 23.

40. Simon Gikandi, *Reading Chinua Achebe* (London: James Currey) 1991),47.

41. Kirsten Hoslt Petersen, and Rutherford Anna, eds. *Chinua Achebe: A Celebration* (London: Heinemann 1991), 20.

42. Chantal Zabus, "The Logos-Eaters: The Igbo Ethno-Text" In: *Chinua Achebe: A Celebration*, eds Kirsten H. P. and Anna Rutherford, *Op. cit.*, 19.
43. Chinua Achebe, *No Longer at Ease* (London: Heinemann Educational Books [1962, 1975]), 9.
44. Chantal Zabus, "The Logos-Eaters: The Igbo Ethno-Text" In: *Chinua Achebe: A Celebration*, eds Kirsten H. P. and Anna Rutherford, *Op. cit.*, 20.
45. Egejuru, *Op. cit.*, 6.

BIBLIOGRAPHY

Achebe, Chinua. *Anthills of the Savannah*. Ibadan: Heinemann Educational Books, 1987.
Achebe, Chinua. *Things Fall Apart*. Ibadan: Heinemann Educational Books, [1958, 1965].
Amuta, Chidi. *The Theory of African Literature: Implications for Practical Criticism.*London: Zed Books, 1989.
Booker, Keith. *The African Novel in English: An Introduction*. Oxford: James Currey, 1998.
Cabakulu, Mwamba. *Dictionnaire des proverbes africains*. Paris: L'Harmattan-ACIVA, 1992.
Chevrier, Jacques. *La Littérature négre*. Paris: Armand Colin, 1998, 2éme édition.
Chevrier, Jacques. *Littérature africaine: Histoire et grands thèmes*. Paris: Hatier. 1985.
Dia, Alassane Abdoulaye. "Achebeism: Verbal Artistry and Style in the Writings of ChinuaAchebe." *AFRREV: LALIGENS: Journal of Language, Literature and Gender Studies: Ethiopia*, vol 3 n° 1, (February 2014): 56–75.
Dia, Alassane Abdoulaye, *The Voice of the Tradition in the African Novel: Chinua Achebe's Artistic Use of Orature in Things Fall Apart and Anthills of the Savannah*. New Jersey: Goldline and Jacobs Publishing, 2015.
Dictionnaire des mythes littéraires, ed. Jean-Paul Bertrand, Paris: Editions du Rocher, 1988.
Emenyonu, Ernest N. ed. *Emerging Perspectives on Chinua Achebe OMENKA: The Master Artist*. Vol.1 Trenton-Asmara: Africa World Press, Inc., 2004.
Gagiano, Annie. *Achebe, Head, Marechera on Power and Change in Afric*. London: Lynne Rienner Publishers, 2000.
Gikandi, Simon. *Reading Chinua Achebe*. London: James Currey, 1991.
Jones, Eldred Durosimi. *African Literature Today, N° 1-2-3-4: A Journal of Literary Criticism*, London: Heinemann Educational Books, 1972.
Jones, Eldred Durosimi. *African Literature Today No 5: The Novel in Africa*, London: Heinemann, 1975.
Kane, Baydallaye. "From the Tick to the Brontosaurus: Animal Imagery in Alex La Guma's Novels." *GELL (Revue de Langues et Littératures)* no. 7, Saint-Louis: XAMAL, janv. (2003): 119–136.
Killam, G. D. *The Novels of Achebe*. London: Heinemann, 1969.

Killam, G. D. *The Writings of Chinua Achebe*. London-Ibadan-Nairobi: Heinemann Educational Books, 1975.

Kirsten Hoslt Petersen, and Rutherford Anna eds. *Chinua Achebe: A Celebration*, London: Heinemann 1991.

Lindfors, Bernth and Innes C.L. eds. *Critical Perspectives on Chinua Achebe* (1stedition) Washington, D.C.: Three Continents Press, 1978.

Makward, Edris *et al*. *The Growth of African Literature* (Twenty-*Five Years After Dakar and Fourah Bay*). Asmara: Africa World Press, 1998.

Ong, Walter. *Orality and Literacy: The Technologizing of the World*. New York: Methuen, 1982.

Reddy, Indrasena K. *The Novels of Achebe and Ngugi: A study in the Dialectics of Commitment*. Delhi: Prestige Books, 1994.

Rowe, Ruth and Douglass Killam, eds. *The Companion to African Literature*. Oxford: James Currey, 2000.

Sougou, Omar. "Language Foregrounding and Intertextuiality in *Anthills of the Savannah.*" In *Critical Approaches to Anthills of the Savannah."* Ed. Holger G. Ehling (*Matatu* n° 8), Atlanta and Amsterdan: Rodopi, 1991, 35–54.

Sougou, Omar. "Didactic Aesthetics: Achebe the Griot and the Mbari Artist." *GELL (Revue de Langues et Littératures) n° 2*, Saint-Louis: XAMAL, (Mars 1998): 69–84.

Tutuola, Amos. *The Palmwine Drinkard.* London: Faber and Faber Limited, 1961.

Chapter 3

Symbols and Imageries in Chinua Achebe's *Things Fall Apart*

Nureni Oyewole Fadare

Chinua Achebe's *Things Fall Apart*,[1] published in 1958, was the first African novel to be published by Heinemann Publishers, London, and the first in their African Writers' Series. Achebe is concerned about rewriting the history of African people by an African writer with the practical knowledge of African culture. Achebe's *Things Fall Apart* deconstructs the erroneous notions about Africaby Eurocentric writers such as Joyce Cary's *Mister Johnson*[2] and Joseph Conrad's *Heart of Darkness*.[3] Most of Achebe's works focus on the culture of the Igbo people as narrated from the perspective of an Igbo man. Through local imageries and symbols, Achebe recreates and reflects on the culture of his people. In his works, generally, he focuses on issues of marriage, naming ceremony, gods and goddesses, occupation and jurisprudence. This, undoubtedly, helps him to project the culture of his people to the world. Based on the above, this chapter seeks to examine how Chinua Achebe deploys symbols and imageries in presenting the culture of Igbo people in *Things Fall Apart*.

THE SOCIAL-CULTURAL FUNCTIONS OF AFRICAN LITERATURE

According to Tanure Ojaide, "There is culturally speaking, no art for art's sake in Africa. Every literary work has a social function: songs, prayers, praise chants and abuse are placed at the service of the community."[4] African literary works are responsive to the social realities of the society where they are produced. Each of the African literary writers across the ages reflects on the social reality in their communities projecting the individual and the collective unconscious of their people in their works. The literary writers, therefore, assume the role of the mouthpiece of their various communities. Most of the earlier literary writers such as, Chinua Achebe, Wole Soyinka, J. P. Clak-Bekederemo, and Ngugi wa Thiongo were committed to the re-awakening of African consciousness and culture in their works. They condemn the Europeans' occupation of Africa and eulogize the beauty of African culture. This led to the establishment of the negritude movements.

The negritude poets such as Leopold Sedar Sengor, David Diop, Birago, Diop, and Bernard Dadie were committed to the glorification of black culture and heritage. They denounced Eurocentricism in their works and upheld the sanctity of African ways of life. The negritude movement was established by Aime Cesaire, Leon-Gontran Damas and, Leopold Sedar Senghor.[5] Negritude movement was a movement against colonialism and imperialism. Senegal and other Francophone African countries suffered from the French policy of assimilation or what is christened, in history, as "frenchification" of Africa. According to Williams and Chrisman,

> Colonialism, the conquest and direct control of other people's land, is a particular phase in the history of imperialism, which is now best understood as the globalization of the capitalist mode of production, its penetration of previously non-capitalist regions of the world, and destruction of pre or non-capitalist forms of social organization.[6]

The import of the above quotation is that it is the issue of colonialism that prompted African writers to uphold negritude as an alter-Native to the colonial usurpation and hegemony. Mohammed Alquwaizani argued that the Senegalese poet and writer, Leopold Sedar Senghor rejected the Descartesian rule of "I think, therefore, I am." Senghor says, "I feel, I dance the other." He further argued that passion is not inferior to reason but its equivalent.[7]

Chinua Achebe is a quintessential postcolonial literary artist who devotes his writings to the battered image of Africa by Eurocentric writers. Chinua Achebe in *Home and Exilesubmitted*, "Until the lions produce their own historians, the story of the lion will glorify only the hunter."[8] Chinua Achebe sees the centrality of narrating one's stories by oneself as a panacea to the distorted history, rumor and half-truth about Africa by non-African writers of African stories. Therefore, *Things Fall Apart* is a re-creation of African history from African perspectives. Achebe in *Morning yet on Creation Day* stated that,

> I would be quite satisfied if my novels (especially the ones I set in the past) did no more than teach my readers that their past with all its imperfections-was not

long night of savagery from which the first Europeans acting on God's behalf delivered them.⁹

THE IGBO WORLDVIEW

The Igbos are unique people with distinct culture and belief system. The Igbos, for instance, are polytheistic in nature, that is, "Both nature and the universe held in awe and revered."¹⁰ The Igbos also believe in supernatural and the significant impacts of the dead over the livings. The belief in the potency of the ancestral is the main basis for the presence of Egwugwu during important festivals or when serious cases are to be settled between individuals or communities. Romanus Ogbonnaya Ohuchesubmitted that, "There is a set of ancestral spirits made up of the dead members of the community. Events in the world are explained in terms that are not always in agreement with explanations proffered by modern science."¹¹ He further stated that life among the Igbos is communalistic and the community consists of the living and the dead. Quoting Professor V. E. King, he further asserted that, "The land is the principal bond of unity . . . the begetter of the unborn, the upholder of the living, the custodian of dead."¹²

It is also important to note that among the Igbos, the idea of a central supreme god doesnot exist. The society is highly fragmented with every human and his/her god, Michael, J. C. Echeruo in his 979 Ahiajoku Lecture affirmed that among the Igbos

> Every man, they said, was a god in his house, every village was an autonomous community; federations and alliances were exactly that: affiliations of convenience which did not pretend to be new political entities capable of transforming the primary pattern of political sovereignty in the federating units.¹³

The Igbos are independent minded. They are community of people that eulogize chivalry while condemning indolence. Olaudah Equiano, an American slave of Igbo origin once in his autobiography published in 1798, praised the contributory roles of every individual among the Igbos communities. He further affirmed that, "everyone contributed something to the common stock, and as we are unacquainted with idleness, we have no beggars."¹⁴

Also, central to the worldviews of the Igbos is religion/spirituality. The Igbos do not have a universal supreme God although this assertion is debatable. The idea of god is individualized and personalized. According to Echeruo, the Igbos only respect the gods who respect themselves, and when the gods "consistently fail to prove themselves powerful, we reserve the right to discard them and seek out new gods. In fact, circumstances greater than the gods themselves will take care of the matter."[15] Echeruo further affirmed that the only exception to this rule is Ala, the goddess of the earth, which Achebe makes copious references to in *Things Fall Apart*. The Igbo society is observed to be highly decentralized. The political and the religious structures of the Igbos are made in a way that care were being taken not to concentrate power in a single hand.

Closely related to the concept of religion and god is the issue of superstitions and rituals. The Igbos are ruled and governed by superstitions such as the belief that a particular plant could grant victory in fight or that a raffia palm hears words when its ownership is being disputed. D. I. Nwoga, supported by I. A. Richard, states that ritual is important among the Igbos because it is believed among the people to facilitate their farming and it is also "a means of enforcing tribal ethics supporting authority, making possible the re-forming of groups and assumption of new roles after marriage, peacemaking or death."[16] In sum, Igbo society is a decentralized society both politically and religiously. Rituals and superstitions sustain the society with the *Dibia* wielding enormous power among the people.

SIGNS, SYMBOLS, AND SIGNIFICATION

Human world is coded with universal signs and symbols. Ernest Cassier described man, "as a symbolic animal" while Richard C. Onwuanibe described symbol as "a sign which points to the presence of another with additional value(s) according to the intentionality of the user."[17] Symbol, according to Ricoeur, is "any structure of signification in which a direct, primary literal meaning designates in addition another meaning which is indirect, secondary and figurative and which can be apprehended only through first."[18] Symbols communicate universal meanings; therefore, in the deployment of symbolism in literature, the relationship between the signifier and the signified is natural.

The system of signs and symbols are paramount in literary criticism. According to Jonathan Culler, "Criticism is the pursuit of signs, in that critics, whatever their persuasion, are incited by the prospect of grasping, comprehending, capturing in their prose, evasive signifying structures."[19] Referring to Ferdinand de Saussure, Jonathan Culler affirmed that,

> linguistics would one day be part of a comprehensive science of signs which would study the production of meaning in culture and society ... The prospect of placing literary studies within a larger science of signs and seemed not only possible but desirable-the key both energizing literary Studies and to solidifying their central place within the humanities and social sciences.[20]

He concludes by stating that literature is an embodiment of signs and symbols. Literary works deploy language to create permanent images and totems in the minds of the readers. What is left to the literary critics is to identify such totems and create meaning out of them. Whatever interpretation given by the critics would be predicated on his/her background and the understanding of the text.

SYMBOLS AND IMAGERIES IN CHINUA ACHEBE'S *THINGS FALL APART*

Symbols and imageries are wrapped in metaphoric expression to beautify a literary work. Without imageries and symbols, the literary work would be too watery and ordinary. *Things Fall Apart is* beautified with imageries and symbols. This has added to the aesthetics of the work and has great impacts on its readability and meanings. In Achebe's *Things Fall Apart*, Okonkwo, the protagonist of the text is presented as a man of valor. Okonkwo epitomizes a typical African hero. He becomes famous after he succeeds in throwing "Amalinze the cat at eighteen"[21] during the yam festival ceremony. This is monumental because Okonkwo had rewritten Amalinze the cat's history whose back now "touch the earth"[22] in the wrestling duel against his performances in his previous outings. Okonkwo is probably thirty-eight years old when the story begins. The writer presents Okonkwo thus, "Okonkwo's fame had grown like a bush fire in the harmattan. He was tall and huge and his bushy eyebrows and wide nose gave him a severe look."[23] Okonkwo chivalry contradicts his father's acts of laziness. Okonkwo's father, Unoka is a worthless man who spends most of his lifetime drinking and singing. Through binary opposition, the narrator compared the chivalry of Okonkwo with the ineptitude of his father "Unlike his father he could stand the look of blood. In Umuofia latest war he was the first to bring home a human head. On great occasions such as the funeral of a village, celebrity he drank his palm-wine from his first human head."[24] Having the courage of withstanding the flowing of "blood" especially during war is counted as a symbol of chivalry among the Igbos.

Okonkwo's father Unoka is regarded as an *Agbala,* a man without a title just like women who are not allowed to take titles among the Igbos. Unoka always has a poor harvest. The priestess of Agbala let Unoka know that his bad harvest is because of his laziness. Among the Igbos, chivalry is applauded while indolence is rebuked. Unoka dies of swollen stomach, an abominable disease and death that confines the sufferer to be buried in the evil forest; Unoka dies without title nor grave. He dies shamefully. African society is mostly patriarchal and being a man confers some privileges on one but Unoka is relegated to being a woman, which is an insult to his personality. Nwakibie is a great man in Umuofia with nine wives, over thirty children, and three barns of yam. Anasi, the eldest wife of Nwakibe wears the "anklet of her husband's titles which the first wife alone could wear."[25] The anklet is a symbol of affluence, power, and authority.

Okonkwo has been widely acknowledged by critics as an embodiment of Igbo culture and the symbol of masculinity and patriarchy. Okonkwo is a model; a perfect representation of what is expected in a man of valor, strength, energy, determination and courage. Abiola Irele sees Okonkwo as, "the incarnation of his society's ideal of manhood."[26] Okonkwo is a patriarchaland fatherly figure who takes care of his father, mother, and two sisters. He allows his wives to grow women's crops such as cocoyam, beans and cassava while he exclusively grows "yam the king of crops."[27] From the above, it could be deduced, that the Umuofia society is a male dominated society where women are restricted from growing economic and viable corps like yams but are allowed to grow less economic viable crops like beans and cocoyam. Yam, the king of all food is highly symbolic among the Igbos. Michael J. C. Echeruo in his 1979 Ahiajoku lecture affirmed that, "the yam was the reincarnation of the first son of an Afikpo woman sacrificed on the orders of the oracle, Ibu Ukpabi."[28] It is also reported by the same authority that when the woman sacrificed a slave to the god, the community harvested bastard yams but when she sacrificed his son, the community had a bountiful yam harvest. It is, therefore, believed among the Igbos that when the year yam harvest is poor, the entire community is doomed to be starved. It is as a result of this that Echeruo concluded that among the Igbos, yam assumed the "status of a god of life"[29] The essence of making yam an exclusive crop of men is to preserve patriarchal hegemony and male chauvinism while cocoyam, also known as *ede* is permissible to be planted by women. As parts of the tradition of the people, it is not permissible to eat the new yam prior the Ahiajoku festival, that is, festival of propitiation to the god of yam called njoku. Donatus I. Nwoga affirmed that the Ahiajoku festival or yam festival is a period of thanksgiving and cleansing. The community is cleansed against misfortune and illnesses. The festival is also a communion between the livings and the dead.[30]

Okonkwo, the representative of Igbo culture and tradition in the novel, is a male chauvinist who believes so much in strength and his life is characterized by war, fighting, and struggle. At a tender age, he has won the title of the best wrestler in Umuofia. Okonkwo always discourages his sons from listening to woman stories, which revolve around tortoise and the bird *eneke—nti—oba,* he believes that a real man must listen to stories about war and bloodshed.

Chinua Achebe's *Things Fall Apart also* delves into the African Philosophy and the belief in re-incarnation. The Igbos' philosophy according to Donatus I. Nwoga is rooted in duality. That is "all beings with agency have their physical existence and their deistic counterparts."[31] This has resulted in their belief in the concepts and existence of *Chi*. This belief is evident in the traditional beliefs such as the Egwugwu tradition and the belief in *Abiku/ Ogbanje*. The *Ogbanje* children among the Igbos, *Abiku* in Yoruba or *Dan Wahabi* in Hausa is a child that belongs to the spirit world. Achebe refers the *Ogbanjes* as "those wicked children who when they died entered, their mother's womb to be born again."[32] Ezinwa, Okonkwo's daughter is believed to be an *Ogbanje* and a *Dibia* (medicine man or traditional healer) called Okagbue has to be invited to severe the bond between Ezinwa and the spirit world by excavating Ezinma's *Iyi Uwa*. The *Ogbanje* children are known for their frequent deaths and their endless return to the same family. Among the Igbos, just like most other African societies, there is mutual interrelationship between the living and the dead. The presence of the ancestors among the Igbos is respected and perceived as real.

The *Egwugwus* symbolize the ancestral fathers on earth and patriarchal figures. The *Egwugwu* shrine allows only men to enter the groove despite that the groove is always taken care of by women. The *Egwugwu* are symbols of male dominion over women. They are maintained as an element of social control towards the sustenance of male hegemonic society. The nine *Egwugwus* are symbolic representationsof the component villages of Umuofia. The Egwugwus are also the symbolic representation of the ancestral fathers on earth and it authenticates the belief of the Igbos about the harmonious interrelationship between the dead and the living.

The *Egwugwus* represent the highest court of appeal in Igbo land. The *Egwugwus,* as the symbols of the ancestors, wield enormous powers and this explains why they adjudicate the dispute between Uzowulu and his wife. The second case they look into is a serious land dispute. Egwugwu are symbols of male power. Their characterization in the story further lends credence to the fact that the African people are highly civilized and organized before the arrival of the Europeans. Their presence in the story further affirms the fact that the Igbos have a well-organized judicial system before the European incursion into the land.

However, in the Igbo traditional society, characters like Chielo, the priestess of *Agbala*, the oracle of the Hills and Caves[33] deconstructs the male hegemonic syndrome as she gives order, just like men and wields enormous powers over the *Ogbanje* children and other sundry issues. Life in African's worldview is transitional and cyclical. This means that death is not the end of human life. Those who lived their life to the brim and died at old age would be welcome into the guild of ancestors, oversee and exert significant control over the lives of the livings. This explains why the ancestral fathers are earthly represented by the *Egwugwus*. Reviewing the African Cosmology and worldview, the narrator states:

> The land of the livings was not far removed from the domain of the ancestors. There was coming and going between them, especially at festivals and also when an old man died because an old man was very close to the ancestors. A man is life from birth to death was a series of transition rites which brought him nearer and nearer to his ancestors.[34]

African Cosmology also relies on fate and destiny. Human's life is timed and predestined. Okonkwo's life has been disturbed by pathological fear, the fears of failure. His father, Unoka, lived a failed life which Okonkwo is working assiduously to erase in his life. He starts his early in life as a highly focused and ambitious young man. He sets out early in life to meet Nwakibie who grants him four hundred seeds of yams to begin his life towards becoming a great farmer. At a very tender age, he assumes the responsibility of taking care of his parents and two sisters. However, there is a higher order that controls his ambition as reflected in the upheavals that characterize his life.

The Igbos also believe in Chi or personal god. It has been earlier submitted that the belief in the existence of Chi further corroborates the Igbos belief in duality. The narrator expresses the symbolic life of Okonkwo who has to be banished from his father's land after inadvertently committed a murder. His life has been arm stringed by his *Chi*. The narrator acknowledges this by stating that,"A man could not rise beyond the destiny of his chi; the saying of the elders was not true that if a man says yea his chi also affirmed. Here was a man whose chi said nay despite his own affirmation."[35] On the Igbo belief in *chi* Edward Okoro writes,

> *Chi* is a good example of a symbol with accumulative intention, a traditional sapiential and religious symbol which has taken on so many contradictory values that tend to neutralize one another. The *Chi* symbol also demonstrates the potentiality of some symbols to acquire oppositional values and function that make polysemy one of the prime problems of semantics.[36]

Okonkwo has been banished at the peak of his career in line with the dictate of his destiny. He commits an inadvertent murder and has to be banished in line with the tradition of their people. The departure of Okonkwo from Umuofia marks the end of the pre-colonial era and what happens afterwards is an anti-climax-the reign of the white people all across the surrounding villages of Umuofia and even Mbata, Okonkwo's mother village. The white men arrive as the breakers of the nation. The news of the arrival of the white men is broken to Okonkwo at Mbata by his friend, Obierika who reports to him that, the white man "was not an albino. He was quite different . . . And he was riding an iron horse . . . The elders consulted their oracle and it told them that the strange man would break the clan and spread destruction among them."[37] The oracle further prophesies that other destroyers are on their way to the clan and the worst might have not been heard about the coming of the white people. The people of Abama kill the first white man they come across while his bicycle is tied to a tree. In a reprisal attack, the Whites massacre the people of Abame, and the ruin they left in Abame is reported thus, "Their clan is now completely empty. Even the sacred fish in their mysterious lake have fled and the lake has turned the colour of blood. A great evil has come to their land as the oracle had warned."[38] The implication of this is that the coming of the white people had caused destruction to both the fauna and flora components of the Umuofia Communities.

The people despise those that join the white men's ways of life as *efulefu*— "worthless empty man."[39] According to Chielo, the priestess of Agbala, those who have joined the new religion are "the excrement of the clan, and the new faith was a mad dog that had come to eat it"[40] The missionaries want the people of Mbata to leave their gods and worship their new God. The people including Okonkwo find this to be an affront against their tradition and culture of Igbos. Meanwhile, Nwoye, the son of Okonkwo and his likes have already abandoned the African ways of life and are now adherents of the new religion. At Mbata the new Catechist named Kiaga has got his first convert, Nneka, the wife of Amadi. Nneka is converted based on some of the challenges that he has suffered under the yolk of the Igbo tradition. The Igbo traditions see the birth of twins as evil and as a result, twins are always thrown into the evil forest. The new converts see the new religion as a viable alternative to the tradition religious practices under the new religion; twins are welcome and the idea of throwing the twins into the evil forest is abolished. According to the narrator, "Nneka had four previous pregnancies and child birth. But each time she had borne twins, and they had been immediately thrown away."[41] The people of Mbata see the conversion of Nneka into Christianity as a good riddance.

The new religion serves as a symbol of hope to the new converts. The catechists are deus ex machina and harbinger of hopes and succor to the ostracized people in Umuofia communities. Another convert to the new religion is Nwoye, the son of Okonkwo. Okonkwo perceives the conversion of Nwoye into Christianity as unfortunate and as a reincarnation of Unoka, the effeminate father of Okonkwo. Okonkwo who is feared across the nine villages of Umuofia begets Nwoye. Okonkwo is called "Roaring Flame" and he wonders why he could beget a degenerate and effeminate brat like Nwoye.[42] Though in his sub-conscious mind, the truth stacks him in the face that "Living Fire begets cold impotent ash"[43] Nwoye's character is in binary to the enviable and chivalric character of Okonkwo.

The arrival of the white people brings a lot of polarization and disunity to the African people. The umbilical cord that binds the people has been severed and things are fallen apart. The missionaries are accepting the rejected twins dumped in the evil forest and raising them in the church. They have no problem with this. Beyond the religion and the campaigns against the killings of twins, the white people have also brought government. They have brought court where those who violates the laws of the white man are tried and convicted. According to the narrator.

> But stories were already gaining ground that the white man had not only brought a religion but also a government. It was said that they had built a place of judgment in Umuofia to protect the followers of their religion. It was even said that they had hanged one man who killed a missionary.[44]

The Igbo tradition also operates a caste system whereby those that are tagged as *osu* are treated as the descendants of slaves and thereby not allowed to enjoy the same privilege and rights with the freeborn. The new religion abolishes the *osu* caste system and treats all the entrants into the new religion as equal. The church adopts this new system because according to the tenet of their religion, "Before God . . . There is no slave or free. We are all children of God and we must receive these brothers"[45] This new step by the church is symbolic and a major turning point in the life the Igbos. It changes the worldviews of the Igbo people. The narrator gives a vivid description of the *osu* caste system and why the Igbos always ostracize and outcast them. The narrator explains who an *osu* is. Achebe states that an *osu* cannot marry the free born, they are confined into an area different from the freeborn. They are denied access to community gatherings and meetings and they are buried in the evil forest whenever they die.[46]

Things Fall Apart displays high level of philosophical statement laden with animal imageries. The Igbo society portrayed in the text considers every man's problem as everybody's problem. This explains why it is easier for Okonkwo to be easily integrated and accommodated in Mbata community. At Okonkwo feast organized for him by his maternal relatives at Mbata, Uchendu, his uncle says the following prayers.

> We do not ask for wealth because he that has health and children will also have wealth. We do not pray to have more money but to have more kinsmen. We are better than animals because we have kinsman. An animal rubs its itching flank against a tree a man asks his kinsman to scratch him.[47]

The word "wealth" above is symbolic. It represents material accumulation. African societies cherish good health and children above material accumulation. They also take as important, kinsman and relatives. A man that has kinsman has wealth, if he runs into trouble his kinsman will be at his aid. The narrator further states that when kinsmen gather, they do so not because they lack food in their various houses or cannot see the moonlights in their respective houses but "We come together because it is good for kinsman to do so."[48]

PROVERBS AS SYMBOLS IN CHINUA ACHEBE'S *THINGS FALL APART*

Africans love speaking with riddles and proverbs among the Igbos, and its appropriate usage, are marks of wisdom. *Things Fall Apart* highlights the richness of African proverbs. The characters in the novel, especially the elders among them, make use of proverbs to add meanings to their words. The coming together of people in the text brings about proverbs.

To start with, the use of kolanut to entertain visitors among Igbos is predominant. The Igbos use Kolanuts to entertain their guests especially during peace period. Okoye in a conversation with Unoka, Okonkwo's father says "He who brings kola brings life"[49] The kola in the above proverb is a symbol of peace and admittance. To offer kola to the visitors signifies that the host is welcoming the visitor wholeheartedly.

Another proverb used in honour of Okonkwo is "if a child washes his hands he could eat with the kings."[50] Okonkwo is a young man who is accepted into the folds of the elders because of his Chilvary and hardwork. Despite his hardwork, Okonkwo is always hunted with his birth—his origin. His late father Unoka is a weaking, a titless *Agbala*, so when people talk about lazy people, he has a way of not laughing at them rather he always feels sober about his birth. The narrator says "an old woman is always uneasy when any bones are mentioned in a proverb"[51] This proverb justifies while Okonkwo cannot laugh at the humble background of Obiako. Proverbs serve as the conversation tools among adult population. In a conversation between Okonkwo and Nwakibie, Okonkwo says, "The lizard that jumped from high iroko tree to the ground said he would praise himself if no one did."[52] Nwakibie adopts another proverb to reply him thus: " Eneke the birds says that since men have learnt to shoot without missing, he has learnt to fly without perching."[53] He adds, "You can tell a ripe corn by its look."[54] One major attribute of the above proverbs is that they are decorated with local imageries as exemplified by words such as lizard, iroko, Eneke the birds, corn etc. These are familiar totems in a typical agrarian community such as the Umuofia where the story is set.

Okonkwo, the protagonist of the text, calls a man named Osugo a woman because he has taken no title. One of the elders rebuked Okonkwo for his insolence and says "those whose palm-kernels were cracked for them by a benevolent spirit should not forget to be humble"[55] This proverb is significant because Okonkwo could have lived to become inconsequential like Osugo in Umuofia if not for the benevolence of the likes of Nwakibie who lends him a helping hand. By looking down on the character of Osugo, Okonkwo seems to have forgotten about his own humble background.

Ikemefuna, the sacrificial lamb given to the people of Umunofia after an Umuofia woman is killed by another person from the neighboring village who is kept in the house of Okonkwo as slave. The growth of Ikemefuna is described thus, "Ikemefuna . . . grew rapidly like a yam tendril in the rainy season and was full of the sap of life."[56] The " yam tendril" above, conveys an image of youthfulness, freshness, beauty, fragility, healthiness and innocence. This description of Ikemefuna later makes his death more tragic in the later part of the novel.

Also the narrator foregrounds the coming of locusts in the novel as harbinger of tragedy and death. The period and time of arrival of the locusts symbolize calamity. According to the narrator, the locusts come during "the cold harmattan season after the harvest had been gathered."[57] The locusts are known as insects of destruction while the harmattan period, equivalent to the winter season in Europe, is always associated with death. The locusts' arrival is accompanied with gloom and darkness, "And then quite suddenly a shadow fell on the world, and the sun seemed hidden behind a thick cloud."[58] The narrator continues,

> And then appeared on the horizon a slowly mooning mass like a boundless sheet of black cloud drifting towards Umuofia—soon is covered half the sky, and the solid mass was now broken by tiny eyes of light like shinning star. Dust[59]

The locust arrived as a large dark body with sinister intent. The imagery used gives the idea of how the locust arrives and the impression they form in the mind of the people. At connotative level of interpretation, the locusts are the white men, the intruders whose presence in Umuofia destroy the culture and tradition of the people.

The novelist sometimes employs imagery and hyperbolic statement in his work. The narrator describes the market of Umuike thus: "The market of Umuike is a wonderful place . . . There are so many people on it that if you threw up a grain of sand it would not find away to fall to earth again."[60]

In the novel, song is also used as a symbol especially the type that is laden with sexual imagery as found in the text. Some of the songs such as the bridal song rendered at Obierika's daughter's wedding. The rendition goes thus:

If I hold her hand she says "Don't touch!" if I hold her foot she says "Don't touch!" but when I hold her waist-beads she pretend not to known.[61]

The above bridal song further accentuates the fickleness of women. Bridal songs across the major ethnic groups in Nigeria always highlight the richness of African cultures. Through marriage ceremonies in *Things Fall Apart*, Achebe grants us the opportunity to have more knowledge about Igbo traditions. To achieve this, the audience come in contact with Obierika's daughter, Akueke wedding ceremony in the text. It is narrated in the story that her bride price is fixed at "twenty bags of cowries."[62] The bride price is symbolic because it portrays the precolonial Igbo society as a society where young women are seen as commodities to be sold into marriage. In Mbata, Uchendu's son, Amikwu also gets married.

NAME AS SYMBOLS IN ACHEBE'S *THINGS FALL APART*

The setting of the novel is symbolic. The name "Umuofia" means "Children of the forest." The name is highly symbolic as it aptly captures the agrarian nature of the Umuofia communities. Africa names are generally symbolic and reflective of the mood and the circumstance that surround the birth of a child. In *Things Fall Apart,* names of characters are used symbolically for instance, the *Ogbanje* children, "one of those wicked children who, when they died, entered their mother's wombs to be born again"[63] are named differently. Some of the names the igbos give to the Ogbanje children are "'Onwumbiko'—'Death I implore you'—Ozoemena—'May it not happen again'—and Onwuma—'Death may please himself.'"[64]

When Okonkwo moves to Mbata, his mother's village. Okonkwo organizes a feast for his mother's clans people. At the reception, Uchendu, Okonkwo's uncle asks rhetorically, "why it is that one of the commonest names we give to our children is Nneka, or mother is supreme?"[65] The above name is symbolic and renders a valid justification on why Okonkwo has to seek refuge in his mother's village when he is chased away in Umnofia after committing an inadvertent murder. Based on the naming system, Okonkwo gives the name of the first child he has in exile as Nneka "mother is supreme."[66] When he gives birth to a male child, he names him "Nwofia-Begotten in the wilderness."[67]

CONCLUSION

This chapter examined how the foremost African writer and novelist, Chinua Achebe deploys imageries and symbols in projecting Igbo cultures. The chapter focuses on local imageries used in the text as well as the symbolic use of proverbs and names. The common feature of most of the instances cited is that symbols and imageries that are used in the novel help to give a detailed picture of the Igbo culture. It also adds glamor and embellishment to the work. The appropriate deployment of symbols and imageries in the text has also portrayed Chinua Achebe as a quintessential African literary artist, an Igbo/African cultural activist and a master storyteller.

NOTES

1. Chinua Achebe, *Things Fall Apart* (London: Heinemann, 1958).
2. Joyce Cary, *Mr Johnson*, (London: Thirstle Publishing, 2016).
3. Joseph Conrad, *Heart of Darkness*, (California:Coyote Canyon Press, 2007).
4. Tanure Ojaide, "Modern African Literature and Cultural Identity," *African Studies Review*, Vol. 35 Issue 3 (1992): 43–57.
5. Souleymann Bachir Diagne, "Reading Aime Cesaire Negritude as Creolization," *Small Axe*, 19(3) (48),(2015): 121–128.
6. Patrick Williams, Laura Chrismas, (ed.) *Colonial Discourse and Post-Colonial Theory: A Reader.* (New York: Columbia University Press, 1994), 2.
7. Mohammed Alquwaizani, "Internationalizing the Domestic: The Harlem Renaissances and the Third World anti-colonial Movements." Retrieved from https://reader.elsevier.com, (April 2010, Accessed on July 23, 2019), 62
8. Chinua Achebe, *Home and Exile*, (New York: Penguin, 2001), 73.
9. Chinua Achebe, *Morning yet on Creation Day* (London: Heinemann, 1975).
10. Romanus Ogbonnaya Ohuche, *Ibu Anyi Ndanda: The Centrality of Education in Igbo Culture. 1991 Ahiajoku Lecture*, retrieved from, http://ahiajoku.igbonet.com/1991/. 1991 (1)
11. Romanus Ogbonnaya Ohuche, "Ibu Anyi Ndanda: The Centrality of Education in Igbo Culture,"1.
12. Ibid.
13. Michael J. C. Echeruo, "A Matter of Identity: 1979 Ahiajoku Lecture" (Owerri: Ministry of Information and Culture, 1979), 1.
14. Cited in Echeruo, "A Matter of Identity," 1.
15. Echeruo, "A Matter of Identity," 1.
16. Donatus I. Nwoga. "Nka Na Nzere: The Focus of Igbo Worldview" *Ahiajoku Lecture Series*, Retrieved from http://ahiajoku.igbonet.com/1984, (1)
17. Edward Okoro, "Chi Symbols in Achebe's *Things Fall Apart*: A Hermeneutic Understanding." OGIRISI: A New Journal of African Studies, Vol. 5 (2008): 56.
18. Paul Ricoeur, *Symbolism of Evil*, E. Buchnam (Trans.) (New York: Harper and Row, 1967), 12.
19. Jonathan Culler, *The Pursuits of Signs Semiotics, Literature, Deconstruction*, (London and New York: Routledge, 2001), vii.
20. Ibid., *xiii*

21. Achebe, *Things Fall Apart*, 3.
22. Ibid.
23. Ibid.
24. Ibid., 8–9.
25. Ibid., 10.
26. Abiola Irele *The African Imagination: Literature in Africa and the Black Diaspora*, (Oxford: Oxford University, 2001), 129
27. Achebe, *Things Fall Apart*, 18.
28. Echeruo, "A Matter of Identity," 1.
29. Echeruo, "A Matter of Identity," 1.
30. Nwoga. "Nka Na Nzere," 1.
31. Ibid.
32. Achebe, *Things Fall Apart*, 62.
33. Ibid., 85.
34. Ibid., 97.
35. Ibid., 104
36. Okoro, "Chi Symbols in Achebe's *Things Fall Apart*,"62.
37. Achebe, *Things Fall Apart*, 110–111.
38. Ibid.,112.
39. Ibid., 115.
40. Ibid.
41. Ibid., 121.
42. Ibid., 123.
43. Ibid.
44. Ibid., 124.
45. Ibid., 125.
46. Ibid., 125–126.
47. Ibid., 132.
48. Ibid., 133.
49. Achebe, *Things Fall Apart*, 5.
50. Achebe, *Things Fall Apart*, 7.
51. Achebe, *Things Fall Apart*, 16.
52. Achebe, *Things Fall Apart*, 17.
53. Ibid.
54. Ibid.
55. Achebe, *Things Fall Apart*, 21.
56. Achebe, *Things Fall Apart*, 42.
57. Achebe, *Things Fall Apart*, 44.
58. Achebe, *Things Fall Apart*, 41.
59. Achebe, *Things Fall Apart*, 45.
60. Achebe, *Things Fall Apart*, 90.
61. Achebe, *Things Fall Apart*, 95.
62. Achebe, *Things Fall Apart*, 51.
63. Achebe, *Things Fall Apart*, 62.
64. Achebe, *Things Fall Apart*, 61.

65. Achebe, *Things Fall Apart*, 106.
66. Achebe, *Things Fall Apart*, 130.
67. Ibid.

BIBLIOGRAPHY

Achebe, Chinua. *Things Fall Apart.* London: Heinemann Educational Books, 1958.
———. *Home and Exile.* London: Oxford University Press, 2000.
———. *Morning Yet on Creation.* London: Heinemann Educational Books, 1975.
———. "Named for Victoria, Queen of England." In *Hopes ad Impediments: Selected Essays 1965–1987*. London: Heinemann, 1988, 22–23.
Alquwaizani, Mohammed, "Internationalizing the Domestic: The Harlem Renaissance and the Third World anti-colonial Movements." *Journalof King Saad University: Languages and Translation*, 23 (1), (2011): 59–64.
Cary, Joyce. *Mister Johnson.* New York: Thistle Publishing, 2016.
Conrad, Joseph. *Heart of Darkness.* California: Coyote Canyon Press, 2007.
Culler, Jonathan. *The Pursuits of Signs Semiotics, Literature, Deconstruction.* London and New York: Routledge, 2001.
Diagne, Souleymane Bachir. "Reading Aime Cecaire Negritude as Creolization." In *Small Axe,* (19) 3, 48, (2015), 121–128.
Echeruo, Michael J. C. "A Matter of Identity." *1979 Ahiajoku Lecture Series*, Retrieved from, http://ahiajoku.igbonet.com/1991, Accessed on 28/8/2019
Irele, Abiola. *The African Imagination: Literaturein Africa and the Black Diaspora.*Oxford: Oxford University Press, 2001.
Lar, Isaac B. "Eurocetricismand Artistic Creation in Chinua Achebe's *Things Fall Apart*." *African Research Review: An International Multi-Disciplinary Journal Ethiopia,* 4 (1), (2010): 93–108.
Nwoga, Donatus I. *"Nka Na Nzere:The Focus of Igbo Worldview. The 1984 Ahiajoku Lecture Series*, Retrieved from, http://ahiajoku.igbonet.com/1984. Accessed August 28, 2019
Ohuche, Romanus Ogbonnaya. *Ibu Anyi Ndanda: The Centrality of Education in Igbo Culture. 1991 Ahiajoku Lecture Series*, Retrieved from, http://ahiajoku.igbonet.com/1991/, Accessed 25/8/2019
Ojaide, Tanure. "Modern African Literature and Cultural Identity." *African Studies Review.* 35(3), (1992): 43–57.
Ojike, Mbonu. *My Africa.* New York: The John Day Company, 1946.
Okoro, Edward. "Chi Symbols in Achebe's *Things Fall Apart*: A Hermeneutic Understanding." *OGIRISI: New Journal of African Studies*. 5 (1), (2008), 55–56.
Ricoeur, Paul. *Symbolism of Evils.* Trans. E. Buchnam. New York: Harper and Row, 1967.
Whittaker, David, and Msiska Mpalive-Hangson. *Chinua Achebe's Things Fall Apart.* New York: Routledge, 2007.
Wiredu, Kwesi. *Philosophy and an African Culture.* London: Cambridge University, 1980.

Chapter 4

Igbo Communal Ethos
A Reading of Chinua Achebe's Things Fall Apart *and* Arrow of God

Ijeoma Nwajiaku

ON INTERPRETATIONS OF IGBO LIFE

The literary corpus of the world-renown but now late Chinua Achebe will continue to furnish scholars with invaluable resources for the interrogation and interpretation of diverse facets of Igbo life and culture. Anthonia Kalu notes how "Achebe's interpretations of Igbo life place him among the artists and philosophers of Igbo tradition."[1] Kalu's observation assumes relevance here because it underscores the conviction that Achebe's texts present a view of Igbo tradition from the inside.

Very deliberately, Achebe utilizes Igbo cultural references to create what Kalu further describes as "an Igbo (African) epistemological congruity that traverses all aspects of social and political interaction."[2] Irrefutably, this accounts for the current trend of recusing to Achebe's works for glimpses of sociological/anthropological data on Igbo life. Thinking along similar lines, Joseph McLaren equally enthuses:

> Though considered a work of fiction *Things Fall Apart* is also a literary ethnography of Igbo culture and a semi-historical novel implicitly addressing late-nineteenth-and early-twentieth-century developments in Igbo land.[3]

Although McLaren's specific focus is *Things Fall Apart*, one remains persuaded that the above assertion readily holds for all of Achebe's other works. Writing further, this scholar proclaims how "Achebe's novel offers an alternative way of presenting political and anthropological analysis."[4] For McLaren really, Achebe's undisguised intention to counter records presented from European perspectives and to offer alternative but more accurate views of Igbo life and traditions "can be paralleled to other texts concerned with the Igbo, such as histories and ethnographic studies."[5]

In several ways, Achebe appears to have gone beyond other modern writers in the description and interpretation of Igbo sociopolitical, economic, and religious realities, while remaining as Kalu again notes "within the Igbo art tradition by couching Igbo thought in the "metaphor of myth and poetry."[6] Symbolically speaking, it is to this 'myth and poetry,' that scholars ceaselessly recourse in the boundless efforts to unearth layers of knowledge for the continued comprehension and assimilation of what defines Igbo reality.

The above viewpoints have been outlined for they principally concretize the assumption that Achebe's texts customarily reconstruct and depict a formalization of Igbo traditional life and collective identity. Such assumptions consequently yield an adequate framework for exploring the concept of *ohaka* within the Igbo worldview, as illustrated in Achebe's *Things Fall Apart* and *Arrow of God*.

OHA **AND** *OHAKA*

> Leadership is neither a one-man show nor a matter of hierarchical or aristocratic machination. In it, there is the solidarity of decision and implementation of decision by the members in matters that affect the members. In it, the *oha* is the central focus. For the individual is so, but in *oha*. The *oha* is a community of individuals and the individuals are individuals in oha.[7]

In very ordinary parlance, *oha* symbolizes the people, the populace, or even the community. The communal spirit has a very strong binding force in the Igbo world-view. F.O.C. Njoku in a discourse on the African philosophy of rights enthuses that the community is the 'gravitational force' that pulls and determines the individual.[8] *Oha* is thus a concept that is reiterated, recaptured, and rephrased in diverse ways to convey its significance among the Igbo. In his very informative paper, "Developing Political Leadership in Alaigbo," Osuji presents *oha* thus:

> The oha, that is the gathering of the free-born, adult male population of each Igbo village ruled the village. The oha (public) passed a law and it was obeyed.

Ohanaka (the people makes (sic) the law, Ohaegbulam (the people can make laws that determine people's life and death, hence they should not kill one), ohakwe (the people should agree, form consensus, pass laws). The Igbos placed enormous emphasis on what oha said. In fact, every Igbo is constituted in such a manner that if he did not obtain his village's oha approval, he felt like he was nothing and that he did not exist.[9]

While the Igbo disparate towns did not have a central unified administration, which governed them as a whole, they certainly had structures for self-governance in individual villages. It is generally believed that adult male members of Igbo villages gathered and made decisions as to how to run their affairs. Osuji further notes that the gathering of the collective free-born in Igbo land villages made the laws and rules that governed their people. A few people could 'temporarily' be conferred with executive powers to implement specific rules.[10] The word temporary is significant and underscores the rights of *oha* to withdraw such powers at any time.

The above is significant for it again enables one to understand why the Igbo societies are generally classified as stateless. A description that emanates no doubt from the documented absence of a political structure that encompassed all of Igboland.[11] In "OHAZURUME: The Philosophy and Practice of Decision Making and Consensus Building Among the Ndigbo of Nigeria," Muo and Oghojafor critically identify how traditional African societies are broadly classified into decentralized and centralized systems for administrative/governance purposes. The Igbo are located within the decentralized system, and through its consensus-based apparatus ensures that issues of law-making, social control, and allocation of resources are presided over by entities such as clans, village groups, kindred groups ('Umunna') age grades, and so on.

The implication of the decentralized administrative structure is relevant to the thrust of this study for it primarily takes into consideration respect for and acceptance of communal interests. Alongside is the fact that individual rights and views are respected just as minority views are accommodated, such that this ensures conflict reduction in the society. Significantly, the direct and well-defined participation of the people in decision-making becomes definitive of the *oha* ideology. Symbolically, this idea practically plays out in the fact that the village or town is representative of its socio-political organization. Thus a gathering of *oha*—(the entire free-born, adult male population) made the laws that governed them. Such laws were overtly binding on all. Some men were thus charged with ensuring adherence, and offenders were punished.

It is this crucial involvement of *oha* in the formulation and execution of societal laws (or codes of conduct), that is to say in general governance, and in ensuring that stipulated punishment is apportioned to violators that underscore the notion of "Igbo enwe eze" which simply infers that the Igbo do not have kings. The import of this then is that power resides in *oha,* not in any single individual. Put differently, pre-colonial Igbo societies were predominantly characterized by the absence of any structured hierarchical arrangement headed by a sovereign entity. Describing this trend in his Igbo community, Chidi Osuagwu observes:

> In Obowo we say *oha na awu eze* which is a better framing of Igbo enwe eze. If you come to Obowo and want to address the people assembled, you greet them as *oha na wu eze*—people who are king or people who are the sovereign. It is the argument of who is eze for the Igbo. So when we say Igbo enwe eze, we are saying that no individual is greater than the people (oha). We say that no individual is the Lord of the people because *oha ka nmadu nile* (ohaka), the people are greater than any single individual. It is the issue of where does sovereignty repose? And the Igbo say it reposes in the people.[12]

Although Osuagwu here speaks specifically of the experience in his own locality, the situation readily portrays that in other parts of Igbo land. Accordingly, the significance of the principles embodied within the concept of *oha* in Igbo worldview is such that the term itself remains recurrent in some form or another in every Igbo society and dialect. The following are insightful:

- Ohabudike—oha is valour
- Ohabundu—oha is life
- Ohazurukwe—meaning oha came together to agree or collectively agree.
- Ohazurume—the community collectively act
- Ohazuru—oha is enough/sufficient
- Ohamuru—oha gives life
- Igwebuike—(a variant of oha, implying that the people signify strength)
- Igwedinma—(variant also, meaning that the majority or oha is preferred)
- Ohamara—the people or oha know
- Oradiegwu—the community is terrifying
- Oraegunam—the community should not kill me
- Oranekwu—the community speaks
- Oraneke—the community creates
- Oranedu—the community guides

This list though inexhaustive does highlight the very common usage of *oha* in Igbo discourses; while equally reaffirming its importance over and above the individual. It is important to note also how the word in its diverse dialectical occurrences and usages invariably almost always convey similar meanings. Thus, words like *Ohabudike, Ohadike, orabudike, oradike,* and *Igwebuike* can all translate to mean that "the community is might (mighty), or that the "community is strong."

Muo and Oghojafor's germane study of the principles and philosophy of *Ohazurume* in Igbo Society further serves to sharpen our understanding of governance structures in pre-colonial Igbo land. The study which presents *"OHAZURUME"* literarily as "'the community did this collectively'; 'the people have concurred'; 'it is the people's will'; 'the people have spoken,'" equally examines this concept as the fundamental approach to decision making and consensus-building among the Igbo. Describing the concept further, they write thus:

> It is a concept, philosophy and practice in the management of affairs among Ndigbo that ensures that decisions are easily accepted and implemented because the people have collectively decided. Consensus on the other hand is a situation where all people involved in a decision or an issue can say 'they either agree with the decision or have had 'their day in court' and were unable to convince others of their viewpoint. In the final analysis, everyone agrees to support the outcome.'[13]

The implication of this is crucial. To assert that people have spoken as 'oha,' and therefore as one voice does not necessarily denote the absolute consent of each individual. It does connote, however, that a consensus or general agreement has been reached such that hitherto dissenting voices (unable to alter the position and outlook of others), must now abide by a law adopted or lend their backing to decisions reached. This means again that whatever matter or subject in question is generally presented before the people (adult men), for open dialogue.

Within this public forum, everyone who wishes is allowed to express an opinion and thus contribute to the tabled discussion. At some reasonable point what emerges as the preponderant public view is upheld as the communal decision. The dissenting individuals or those whose opinions run contrary to the favored one(s) receive clarification in the form of a summation of the dominant public agreement. This reemphasizes the *"Ohazurume"* paradigm that esteems individual rights and viewpoints. However, individuals in reciprocation assent and defer to the interest of the community or indeed face communal censor. We proceed therefore to determine how Achebe depicts the ideology of *oha* in his narratives selected for this study.

DISCORDANT PARADIGMS: OKONKWO, EZEULU AND THE COMMUNAL VOICES

Things Fall Apart and *Arrow of God* are both examples of Chinua Achebe's relentless exploration of Igbo life and Igbo world-view. Both texts are set within rural Igbo villages in pre-colonial/colonial Nigeria. Instructively, both texts significantly demonstrate how the communal process of decision-making plays out in the societies examined in the texts. The point has already been made that Igbo society is predominantly "*oha* centered." At a psychological level, therefore, the adult in such a society is mostly influenced by values, norms, and standards which convey and underscore widespread notions. Again, this is because the Igbo traditional society has a strong sense of solidarity and communalism.[14] This notwithstanding, the Igbo people endorse an individual's right to choose and to self-affirmation.

Personal attainments and outstanding achievements are applauded within this society for such factors greatly influence societal assessment and evaluation of an individual. Thus, Achebe writes in *Things Fall Apart* "among these people, a man was judged according to his worth and not according to the worth of his father."[15] Needless to point out how several acclaimed societal attitudes and norms become ingrained over time in the psyche of individuals growing in any society. Okonkwo in *Things Fall Apart* consequently observes with much dismay the disdain with which his lazy, but fun-loving father is treated among his kindred and within the society at large.

From his youth, Okonkwo's vision was visibly formed by his society's definition of an accomplished man. This understanding becomes so embedded in his consciousness that it not only generates an outright repudiation of all that typifies failure but also acts as a catalystic force motivating and manipulating his attitude and actions. His life was in reality controlled by a livid fear of failure. The word "fear" is revealing, for it affords one much relevant insight into the inner working of Okonkwo's mind. We read thus:

> Perhaps down in his heart, Okonkwo was not a cruel man. But his whole life was dominated by fear, the fear of failure and weakness. It was deeper and more intimate than the fear of evil and capricious gods and of magic . . . Okonkwo's fear was greater than these. It was not external but lay deep within himself. It was the fear of himself, lest he should be found to resemble his father.[16]

One notes how this abysmal apprehension metamorphoses into a phobic obsession that dominants Okonkwo's life often transcending normal reasoning. Judged by the standards of his society (also *Oha* here), Unoka his father was deemed a failure, and Okonkwo in desperation seeks to create a counter-image of himself, one that would be in consonance with acceptable communal standards. The extent of emotional pain which he suffered when a playmate referred to his father as *agbala* left Okonkwo with a lasting resentment for all that his father symbolized. Without reservation, he allowed himself to be "ruled by one passion—to hate everything that his father Unoka had loved."[17]

One wonders though how justifiable Okonkwo's perceptions are. Convinced that whatever smirks of gentleness is analogous to weakness, he persistently embraces a flagrant display of aggression which repeatedly has him embroiled in conflict with people, oftentimes quite unnecessarily. The interest here though is particularly in how Okonkwo's inert abhorrence for whatever would portray him as weak before *oha*, pushes him to ludicrous heights and inevitably pitches him for a catastrophic downfall. A few outstanding incidents readily come to mind.

The week of peace was observed by all in Umuofia community. It was usually a period long ordained by the forefathers of the land during which "a man does not say a harsh word to his neighbor." Every member of the community consequently strove to live in peace with the other in order to honor their great goddess of the earth, without whose blessings (it was believed), their crops would not grow. The narrative clearly records how it "was unheard of to beat somebody during the sacred week."[18] Ezeani the priest of the earth goddess, Ani, described Okonkwo's action as a great evil which was capable of unleashing ruin upon the entire clan.

Although Okonkwo was penalized and made to pay a fine, perhaps to appease the goddess, the fact remains that Okonkwo was not one to readily succumb to the desire of the majority, if it required acting differently from his preferred and chosen way. Conceding that in his anger he had forgotten it was the week of peace, but when he began to beat the offending wife, his other "wives ran out in great alarm pleading with him that it was the sacred week."[19] We read however that "Okonkwo was not the man to stop beating somebody halfway through, not even for fear of a goddess."[20] One can well imagine how Okonkwo would deem it an act of weakness if he were forced to stop battering his wife. Thus, his unbridled desire cum need to constantly assert strength and observe all indices of masculinity override simple caution and reason and thus even the voice of *oha*, located this time in the joint pleas of his wives and immediate neighbors all fail to stop his wrong act.

In a most insightful paper, "And the Truth is Made Manifest: The Strong Ones Behind Okonkwo," Chioma Opara, makes the following relevant observations about Okonkwo:

> The Patriarch, Okonkwo, was high-handed and insensitive in his patrilocal, patrilineal and patriarchal household where his word was law. Beneath the veneer of brashness and intransigence was a vein of inferiority complex as well

as weakness. . . . In his will to power, the ambitious Okonkwo, overwhelmed by daunting social realities surrounding his lowly circumstances and embarrassing parentage, suffers from a vitiating inferiority complex.[21]

While one may empathize with Okonkwo in consideration of the psychological trauma which his natal background thrust on him, and even strive to apprehend his overwhelming desire and effort to sever all connections to this daunting background, one nonetheless struggles to justify the extent of his deep-rooted psychological blotches. Opara again notes the dual manifestation of Okonkwo's inner turmoil. First, he "invariably displays fitful bouts of aggression which may be misplaced"[22] and second, his "psychological blotches constitute a patent chink in his amour."[23] Certainly his inability to control his emotional outbursts stemming as it does from a tight maze of fear become representative of a tragic flaw pitching him for an eventual downfall.

Whatever argument may be proffered as justification for Okonkwo's dominating fear, it sadly pales before consideration of acceptable societal standards. The instance where he aims his gun at his wife and pulls the trigger readily comes to mind also. His repugnance for idleness had put him in a sour mood. The period was a festive one, but "he was always uncomfortable sitting around for days waiting for a feast or getting over it. He would be very much happier working on his farm."[24] Consequently, his barely suppressed anger found some vent on his second wife, whom he gave a "sound beating," in order to satisfy his mounting rage, she had merely picked a few leaves off a banana tree, but Okonkwo translated that to killing the tree and thrashed her.

As if this was not enough, her subsequent under-the-breath mutter about a gun that never shot had Okonkwo (who overheard her) run "madly into his room for the loaded gun." We read further that "he ran out again and aimed at her as she clambered over the dwarf wall of the barn."[25] Describing this incident, Achebe narrates:

> He pressed the trigger and there was a loud report accompanied by the wail of his wives and children. He threw down the gun and jumped into the barn, and there lay the woman, very much shaken and frightened but quite unhurt. He heaved a sigh and went away with the gun.[26]

It comes across clearly as aforementioned how Okonkwo's inert personal fear of being perceived as weak in any way at all, assumes the status of a formidable force that overpowers and compels him to act almost subconsciously. Indeed, it would seem that even when he realizes afterward that an action has exceeded the boundaries of acceptable conduct (within the purview of *oha*) in his society, Okonkwo is loath to betray any visible remorse. Thus, when he desecrated the week of peace he was inwardly repentant but since "he was not the man to go about telling his neighbor that he was in error," people generally mistook his ambiance for arrogance and utter disregard for the gods of the clan. Also, when he shot at his wife in blind fury, the realization of what he had done caused him to quickly clamber into the barn after her. Again, his relief at her unhurt state was a heavy but controlled sigh.

Perhaps though the most outstanding incident in Okonkwo's life which stands him against the majority view is his involvement in the killing of Ikemefuna. Quite unexpectedly, Ogbuefu Ezeudu, (the oldest man in Okonkwo's quarter of Umuofia), comes to visit. Without taking a seat, and after refusing the offer of a meal, he simply asks to have a word with Okonkwo outside. In very serious tones, and giving Okonkwo no chance to say anything, this old man enjoins the latter to have nothing to do with the death of Ikemefuna. Reiterating the premise that the boy calls Okonkwo "father," Ogbuefi Ezeudu repeats his injunction and leaves.

For whatever reason, Okonkwo elects to disregard the old man's wise counsel and goes along with others to carry out the unpleasant assignment. While on the mission to kill the boy, Okonkwo's phobic dread of being considered weak again overtakes him, so he raises his machete and cuts down the young boy running towards him, obviously for help with a frightened cry of "my father, they have killed me!" The group's disdain for those who opted not to accompany them shows clearly in their comments about "some effeminate men who had refused to come with them."[27] One wonders at subsequent developments in Okonkwo's life. In a most bizarre twist of events, for instance, his gun explodes at the burial rite activities of Ogbuefi Ezeudu leaving the man's sixteen-year-old son lying dead in a pool of blood. This catalystimatic incident triggers off a chain of events with multi-ripple effects.

While the text does not provide a clear correlation between these two occurrences, one takes into cognizance the strong kinship spirit among Igbo people. Within this society also biological bonds are solid and respected, just as blood, considered the live wire of human life is held very sacred. Okonkwo consequently violates several communal codes when he spills Ikemefuna's blood. Obierika his bosom friend is sharp in his retort that he did not want to go on the mission to kill Ikemefuna because he had something better to do. His reprimand of Okonkwo's complicity is clear. Okonkwo defensively disagrees with Obierika and struggles to justify his role in carrying out the bidding of the god.

This dialogue ends in a dead-lock as the men are interrupted by the arrival of a visitor. Yet it comes across glaringly that Okonkwo's views frequently diverge from those of the majority-*oha*. Perhaps Obierika had refrained from going along on the basis of his close-knit relationship with Okonkwo and his household, which at this time obviously includes Ikemefuna also, (noticed when his daughter got married). If this Obierika recognizes and respects existing family/friendship ties as is expected, one is more perplexed at Okonkwo's utter disregard for the bond (akin to parental adoption), which had existed between himself and Ikemefuna. One notes how in his moments of turmoil and anguish he had wondered how he who had killed men in battle could fall to pieces because he had added a boy to their number.[28] Speaking to Obierika too, he had wondered aloud why the former failed to go along to "kill that boy."[29] The words "that boy," coming from Okonkwo raise questions.

Would one be right to assume that in spite of the existing relationship described in the text, Okonkwo somehow still perceives of Ikemefuna as an outsider? Again, Okonkwo's inquiry about his friend's unwillingness to go with the group reveals his utter disregard of Ogbuefi Ezeudu's rather peculiar visit and equally peculiar warning. Indeed, his question to Obierika suggests rather that he had neither given the revered old man's counsel a thought nor contemplated its implementation. Sad indeed that the gravity of the situation was utterly lost on him.

A further conundrum arises from the incidental killing of Ogbuefi's son during the old man's burial. The inexplicability of the ironic event is not lost on a reader. Why indeed did a piece of iron from none other than Okonkwo's exploding gun kill Ogbuefi's son? Is there a possible link between the old man's visit to Okonkwo, the latter's subsequent disobedience and the accident of the young lad's violent death. One recalls Obierika's words to his friend:

> And let me tell you one thing, my friend. If I were you I would have stayed at home. What you have done will not please the earth. It is the kind of action for which the goddess wipes out whole families.[30]

Would one suggest that perhaps the gods did have a hand in the misfortune that befell Okonkwo; causing him and his family to be banished from the land for seven years and by extension precipitating the loss of all that he had laboriously striven to build? Whatever the answers to these complex inquiries, one factor underscores the triggering impulse of Okonkwo's action—his fear of being considered a weakling. This apprehensiveness overrides all reason, and constantly sets the valiant Okonkwo against *oha* to his detriment and eventual downfall.

By the end of the narrative, this great persona is overwhelmed by rage, blinded by hatred and choking with fury over the maltreatment of Umuofia leaders (including himself), by the white administrators. He is persuaded that the only solution to the complex problem was a war aimed at annihilating all the white men and their agents. He however nursed the secret fear that the cowardly Ugonwanne whose "sweet tongue" could "change fire into cold ash," would dissuade the assembly of men from going to war.[31] Ironically though, Okika spoke first and did speak persuasively in favor of a war. Subsequently, events seem however to have been taken out of everyone's hands. Okonkwo's uncontrollable ferocity causes him to behead one of the messengers who had been sent to put an end to the gathering of Umuofia men.

Again, Okonkwo stood and acted alone. The assembly of *oha* did not appear to be in support of his action. As he overheard voices asking why he did it, he rightly discerned the fright in the tumult and knew that his people would not go to war, for they had allowed the other messengers to escape. Alone in these thoughts and action and disappointed in his people, Okonkwo opted for a lonely and miserable death.

One would say that Okonkwo's stand against the community was not premeditated but was on the contrary often based on sudden impulses attributable to his peculiar disposition. An exception may be the period he returned to Umuofia with the other elders after a period of incarceration at the white colonial administrator's office. His deep resentment and pain at the humiliation and ill-treatment they are subjected to cause him to deliberately plan retaliation. He thus decides to avenge himself and resolves to act alone, if Umuofia elected to do nothing.

In several ways, Ezeulu's conflict with his community stands in sharp contrast to Okonkwo's in *Things Fall Apart.* In *Arrow of God*, Achebe again explores the sensitive subject of an individual versus *oha*. In Igbo cosmology, it comes across quite clearly as Akuebue declares that "no man however great can win judgment against a clan." Thus, in this text, what commenced as mere disagreements over critical communal issues sadly assumed heightened proportions and gradually evolved into a major catastrophe that culminated in the disintegration of the society's unifying forces. Ezeulu acting in his capacity as chief priest tries to dissuade his community from sending "an emissary to Okperi with white clay for peace or new palm frond for war."

The community (made up of adult males and leaders) met to deliberate over the issue of a piece of land which was in dispute between them (Umuaro) and the neighboring Okperi. Ezeulu strongly advised his community against the attempts to try to gain ownership of the land, recalling how his late father had told him that the land in question belonged to the Okperi people. Another elder Nwaka (a self-avowed enemy of Ezeulu's), narrates a different version of the story and successfully persuades the people to seek ownership of the land. Emissaries are sent to Okperi. Unfortunately, events take a negative turn during the trip and a life is lost. Subsequent developments culminate in a war between the two towns and attract the immediate intervention of the white administrators who use soldiers to put a stop to the war.

During the investigation into the dispute Ezeulu in the witness stand reaffirms Okperi's ownership of the land to the annoyance of his people. The ensuing feeling of betrayal carries distrust and suspicion and further exacerbates

Nwaka's resentment and hatred. In many ways, these developments culminated in pitching Ezeulu against his community as it were. During this time Nwaka exploits the Igbo abhorrence for any form of authoritarian leadership to further widen the gap between Ezeulu and members of the community. He reiterates that the people did not need to seek nor obtain permission from any priest of Ulu, before fighting a war. His words are most insightful:

> Nwaka began by telling the assembly that Umuaro must not allow itself to be led by the chief priest of Ulu . . . The man who carries a deity is not a king . . . But I have been watching this Ezeulu for many years. He is a man of ambition; he wants to be king, priest, diviner, all . . . But Umuaro showed him that Igbo people knew no kings. The time has come to tell his son also.[32]

Nwaka here presses his acclaimed oratorical skills to maximal advantage. Preying on the psychology of his people, he evokes their collective distaste for imposed leadership by pointing at Ezeulu's quest for leadership (real or imagined), and enjoins them "not to listen to anyone trying to frighten us with the name of Ulu." Thus, even a chief priest as important as his position is and as sacred as the deities are in the psyche of the people, does not counteract the collective rejection of centralized authority. To seal off this fact, he reminds the assembly about what the people of Aninta did with their deity when it failed them. They carried "it to the boundary between them and their neighbors and set fire on him." By implication, the wish or voice of *oha* holds supreme. Not even a god could at random thwart the will/voice of the majority.

Years later when Ezeulu is incarcerated in the white man's cell, he recalls these incidents as he derives pleasure from the thoughts of his revenge which had formed in his mind as he sat listening to Nwaka in the marketplace. We catch a glimpse of these musings:

> His quarrel with the white man was insignificant beside the matter he must settle with his own people. For years he had been warning Umuaro . . . But they had stopped both ears with fingers. They had gone on taking one dangerous step after another and now they had gone too far. Now the fight must take place . . . Ezeulu's muscles tingled for the fight.[33]

Perhaps this desire and intent heralded the beginning of Ezeulu's complications. In addition, the eventual outcome attests to the superiority of *oha* over the individual and buttresses the assertion that *ohabudike*, which means that the people embody might. Another fallout of the above is that the scenario raises crucial questions as to who or what was responsible for Ezeulu's eventual downfall? His apparent weapon of fight was the people's deity. While in custody at the seat of government, his thoughts clearly reveal his secret hope thus: "Let the white man detain him not for one day but for one year so that the deity not seeing him in his place would ask Umuaro questions."[34]

The question becomes apparent at this point. Was Ezeulu truly fighting a battle on behalf of his deity, Ulu, or was he in actuality using the situation to pursue a personal vendetta in order to prove a point and to reassert his authority? His inner musings above reveal some measure of concealed pride. He appears piqued at his people's rejection of his (perhaps) wise counsel in favor of Nwaka's prejudice and malice-laden one (which also aimed to undermine Ezeulu's authority). A further pointer to Ezeulu's pride can be seen in the incident between him and the white man. An intelligent man, the chief priest knew that his not appearing before the administrator for days after his arrival at Okperi was deliberate. Apparently, it was some retribution for Ezeulu's initial refusal to come at once in response to the messenger's summons. If the white administrator had felt insulted by Ezeulu's reaction and attitude, the latter did not feel any less humiliated by his detention of many days.

It was thus with much disdain and satisfaction that the chief priest turned down the proposal to be made paramount chief, asking the interpreter to "tell the white man that Ezeulu will not be anybody's chief."[35] Afterwards we again observe his private reflections: "Ezeulu himself was full of satisfaction at the way things had gone. He had settled his little score with the white man and could forget him for the moment."[36] Even when the quiet consideration that his friend 'Wintabota' could not mean him harm tries to assert itself, Ezeulu quickly justifies himself: "But what was the value of goodwill which brought him to this shame and indignity?"[37]

Afterwards, Ezeulu is able to set his issue with the white man aside albeit temporarily for he believes he had not yet said the last word to him. His immediate need was to concentrate his energy and resources on his "real struggle" which "was with his own people and the white man was, without knowing it his ally." Consequently, the longer Ezeulu stayed in Okperi, "the greater his grievance, and his resources for the fight" were. In all, he was detained for thirty-two days, and he returned home much more determined to avenge himself on his community for all the shame, humiliation and suffering to which he had been subjected.

The sad scenario which plays out subsequently symbolically captures the conflict between the community (*oha* here) and an individual (albeit a highly placed one). Ezeulu resolves not to announce a date for the New Yam Feast. This expectedly throws the entire community into panic, shock and confusion as nothing like it had ever happened in living memory. From the team of his assistants to a delegation of the most powerful leaders of the land (representing the entire villages of Umuaro), Ezeulu maintains a stoic stance when he rejects their pleas. This was his master ace, and he was not about to renege on the greatest opportunity he had. Refusing all entreaties to call the Feast,

Ezeulu calmly explains to the leaders that the Feast could not be announced until the very last yam had been eaten in accord with tradition.

Although the presentations and arguments of the leaders sound plausible and logical, and they in desperation ask to be liable for whatever the consequence of eating up the remaining yams and calling for the Feast would be, the priest counters their arguments by pointing out that what they ask had never been done and was tantamount to inviting death. At this, the complexity of the conundrum heightens. Ezeulu on the one hand tries to justify his unyielding position by rationalizing how it "was a fight of the gods"[38] and how "he was no more than an arrow in the bow of a god."[39] At the other end, however, is the fact that Ezeulu had "had a long period of silent preparation" before revealing his intention to "hit Umuaro at its most vulnerable point-the Feast of the New Yam."[40] And hit them he did, with a most formidable blow.

The ensuing battle is a long drawn-out one. The priest deigns to say that the gods sometimes use humans as whips.[41] If this was the case, Ezeulu does unleash a most severe thrashing on the community. We read that almost overnight he becomes more of a public enemy in the eyes of all. Ogbuefi Ofoka, one of the elders of the community almost feels that Ezeulu has inherited some of his mother's madness. The majority believe that Ezeulu would rather see the six villages ruined than eat two yams. While the crisis generated by the conflict raged on, the hardship on the populace becomes intolerable. Thus, as the people's harvest gradually wasted away in the hardening soil, they become forced to seek whatever survival strategy offered itself. The catechist of the formerly struggling church in Umuaro suddenly finds opportunity in the deteriorating situation and offers a much-needed respite.

Neighboring towns also cash in to prey on the people of Umuaro. They brought in new yams on the market days and sold them at exorbitant prices. While neither of these two options was palatable to the Umuaro community, the challenges of hunger and impoverishment from ruined harvests continue to compel them to reconsider these. Amid all the confusion which engulfed the community at large, Ezeulu's son Obika dies unexpectedly. Ezeulu himself (not spared from the calamitous situations around him), is unable to apprehend this action of his god, his magnificent mind disintegrates and he lives the rest of his life as a demented high priest. As for his enemies, their summations were simple:

> Their god had taken sides with them against his headstrong and ambitious priest and thus upheld the wisdom of their ancestors-that no man however great was greater than his people; that no one ever won a judgment against his clan.[42]

CONCLUSION: THE SUPREMACY OF OHA

Both Okonkwo and Ezeulu, the great warrior and the renowned priest, come to very tragic ends, thus upholding the notion that the communal voice would ultimately prevail. Ezeulu himself and his arch-enemy Ezeidemili separately attribute Obika's death to a direct action of the god. They could not have known that Obika had been too ill on that fateful night to carry the *Ogbazuluobodo*. His consent under pressure from Aneto was an attempt to avert further accusations of malice at his family. If indeed Ezeulu's god had so afflicted him through this misfortune, one wonders to what purpose and to what end? Would Ulu as Akuebue queries have spared him if he had eaten the yams at once? While clear-cut answers to these questions remain elusive, the truth remains that Ezeulu had engaged his community in a battle and so like Okonkwo also the verdict could only be failure, for the Igbo insist that community is supreme.

NOTES

1. Anthonia Kalu, "Achebe and Duality in Igbo Thought," *The Literary Groit-International Journal of Black Expressive Culture Studies* Vol.10, No. 2, (Fall 1998): 16.

2. Ibid., 19.

3. Joseph McLaren, "Missionaries and Converts: Religion and Colonial Intrusion in *Things Fall Apart*," *The Literary Groit-International Journal of Black Expressive Culture Studies* Vol. 10, No. 2, (Fall 1998): 48.

4. Ibid.

5. Ibid., 49.

6. Kalu, "Achebe and Duality," 23.

7. Pantheleon Osondu Iroegbu, "African Vicious Circles-A Plea for Ohacracy: The Socio-political Lee-Way," Text of Lecture Delivered to the Chaire Hoover, Catholic University of Louvain, Louvain-la-Neuve. November 1997), 3.

8. F. O. C. Njoku, "A Theoretical Foundation for Understanding Law Subjects & Rights in Igbo Philosophy of Law," *Open Journal of Philosophy* Vol. 3. No 1A (2002): 255–265. Cited in D. A. Osuagwu and A. Anyanwu, "A Study of the Concept of Freedom in Igbo Traditional Worldview," *Maryland Studies* Vol 10 (Nov. 2011), 109.

9. Ozodi Osuji,"Developing Political Leadership in AlaIgbo," *BMW Magazine*, 2005<http://magazine.biafranigeriaworld.com>, 12.

10. Ibid.

11. Chinyere Ukpokolo, "Gender Space and Power in the Indigenous Igbo Socio-Political Organization," *Pakistan Journal of Social Sciences* Vol. 7. no 2, (2010): 177–186. Ik Muo and B.E.A. Oghojafor, "OHAZURUME: The Philosophy and

Practice of Decision Making and Consensus Building among the Ndigbo of Nigeria," *American Journal of Business and Management* Vol 1, No 3, (2012): 154–156.

12. The Igbo World-Interview with Professor Chidi Osuagwu (http://groups.yahoo.com/neo/groups/worldIgbocongress/).

13. Muo and Oghojafor, "OHAZURUME," 156. *Italics are mine.*

14. Osuagwu and Anyanwu, "A Study of the Concept."

15. Chinua Achebe, *Things Fall Apart* (Oxford: Heinenamm Educational Publishers, 1958), 6.

16. Ibid., 9–10.

17. Ibid., 11.

18. Ibid., 23.

19. Ibid., 21.

20. Ibid., 21.

21. Chioma Opara, "And the Truth is Made Manifest: The Strong Ones Behind Okonkwo," *Achebe's Women-Imagism and Power*, ed. Helen Chukwuma (Trenton, NJ: Africa World Press, 2012), 28–29.

22. Ibid.

23. Ibid.

24. Ibid.

25. Achebe, *Things Fall Apart*, 27.

26. Ibid., 28.

27. Ibid., 43.

28. Ibid., 45.

29. Ibid., 46.

30. Achebe, *Things Fall Apart*, 40.

31. Ibid., 141.

32. Chinua Achebe, *Arrow of God* (Oxford: Heinemann International Literature and Textbooks, 1964), 27–28.

33. Ibid., 160.

34. Ibid.

35. Ibid., 175.

36. Ibid.

37. Ibid.

38. Ibid., 192.

39. Ibid.

40. Ibid.

41. Ibid., 208.

42. Achebe, *Arrow of God*, 230.

BIBLIOGRAPHY

Achebe, Chinua. *Arrow of God*. Oxford: Heinemann International Literature and Textbooks, 1964.

Achebe, Chinua. *Things Fall Apart*. Oxford: Heinemann Educational Publishers, 1958.

Iroegbu, Pantheleon Osondu. "African Vicious Circles-A Plea for Ohacracy: The Socio-political Lee-Way," Text of Lecture Delivered to the Chaire Hoover, Catholic University of Louvain, Louvain-la-Neuve. November 1997.

Kalu, Anthonia. "Achebe and Duality in Igbo Thought." *The Literary Groit-International Journal of Black Expressive Culture Studies* Vol. 10, No. 2, (Fall 1998): 16.

McLaren, Joseph. "Missionaries and Converts: Religion and Colonial Intrusion in *Things Fall Apart*." *The Literary Groit-International Journal of Black Expressive Culture Studies* Vol. 10, No. 2, (Fall 1998): 48.

Muo, Ik, and B. E. A. Oghojafor. "OHAZURUME: The Philosophy and Practice of Decision Making and Consensus Building among the Ndigbo of Nigeria." *American Journal of Business and Management* Vol. 1, No. 3, (2012): 154–156.

Njoku, F. O. C. "A Theoretical Foundation for Understanding Law Subjects & Rights in Igbo Philosophy of Law." *Open Journal of Philosophy* Vol. 3. No. 1A (2002): 255–265.

Opara, Chioma. "And the Truth is Made Manifest: The Strong Ones Behind Okonkwo." In *Achebe's Women-Imagism and Power* ed. Helen Chukwuma. Trenton, NJ: Africa World Press, 2012.

Osuagwu, D. A., and A. Anyanwu. "A Study of the Concept of Freedom in Igbo Traditional Worldview." *Maryland Studies* Vol. 10 (Nov. 2011) 109.

Osuji, Ozodi. "Developing Political Leadership in AlaIgbo." *BMW Magazine*, 2005, 12.

Ukpokolo, Chinyere. "Gender Space and Power in the Indigenous Igbo Socio-Political Organization." *Pakistan Journal of Social Sciences* Vol. 7. No. 2, (2010): 177–186.

Chapter 5

Things Fall Apart and Igbo Leadership

Learning and Unlearning the Lessons of Okonkwo's Life

N. Tony Nwaezeigwe

One of the intractable problems confronting the Igbo ethnic group in the stream of Nigerian politics is unsustainable populist leadership. This problem is no doubt the result of the inability of the emerging leaders to fully understand the strong link between the traditional Igbo concept of popular leadership constructed on their characteristic individualism and their culture of followership. Chinua Achebe's main character in his novel, *Things Fall Apart*—Okonkwo no doubt presented a graphic example of the inherent limitations in the traditional Igbo pattern of popular leadership. This chapter attempts to look at the current problem of contemporary Igbo political leadership through the literary historiography of Achebe's *Things Fall Apart*. The novel, being a classic literary replay of pre-colonial political dynamics of the Igbo society is thus an important lever for the understanding of the problems of contemporary Igbo leadership in the context of Nigerian national politics.

Things Fall Apart is an account of a society, a people whose descendants are still living and a culture partly still existing. It is therefore unlikely that Chinua Achebe might have written the novel without casting his mind on a particular sub-cultural setting of the Igbo society. Achebe could not, therefore, be said to have constructed his ideas solely from a holistic standpoint of the entire Igbo society. As G. C. Mutiso noted:

> All literature depicts the values of the people and the period. This is to say that however imaginative a writer may be, the framework of his writing must always

be the society he knows. Even when he transcends his own historical period, he is choosing other periods for comparison with his understanding of the historical present.¹

Looking at the ethnohistorical setting of *Things Fall Apart,* it is obvious that any historian familiar with traditional Igbo society will not escape being struck by the veiled historicity of the work. It is like, as James Kerr described Walter Scott: "He deliberately played fiction and history off against one another, not only as 'artifice' against 'reality,' but as codified forms of discourse."² There is no doubt that the characteristic content and setting of *Things Fall Apart* present a strong ground for historical inferences, a basic source for a non-historian's understanding of the historical setting of a typical pre-colonial traditional Igbo society at the first stage of confrontation with European colonialism. Innes and Lindfors seem to agree with this fact when he noted that Achebe built *Things Fall Apart* around the setting of a traditional Igbo village at the dawn of European missionary and colonial intrusions into Igboland.³

It thus follows that while it is not improper to state that within every molecule of fiction there should be an atom of historical reality. While it is not improper to state that within every molecule of fiction lays an atom of reality, for *Things Fall Apart*, however, the case would appear to be that of an atom of fiction in a molecule of reality. Thus, as Biodun Jeyifo argued, the root of the novel's exceptional critical success is found in the general agreement that it created a scene of unquestionable reality.⁴ One could therefore assert that *Things Fall Apart* is not just an isolated imagination of Achebe's contraption of traditional Igbo society in action. Rather the work presents a factual historical scenario from which inferences could markedly be drawn for the interpretation of traditional Igbo values and practices, patterns of inter-group relations, socio-economic patterns, as well as political dynamics of the society.

Earlier European anthropologists and ethnographers could have recorded the state of traditional African society, but they never recorded its movement. Achebe recorded an African society in motion. The society was moving as if it is happening in the present. It is therefore not apparent to see *Things Fall Apart* representing the classic point of inference for the first-hand understanding of a typical traditional Igbo society from the perspective of literature.

It is an acceptable reality therefore that *Things Fall Apart* did not present an isolated imagination of Achebe's conception of traditional Igbo society with all the associated movements in time. Achebe wrote from existing historical phenomena. But it is the depth and significance of these phenomena in relation to the present society that placed the novel on the saddle of realism. Oladele Taiwo conveys a similar opinion when he asserted that Nigerian writers are often influenced by the factors of their environment and the historical circumstances that created such environments. He further noted that such writings were similarly predicated on the attempts of the authors to explain the social mechanisms and dynamics of the society in general in their original forms before succeeding events intervened to undermine them and subsequently created in the Africans a new attitude of themselves in relation to what other people thought of them.[5]

Having outlined the conceptual historical background of the novel, it becomes necessary now to focus on its interpretational dimension. The fact that the novel portrays the enormous realities of traditional Igbo society is a matter already out of the debate. But whether these realities, be they cultural or historical, are essentially holistic in dimension or restricted to a given sub-culture is something worth establishing. Concerning his opinion in this matter, William Walsh had written:

> Whether the vision of Igbo society given to novels is justified by history is almost irrelevant. What we have in this work is a conception of civilization which has a root in reality. It includes a world and a group with coherent anatomy of standards and beliefs and a solid convincing body.[6]

But against Walsh's conception, it is unlikely that in the context of *Things Fall Apart* a reality could exist in isolation to its historical significance. To dismiss the historical character of such a novel as being irrelevant to its main theme is like removing the wheels of a vehicle and attempt to move it.

In relating the novel to this characteristic historicity Dan Izevbaye has argued that Achebe through *Things Fall Apart* provided a concise cultural history of the Igbo in particular and Africans in general which has helped to counter the age-long myths and prejudices against Africans and their continent. He further argued that even though the setting of the novel remains fictional by its broader definition, its characteristic stream of episodes remains historical and definitive within the time perspective of European colonization of the continent.[7] One may agree with Izevbaye through the telescopic lens of a literal critic that the characters of the novel are definitely fictional. But to the historian of Igboland, this cannot be true of the setting.

TRADITIONAL IGBO SOCIETY IN PANORAMA

> The missionaries spend their first four or five nights in the market-place and went into the village in the morning to preach the gospel. They asked who the king of the village was, but the villagers told them that there was no king. "We have men of high title and the chief priest and the elders," they said.[8]

The above episode clearly depicts the pattern of political leadership found in most parts of traditional Igbo society before the coming of the Europeans and even up to the recent past when the rush for the creation of artificial monarchies became fashionable among the people. In a general sense, therefore, the greater part of Igboland in its most unadulterated indigenous form showed a markedly high level of political decentralization and democratization. In other words, there was a clear absence of strong centralization of authority in any one individual or group of individuals which gave rise to a situation where some scholars erroneously classify the Igbo society as part of the territorial political complex popularly, but in certain circumstances erroneously known as "stateless societies."[9]

One fact which should not be overlooked in relation to the present study is that the leadership pattern of any people, both in its unadulterated traditional form and its modern system of Western-induced pattern, is historically subject to the form and structure of the society. And since the form and structure of such a society are defined by its peculiar culture, for its pattern of leadership to be functionally acceptable, it must conform to the values set by the society.

However, when such peculiar culture of those people comes into contact with a more sophisticated culture, the tendency is often for the invading culture to impose its domineering features, which might include but not limited to its set of foreign norms and values, which subsequently became equally acceptable to the indigenous people as the foreign feature within their traditional value system. It, therefore, follows that the degree of the hosts' receptivity to the invading culture and subsequent values will eventually determine the degree of their subsequent attachment to their indigenous culture.

In Igboland, as with most other indigenous African societies, three but complementary agents of social control stand out prominently as the points of reference in the understanding of their traditional value system. These are religion, economics, and politics; with politics occupying the domineering position. However, although we are mainly concerned in the present study with the patterns of political relationship, the nature and means of social control in traditional African society demand that one cannot conveniently study one aspect without reference to the other. In fact, in pre-colonial African society, it is often difficult to study the political and economic patterns of the people's culture without reference to the part being played by their religion. For while it is evident that political authority seeks to anchor its legitimacy on the bastion of religion, economic control, which, under normal circumstances is implicitly bound to the agency of political control, equally seeks to obtain protection and guide from religious sanctions.

Religion, as Max Muller rightly defined it as "the perception of the infinite under such manifestations as are able to influence the moral conduct of man."[10] Thus, being that the maintenance of a degree level of moral principle has always remained the main goal of every organized society, the prominence of religion as a factor of social control leaves no one in doubt. In fact, Major A. G. Leonard was quick to recognize this factor as essential to his understanding of the Igbo society, which was under his investigative armpit at that period when he stated:

> To get a clearer and thorough insight into the characteristics and temperaments of a people, it is, I think, essential first to obtain a comprehensive grasp of their religion, even before attempting to master their laws and customs.[11]

Even Professor Radcliffe-Brown did not spare much time in putting more emphasis on the above position when, partly parodying Fustel de Coulanges, he stated that it is impossible for us to understand the social, juridical, and political institutions of what he termed ancient societies unless we take religion into account, just as it remains a fact that we cannot understand religion unless we examine its relations to the institutions of the given society.[12]

Igbo belief system forms part of the African traditional religious complex, which has in its diversified forms one common underlying principle—the belief in a supreme being who is approached in worship through a number of media of both transcendental and human characters. It is based on what G. T. Basen refers to as "a circumscribed belief in a Supreme Being and a future life."[13] This was further characterized by Dike and Ajayi to include "a belief in the continuity of life, a life after death, and a community of interest between the living, the dead, and the generations yet unborn is fundamental to all African religious, social, and political life."[14]

TRADITIONAL IGBO POLITICAL ORGANIZATION

In his preface to *African Political Systems*, A. R. Radcliffe Brown stated:

> In seeking to define the political structure in a simple society, we have to look for a territorial community that is united by the rule of law. By that, it meant a community throughout which public sentiment is concerned whether with the application of direct or indirect penal sanctions to any of its own members who offend in certain ways or with the settlement of disputes and the provision of just satisfaction for injuries within the community itself.[15]

In Igboland therefore, we have, as representing the territorial community, the village-group—defined as the town. This forms the traditional superstructure of the Igbo political community. Any other level beyond this structural definition was considered a confederate arrangement for purposes of mutual defence against a defined common enemy. Although there is marked evidence of foreign political influence in certain parts of Igboland, especially among the Riverain and Western Igbo where Benin (Edo) influence on their political structure is found, the basic political structure of the Igbo in all the cases, including even the Edo remains the same. *Umuofia* of *Things Fall Apart* represents the formal Igbo territorial community.

At the material base, the political structure, like the social organization follows the kinship pattern. Within each level of lineage organization, the *Okpala*—most often the oldest surviving male descent of a given act as the titular head of the community presiding over the allocation of communal resources and the settlement of disputes between members, as well as enforcing the set standard of the community's value system. He also acts as the chief priest to the community at the appropriate level, particularly with regard to the *Ana*—the Earth-force deity that defines the abode of the ancestors and regulates the social norms of the community. He thus acts as the link between the living and the dead defined as the ancestors. This aspect of relationship forms the back-bone of Igbo cosmology on which are predicated the functional definition and regulation of other inter-connecting socio-political and economic dynamics of the society. Chinua Achebe mirrors this further in *Things Fall Apart*:

> The land of the living was not far removed from the domain of the ancestors. There was coming and going between them, especially at festivals and also when an old man died, because an old man was very close to the ancestors. A man's life from birth to death was a series of transition rites which brought him nearer and nearer to his ancestors.[16]

Although his office is sanctioned by the possession of the *Ofo*—the ancestral staff of authority handed down from one generation to the other, his authority is however generally nominal. He does not possess overriding authority but relies on the majority decision which often comes by way of consensus. But his words have the sanction of the ancestors and thus are held sacrosanct with every necessary respect. The *Okpala* is variously known by different names among the various dialectal subgroups of the Igbo. These include *Okpala, Diokpa, Ezeani, Ezeala, Onyeishi, and Ogene*. In the case of *Umuofia* of *Things Fall Apart*, *Ezeani* occupies this defining role of the *Okpara*. The *Okpara* whose mode of appointment is based on age-grade system, in some cases supplemented by the acquisition of social title defined in the context of the *Ozo* title complex, is assisted in the business of governance by titled men of various categories, including age-grade societies, masquerade and warrior cults, as well as women societies.

In all these categories of roles in society, there is no provision for hereditary succession to titles, offices, and roles. Every man's role and standing in the society is dependent upon his personal effort as dictated by the twin-forces of his *Chi*—the personal guardian spirit that defines a man's destiny, and *Ikenga*—the cult of the right hand that dictates his achievements—successes and failures in life. In Igbo cosmology, however, a man has to activate his destiny by his personal efforts—*Ikenga*. Achebe expresses this belief concept in the following scenario when Okonkwo referred to Osugo as a woman in reference to a man without a title. In admonishing Okonkwo, the oldest man in the meeting had stated in Achebe's words, "that those whose palm kernels were cracked for them by a benevolent spirit should not forget to be humble."[17] But Achebe in contradicting this thesis of admonition went further to state:

> But it was really not true that Okonkwo's palm-kernels had been cracked for him by a benevolent spirit. He had cracked them himself. Anyone who knew his grim struggle against poverty and misfortune could not say he was lucky. If ever a man deserved his success that man was Okonkwo. At an early age, he had achieved fame as the greatest wrestler in all the land. That was not luck. At the most one could say that his *chi* or personal god was good. But the Ibo people had a proverb that when a man says yes, his *chi* says yes also. Okonkwo said yes very strongly, so his *chi* agreed. And not only his *chi* but his clan too, because it judged a man by the works of his hands.[18]

The *Ikenga* is thus a cosmological concept of the Igbo belief in an open society, which recognizes that talent leads to enterprise and enterprise to achievement, and achievement to customary privileges. Hence the Igbo society with its characteristic republicanism is oriented towards a highly competitive achievement-driven spirit, which is anchored on a generative life-force cosmologically defined as the *Ikenga*. A. E. Afigbo describes the *Ikenga* as the cult of the right hand with which "a man hacks his way through the jungles of sweat and bitter experiences known as life."[19]

The Igbo spirit of enterprise is therefore strongly anchored on the premise that man is created by *Chukwu*—the Almighty God who dumps him with hands and feet a world-like jungle, giving him the option of either to conquer or be conquered. The *Ikenga* in this case provides the impetus for strong bargaining power. Hence, while intelligence and strength are recognized as natural gifts from *Chukwu*, the ability to harness them into tangible substance is attributed to *Ikenga*. M. D. W. Jeffreys explains this in these terms:

> Even if a man is naturally strong and vigorous, this virility is attributed to the power of his Ikenga; furthermore, if a weak man by accident throws a stronger one or makes money more easily than others, people give the credit to his Ikenga.[20]

In his study on the forces of change in Igbo society, Simon Ottenberg had pictured the pattern of the inherent individualism among the Igbo thus:

> The Igbo are highly individualistic people. While a man is dependent on his family, lineage, and residential grouping for support and backing, strong emphasis is placed on his ability to make his own way in the world. The son of a prominent politician has a head start over other men in the community, but he must validate this by his own ability. While seniority in age is an asset in secular leadership, personal qualities are also important. A secular leader must be aggressive, skilled in oratory, and able to cite past history and precedent.[21]

Ottenberg summed up the above description by pointing out that prestige in traditional Igbo society came by way of individual accumulation of capital which was formerly defined by foodstuff but has now been converted to money, needed to join title societies and perform other traditional ceremonies that tended to enhance a man's status in the society. In other words, traditional Igboland was an open society where every man could rise to the highest leadership status of the society without lineage or clan restrictions.

Going through the above excerpts one may be tempted to believe that either Chinua Achebe must have read Ottenberg before designing the character of Okonkwo in *Things Fall Apart,* or that Ottenberg must have read *Things Fall Apart* before arriving at the above characterization of Igbo society. This is because it is strikingly evident that Okonkwo's character clearly fits into Ottenberg's description of the pattern and character of socio-economic and political mobility in a typical Igbo society.

The fact however is that there is no possibility that both Achebe and Ottenberg might have read each other's work since both came out of the press almost at the same time; *Things Fall Apart* in 1958, and Ottenberg's work in 1959. It is reasonable therefore to say that both writers saw the same reality from different perspectives—literature and anthropology respectively—like two men dancing the same tune of music from different rooms.

THE IGBO PHENOMENON OF ACHIEVEMENT AND LEADERSHIP IN OKONKWO

In looking at the ideal traditional Igbo achievement instinct transformed into popular leadership Okonkwo's personality presents a perfect picture. This is clearly portrayed by his very humble beginning, a history not very much uncommon with many successful Igbo leaders in both business and politics. Achebe opens the story with a headline-like sentence constructed on a poetic paragraph of motivating spirit, which clearly defines the lives of many Igbo leaders in present times: "Okonkwo was well known throughout the nine villages and even beyond."[22] Okonkwo became famous by the single act of personal achievement. At the age of eighteen he brought honor to his village when he defeated the unbeaten Amalinze the cat in one of the most celebrated wrestling contests in his clan. Amalinze had been unbeaten for seven years from Umuofia to Mbaino, and it was for that reason he was called the cat because his back never touched the ground during the contest. It was this man that Okonkwo defeated in a wrestling contest, a feat that catapulted him from his humble background to the status of a hero among his people.[23]

Achebe then raps up this act one episode of scene one episode of Okonkwo's window to success with a graphic description of his personality:

> That was many years ago, twenty years or more, and during this time Okonkwo's fame had grown like a bush-fire in the harmattan. He was tall and huge, and his bushy eyebrows and wide nose gave him a very severe look. He breathed heavily, and it was said that, when he slept, his wives and children in their out-houses could hear him breathe. When he walked, his heels hardly touched the ground and he seemed to walk on springs as if he was going to pounce on somebody. And he did pounce on people quite often. He had a slight stammer and whenever he was angry and could not get his words out quickly enough, he would use his fists. He had no patience with unsuccessful men. He had had no patience with his father.[24]

This was the description of a man whose father could neither fend for himself nor his family. His father was a pauper by every sense of the word. Achebe in his impolite description of Unoka—Okonkwo's father did not spare any word: "Unoka, for that was his father's name, had died ten years ago. In his day he was lazy and improvident and was quite incapable of thinking about tomorrow."[25] He went further to describe Unoka as a failure in life who was so poor that he could not provide enough food for his wife and children as required of a man in the community and thus was mocked as a loafer who was never able to repay any money given to him on loan.[26] Not only in achievement instinct was Unoka a direct contrast of his son Okonkwo, in physiognomy too, the difference was mournfully striking as Achebe was apt to described Unoka as a man of tall and very thin stature with a slight stooping feature wearing a haggard and mournful look except when he was drinking or playing his flute.[27]

That was the description of Okonkwo's father, the man Achebe presented as the model of Igbo individualism and achievement instinct—under the motivational instinct of *Ikenga*. Okonkwo was no doubt the kind of person who could succinctly be described as a self-made man, whose *Ikenga* enabled him to hack his way to success through the jungle of sweet and bitter experiences of life. His father Unoka lived a pauper and died a pauper. Okonkwo, therefore, had nothing to inherit from his father. With a father like Unoka, Okonkwo did not have a pleasant start in life which many young men had. He neither inherited a barn nor a title nor even a young wife as was the custom in those days. But despite these disadvantages, he had begun even in his father's lifetime to lay the foundation of a prosperous future.[28]

It could therefore be argued that through the kind and timely intervention of his *Ikenga*, Okonkwo first gained fame by engaging and beating in a wrestling contest, the once invincible Amalinze the Cat. In the same vein, it could also be argued that through the dint of hard work and the further intervention of his *Chi*, he soon rose to economic and socio-political stardom in his community. But as Achebe further puts it, "It was slow and painful".[29] Part of this slow and painful experience was that Okonkwo had to seek seed yam loans from successful and prominent farmers, a risk which a lot of his contemporaries could not surmount.

As Achebe dramatically described how Okonkwo explained his predicament to Nwakibie applying every convincing anecdote in the most humble way to prove his sincerity and seriousness. Applying the anecdote of the lizard praising itself for its ability to jump from the high Iroko tree, Okonkwo concluded by assuring the man that given his track record of hard work from his early stage of life he would not renege the magnanimity.[30] Okonkwo's success in life as a prosperous farmer was no doubt dramatic as much as it was pains-taking. His success in farming soon not only elevated his doggedness in wrestling to the status of an all-round fighter but equally afforded him the necessary means for further elevation to the leadership status of his community. In describing the height of Okonkwo's elevation in status, Achebe succinctly noted his destined pattern of achievements right from his early age in life. These include his fame as the greatest wrestler in the nine villages that make up his town; his noted status as a wealthy farmer with two barns full of yams, crowned with three wives, two titles, and incredible prowess in two inter-tribal wars. All these he achieved at a very young age thus putting him forward as one of the greatest men of time. It is therefore plausible to say that Okonkwo even though young in age, his achievements when measured within the social parameter of his community, clearly placed him on the saddle of a leader by right of personal achievement.[31]

There is therefore no doubt that Okonkwo presented a perfect illustration of the pattern of achievement-driven status elevation in Igbo society, which is still in vogue up to the moment. In other words, leadership among the Igbo emerges by the dint of individual exhibition of high standard of quality achievement in the society.

LACK OF A SENSE OF HISTORY— OKONKWO'S TRAGEDY

It might be totally wrong to say that the tragedy of Okonkwo was solely predicated on the lack of understanding of his past. Okonkwo was fully aware of his humble past which indeed was the one major driving force that created in him the fear of what might be described as a chronic failure. To state the obvious, he was fully aware of his humble past which he quite often used to justify his high-handed approach in his dealings with his household. Achebe graphically describes the element of Okonkwo's personality as someone who ruled his household with a heavy hand. Although he might not be a cruel man down his heart but as a man haunted by the fear of failure and weakness for which his father was marked out, he tended to instil in himself that carriage of a tough man in and out of his immediate household. As Achebe further noted, it was a fear "deeper and more intimate than the fear of evil and capricious gods and of magic, the fear of the forest, and of forces of nature, malevolent, red in tooth and claw."[32]

To Okonkwo, therefore, everything he saw about his past was his father who defined failure in him, and so his past became a no-go area for him. He did not attempt to see his past in terms of his humble beginning and how such a humble experience should be applied in positive terms to mould his pattern of inter-human relations. And it was this failure to recognize the positive angle of his past that divest every element of humility in him, consequently creating in him an iniquitous arrogance. He became what is called in local parlance "full of himself." He forgot so soon that his own father during his life-time was unable to fend for himself and his family. Indeed, his father's poverty was so chronic that it even formed part of past-time tales of Umuofia clan. Thus, unlike most of his peers, Okonkwo did not have the opportunity of an economic soft-landing pad to begin a life as a young man. There was nothing for him to inherit from his father there was no yam barn or seed yams to inherit. Indeed, the story of what the Oracle of the Hills and Caves told Okonkwo's father Unoka when he went to consult on why his harvest had remained miserable all the time became a proverbial tale among the people of Umuofia.[33]

The rest of Unoka's story was a tragic one. Achebe partly recounted his conversation with the Priest of Agbala Oracle. The priestess was reported to have told Unoka directly on his face that he was noted throughout the clan as a lazy man euphemistically described as the weakness of his matchet and hoe. Unoka was further reminded that while his neighbors used axe to cut down virgin forests, he sowed his yams on exhausted farmlands that required little labor to clear, and when his neighbors crossed seven rivers to farm he stayed back at home to sacrifice to reluctant soil. He was subsequently admonished by the Oracle to go home as work like other men.[34]

This same Okonkwo also forgot so quickly that this same father of his died an ignoble and abominable death and had no grave as he was dumped in the evil forest to die. So unlike other people whose fathers died an honorable death and had the privilege of celebrating their fathers in form of traditional burial rites, Okonkwo did not have such privilege. But his history did not matter to his clan. What mattered to them was what Okonkwo could offer to the clan as an individual and not as the son of the loafer called Unoka. But the overt magnanimity of the clan in according him his rightful place on the ground of his personal achievements did not condition Okonkwo's arrogance towards those people he saw as less successful. This arrogance went further to include the disobedience of the sacred laws of the land regarding the Week of Peace when he beat his wife Ojiugo, an action he was made to atone for by the *Ezeani*. But it revealed a precipitous alienation of Okonkwo from the guardian forces of the ancestors. Achebe was dramatic when he recounted the episode. The Ezeani was stern to Okonkwo in the most authoritative manner, reminding him that it was obligatory for him to know the importance of the traditional Week of Peace as instituted by their ancestors. He went further without equivocation to indict him for desecrating the time-honored tradition of the people, reminding him that his action could ruin the entire clan through the refusal of the earth goddess to provide sumptuous harvest for them. Okonkwo was subsequently fined one she-goat, one hen, a length of cloth, and a hundred cowries without option of appeal.[35]

In his response to the above sanction, Okonkwo, even though he obeyed the command to its letter, he was not remorseful of his actions, an attitude which might have angered the ancestors. Achebe noted in Okonkwo what could be described as an attitude of iniquitous arrogance, for not only did he obey the priest but added to the defined penalty a pot of palm wine possibly to prove not his remorse but rather his wealth. His attitude of refusing to accept the fact that he was in error had become so disgustingly to the extent that his people often described him as someone who had no respect for the gods of his clan. To his enemies, he had become over-drunk with his unimaginable fortune, and thus was like "the little bird Nza who so far forgot himself after a heavy meal that he challenged his Chi."[36]

Gradually he began to experience the creeping presence of the malevolent spirit of *Ogbo n'uke*—the junior negative counterpart spirit to *Ikenga* responsible for individual-based violent crimes such as affray, manslaughter, and murder. The first sign of *Ogbo n'uke* in his household emerged when he nearly shot his second wife Ekwefi after giving her a thorough beating.[37] Then followed the killing of Ikemefuna—a boy who had by accident of history become his son by right of adoption safe for the associated misfortune through which the young boy found his way to Umuofia clan.

In a characteristic compassionate admonition loaded with ominous consequences, *Ogbuefi* Ezeudu who came to convey the Umuofia's decision to kill Ikemefuna to Okonkwo warned Okonkwo against his participation in the killing of Ikemefuna in the following stern terms: "'That boy calls you father. Do not bear a hand in his death.'"[38] But Okonkwo did not adhere to the advice, for the reason of not being thought a coward. For he not only joined the killing squad but became the executioner himself. The ensuing emotionally enveloped episode is indeed worthy of a recap:

> As the man who had cleared his throat drew up and raised his matchet, Okonkwo looked away. He heard the blow. The pot fell and broke in the sand. He heard Ikemefuna cried, 'My father, they have killed me' as he ran towards him. Dazed with fear, Okonkwo drew his matchet and cut him down. He was afraid of being thought weak.[39]

At the end of the episode, Okonkwo's closest friend and ally Obierika was up in arms against him for bearing arms against Ikemefuna in the name of proving his valor before Umuofia in proving to Okonkwo he was not the only brave man in Umuofia and he himself to Okonkwo's deepest knowledge was neither a coward nor someone afraid of blood. Directly expressing his gross displeasure over Okonkwo's unmanly and unfatherly act by killing Ikemefuna Obierika admonished him in the sternest manner a trusted friend could. Obierika reminded Okonkwo that he, Okonkwo was aware that he was not afraid of blood and that if anyone said so such a person would be speaking lies. He went further to admonish Okonkwo telling him that if he were him he would have preferred to stay back at home and not be part of the killing of Ikemefuna for very serious moral reasons; since such action could cause the goddess of the land to wipe out a whole family.[40]

Indeed, Obierika's emphatic admonition was as judgmental as it was predictable, for not long after the inevitable happened. *Ogbo n'uke* had taken a permanent abode with Okonkwo, demanding more blood, this time going beyond the traditional wall fence of Okonkwo's compound. Ironically, the next episode of *Ogbo n'uke* intervention centered on manslaughter committed during the funeral rites of the very man—*Ogbuefi* Ezeudu who warned Okonkwo against participating in the killing of Ikemefuna. It was however unfortunate that it was the former's son that became the victim.[41]

This crime of manslaughter subsequently resulted in a punitive seven-year exile. The dramatic manner with which the judgment was executed reveals the inherent powers of the Igbo society over its leaders in dealing with any serious act of contravention of the laws of the land. Indeed, once an act is clearly defined as an irredeemable taboo—*nso-ana* in the class of manslaughter and murder, the apportioned penalty does not need any form of deliberation other than instant execution of judgment. According to Achebe, early in the morning a large number of men from Ezeudu's quarter dressed as if in war invaded Okonkwo's compound and set his houses ablaze, demolishing the earthen walls, destroying the animals, including his yam barn. To them they were in a mission to execute the judgment of the earth goddess and not as Okonkwo's enemies, which had the sole objective of cleansing the land desecrated by Okonkwo. This explains the reason for the presence of his closest friend Obierika was among them.[42]

Like a flaming fire which he was, within a moment of fewer than twenty-four hours, all he had toiled with a strength enveloped in the fear of failure had been consumed by the same wildfire. What an irony of life who had toiled from his early beginning to defeat the stigma of power with which his father was identified. But was that instructive to him enough? The answer is no. For after seven years of exile Okonkwo again did not attempt to learn from history or to realize from his experience that without him Umuofia could still forge ahead with their formal political activities. Indeed, as Achebe noted, there was no striking effect of Okonkwo's absence from the clan during his period of exile in seven years. Life continued as normal as it had always been when a prominent member of the clan left the community as in the case of even death. Even Okonkwo accepted this fact which he believed could still be recovered with the same fervent spirit of achievement.[43]

However, returning with a rage of hatred against the white colonial administrators, who not only appropriated his first son—Nwoye but desecrated the clan's traditional values, he sought to reclaim his erstwhile position as one of the prominent leaders of the clan by leading the vanguard of the opposition against the Christian missionary invaders and their patron-colonial officers. Bearing in mind that while at his mother's clan of Mbanta where he served his seven-year exile he had described the people as a clan of women for refusing to buy his idea of a frontal confrontation against the white colonial masters and their church, he was determined to make a difference in his clan as a bona fide leader of the clan.

But Okonkwo forgot that while he was away in exile, both the missionaries and the white administrators had not only entrenched themselves firmly in his clan, by gaining substantial members of the clan as followers such as his compatriot *Ogbuefi* Ugonna, but equally introduced certain political and economic institutions like schools, courts and trading store from where the people could now make substantial incomes from the sale of their agricultural produce, which many members of the clan had come to accept. It was clear that a section of the clan did not see the new dispensation as Okonkwo.

These people were quick to notice the positive aspect of the intervention of the white man which came alongside the lunatic religion. Most noticeable was the economic aspect that came through the sale of palm produce with the resultant inflow of cash to the community. Even in the same lunatic religion could be seen some embedded positive characters.[44]

But being driven by the precipitous force of *Ogbo n'uke* Okonkwo was like, as the Igbo say, a dog whose sense of the smell of shit had been destroyed because it was destined for destruction. Every sense of reason on the changing circumstances of the moment seemed to have fled from Okonkwo's mindset, his exile experience notwithstanding. Thus, he allowed himself to become one of the instruments of Umuofia's anti-Christian vanguard and soon found himself becoming the first in Umuofia clan to cut off the white agent's head, for which he paid the ultimate price—suicide, for against his expectation of military action by his Umuofia kinsmen, the spirit of resistance was no longer there. He had hoped that with his personal charm as a renowned warrior he would sway the people into action. But it was not to be so.

According to Achebe, as soon as the court messenger's head fell from Okonkwo's matchet the dazed crowd went into disorderly life, a sign that he was standing alone. He was disappointed that even the people could not stop the other messengers from escaping. He felt abandoned especially when he heard some people among the crowd question his action. Seeing himself abandoned by the same people he devoted his life to serve and defend, Okonkwo thus felt there was no further reason for living among them. He wiped his matchet on the sands of his ancestors for the last time and departed from the people to the land of his ancestors forever.[45]

True to the title of the book—*Things Fall Apart* and for that reason, the center could not hold, but by the fundamental focus of the book, "things" actually began to "fall apart" from the angle of Okonkwo's personality syndrome—the fear, instead, the lessons, of his past, as the impetus to his achievement-driven orientation. Since fears are mostly founded on despondency, the question of moral judgment does not quite often take precedence in the actions of anyone whose mindset is predicated on fear. On the other hand, lessons often go with value judgments, and value judgments are often predicated on a moral sense of judgment. Okonkwo was a victim of the former, and so became a victim of all the negative presumptions of a man's life that grow out of the mindset of fear. The result was that he was, like his father Unoka, buried in an abnormal manner undeserving of a man of his achievement and status in his clan. Thus, part of what he feared most consequently came to become part of him in his departing moment from mother earth.

For Okonkwo therefore, who mattered to him were those fundamental factors that defined a successful man in his society—wealth and prowess in wars, which his father Unoka lacked. It did not matter to him that these elements of success must be defined within the set standard of his clan's moral values, hence the thought of remembering his father became anathema to him, forgetting that even within the context of aggregate individual contributions to the society, his father—Unoka was not a total failure, his role as a flutist had its own incidental contributions to the entertainment industry of his clan.

His misdirected sense of judgment similarly led him to understand the fact that his recognition as a leader in his Umuofia clan was predicated more on consensus opinion than his personal qualities as an achiever in both farming and valor. Thus, where a person's position of leadership was made possible by virtue of his personal qualities and achievements, and such a person at any moment attempted to exercise absolute authority without regard to consensus opinion, such a person was bound to face outright opposition and possible sanction by his people.

Among the Igbo therefore, absolute power is an alien contraption. The concept of absolute authority given the framework of Igbo cosmology does not even have a place among the ancestors—the transcendental custodians of the guardian earth-force deity (*Ana*), since it is believed that even in the land of the dead, decisions are taken in-council and not on an individual basis, hence the pluralistic conception of the term (*Ndichie*), meaning titled elders—both living and dead. One may offer supplications to his late father in the form of libation and prayer through the ritual breaking of kola-nut, but he cannot conclude without beaconing on the associated ancestors represented by the *Ndichie,* of which his late father formed apart.

Taking the case of Okonkwo as an instance, it is found that despite his monumental achievements as the greatest wrestler of his time, warrior *par excellence*, wealthy farmer, senior titled man, and above all, a revered leader among his people, he enjoyed the praise and confidence of his Umuofia clan so long as he acted within the acceptable moral orbit of his society. But once he changed from these moral rhythms of leadership to unguarded pride, dictatorial tendencies, or general conduct unbecoming of a leader, he was slammed with the appropriate sanctions.

CONCLUSION

A number of factors clearly accounted for Okonkwo's tragedy. First, at the height of his achievement, he suddenly forgot his humble beginnings and became clouded with over-bearing arrogance. He forgot that his father, Unoka was a pauper to the most disgusting extent. As the Igbo saying, "A man who does not know where the rain began to beat him will not equally recognize where it stopped to beat him," would indicate. It was clear that Okonkwo forgot his humble beginning in the celebration of his achievements and by the same token, forgot the limitations of personal achievements in his society. There is no doubt that the said attitude was bound to distance him from the people since Igbo followership abhors any leader with a penchant for arrogance.

Another factor was Okonkwo's vile tendency to believe that his achieved status was a license to contravene the customary regulations guiding his community, as in the case of the assault on his wife, Ojiugo during the week of peace, believing in the same wise that money alone, especially with the addition of the unsolicited extra keg of palm-wine would appease the ancestors. Finally, Achebe in describing the decision-making process of Mbanta was indeed speaking of the typical traditional Igbo political system. In other words, he vividly showcases the democratic character of traditional Igbo society, which still forms not just the political framework of many Igbo communities, but an internalized aspect of Igbo individualism.

It was obvious that Okonkwo's restiveness clouded by his intense sense of the unexpected rise in substance and valor in his community led to his crowning tragedy. He never waited to allow the democratic process offered by the people to decide on the final action on the problem before them, before unilaterally beheading the white man's chief messenger. He had been away from the community for seven years in exile. He did not understand that Umuofia society was not so static as to wait till he came back from exile before it could move. He forgot that a lot had changed in his seven years of absence just as he was actively witnessing the change in his place of exile. Okonkwo failed to note that he came back from exile to meet a new Umuofia with a clearer understanding of the emerging and obvious superior firepower of the white man.

It is pertinent to state that the underlying character of traditional Igbo leadership lies on the customary limitations of the two types of leadership—ascribed and achieved, which permit one to exercise his authority and influence as long as the circumstances that gave rise to his ascendancy persisted. Once the occasion ceases, the said leader is expected to revert to his original status as a member of his community. Otherwise, any further attempt by such a person to exercise power beyond the given situation would often be resisted.

The strength of Igbo leadership thus lies in understanding its basis of traditional authority, as well as the potency of the people's sentimental attachment to the concept of individualism and democratic principles. Most present-day Igbo leaders bore Okonkwo's characteristic pattern of rising and fall, even though the forms may differ, particularly among the present-day political class. Like Okonkwo, these people had sought to view their time-bound circumstantial leadership roles among their people as an imprint of timeless authority and influence. But the Igbo society where a truck-pusher today could become a successful big-time businessman tomorrow in the manner of Okonkwo rising from pauper to prosperity, will not permit any form of dictatorial tendency founded on individual achievements to thrive for so long. *Things Fall Apart* thus presents not just a picture of the limiting character of Igbo leadership in a traditional setting—both past and present, but also a lesson in the failure of Igbo political leadership in contemporary times.

NOTES

1. G. C. Mutiso, *Socio-Political Thought in African Literature* (London: Barnes & Noble Books, 1974), 3.

2. James Kerr, *Fiction Against History: Scott as Storyteller* (Cambridge: Cambridge University Press, 1989), 1.

3. C. L. Innes and Bernth Lindfors (eds.), *Critical Perspectives: Chinua Achebe,* (London: Three Continents Press, 1978), 47.

4. Ibid., 113.

5. Oladele Taiwo, Culture *and the Nigerian Novel* (London: Macmillan, 1979), 1.

6. Taiwo, *Culture and the Nigerian Novel*, 112.

7. Dan Izevbaye, in Innes and Lindfors (eds.) *Critical Perspectives.*

8. Chinua Achebe, *Things Fall Apart* (Ibadan: Heinemann,1958), 105.

9. Robin Horton, "Stateless Societies in the History of Western Africa," in J. F. Ade-Ajayi and Michel Crowther (eds) *History of West Africa* Vol. I. (New York: Columbia University Press, 1972).

10. Quoted from A. G. Leonard, *The Lower Niger and Its Tribes* (London: Frank Cass, 1968), 78.

11. Ibid.

12. A. R. Radcliffe-Brown, "Religion and Society," *Journal of the Royal Anthropological Institute* LXXV, (1941): 37.

13. G. T. Basden *Niger Ibos* (London: Frank Cass, 1966), 37.

14. K. O. Dike and J.F.A. Ajayi, "African Historiography," *International Encyclopaedia of the Social Sciences,* Vol. 6, (1968), 394.

15. M. Fortes and E. E. Evans-Pritchard, (eds) *African Political System* (London, 1967), xviii.

16. Achebe, *Things Fall Apart*, 85.

17. Achebe, *Things Fall Apart,* 19.

18. Ibid.

19. Adiele E. Afigbo, *Ikenga: The State of Our Knowledge* (Owerri: Rada Publishing Company, 1986), 2.

20. M. D. W. Jeffreys, "Ikenga: the Ibo Ram-headed God," *African Studies* Vol. 13, (1954): 34.

21. Simon Ottenberg, "Ibo Receptivity to change," in William R. Bascom and Melville J. Herskovits (eds) *Continuity and Change in African Cultures* (Chicago: The University of Chicago Press, 1959), 13.

22. Achebe, *Things Fall Apart*, 3.

23. Ibid.
24. Ibid.
25. Ibid., 3.
26. Ibid., 4.
27. Ibid.
28. Ibid., 14.
29. Ibid., 4.
30. Ibid., 17.
31. Ibid., 7.
32. Ibid., 9.
33. Ibid, 12.
34. Ibid., 13.
35. Ibid., 21–22.
36. Ibid., 22.
37. Ibid., 27–28.
38. Ibid., 40.
39. Ibid., 43.
40. Ibid., 46.
41. Ibid., 86.
42. Ibid., 87.
43. Ibid.,121.
44. Ibid., 126.
45. Ibid., 144–45.

BIBLIOGRAPHY

Achebe, Chinua. *Things Fall Apart.* Ibadan: Heinemann, 1958.
Afigbo, Adiele E. *Ikenga: The State of Our Knowledge.* Owerri: Rada Publishing Company, 1986.
Basden, G. T. *Niger Ibos.* London: Frank Cass, 1966.
Dike, K. O., and J. F. A. Ajayi, "African Historiography." *International Encyclopaedia of the Social Sciences,* Vol. 6, 1968.
Horton, Robin. "Stateless Societies in the History of Western Africa." In J. F. Ade-Ajayi and Michel Crowther (eds.), *History of West Africa* Vol. I. New York: Columbia University Press, 1972.
Innes, C. L., and Bernth Lindfors (eds.) *Critical Perspectives: Chinua Achebe.* London: Three Continents Press 1978.
Jeffreys, M. D. W. "Ikenga: the Ibo Ram-headed God," *African Studies* Vol. 13 (1954): 25–40.
Kerr, James. *Fiction Against History: Scott as Storyteller.* Cambridge; Cambridge University Press, 1989.
Leonard, A. G. *The Lower Niger and Its Tribes.* London: Frank Cass, 1968.
Mutiso, G. C. *Socio-Political Thought in African Literature.* London: Macmillan, 1974.

Ottenberg, Simon. "Ibo Receptivity to Change." In William R. Bascom and Melville J. Herskovits (eds.), *Continuity and Change in African Cultures*. Chicago: The University of Chicago Press, 1959.

Radcliffe-Brown, A. R. "Religion and Society." *Journal of the Royal Anthropological Institute* LXXV, (1941): 33–43.

Taiwo, Oladele. *Culture and the Nigerian Novel*. London: 1979.

Chapter 6

Achebe and the Pedagogy of Indigenous Knowledge Systems

Gleanings from Arrow of God

Ijeoma C. Nwajiaku

THE INDIGENOUS AND CONTEMPORARY DEVELOPMENT

The sphere of indigenous knowledge is currently gaining attention, not just in academia but also in developmental institutions. An offshoot of this enhanced attention is the multifarious efforts to provide working definitions of the term and concept. One notes however that the interpretations are not fundamentally conflicting in outlook, but rather present several points of overlap. Interestingly though, this truth does not belie the fact that issues emanating from and revolving around indigenous knowledge (popular as IK), remain debatable such that a unanimous notion of the concept appears elusive.

Indigenous knowledge presupposes the existence of an indigenous people who inherently possess such knowledge. Charles Takoyoh Eyong's "Indigenous Knowledge and Sustainable Development in Africa: Case Study on Central Africa" observes that the "term indigenous people" is in itself a contested category of people; so too is indigenous knowledge."[1] Eyong cites Melchias 2001:35, who defines the former as "culturally district ethnic groups with different identity from the national society, [who] draw existence from local resources and are politically non-dominant."[2]

One thing is evident thus far. It is the local nature of indigenous knowledge. Clearly, it is domiciled within the domain of a particular place and set of experiences; it is thus generated by the people resident in those areas. One might argue then that transferring such knowledge to other places might amount to dislocating it. This thought notwithstanding developmental policymakers at a global level are persuaded that indigenous knowledge systems having sustained numerous human communities for centuries could lend with valuable and constructive principles for enhanced societal advancement. Nicolas Gorjestani consequently highlights this characteristic feature of indigenous knowledge:

> Indigenous knowledge (IK) is used at the local level by communities as the basis for decision pertaining to food security, human and animal health, education, natural resources management, and other vital activities. Ik is a key element of the social capital of the poor and constitutes their effort to gain control of their own lives. For these reasons, the potential contribution of Ik to locally managed, sustainable and cost-effective survival strategies should be promoted in the development process.[3]

Gorjestani's study titled, "Indigenous Knowledge for Development—Opportunities and Challenges" seeks to introduce "indigenous knowledge as a significant resource which could contribute to the increased efficiency, effectiveness and sustainability of the development process." Evidently aware of these possible potentials, the African Development unit of the World Bank in a bid to facilitate the integration of indigenous knowledge into operation launched the indigenous knowledge for development program in 1998. Gorjestani's study consequently reflects on the program's experiences over three years and highlights steps that could be taken to further assist indigenous communities and governments to integrate indigenous knowledge into the development process.

To assess the potential development impact of indigenous knowledge system some examples of what it has already achieved are recorded in Gorjestani's study. Two of such examples would suffice for our purposes here:

> After fifteen years of civil war, community leaders in Mozambique reportedly managed about 500,000 informal "land transactions" and helped in the settlement of about 5 million refugees and displaced persons in two years. Most significantly, they achieved this without direct external help from donor or central government. How did this happen? Traditional, local authorities relied on indigenous, customary laws to resolve potential conflicts arising.[4]

CASE TWO

In the Iganga district of Uganda, leveraging traditional knowledge systems with simple and appropriate modern communications helped to dramatically reduce high maternal mortality rates. To address the high mortality rates, local communities and officials built on the local traditional institutions to improve the reach and impact of modern prenatal and maternal healthcare services. The local initiative used and leveraged the system known and trusted by Ugandan women—the traditional birth attendant.[5]

Several other examples abound in the study, but of relevance are the inferences that could be drawn. The positive yield of applying indigenous knowledge systems to critical situations in the outlined cases effectively underscore the significance of these systems and particularly accentuate their capacity to bear the full weight of the people's burden as well as proffer solutions to emanating difficulties. This point is crucial and validates the Igbo saying "*nku di be ndi, na eghe lu ndi nni,*" which simply states that the firewood within a people's community cooks their meals for them.

INDIGENOUS KNOWLEDGE: CONCEPTIONS AND PARADIGMS IN AFRICAN LITERATURE

It has severally been reiterated that African communities and peoples generally had (in the majority), fairly well-structured systems of societal existence that quite adequately catered to the needs of the individual(s) in the area. In other words, several peoples had well-organized leadership structures at different levels depending on the community. Established patterns or procedures in the form of traditional rites were in place to guide and direct ceremonies, festivals, marriages, births, deaths, and other activities. In addition, unwritten but nonetheless robustly articulated codes of conduct and ethics generally governed the ways of life of the people.

From the foregoing, and for this study, the concept of indigenous knowledge system is viewed as "the sum total of the knowledge and skills which people in a particular geographic area possess and which enables them to get the most out of their natural environment."[6] One notes how a major feature of this knowledge system lies in its oral mode of transition from generation to generation. Taking cognizance of this fact, Odora Hoppers observes:

> Most of this knowledge and these skills have been passed down from earlier generations, but individual men and women in each new generation adapt and add to this in a constant adjustment to changing circumstances and environmental

conditions. They in turn pass on the body of knowledge to the next generation, in an effort to provide survival strategies.[7]

This method of transferring information (and wisdom) is clearly depicted in *Arrow of God*. During one of the elders' meetings, we encounter the following statements:

> 'I know,' he told them, 'my father said this to me that when our village first came here to live . . . This is the story as I heard it from my father.'

Nwaka speaks afterward:

> Wisdom is like a goatskin bag: every man carries his own. Knowledge of the land is like that. Ezeulu has told us what his father told him about the olden days. We know that a father does not speak falsely to his son . . . My father told me a different story. He told me that . . . He told me that . . . But let us not tell ourselves or our children that we did it because . . . Let us rather tell them that their fathers did not choose to fight. Let us tell them that.[8]

The foregoing is just an example which serves to underscore Achebe's deliberate focus and interest in unearthing and inculcating the indigenous culture into his works. For him, art in Africa cannot just afford to be art for art's sake. Art ought to be able to serve a higher purpose in the human experience. Anthonia Kalu notes in a study how "Achebe considers himself and other African artists teachers and recorders of African history and culture."[9] One consequently notes an apparent correlation between the Igbo thought life and Igbo art tradition. Kalu's study provides an excellent summation of Achebe's engagement of the indigenous in his literary oeuvre:

> In his works, Achebe identifies certain major characters and situations in Igbo life, using these as the people do in their oral art tradition to portray their perception of the harmonizing principle in their lives. Achebe's interpretation of Igbo thought through art reveals a relationship between political and religious institutions. It is in these relationships that the Igbo artist and art traditions are most important. In recreating and revealing these connections, Achebe assumes the venerable role of Igbo priest and artist.[10]

One perceives therefore that indigenous knowledge embraces and encapsulates the totality of all knowledge and habitual actions whether categorically defined or implied, but which are adopted and utilized in the administration of the social, economic, political, spiritual, and ecological aspects of human life in society. Expressed differently, indigenous knowledge encompasses the width and breadth of what Anthonia Kalu in another study, quite appropriately refers to as "ways of knowing."[11] For Kalu, this descriptive tag appears more pliable and allows "for a broad-based discussion of what is known and the structures in which such knowledge becomes relevant."[12]

Writing more specifically about Africa and Achebe's Igbo society, Kalu makes the following relevant observation:

> Equilibrium and harmony are maintained by *"those who know"* that is, members of the knowledge-seeking community of elders. The totality of what they know is what I refer to here as Igbo (African) ways of knowing. I am not using the term "epistemology" because its definition, which is tied to that of the word "know" makes it less encompassing and locks this discussion about methodological shifts into familiar, authenticated western-based definition.[13]

Kalu's point here emphasizes a distinguishable relationship between an indigenous pool of knowledge and the community of elders in traditional Igbo society. In addition, she notes how Achebe's works promote the community of elders as one of the locations of Igbo self-re-creation. One could quickly enthuse that the described scenario cuts across much of Africa, prompting Kalu once again to affirm the recognizable existence of this community of elders all over Africa and indeed the Africa Diaspora in their forms.[14] According to her, in "most African and African Diaspora literature, the elders are a group of individuals who represent strongly held beliefs and practices."[15]

Evidently, this explains and accounts for Achebe's recurrent presentation of the elders in Igbo villages and communities as the major custodians of wisdom/knowledge in his writing. Their role in providing guidance or direction in society is thus as critical as it is indispensable. This point is clearly illustrated during the meeting held by leaders of Umuaro referred to in the opening pages of *Arrow of God*. Although Ezeulu, the chief priest of the Ulu deity (and the protagonist of the story) had expressed strong objection to the decision to send an emissary to Okperi, he and Ogbuefi Egonwanne further expressed similar sentiments about the duties of the elders in the meeting.

Thus, Ezeulu vehemently declares that "when an adult is in the house the she-goat is not left to suffer the pains of parturition on its tether."[16] The figurative employ of words here sharply censures the inability of certain elders in the gathering to counter the decision to go to Okperi. An enraged Ezeulu speaks further:

> That is what our ancestors have said. But what have we seen today? I would not have spoken again today if I had not seen adults in the house neglecting their duty. Ogbuefi Egonwanne, as one of the three oldest men in Umuaro should have reminded us that our fathers did not fight a war of blame.[17]

Ogbuefi Egonwanne had also spoken. Reputed to be one of the oldest men in the community, he had declared a desire to speak to the men being sent to Okperi. Apparently, he considers his role as vital in bringing "wise" counsel to the young men. It is through the words of the elderly that knowledge is transferred, and so Ogbuefi adds:

> But I am an old man, and an old man is there to talk. If the Lizard of the homestead should neglect to do the things for which its kind is known, it will be mistaken for the Lizard of the farmland.[18]

Like Ezeulu's figurative contention, Ogbuefi Egonwanne's equally underscores the duty or perhaps obligation of elders towards upholding and expounding indigenous knowledge as it pertains to their ways of life. Unarguably, the body of knowledge localized within any area sums up that which is required for their very existence. As already noted, it encapsulates all the information, data, and practices for managing their resources—human, material and natural. Additionally, it provides a framework for formulating individual and collective ideology. Thus, Ezikeojiaku in an insightful paper on understanding the Igbo and their cosmology notes:

> It has been observed that the behavioral pattern of *ndi Igbo* derives from their conception or perception of their worldview. To understand the world-view is, therefore, to understand how they behave in any society they find themselves. And to make the Igbo aware of the resources at their disposal; and to motivate and energize them to collectively utilize such resources for the improvement of their spiritual and material condition of living, a clear understanding of their cosmology is crucial.[19]

THE DYNAMICS OF THE INDIGENOUS IN *ARROW OF GOD*

Achebe's unrelenting appropriation of a totalizing narrative of culture repeatedly finds expression in his novels. *Arrow of God* re-enacts periods of the pre-colonial and colonial traditional structure in African history. He thus focuses on significant moments of ideological crises in Umuaro community. Published in 1964, the novel is at once cultural and political. Its eastern Nigerian setting depicts an era in the early twentieth century when colonization by the British government officials and Christian missionaries was well underway.

The narrative is as intricate as it is complex. The writer presents Ezeulu, his protagonist as a dynamic chief priest of Ulu, a god unanimously instituted by the six villages of Umuaro, decades earlier to ward off attacks by

Abam slave raiders. Ezeulu's role as chief priest is thus significant, as he is ultimately responsible for preserving the rituals and traditions of his people and community. That Ezeulu is deeply and extensively versed in Umuaro traditional knowledge is clearly apparent. Consequently, his words and speech recurrently delineate a cognitive structure in which theories and perceptions of nature and culture are well conceptualized.

One is confronted quite early in the story with the conflict which stems from Nwaka's overriding decision to send emissaries to Okperi "to place a choice of war or peace before them."[20] Ezeulu had tried fruitlessly to dissuade the people from engaging in what the culture regarded as an unjust war. One reads the chief priest's thoughts as he afterward reminisces on the events of that period:

> Ezeulu's often said that the dead fathers of Umuaro looking at the world from Ani-muo must be utterly bewildered by the ways of the new age. At no other time but now time but now could Umuaro have taken war to Okperi in the circumstances in which they did. Who would have imagined that Umuaro would go to war so solely divided? Who would have thought that they would disregard the warning of the priest of Ulu who originally brought the six villages together and made them what they were? Umuaro challenged the deity which laid the foundation of their villages. And—what did they expect? He thrashed them, thrashed them enough for today and for tomorrow.[21]

The above passage perceptibly illustrates a wisdom-laden expression pattern that typically conveys the ideological stance of the people. Ideally, such thoughts and viewpoints collectively highlight the knowledge base system of a people and their existence consequently revolves around the framework thus provided. In this stance, Ezeulu's wise and noteworthy thoughts serve to highlight two significant aspects of Umuaro culture. One, Umuaro ought not to go to a war disunited and divided. In other words, communal unity was of essence, and its value as a survival strategy is thus emphasized. Moreover, in dealing with the outside world especially, the need to present a unified front becomes even more vital.

The second fallout of Ezeulu's summations here derives from the circumstances which lead to the war. Although Ezeulu and Nwaka insist on the veracity of their conflicting versions of the historical account of the disputed land, Ezeulu insists that the war the community wanted to engage in was "an unjust war." As a chief priest, he maintains that "Ulu would not fight an unjust war."[22] The belief here is that their deity to whom they look for support would always favor the side of justice and truth. Convinced that the land in dispute was in reality, not theirs, Ezeulu cautions against initiating a war, but the people swayed by Nwaka's eloquence refuse to heed counsel. Finally,

Ezeulu makes a proclamation which has spiritual undertones: "if in truth the farmland is ours, Ulu will fight on our side. But if it is not we shall know soon enough."[23]

Needless to say, Umuaro eventually loses the land to Okperi. But the tragic turn of events results in disastrous circumstances and eventual loss of lives creating a major fragmentation within the community, from which it sadly never recovers. Difficult as it is to ascertain the actual role of Ulu in the outcome of the war, (given contemporary scientific awareness); one still perceives a society which sought to hinge its ideological stance on strictures of honesty and integrity. In other words, such functional systems of IK operated in communities to guide, direct and standardize the lives and ways of the people.

In a detailed and insightful study titled "Culture, Indigenous Knowledge and Development: The Role of the University," Catherine A. Odora Hoppers makes this very relevant observation about the nature and capacity of Indigenous Knowledge:

> it includes definitions, classifications and concepts of the physical, natural, social, economic and ideational environments. People own, manage and manipulate the knowledge according to their level of expertise in the particular domain.[24]

Arrow of God extensively demonstrates a solid and comprehensive knowledge of Igbo cosmology not just in a theoretical form, but quite vividly in practice. Thus, Odora Hoppers' summations here about IK's ability to define, clarify and conceptualize virtually all ramifications of existence within a human community can be authenticated within the narrative. One notes the organized structure and order in the purifying ritual of the Feast of the Pumpkin Leaves. Apparently, an age-old tradition in Umuaro is that the High Priest must necessarily take the six villages together through a purification process before the planting of their crops. It is instructive to note here how the Chief Priest recognizes his own need for a clear "heart" (conscience) before embarking on the grave assignment of cleansing the entire community.

His proportionate though concealed anxiety over Oduche's imprisonment of the sacred python is thus understandable. The sacrilegious act occurring shortly before this important festival leaves Ezeulu with perplexing thoughts:

> it was the kind of offence which a man put right between himself and his personal god. And what was more the Festival of the New Pumpkin Leaves would take place in a few days. It was he, Ezeulu, who would then cleanse the six villages of this and countless other sins, before the planting season.[25]

It was therefore a relief to Ezeulu that his in-laws suddenly visited his home to negotiate the return of his daughter Akueke to her husband's home. (She had fled her marital home on account of gross domestic violence). Ezeulu was immensely grateful to Ulu (his deity), who he believed used this reconciliatory incident to "cast him in the right mind for purifying the six villages before they put their crops into the ground."[26] This incident minor as it may seem serves to accentuate the importance of having a proper and acceptable frame of mind before participation in the festival. Within this culture, tradition demands that everyone would (communally) be cleansed in the ceremonial rites of the festival to prepare them for planting their crops in the ground.

One perceives therefore that the earth '*ani*' would fail to cause growth to what was sown into it if sown with malice, impurity, or other negative emotions. Hence the need for cleansing. To buttress the importance of this cultural demand, Umuaro would consent to present a unified front, at least on the day of the feast itself. We read therefore that, in the atmosphere of the gathering, "the great hostility between Umunneora and Umuachala seemed momentarily to lack significance."[27] Achebe notes further:

> Yesterday if two men from the two villages had met, they would have watched each other's movement with caution and suspicion; tomorrow they would do so again. But today they drank palm wine freely together because no man in his right hand would carry poison to a ceremony of purification; he might as well go out into the rain carrying potent, destructive medicines on his person.[28]

Clear reverence for the tradition and law of the land is unmistakable here. No doubt though this stems from widespread knowledge of what is indigenous to the community and what directs their affairs. It is also described as a special day for women. The women accordingly adorn themselves in "their finest clothes and ornaments of ivory and beads."[29] One wonders if the festival is linked to women, because of their procreative abilities. The women and 'ani' thus share an affinity which derives from their "seed-bearing attributes—children in the case of the female to sustain progeny (and ensure family lineage continuity); and 'ani' to yield food which equally does the work of sustenance of human life.

The overall organization of the festival is as impressive as is its ambiance. In spite of crowds involving the entire villages of Umuaro, everyone instinctively seems to know what to do and when to do it. For instance, as soon as the Chief Priest completed his circle of runs round the square and disappeared back into the shrine with his assistants, we read thus: "As if someone had given them a sign, all the women of Umunneora broke out from the circle and began to run round the marketplace stamping their feet heavily."[30] Describing the rest of the event, we again read:

> At the beginning it was haphazard but soon everyone was stamping together in unison and a vast cloud of dust rose from their feet . . . when they had gone round they rejoined the standing crowd. Then the women of Umuagu burst through from every part of the huge circle to begin their own run. The others waited and clapped for them; no one ran out of turn.[31]

It is noteworthy that without the aid of microphones, amplified loudspeakers, or even scores of armed policemen or security agents, a traditional society is able to hold festivals of this magnitude successfully, with no violence or deaths from a stampede recorded. As in this area so do other aspects of life in the community thrive based also on their scope of knowledge.

Writing about Achebe's *Things Fall Apart*, Kwadwo Osei-Nyame observes how masculine traditions "operate as forms of consciousness that act foremostly to legitimize specific ideals and values and to distribute and restrict authority within Umofia."[32] Without a doubt this assertion captures the scenario in Umuaro, which is also an Igbo community. Similar to *Things Fall Apart* also, titled and wealthy subjects, war heroes, and other revered and celebrated figures are predominantly male in *Arrow of God*. Although Achebe's over-riding portrayal of male figures has earned him accusations of favoring and promoting patriarchy and female negation, one would like to reassess this allegation.

When Akueke (Ezeulu's daughter), is introduced in *Arrow of God*, she lives in her father's home, having fled from a battering husband. Much as her father wanted her to return to her husband's home, he remained mindful of the fact that manifesting any attitude of intolerance amounted to "telling her husband to treat her as roughly as he liked."[33] It is easy to discern from the narrative that Umuaro tradition does not promote the beating and ill-treatment of the womenfolk. Thus, when the fiery Obika rises in defense of his half-sister Akueke, he is not really blamed for beating up her husband in retaliation, but only for tying him up and carrying him away from his home in a most disgraceful manner. Plainly, the "men agreed that Ibe stretched his arm too far, and so no one could blame Obika for defending his sister."[34]

Eventually, Ibe (Akueke's husband) goes with a group of his kinsmen as required by tradition to Ezeulu's home to be reconciled to his wife and to take her back home. Before the gathering ended, Ezeulu's younger brother Okeke Onenyi who was in the meeting carefully makes the following interjection:

> Since you began to speak I have been listening very hard to hear one thing from your mouth, but I have not heard it. Different people have different reasons for marrying. Apart from children which we all want, some men want a woman to cook their meals. Some want a woman to help on the farm, others want someone they can beat. What I want to learn from you is whether our in-law has come because he has no one to beat when he wakes up in the morning nowadays.[35]

Thus said, Okeke Onenyi was able to extract a firm promise from Ibe's relatives that "Akueke would not be beaten in future."[36] On his part, Ezeulu a major custodian of the norms of Umuaro admonishes his in-law thus:

> Akueke will return, but not today. She will need a little time to get ready . . . When she comes treat her well. It is not bravery for a man to beat his wife. I know a man and his wife must quarrel; there is no abomination in that . . . No, you may quarrel, but let it not end in fighting.[37]

Noticeably, the tradition of Umuaro does not encourage nor condone mistreatment of women or wife-beating. The Igbo society is inherently patriarchal, and Achebe's representations merely seek to depict the picture. However, while masculinist traditions hold fort and reign supreme, a few women could on occasion also prosper. During the Feast of the Pumpkin Leaves, for instance, the narrative describes the finery of the women's outfits and ornaments which were often determined by the "wealth of their husbands," but it also records "the few exceptional cases," where women were adorned on "the strength of their own arms.[38]

Notably, Umuaro has well-defined procedures for conflict resolution, as well as for taking decisions that affect the welfare of the community. One encounters several meetings in the text. The elders of the town meet for instance before deciding to send emissaries to Okperi. Another meeting holds immediately afterward, to discuss the outcome of the visit and to chart a course forward. Ezeulu calls for the elders too when he received the summons to appear before the white man. After Obika was flogged by a white man, his age-grade group held a meeting. Sometimes the meetings may involve smaller groups or a few adult men as in the few elders sent to confer with Ezeulu a number of times on behalf of the community when he refused to announce the day of the New Yam Feast.

Although the meetings may at times end in disarray, they nonetheless provided the critical platform for individuals to air their views as well as lend voices to matters of communal interest. They equally afford the elders and leaders of the land opportunity to poll the opinions of the people and to reach consensus on issues that concern them all. Efforts are made to resolve arising and outstanding conflicts within the community and even between the community and the outside world. It is important to observe that at these gatherings, usually of all adult males in the community, whoever wishes to express an opinion is granted the space. He could thus speak in support or against raised matters. When a consensus is reached, however, everyone is expected to comply, for it becomes adopted as a communal decision which is binding on all.[39]

Instances abound in the text. When Obika is whipped by the white man, Mr. Wright, his age-grade members, quickly and in the aftermath of the ensuing anger and bewilderment arrange a meeting for themselves. In spite of conflicting emotions, the assembly is able to resolve to send Moses Unachukwu (who works with the white man) to find out why they were not being paid for the work they were compelled to do, even though people in other places were being paid for similar work.

One also notes Ezeulu's immediate and sudden summon of "the elders and *ndi chie* to an urgent meeting at sunset"[40] after he receives the order to appear before the white man. The old man who beats the *ikolo* responds at once and "the *ikolo* began to speak to the six villages. Everywhere men of title heard the signal and got ready for the meeting."[41] Uncertain what the issue at stake was—a threat of war or a revelation from their deity, which required express attention—the people were nonetheless aware of the urgency of the invitation. They thus responded with haste and deliberated upon the matter which was presented to them. This fact that communal gatherings are an integral feature of Umuaro (and by extension Igbo) life and culture is further validated by:

> The meeting took place under the timeless ogbu tree on whose mesh of exposed roots generations of Umuaro elders had sat to take weighty decisions. Before long most of the people expected had come.[42]

While the majority of crucial formal meetings were held at this designated area of the town's market square, other meetings could of course hold at other agreed locations as dictated by circumstances or other factors pertaining to the gathering. Thus, when Umuaro broke up from a meeting in confused disagreement over the decision to go war or not against Okperi, Nwaka held a meeting of very select people in his compound on the same night. There they resolved to fight.

After Ezeulu's return from the protracted detention at the white administrator's office, he refuses to announce a day for the New Yam Feast. This feast which is, in reality, a festival preceding the harvest of new yams from the soil was absolutely indispensable as no one would dare to eat new yams until it had been celebrated in the feast. Perhaps, the deliberate focus on the yam here allows Achebe to further project the 'YAM,' with its production and consumption as being central and integral to Igbo identity and political economy. Generally considered to be chief of all crops, the yam clearly enjoys an elevated status among the Igbo. In his pioneering epochal work, *Things Fall Apart*, Achebe refers to the yam as the "king of crops," and one sees how the successful cultivation of this revered crop epitomized Igbo male achievement and prestige.[43]

Korieh's study further traces a historical dimension to the peculiar significance of the yam. One comes to understand how the cultivation of yams was guided by stringent rules, often involving elaborate ceremonial rituals at both planting and harvesting seasons. He notes moreover, how the evidence supports that "the Igbo were a yam people at heart" and cites Basden's observation that a shortage of yam supply "was a cause of genuine distress because no substitute gave the same sense of satisfaction."[44] Phanuel Egejuru in *The Seed Yams have been Eaten* equally dwells extensively on the idolized position of yam within Igbo culture. Her protagonist consequently loses his mental stability when his mind is unable to comprehend what he considers a major sacrilege—the eating of yam seedlings by soldiers who invaded his town during the Nigeria-Biafra civil war. [45]

To return to *Arrow of God*, the implication of this reality (Ezulu's refusal to announce a date for the celebration of the new yam season), lay heavily on the minds of Umuaro elders and prompted a number of small group meetings with Ezeulu as they conferred together and sought a way out of their dilemma. On occasion, the elders assembled elsewhere and held a meeting prior to going to Ezeulu's house to hold yet another meeting. The point is that even within the bounds of this traditional society, meetings are frequently convened to provide the forum for deliberations on issues of communal concern. (On rare situations, even cases pertaining to individuals or smaller sects may also be tabled before the gathering if such matters require general input).

It is noteworthy that the meeting often involved male adults of the community. Obviously, this is because the society wholly endorses a phallocentric tradition where masculinist ideologies serve to influence and structure outlook as well as values. Interestingly, adult males and especially the very old men consistently perceive themselves to be custodians of the traditions of the land. They thus seek to accomplish the impartation and transference of these norms to younger people. Of course, the sole available means for accomplishing this was the oral medium. This fact invariably draws attention to the language pattern of the discourse in *Arrow of God*. Achebe had stated explicitly in *Things Fall Apart* that "[a]mong the Ibo the art of conversation is regarded very highly and proverbs are the palm-oil with which words are eaten."[46] Perhaps *Arrow of God* much more than his other narratives exemplifies this trend. Indeed, one notes how the utterances of the several adult men in the text are visibly laden with proverbs, anecdotes, symbolisms, allegorical expressions, sarcasm, and other language forms. Imagery is thus intense and functions to drive home the message of a speaker. Oratorical skills are valued and time and again, a good orator easily carried the day at communal gatherings.

It would hardly be an understatement to assert that elderly men in the narrative rarely spoke in plain ordinary speech. Their words frequently divulge deep knowledge of the values and traditions of the land. This was as true of formal gatherings as it was of ordinary domestic settings. Ezeulu and his close friend Akuebue exchange visits and their duologue is a great pleasure to read. One notes how the casual banters, jokes, and interjections of humorous lines amidst the serious discussions all combine to heighten the value of the spoken word in Igbo tradition. Aside from the eloquence of delivered speeches and arguments during communal meetings and gatherings, other notable communication contexts requiring carefully crafted word choices abound in the work.

When Ezeulu returns to Umuaro from detention, several of the town's people visit him. Ogbuefi Ofoka's was however outstanding. He appeared to have come specifically to convey thoughts, which had formed in his mind precisely. His words impressive, honest, and imbued with wisdom have a profound effect on Ezeulu who admits that Ofoka's remarks sum up all the argument that had been going on in his mind for days. Other instances of articulate renditions can be glimpsed when Ezeulu's assistants attempt to reverently remind him that the Feast of the New Yam was due to be announced. During this meeting, Nwosisi's flow of cautiously strung words was interrupted by Obiesili's unwarranted interjection. A bout of silence follows, and the reader is at once informed that "he was always a tactless speaker" and that "no one had asked him to put his mouth into such a delicate matter."[47]

The negative effect of these ill-spoken words is not lost, as Ezeulu's reaction reveals. Even Chukwulobe's attempt to remedy the situation and to placate the chief priest fails woefully as his statement only infuriates Ezeulu the more. Plainly, appropriate verbal expression (including selection and arrangement of words), matter in this society. Close attention is paid to anyone speaking and his utterances are carefully interpreted to decode meanings. Misunderstandings frequently arise on account of spoken words and so word use remains important. Sometimes one notes how speakers deliberately phrase their statements in manipulative forms to arouse emotion, win support or even gain favor. At other times, ironies and sarcasms drip from words in order to undermine an enemy or to ridicule an opponent.

When the elders of Umuaro visit Ezeulu to confer about the New Yam Feast, the solemnness of the meeting is again emphasized by the enormity of tact and wisdom with which these revered leaders of Umuaro speak. At intervals, each party applauds the other's well-delivered presentations. Thus, Onenyi Nnanyelugo salutes everyone and remarks: "I think that Ezeulu has spoken well. Everything he said entered my ears. We all know the custom and no one can say that Ezeulu has offended against it."[48]

After Onenyi Nnanyelugo's speech, Ezeulu himself affirms that he had spoken well.[49] During this critical dialogue, one senses much tenseness in the atmosphere (because of the subject of discussion) and can thus appreciate the dexterity of the elders in their consequent employment and deployment of word expressions couched in traditional norms and parlance. The great art of conversation plays out here, and the proverbs serving as palm oil for "eating" the words are in abundant supply too. Again, as in the case with the assistant's visit, when a temper rises, the others quick and skillful interventions strive to douse such flaring emotions. In this instance, Nnanyelugo and later Ezekwesili strive to stir Ofoka away from the direction his words were heading:

> "If you will listen to me, Ofoka, let us not quarrel about that," said Ezekwesili. We have come to the end of our present mission. Our duty now is to watch Ezelu's mouth for a message from Ulu. We have planted our yams in the field of Anaba-nti.[50]

As the other elders agreed with the speaker, Nnanyelugo "deftly steered the conversation to the subject of change."[51] One cannot but be impressed at this expert avoidance of conflict as well as the willingness of the people present to put all differences aside to speak in unison as demanded by the situation at hand.

Achebes's narrative equally emphasizes the importance of being armed with a sound knowledge of the ways of the land. This is of essence to the people and the younger generations are expected to acquire and imbibe this knowledge as they listen intently to the words of the elders. In the opening pages of the narrative, Ezeulu's sons approach him to ascertain what assignment they would carry out for him on Afo market day as the custom was. Oduche informs his father that he had been selected along with other pupils to perform a task for the school. Without mincing words, Ezeulu's retort is sharp: "Your people should know the custom of this land; if they don't you must tell them. Do you hear me?"[52]

In summary, the many customs of the land seek in diverse ways to direct, standardize and even legalize the affairs of the people at personal and communal levels. Thus, the people could conduct their marriage rites, child-birth, funeral, and all other rites according to the guidelines outlined within their own culture. Belief in a supreme being "Chukwu" or "Chi" (the name for God) as well as in many lesser gods who intervened to varying degrees in man's affairs was evident. Other deities also exist for these people and also rule or preside over different spheres of their lives. Ceremonies and religious feasts were celebrated at stipulated times and in structured patterns. Indeed, the people had adequate knowledge within their environment to cater for their existence.

CONCLUSION

It is apparent at this time that the world again stands at major intersections seeking what Odora Hoppers calls "new human-centered visions for development." This quest has led development consultants and international agencies to recognize in an increasing measure the immeasurable value of the resources and insights located in traditional knowledge systems. Because these systems are broad and encompass virtually all aspects of life, contemporary players at all levels of government and nongovernmental policy structures strive to incorporate this knowledge into current programs that aim to achieve and uphold sustainable developmental paradigms.

Thus far we have sought to reaffirm the indisputable significance and adequacy of indigenous wisdom. Its relevance and uniqueness have equally come across quite vividly. It is thus a welcome development to observe how the modern world is reassessing this source of knowledge to harness its limitless potentials in diverse areas of contemporary life. James D. Wolfensohn a one-time president of the World Bank had made the following insightful assertion: "indigenous knowledge is an integral part of the culture and history of a local community. We need to learn from local communities to enrich the development process." No doubt this statement rings true and much benefit has accrued as noted earlier in this study, from attempts to adopt and adapt such knowledge in spheres of modern life.

It is important of course to note that African ways of knowing have not been static but have over the years incorporated changes following its contacts with colonialism, Christianity, Islam, and more recently influences from other world cultures as globalization continues to sweep across continents. These changes notwithstanding, the traditional way of life as Tanure Ojaide notes "still persists in mainly rural areas in many parts of Africa today"[53] No doubt this is the life that generations of Africans have proved for centuries. Ojaide consequently asserts further: "The communal, democratic, and spiritual life still imbues traditional African society with many of the mores and values that sustained African forefathers.[54] To this end, therefore, concerted efforts by African writers with Achebe perhaps in the foremost position to represent indigenous knowledge have not been futile. Because literature informs, educates, and instructs, these texts remain invaluable assets in teaching younger generations of Africans about their culture and tradition and thereby urging a reincorporation of these values into contemporary life and society commencing at individual levels.

NOTES

1. See Charles Takoyah Eyong's work on Indigenous Knowledge and Sustainable Development, 120. Accessed April 12, 2021. www.krepublishers.com/06-Special
2. Ibid.
3. Nicolas Gorjestani's work documents outstanding successes recorded under a world Bank assisted program of incorporating indigenous knowledge into developmental policies. www.worldbank.org/afr/ik/ikpaper_0102.pdf.
4. Ibid.
5. Ibid.
6. Grenier,1998, cited in Odora Hoppers, 2004
7. Odora Hoppers, 2.
8. Achebe, *Arrow of God*, 16.
9. Kalu, "The Priest/Artist Tradition," 51.
10. Ibid., 51.
11. Anthonia C. Kalu, "The Priest/ Artist Tradition in Achebe's Arrow of God," *Africa Today*. Vol. 41, No 2, Arts and Politics in Africa (2nd Qtr., 1994)," 38.
12. Ibid.
13. Ibid., 38.
14. Ibid., 37.
15. Ibid., 37.
16. Achebe, *Arrow of God*, 18.
17. Ibid., 18.
18. Ibid.,17.
19. P. A. Ichie Ezejiaku, "Towards Understanding Ndi Igbo and their Cosmology," in *Radical Essays on Nigerian Literatures*, ed. G.G. Darah (Lagos: Malthouse Press, 2008), 37.
20. Achebe, *Arrow of God*, 17.
21. Achebe, *Arrow of God*, 17.
22. Ibid., 15.
23. Ibid., 18.
24. Odara Hoppers, 3.
25. Achebe, *Arrow of God,* 60.
26. Ibid., 64.
27. Ibid., 66.
28. Ibid.
29. Ibid.
30. Ibid., 73.
31. Ibid.
32. Kwadwo Osei-Nyame, 1999, 150.
33. Achebe, *Arrow of God*, 62.
34. Ibid., 12.
35. Achebe, *Arrow of God*, 63.
36. Ibid.
37. Ibid.

38. Ibid., 66

39. Ijeoma Nwajiaku's 2014, study examines the principle of 'oha' and its supremacy in reaching a consensus during communal gatherings in Igbo societies.

40. Achebe, *Arrow of God*, 140.

41. Ibid.

42. Ibid., 141

43. Chima J. Korieh, "Yam is King! But Cassava is the Mother of all Crops: Farming, Culture and Identity in Igbo Agrarian Economy," *Dialectical Anthropology*, Vol. 31, No. 1/3. (2014), 222.

44. Ibid.

45. Phanuel Akubueze Egejuru, *The Seed yams have been eaten* (Heinemann Educational Book, 1993).

46. Achebe, *Things Fall Apart*, 5.

47. Achebe. *Arrow of God*, 203.

48. Achebe, *Arrow of God,* 207.

49. Ibid.

50. Ibid., 209.

51. Ibid.

52. Ibid., 14.

53. Tanure Ojaide, *Contemporary African Literature: New Approaches* (Durham, North Carolina: Carolina Academic Press, 2012), 10.

54. Ibid.

BIBLIOGRAPHY

Achebe, Chinua. *Arrow of God*. Oxford: Heinemann International Literature and Textbooks. 1964 (1986 edition).
———. "What Has Literature Got to do with it?" *Radical Essays on Nigerian Literatures*. Ed. G.G. Darah. Lagos: Malthouse Press, 2008.

Egejuru, Phanuel Akubueze. *The Seed Yams Have Been Eaten*. Heinemann Educational Book, 1993.

Eyong, Charles Takoyah. "*Indigenous Knowledge and Sustainable Development in Africa: Case Study on Central Africa.*" Accessed April 12, 2021. www.krepublishers.com/06-Special.

Ezejiaku, P. A. Ichie. "Towards Understanding Ndi Igbo and their Cosmology." *Radical Essays on Nigerian Literatures*. Ed. G.G. Darah. Lagos: Malthouse Press, 2008.

Gorjestani, Nicolas. "Indigenous Knowledge for Development: Opportunities and Challenges." Accessed April 12, 2021. www.worldbank.org/afr/ik/ikpaper_0102.pdf.

Kalu, Anthonia C. *Women, Literature and Development in Africa.* Trenton, NJ: Africa World Press, Inc. 2001.

Kalu, Anthonia C. "The Priest/ Artist Tradition in Achebe's Arrow of God." *Africa Today*. Vol. 41, No 2, Arts and Politics in Africa (2nd Qtr., 1994): 51–62.

Korieh, Chima J. "Yam is King! But Cassava is the Mother of all Crops: Farming, Culture and Identity in Igbo Agrarian Economy." *Dialectical Anthropology*. Vol. 31, No. 1/3. (221–232).

Madubuike, Ihechukwu. *Literature, Culture and Development: The African Experience*. Abuja: Roots Books & Journals Limited. 2007.

Nwajiaku, Ijeoma C. "The Communal, the Supreme—A Reading of Chinua Achebe's *Things Fall Apart* and *Arrow of God*." *Igbo Studies Review*. Number 2, 2014.

Odora Hoppers, Catherine A. *Culture, Indigenous Knowledge and Development—The Role of the University*. Johannesburg: Centre for Policy Development. Accessed April 12, 2021. wwwcepd.org.za/files/pictures/CEPDoccasionalpaper.

———. "Indigenous Knowledge Systems: An Invisible Resource in Literacy Education." SGI Quarterly. Literacy—Renewing the Challenge, January 2003. Accessed April 12, 2021. www.sgiquarterly.org/features.

Ojaide, Tanure. *Contemporary African Literature: New Approaches*. Durham, North Carolina: Carolina Academic Press, 2012.

———. *Ordering the African Imagination-Essays on Culture and Literature*. Lagos: Malthouse Press Limited, 2007.

Osei-Nyame, Kwadwo. "Chinua Achebe Writing Culture: Representations of Gender and Tradition in Things Fall Apart." *Research in African Literatures*. Vol 30, No 2, Summer 1999.

Owusu-Ansah, F. E. and Gubela Mji. "African Indigenous Knowledge and Research." *African Journal of Disability*. 2 (1) Art. #30. Accessed April 12, 2021. http://dx.doi.org/10.4102/ajod.v2130.

Zulu M. Hibari. "Critical Indigenous African Education and Knowledge." *The Journal of Pan African Studies*. Vol. 1, No 3 March 2006. Accessed April 12, 2021. www.jpanafrican.com/docs/vol1no1/criticalindiginousAfricanEducationand Knowledge.

PART II

Chinua Achebe and Politics of Representation

Chapter 7

Chinua Achebe's "'Chi' in Igbo Cosmology"
Revisiting a Classic

Chijioke Azuawusiefe

In his seminal 1975 essay, "'Chi' in Igbo Cosmology," Chinua Achebe presents a compact treatment of "chi," outlining its primacy and creative role in traditional Igbo religious thought.[1] Nevertheless, Achebe undercuts his own analysis of the relationship between chi and "the Supreme God (Chukwu)" with his assumption that the ascendancy of the Supreme God in this relationship "is well known in Igbo cosmology"[2] as well as with his assertion that, as a result, chi *proceeds* from Chukwu, "to borrow the words of Christian dogma."[3] Indeed, Chukwu as Supreme God is very much part of Igbo religious consciousness today. Chukwu (sometimes also called Chineke, the Chi that creates), Achebe and the Supreme God advocates maintain, is too big to be approached directly; so, he created "minor deities," as intermediaries between him and human beings. Each individual has his/her chi, which, these scholars argue, is a particle of the great Chi (Chi Ukwu, contrasted as Chukwu), assigned to the individual. Chi returns to *Chukwu* for reassignment at the person's death.[4] However, it remains to be ascertained that this orthodoxy has always been the case.

This chapter revisits Achebe's analysis in the light of the prevailing scholarship on Igbo cosmology as well as on African Traditional Religions, questioning his assumption and expanding the scope of his reading of chi and Chukwu.[5] Drawing examples from traditional cultural and religious conceptions of the Igbo worldview as well as from Achebe's other works which contradict his Supreme God assumption, the paper will first contextualize Achebe within the dominant missionary Christian reconfiguration of colonial

Africa's cultural-religious worldviews. Then, it will establish his subsequent outlook on the relationship between chi and Chukwu and afterward underline the inherent oversights of such a viewpoint. The paper will further problematize the discussion by investigating the arguments for and against the Supreme God orthodoxy by scholars of Igbo and African religions and cultures. It argues that Achebe's uncritical examination of the place and position of the Supreme God in Igbo religious thought led to his assumption, in the mode of the African nationalists who asserted the existence and monotheism of the Supreme God among Africans in reaction to its denial by Western scholarship. This conclusion reaffirms the position of scholars, like Donatus Ibe Nwoga, who have argued that Chukwu as Supreme God is a product of the Christian missionary enterprise among the Igbo people.[6] Achebe agrees with Nwoga on that.[7] As both of them point out, the missionaries, in their quest to establish a Supreme God among the "primitive" people, baptized Chukwu, an oracular deity, turned it into a Supreme God and moved it from its shrine in Arochukwu into the heavens.[8] The paper will examine the central place of Arochukwu in the construction and conceptualization of Chukwu among the Igbo in a later section, "Beyond Achebe." "Supreme God" as used in this essay refers to the Judeo-Christian God who existed from and creates out of nothing.

CONTEXTUALIZING ACHEBE

Among the Supreme God orthodoxy proponents in Igbo religious thought are senior clerics like Francis Arinze and Stephen Ezeanya, a cardinal and an archbishop of the Catholic Church, respectively.[9] But as anthropologist Okot p'Bitek rightly observes, the two typify the orthodoxy scholars' tendency to read Christian catechism into their African religion's scholarship.[10] They represent the majority of the first generation of Igbo scholars to articulate the Igbo religious worldview and cosmology who had their training in Christian theology or Western philosophy grounded in the Christian tradition. Over the years, their articulation has assumed the "well known" standpoint of the Supreme God authorized standard version. However, for the purposes of this essay, I have decided to focus on Achebe, a non-cleric, who, though strove to present elements of Igbo religious thought on their own worth, was nonetheless influenced by his Christian background. Chi is central to Igbo cosmology, Achebe argues, but it derives its essence from Chukwu the Supreme God. To better understand, however, Achebe's treatment of the chi-Chukwu relationship, it is proper to first historicize the evolution of his idea of God.

Born in 1930 to an Anglican evangelist father in Ogidi, southeast Nigeria, Achebe grew up within an environment that was "only part Christianized . . .

and still provided its traditional sights and sounds" from which the little Achebe, as a Christian, was sadly excluded.[11] Christianity had split his village into Christians and heathens, but the two sides still interacted with each other. The divide, together with its attendant exclusion, triggered Achebe's attraction to and curiosity for the traditional religion. That attraction incidentally paralleled that of Wole Soyinka, Achebe's contemporary and literary counterpart to the west, who, although was "formally forbidden" from the world of Orisha (the Yoruba pantheon), insisted that that world still "cast its spell on [his] childhood imagination."[12] The daily dose of Christian religion the two youngsters grew up imbibing within their families' Christian culture (Soyinka's father was also a Methodist minister) could not sate their thirst for the other religion across the divide. Soyinka continues to identify with the Orisha world in his adult life, especially with the primordial *Ogun*—master craftsman, artist, and the god of metallurgy—not only for guidance but also for a backdrop to critique the "competing claims of other worldviews, other spiritual claims, other arrogations of knowledge and truth."[13]

Unlike Soyinka, Achebe's approach to the two religions later in life was informed by a dialectic he inherited from his father and his father's maternal uncle, Udoh—an open-minded community leader, who had received the first missionaries in Ogidi in his compound. Although Udoh "stood fast in what he knew . . . he left room also for his nephew [whom he had raised] to seek other answers. The answer [Achebe's] father found in the Christian faith solved many problems, but by no means all."[14] Nevertheless, Achebe admitted that as a secondary-school student in the 1940s Nigeria, he "did not see [himself] as an African to begin with," neither did he identify with the African characters as he read the so-called colonial classics of the time.[15]

That mindset however underwent a radical transformation few years later. After one year of medical studies in the university, Achebe switched to English, history, and theology. Then, the study of religion became all new and exciting to him because "the focus went beyond Christian theology to encompass wider scholarship—West African religions."[16] For the first time Achebe was able, through the works of his professors, like Geoffrey Parrinder, to see the structures of his Igbo religious system compared side by side other religious traditions. It was then he began to understand and value more his traditional Igbo history and religion. But he also realized that no matter how brilliant his professors were, they could not teach him the essential "introspection, deep personal scrutiny, and connection" required to plumb this worldview.[17] Probing the Igbo conceptions of the world, then, became Achebe's lifelong interest, which he articulated through his many writings, among them the "'Chi' in Igbo Cosmology" essay.

ACHEBE AND THE CHI-CHUKWU RELATIONSHIP

In the 1975 essay exploring the interconnectedness between chi and Chukwu, Achebe notes the two distinct meanings of chi in Igbo language. The first, he aptly observes, has variously been rendered as "god, guardian angel, personal spirit, soul, spirit double . . ."[18] while the second means day or daylight. This essay is concerned with the first meaning which, according to Achebe, is "so central in Igbo psychology and yet so elusive and enigmatic."[19] The complexity of this concept is confirmed by the variety of words and phrases, as could be seen above, with which it has been translated.

Achebe argues that generally one may imagine a man's chi as his other identity in the spiritland—"his *spirit being* complementing his terrestrial human being."[20] This complementarity speaks to the notion of duality which is central in Igbo worldview. Nothing is absolute; nothing ever stands alone, for "wherever Something stands," the Igbo would say, "Something Else stands beside it." Chi, from the spiritland, exercises a special hold over the individual and his or her destiny. That is why the Igbo say, "if one's chi is not present in the plot for his or her downfall, the plot will never succeed." Nevertheless, since nothing is absolute among the Igbo, the complementarity role of the individual limits the exercise of chi's power. Thus, another Igbo proverb, *onye kwe chi ya ekwe* ("if one says 'yes,' his or her chi also says 'yes'"), returns the initiative, or some of it, to the individual.[21]

According to the Igbo, Achebe notes, "a man receives his gifts or talents, his character—indeed his portion in life generally—before he comes into the world"[22] based on the agreement he reached with his chi. So, when an incomprehensible misfortune befalls an individual, the Igbo would say *O bu ihe ya na chi ya kpara* ("that was what she and her chi agreed on"). For the Igbo, Achebe argues, an individual is created by his or her own chi, and no two people, not even blood brothers, are created by the same chi. Each person has his or her own unique chi. Hence, for Achebe, the proverb *ofu nne n'amu, ma ofu chi a naghi eke* means "one mother gives birth, different chi create."[23] In other words, every individual is both a unique creation and the work of a unique creator. However, the no-absolute rule restrains the individual's total freedom, since this freedom is contained within the will of the community.

But whence cometh chi? Drawing from the northeast Awka section of the Igboland where, according to him, shrines of chi are set up through a ritual that brings down the spirit from the face of the sun at day break, Achebe maintains that "a person's chi normally resides with the sun, bringer of daylight, or at least passes through it to visit the world."[24] He thinks that this passage of chi from or through the sun "may have an even profounder implication, for *it is well known in Igbo cosmology* that the Supreme Deity, Chukwu Himself, is in close communion with the sun."[25]

Turning to "the all-important relationship between chi and Chi Ukwu,"[26] Achebe asserts that since Chukwu (Chi Ukwu) means literally Great Chi, "whatever chi may be it does seem to partake of the nature of the Supreme God,"[27] due to the chi/sun/Chukwu relationship. For Achebe, the Igbo "see the sun as an agent of Chukwu to whom it is said to bear those rare sacrifices offered as man's last desperate resort."[28] Thus, although the true relationship among the Supreme Being (Chukwu), the sun, and chi might never be unraveled, if Chukwu literally means Great Chi, "one is almost tempted to borrow the words of Christian dogma and speak of chi as being of same 'substance' as, and 'proceeding' from, Chukwu,"[29] Achebe concludes.

From the foregoing, one can note three key oversights in Achebe's argument. First, Achebe assumes the existence of the Supreme God as "well known" among the Igbo, as something given in Igbo cosmology. As a result, he never bothered to either clarify the sense of his usage or demonstrate the "givenness" of the knowledge. Second, despite the fact that Achebe noted earlier that chi could be imagined as a man's other identity in the spiritland, Achebe now asserts that chi's abode is in the neighborhood of Chukwu's in the heavens,[30] and this neighborhood is also different from *ani mmuo*, the spiritland. At the same time, he maintains, chi is not remote; although it need not appear in person or act directly, it may act through other people who are close by.[31] Yes, there are no absolutes in the Igbo conceptions of the world and Achebe from the outset pointed out the challenges in articulating the chi concept. That notwithstanding, the fact that Achebe fails to reconcile his location of chi in three different spaces—heavens, spiritland, and human world—invests chi with the supremacy which Achebe tries to deny it by subsuming it under Chukwu. Third, by simply positing a literal meaning of Chukwu, Achebe has produced what in fact is remarkably like the Christian God by assuming this Chi Ukwu to be the Supreme God and claiming that chi "does seem" to partake of the nature of this Supreme God. In fact, however, although Chukwu literally means Great Chi, the relationship between this Great Chi and the Supreme God remains to be ascertained.

BEYOND ACHEBE: CHI-CHUKWU IN IGBO SCHOLARSHIP

Scholars like Nwoga, Ibe Chukwukere,[32] and C. N. Ubah,[33] have challenged, albeit in varying degrees, the assumptions that inform Achebe's orthodoxy outlook. Nwoga (a professor of and researcher in Igbo literature and culture, as well as African literature in foreign languages), for example, offers a radical critique of this authorized Supreme God version. Ubah, a historian, on the other hand, although in basic support of the orthodoxy, disagrees with the claim that Chukwu ultimately received all sacrifices and prayers made to "lesser deities." Ubah points out that the Otanchara and Otanzu areas of central Igboland, for instance, are "emphatic on the point that sacrifices offered to any spirit are meant for its own consumption, although it could *invite* any other spirit or spirits to its meal."[34]

With regard, then, to the origin of Chukwu, Nwoga argues that the notion of Chukwu as Supreme God with intermediary deities was an invention of the mid-nineteenth century monotheistic missionaries in search of a Supreme Being among the "primitive" people.[35] He cites anthropologist Thomas Northcote and Catholic priest Joachim Correia in support of his argument. The two researched the Igbo people of Awka in 1913/4 and around Onitsha area in 1920, respectively. The former observed: "It is worthy of note that the old men frequently said that they knew nothing of *Cuku* [Chukwu] before the coming of the white man,"[36] while the latter noted that the concept of Chukwu as Supreme God among the Igbo was due to European influence.[37] Correia, Nwoga maintains, discovered in his research that "wherever *Chukwu* was met among the traditional Igbo, the term referred to the deity touted by the Aro people."[38] Indeed, history seems to show how this particular group of the Igbo spread the concept of Chukwu. While the remaining part of this section outlines this history, a later section, "Along their own way," will examine the ethnographic implications of the understanding and use of Chukwu in Igbo culture, say, in names, language, and rituals.

For the Aro, an Igbo group from Arochukwu, Chukwu was the name of their deity, the deity behind their famous and powerful oracle, "one of the essential bastions of their prestige."[39] The oracle and the cult of Chukwu became particularly influential from the seventeenth century onwards. The Aro spread the cult of this Chukwu throughout most of Igboland and beyond by means of an extensive network of trade. They traded mainly in slaves, stimulated by the European slave trade. But wherever they went, the Aro also took with them "both for protection and as an additional business, the reputation of their *Chi-Ukwu* (Big Chi),"[40] whose status they succeeded in elevating to that of the last arbiter beyond which there could be no surer answer to a problem.

Drawing on data from a 1951 study of the Chukwu Oracle by anthropologist Simon Ottenberg, Nwoga notes: "A strong chain of information gathering was created, mysteries were invented around the [Chukwu] shrine, death and slavery were visited on guilty persons, and generally going 'to consult Chukwu' [*ije Chukwu*] in Arochukwu"[41] became the highest act of judicial process and of solving other problems as well as clarifying situations that required ultimate and drastic solutions: accusation of sorcery, land inheritance disputes, grave illness, or childlessness. However, Nwoga adds, every Aro adult knew about the trick of consulting Chukwu. The British army finally sacked the oracle of Chukwu in 1901 and 1902 in the largest colonial military expedition in Igboland.[42] No doubt, other oracles and deities existed in Igboland, but, after the success of the Aro, none could match Chukwu's overarching hegemony, which they promoted across the region. Non-Aro villages and individuals that received favors from Chukwu, and many did, set up shrines for it in appreciation. According to Nwoga, that was the state of affairs in Igboland when the Christian missionaries arrived there in the mid nineteenth century, as far as can be ascertained.

Given that today "Chukwu" is the dominant name for God in Igbo both among Christians and non-Christians, and that it is interpreted to mean a universal "over-soul" from which each particular chi is derived, one cannot but ask if the Aro thought of their Chukwu deity in this universal sense. As a matter of fact, some scholars think otherwise. Anthropologist Margaret Green, in a study of the Agbaja people in 1930, contends that "any conception of universal Ci [chi] seems doubtful."[43] According to Chukwukere: "*Chukwu* rather appears to be the Aro people's name for their 'town' deity, which the Aro may well have conceived as a kind of their collective or 'national' *chi*, at first peculiar to themselves and later 'adopted' by other Igbo people, which is understandable in the context of collective Aro achievement in Igbo history."[44]

It is not surprising that the characteristics of Chukwu, with cults and shrines almost all over Igboland, seemed to fit the attributes of the Christian God: omnipresence, omnipotence, and omniscience. The missionaries remembered their great "ancestor," St Paul, and his "discovery" of the shrine to the unknown god in Athens. According to Nwoga, they identified Chukwu with the God of the Judeo-Christian tradition and moved it from its shrine in Arochukwu to the heavens. Interestingly, Achebe himself corroborates Nwoga on the point that a concept in Igbo religion was identified with the Christian God. While arguing that Chineke, another name for the Supreme Being among the Igbo (more on Chineke later), does not mean "God who creates," its common understanding today, Achebe notes: "The early missionaries by putting the wrong tone on that little word na [a conjunction in *chi* na *eke*] escorted a two-headed, pagan god into their holy of holies."[45]

AFRICAN RELIGIONS, CHRISTIAN APOLOGISTS, AND AFRICAN NATIONALISTS

If it is the case that Chukwu was the name of an Aro deity and that this deity was not regarded in the universal sense by the Aro, how did most Igbo scholars come to uphold the mistake of the missionaries in making Chukwu a High God? The philosopher, Kwasi Wiredu offers an explanation. He notes that since most people assume that it speaks well of a people's mental capabilities if they are shown to have a belief in God, especially a God of a Christian likeness, generalization about African beliefs in the Supreme God abound in the literature on African religions.[46] Anthropologist Robin Horton concurs, arguing that most scholars of African religions are strongly influenced by their Christian faith as well as a Christian theological methodology and framework.[47]

p'Bitek goes further than Wiredu and Horton in offering an explanation, albeit furiously, to the "agreement" between African scholars and the missionaries. He implicates not only the missionaries (like Edwin Smith, John Taylor and Placide Tempels), but also those he calls the "Christian apologists" (Edward E. Evans-Pritchard, Godfrey Lienhardt and Geoffrey Parrinder).[48] The two groups together with the African pre-independent nationalists, p'Bitek maintains, are "reactions . . . heavily influenced, limited and controlled by the forces against which they react."[49] Horton calls p'Bitek's three categories the "Devout Opposition," and includes within his own classification African scholars like Bolaji Idowu and John Mbiti as well as Evans-Pritchard, Victor Turner, and Harold Turner. "Opposition" in Horton's term describes the members' "adversary attitude to the more established approach" while and the qualifier "devout" refers to the "deep influence of personal Christian faith on their own approach."[50] p'Bitek argues that in their attack on the eighteenth to twentieth centuries Western non-believers, the Christian apologists used African deities to prove that the Christian God does exist "and is known also among African peoples."[51] The missionaries, on the other hand, aimed to win the hearts of the African elites. So, they undermined the earlier portrayal of Africans as "pagan savages," and asserted instead the image of Africans as "highly religious and moral people."[52] Franciscan missionary Placide Tempels typifies the highly religious sentiment in his articulation of "vital force," a life-imbuing spirit from God, present in all living and inanimate things, as the pivot of Bantu thought and behavior.[53] African theologian and philosopher John Mbiti echoes a similar sentiment in his now famous assertion: "Africans are notoriously religious . . . Religion permeates into all the depths of life so fully that it is not easy or possible always to isolate it."[54]

The missionaries' dilemma as regards what name to call their God when they preached to Africans, p'Bitek contends, led the missionaries to name-soliciting. They busily engaged themselves in extracting from the peoples they evangelized names of the Supreme Being. As Horton puts it, "sometimes, it seems, the peoples involved could only produce names of lesser spiritual forces, and it was the missionaries themselves who deceived themselves into thinking that they were in possession of indigenous names for the Supreme Being."[55] p'Bitek gives an example of how in 1911, some Italian Catholic priests engaged some Ugandan Acoli elders in the "Who created you?" questions. Given that *create/creation* is not an independent concept in Luo language, the elders could not make sense of the questions. But in the process of further questioning, an elder remembered *Rubanga*, the hostile spirit which the Acoli people believe causes, "moulds," the hunch or hump on the back, and said "*Rubanga* is the one who moulds people." The missionaries then erroneously upheld Rubanga as the creator of the Acoli.[56]

Although some African cosmologies do have the concept of a Supreme God as creator and sustainer of the world, it should also be noted that that concept is not common in African religions. Instances include the Zimbabwean Shona (among whom it is questioned whether *Mwari* has always been understood as Supreme Being), the Tanzanian Gogo (whose *Maduwo*—world creator—often refers to a foreign malevolent force, and so casts doubt on its understanding as Supreme God), and the Malawian Nyakyusa people (who do not have one indigenous concept of a creator/sustainer of the world).[57]

According to p'Bitek, African nationalists like Jomo Kenyatta, Leopold Senghor, Joseph B. Danquah, Kofi A. Busia, John Mbiti, and Bolaji Idowu added another phase to the process of affirming the "religiousness" of Africans. He maintains that "in the face of the arrogance and insults of western scholarship," the nationalists over-reacted by claiming that African deities not only possess all the attributes of the Christian God, but also that the African peoples knew this Christian God long before the missionaries told the Africans about him.[58] Writing in the late 1960s, p'Bitek argues, "although some of them are priests, the present day African scholars are first and foremost nationalists. Their works are in defense of African culture against the vicious attack of Western scholarship."[59] These devout scholars engaged themselves in "demonstrating equality of mental and cultural capacity between the African and his Western counterpart."[60] That way, the dignity and worth of Africans would be restored in the eyes of the world.

Bolaji Idowu, for instance, talks of African religion as "Diffused Monotheism,"[61] as he argues for a Supreme God with intermediaries. By so doing, Idowu ends up with a construction of "African Traditional Religion" "as a single, pan-African belief system comparable to Christianity."[62] Idowu also talks about the Yoruba sense of a fallen, evil-ridden world, and about the

Yoruba yearning for paradise. By implication, he suggests that there exists in the African religious thought the idea of an imperfect world from which the individual longs to escape into an eternal perfection.[63] Going even further beyond Idowu, Mbiti claims, "God is the ultimate Recipient [of sacrifices and prayers to other deities] whether or not the worshippers are aware of that."[64] Hence, "Diffused Monotheism" is raised as an article of faith, a depiction of what African religious participants "ideally *ought* to think," regardless of their own self-knowledge.[65]

"ALONG THEIR OWN WAY": IGBO APPROACH ROOTED IN CULTURE

The preceding section provides a wider context for understanding Achebe's assumption of the Supreme God among the Igbo. However, to further problematize the discussion, the paper will push back more on Achebe's position by engaging the conversation on the terms of Igbo religious culture itself. Like Achebe rightly observes, "since the Igbo people did not construct a rigid and closely argued system of thought to explain the universe and the place of man in it . . . anyone seeking an insight into their world must seek it along their own way."[66] In light of that position, the essay will now turn to some of these ways, namely proper names, language, folklore, rituals, and morality, to further bolster its argument.

First, proper names: Names are one way through which the Igbo chronicle their encounter with life: their hopes, fears, joys and sorrows; their grievances against their fellow men or complaint about their fortune; and their historical records. "And because chi is so central to Igbo thought," Achebe rightly acknowledges, "we will also find much about it in proper names—more I think than from any other single source."[67] Chika, "Chi is supreme"; Chibuzo, "Chi is in front"; and Nebechi, "look unto chi" are examples of names that illustrate chi's primacy over humankind. Chinonso, asserts chi's nearness; Chinwendu, its power over life; and Chinweuba, its special responsibility for increase and prosperity. Chijioke ("Chi holds one's portion/share—of life") points to chi's role as the great dispenser of gifts.

The Igbo had a tradition of naming children after the oracle or deity that was appealed to before they were born. For example, a child named after *Amadioha*, the thunder god, was called Amadi, for short; while Nwagwu (child of *Agwu*) was given to children named after Agwu, the deity of divination and medicine. Hence, there were some Chukwu names in reference to Chukwu of Arochukwu, like Nwachukwu (child of Chukwu) and Ekenedirichukwu (thanks be to Chukwu). But, given the overarching proselytizing mission of Christianity in Igboland and the prominent place it accorded

Chukwu, the tradition of naming children after deities became mixed up with the tradition of translating Christian theistic ideals into Igbo. Chi names were then transformed into Chukwu ones, the Supreme God, so that Chibuzu now reads Chukwubuzo; and Lebechi, Lebechukwu.[68]

Second, language: Achebe and his co-proponents of the Supreme God orthodoxy often use Chukwu and Chineke interchangeably to buttress their argument that the Great Chi (Chi Ukwu) is the God who creates (Chineke). But there are reasons for thinking that this is a mistaken view, as Achebe's apposite explanation illustrates:

Chineke consists of three words: chi na eke. In assigning a meaning to it the crucial word is *na*, which itself has three possible meanings. a) Said with a high tone, na means *who* or which. Chineke will then mean chi which creates; b) said with a low tone, na can mean the auxiliary verb *does*, in which case Chineke will mean chi *does create*; and finally, c) again said with a low tone, na can mean the conjunctive *and*. Here something fundamental changes because eke is no longer a verb but a noun. Chineke then becomes chi and eke. And that, in my opinion, is the correct version.[69]

Both Nwoga and Chukwukere concur with Achebe's opinion.[70] Nwoga notes that the *ke* ending of Chineke is an Igbo root which always refers to the act of dividing, sharing, and splitting up (*okè* = a share; *okike* = the act of sharing; *èkè* = one who shares; *kèé* = divide) rather than creating *ex nihilo*, as "God the Creator" connotes.[71] Catholic priest and traditional medicine practitioner Raymond Arazu echoes Nwoga's stance when he says, "*Chineke* only apportions to each existing thing its lot and was never conceived by the traditional Igbo religionist as bringing things out of nothing."[72]

If that be the case, then "One mother gives birth, but different chi (plural) apportion" would be a more appropriate rendition of the Igbo proverb *ofu nne n'amu, ma ofu chi a naghi eke*, rather than Achebe's translation, "One mother gives birth, but different chi create." Besides, this alternative translation not only buttresses Achebe's immediate conclusion above that with the understanding of "na" as a conjunctive "eke" ceases to be a verb but a noun, it also confirms his earlier emphasis on how central the concept of duality is in Igbo worldview. It is in standing as discrete two nouns that "chi" and "eke" can withstand the nothing-stands-alone preeminence in Igbo cosmology and consciousness. For indeed, "wherever something stands, something else stands beside it." It would be difficult to imagine that the Igbo did not assign a concept as fundamental to their worldview as chi a complementary being.

Given the above discussion, Chineke, then, does not mean *chi who creates*, but rather a dualistic deity chi and eke which is both "two" and "one." Eke has its standard meaning in tradition, referring to "destiny, and agency of destiny, in each person's life."[73] Its "oneness" with chi explains the use of one or the other in Igbo names: Chinweuba or Ekejiuba (Chi owns or Eke holds wealth) and Lebechi or Lemeke (look unto chi or eke). Achebe acknowledges that the early missionaries could not resist the attraction of Chineke in its seeming lack of ambiguity on "the all-important question of creation. They needed a 'God who creates' and Chineke stood ready at hand."[74] However, as the above description of Chineke has shown, the dualistic conception of Chineke is significantly different from the Judeo-Christian Creator-God image into which early missionaries translated it.

Third, folklore: As an expression of the traditional beliefs of a people, folklore portrays a people's conception of their world, and their relationship with the world. Two examples of Igbo lore appear to undermine the conception of an all-powerful and all-knowing Supreme God. The first, common among the Azia, Ihiala, and Awka people, goes like this:

> Chukwu invited Amachaamifeuwa ("I-know-all-things-in-the-world," hereafter referred to as Amachaam) to shave Chukwu's hair. Amachaam went with a cob of corn which he gave to Chukwu. While he shaved Chukwu's hair, Chukwu ate the corn. When Amachaam was done, Chukwu ran his hand over his head and exclaimed, "Why did you shave my hair; put it back!" Amachaam riposted, "You first put back the seeds of my corn." Chukw could not do it and so he let Amachaam go.

Another story is told of Chukwu and the tortoise (the epitome of craftiness in Igbo lore). Chukwu invited Tortoise to his place and when Tortoise arrived Chukwu offered him a stone and said, "Break this kola nut for us to eat." Tortoise then asked Chukwu to carry the earth on his head. Chukwu retorted, "Does one ever carry the earth?" And Tortoise replied, "Does one ever break stone as kola nut?" Chukwu saw the wisdom in Tortoise's reasoning and surrendered. The two stories point to how this Chukwu is easily outwitted. As such, it seems unlikely that such a god is the omnipotent and omniscient Supreme God who would be honored in sacred rituals, but more likely that he is the oracular deity about whom such stories of tests and defeats might be told.

Fourth, rituals: The Igbo have a ritual system, and therefore a structure of religion consonant with and adequate for their needs. Sacrifices were specific to the different agencies to which offerings were made for different needs or challenges; and there were full personal or communal needs and appropriate rituals for chi and the deities.[75] Religious studies scholar Christopher Ejizu, however, rues the fact that although when it comes to rituals "the divinities, patron spirits and deities, continue to dominate as the objective phenomena of the system,"[76] the concept of the Supreme God has become an "infiltrated alien idea"[77] that has gained prominence in the religious thought of the traditional religionists. This "infiltrated idea" has so penetrated the system that even non-Christian elders in Igboland today conclude their kola nut rituals *n'aha Jesu Christi onye nwe anyi* ("In the name of Jesus Christ our Lord").

Infiltrated ideas notwithstanding, as far as the Igbo were concerned, if a god was not worshipped, it did not exist.[78] This is evident in the cases, among the Azia in the Ihiala region for example, where deities were deserted and their shrines cleared for other purposes when their priests died and there were no replacements. Thus, the acceptance of the Supreme God concept would amount to an imposition on the Igbo of "a god that they could not discipline or do away with if that god became unsatisfactory in his relationship with them."[79] Interestingly, the character Nwaka in Achebe's *Arrow of God* also attests to the fact that the relationship between the Igbo and their gods was a contractual and reciprocal one.[80] In his community-splitting rivalry with the chief priest of *Ulu*, Umuaro's communal deity, Nwaka makes it clear to Ezeulu that Umuaro people would serve their gods but would not hesitate to abandon or even burn any gods, including Ulu, that failed to live up to their functions.[81]

Fifth, morality: The Igbo depended and still depend on *Ala/Ani*, the Earth goddess/deity, for solidarity and continuity. Ala is "the deified counterpart of the group sphere of existence";[82] so, the Igbo assigned to her the morality of the group at all levels. The most serious offenses, the taboos and abominations, like murder, incest, yam theft, birth of twins, suicide, bestiality, etcetera, were, and some still are, referred to as *nso Ala*, tabooed by Ala. No offense was referred to any Supreme God. It was to Ala that sacrifices were offered in cases of any nso Ala; cleansing rituals were performed to appease Ala and avert her wrath on the community.[83] Ala in the Igbo community life was therefore the preeminent recipient of appeal and placation. This position of Ala prompts literary scholar Michael Echeruo to assert: "If there was a supreme god among the Igbo it was Ala."[84] In fact, her place was "so important that she is believed to be older than and superior to all other deities."[85] That explains why in different parts of Igboland, for example, when a diviner sacrificed a cock at his or her shrine, usually housing a number of deities, he or she first offered the head to Ala before distributing the remnant to the rest.

Achebe himself acknowledges this ascendancy of Ala particularly in two of his classical novels set in Igbo traditional societies, *Things Fall Apart* and *Arrow of God*. In *Things Fall Apart,* Okonwko commits three offences (beating his wife during the Peace Week, inadvertently murdering a kinsman, and committing suicide) which are tabooed by Ala and require the cleansing of the Earth,[86] the "proper source of moral law . . ."[87] In *Arrow of God,* Nkechi and Nwafo remind Obiageli (when the latter asks in a song, "Who will punish the Earth for me?"[88]) that there is no greater power than the Earth. In neither of these instances from the two novels does Achebe posit an omnipotent Supreme God to whom morality should have been a concern. And this is in spite of his assertion that he would be quite satisfied if the novels he set in the past "did no more than teach [his] African readers that their past . . . was not one long night of savagery from which the first European acting on God's behalf delivered them."[89]

It is true that Achebe does make a case in *Things Fall Apart* for Chukwu as the creator of the world among the Igbo when, for instance, Umuofia's first white Christian missionary, Mr. Brown, engages community chief Akunna in a God discourse which helps Mr. Brown advance his knowledge on the religion of Umuofia people.[90] However, before that unusually mutual encounter, "an old man" in Mbanta, reminiscent of Achebe's granduncle in Ogidi (see first section of this essay), has been unable to associate this Christian Supreme God with either "the earth goddess or Amadiora, the god of the sky." When the white missionary speaking through an interpreter at the village square tells the old man that "there is only one true God and He has the earth" and everything in it, another Mbanta man asks: "If we leave our gods and followed your god . . . who will protect us from the anger of our neglected gods and ancestors."[91]

To the missionary's response that Mbanta gods are dead and therefore harmless, the gathered men of the community "broke out into derisive laughter. These [Christian] men must be mad, they said to themselves. How else could they say that Ani and Amadiora were harmless? And Idemili and Ogwugwu too? And some of them began to go away."[92] Also in *Arrow of God*—although Soyinka has questioned Achebe's denial of the preeminence of Ulu[93]—it is still Idemili, the river deity, not Chukwu, that is said to have existed from the beginning of things. It is instructive from the references to the two novels to note which gods Achebe chooses to privilege among the pre-colonial and colonial Igbo communities he writes about. The men of Mbanta would not have laughed the missionary to scorn as they left him to his lunacy of considering Ani dead and harmless if the idea of a Supreme God greater than Ani had not sounded insane to them in the first place.

CONCLUSION

Aru gbaa afo, o buru omenaala, ("When an anomaly lasts a year, it becomes tradition") typifies the Igbo resignation to accepting and integrating novel realities into their worldview. The Supreme God orthodoxy is one such reality. Its dominance in Igbo religious thought does not only derive from the overarching Christian enterprise promoted by the Christian missionaries and supported by Christian apologists, but also, albeit sometimes inadvertently, from the reactionary approach of colonial African nationalist scholars like Achebe. Indeed, plumbing the concepts of "chi" and the "Supreme God" as well as the interaction between the two is an enterprise so complex that, like Achebe rightly points out, attempts at describing phenomena that vast and deep can only be approached from parts that one is familiar with.[94] Achebe is first to acknowledge his restricted approach to this discourse.[95] This essay is an invitation to further expand the range of that approach.

NOTES

1. Chinua Achebe, "Chi in Igbo Cosmology," in *Morning Yet on Creation Day: Essays* (Garden City, New York: Anchor Press/Doubleday 1975), 159–175.
2. Ibid., 161.
3. Ibid., 170.
4. See Achebe, "Chi in Igbo Cosmology," 168–170.
5. See Francis Arinze, *Sacrifice in Ibo Religion* (Ibadan: Ibadan University Press, 1970); Emmanuel Edeh, *Towards an Igbo Metaphysics* (Chicago: Loyola Press, 1995); Stephen N. Ezeanya, "The Place of the Supreme God in the Traditional Religion of the Igbo," *West African Religion* 1, nos. 1–4 (1963); Ikenga E. Metuh, *God and Man in African Religion: A Case Study of the Igbo of Nigeria* (London: Geoffrey Chapman, 1981).
6. Donatus Ibe Nwoga, *The Supreme God as Stranger in Igbo Religious Thought* (Owerri: Hawk Press, 1984).
7. Ibid; Achebe, "Chi in Igbo Cosmology," 171.
8. Nwoga, *The Supreme God as Stranger;* Achebe, *"Chi in Igbo Cosmology."*
9. Nwoga, *The Supreme God as Stranger.*
10. Okot p'Bitek, *African Religions in Western Scholarship* (Nairobi: Kenya Literature Bureau, 1970).
11. Chinua Achebe, *The Education of a British-protected Child* (London: Penguin, 2009), 12.
12. Wole Soyinka, *Of Africa* (New Haven: Yale University Press, 2012), 107.
13. Ibid., 107–108. See also Wole Soyinka, *Myth, Literature and the African World* (Cambridge: Cambridge University Press, 1976).
14. Achebe, *The Education of a British-protected Child*, 37.
15. Chinua Achebe, "African Literature as Restoration of Celebration," in *Chinua Achebe: A Celebration*, ed. Kristen Holst Petersen and Anna Rutherord (Oxford: Heinemann Educational Books, 1991), 7.
16. Chinua Achebe, *There Was a Country: A Personal History of Biafra* (London: Allen Lane, 2012), 33.
17. Ibid., 34.
18. Achebe, "'Chi' in Igbo Cosmology," 159.
19. Ibid.
20. Ibid., 160.
21. Ibid., 161.
22. Ibid., 165.

23. Ibid., 166.
24. Ibid., 161.
25. Ibid. Emphasis added.
26. Ibid., 168.
27. Ibid., 169
28. Ibid.
29. Ibid., 170.
30. Ibid., 169.
31. Ibid., 164.
32. Ibe Chukwukere, "Chi in Igbo Religion and Thought: The God in Every Man," *Anthropos* 78 (1983).
33. C. N. Ubah, "The Supreme Being, Divinities and Ancestors in Igbo Traditional Religion: Evidence from Otanchara and Otanzu," *Africa* 52 (1982).
34. Ubah, 92.
35. Nwoga, 24.
36. Ibid., 25.
37. Ibid.
38. Ibid., 26.
39. Elizabeth Isichei, *A History of the Igbo People* (London: Macmillan, 1976), 59. See also Ogbu Kalu, *The Embattled Gods: Chrstianization of Igboland, 1841–1991* (Asmara: Africa World, 2003).
40. Nwoga, 36. See also Adiele E. Afigbo, *Ropes of Sand: Studies in Igbo History and Culture* (Ibadan: Oxford University Press, 1982).
41. Nwoga, 36.
42. See Kenneth Onwuka Dike, *The Aro of South-Eastern Nigeria, 1650–1980: A Study of Socio-economic Formation and Transformation in Nigeria* (Ibadan: University Press, 1990); Elizabeth Isichei, *A History of the Igbo People*.
43. Margaret M. Green, *Igbo Village Affairs: Chiefly with Reference to the Village of Umueke Agbaja* (London: Frank Cass, 1964).
44. Chukwukere, 528.
45. Achebe, "'Chi in Igbo Cosmology," 171.
46. Kwasi Wiredu, "On Decolonising African Religions," In *The African Philosophy Reader*, ed. P. H. Coetzee and A. P. J. Roux (London: Routledge, 1998), 186–204.
47. Robin Horton, *Patterns of Thought in Africa and the West: Essays on Magic, Religion and Science* (Cambridge: Cambridge University Press, 1993).
48. p'Bitek, 41.
49. Ibid.
50. Horton, 162.
51. p'Bitek, 41.
52. Ibid.
53. Placide Temples, *Bantu Philosophy*. Trans. C. King (Paris: Presence Africaine, 1959).
54. John Mbiti, *African Religions and Philosophy,* (Florence: Heinemann, 1990).
55. Horton, 174.
56. p'Bitek, 62.

57. Horton, 174.
58. p'Bitek, 29.
59. Ibid.
60. Horton, 190.
61. Bolaji E. Idowu, *African Traditional Religion: A Definition* (London: SCM, 1973).
62. Rosalind Shaw, "The Invention of 'African Traditional Religion,'" *Religion* 20, 339–53, 1990.
63. See Horton.
64. Mbiti, 58.
65. Shaw, 345.
66. Achebe, "'Chi in Igbo Cosmology," 161.
67. Ibid., 69. The following analysis on Igbo names relies a lot on Achebe's exposition of the same topic.
68. Nwoga, *The Supreme God as Stranger*, 38.
69. Achebe, "'Chi in Igbo Cosmology," 171.
70. See Nwoga, *The Supreme God as Stranger* and Chukwukere, "Chi in Igbo Religion and Thought."
71. Nwoga, *The Supreme God as Stranger*, 56.
72. Raymond Arazu, "The Supreme God in Igbo Traditional Religion," Workshop on The State of Igbo Studies (Nsukka: Institute of African Studies, 1982), 5.
73. Nwoga, *The Supreme God as Stranger*, 56.
74. Achebe, "'Chi' in Igbo Cosmology," 173.
75. Nwoga, *The Supreme God as Stranger*.
76. Christopher Ejizu, "Continuity and Discontinuity in Igbo Traditional Religion," in *The Gods in Retreat: Continuity and Change in African Religions*, ed. Emefie Ikenga Metuh (Enugu: Fourth Dimension, 1985), 150.
77. Ibid.
78. Chukwuemeka Nze, "Pragmatism and Traditionalism in the Concept of God in African Culture," *Uche* 5 (1981), 24.
79. Ibid.
80. Chinua Achebe, *Arrow of God* (New York: Doubleday, 1974).
81. Chinua Achebe, *Arrow of God* in *The African Trilogy: Things Fall Apart, No Longer at Ease, Arrow of God* (New York: Everyman's Library, 2010), 327.
82. Nwoga, *The Supreme God as Stranger*, 16.
83. J. U. Tagbo Nzeako, *Omenala ndi Igbo* (Enugu: Longman, 1979).
84. Michael J. C. Echeruo, *A Matter of Identity: 1979 Ahiajioku Lecture* (Owerri: Culture Division, Ministry of Information, Culture, Youths and Sports, 1979), 19.
85. Nwoga, *The Supreme God as Stranger*, 66.
86. Chinua Achebe, *Things Fall Apart* (New York: Anchor Books, 1994).
87. Achebe, "'Chi' in Igbo Cosmology," 165.
88. Achebe, *Arrow of God*, 66.
89. Achebe, *Hopes and Impediments*, 45.
90. Achebe, *Things Fall Apart*, 179–182.
91. Ibid., 146.

92. Ibid.
93. Soyinka, *Myth, Literature and the African World*, 86–96.
94. Achebe, *The Education of a British-protected Child*.
95. Achebe, "'Chi' in Igbo Cosmology," 160.

BIBLIOGRAPHY

Achebe, Chinua. "African Literature as Restoration of Celebration." In *Chinua Achebe: A Celebration*, ed. Kristen Holst Petersen and Anna Rutherord. Oxford: Heinemann Educational Books, 1991.

Achebe, Chinua. "Chi in Igbo Cosmology." In *Morning Yet on Creation Day: Essays* Garden City, New York: Anchor Press/Doubleday 1975, 159–175.

Achebe, Chinua. *Arrow of God* in *The African Trilogy: Things Fall Apart, No Longer at Ease, Arrow of God*. New York: Everyman's Library, 2010.

Achebe, Chinua. *The Education of a British-protected Child*. London: Penguin, 2009.

Achebe, Chinua. *There Was a Country: A Personal History of Biafra*. London: Allen Lane, 2012.

Achebe, Chinua. *Things Fall Apart*. New York: Anchor Books, 1994.

Achebe, Chinua. *Arrow of God*. New York: Doubleday, 1974.

Afigbo, Adiele E. *Ropes of Sand: Studies in Igbo History and Culture*. Ibadan: Oxford University Press, 1982.

Arazu, Raymond. "The Supreme God in Igbo Traditional Religion," Workshop on The State of Igbo Studies. Nsukka: Institute of African Studies, 1982.

Arinze, Francis. *Sacrifice in Ibo Religion*. Ibadan: Ibadan University Press, 1970.

Chukwukere, Ibe. "Chi in Igbo Religion and Thought: The God in Every Man." *Anthropos* 78 (1983).

Dike, Kenneth Onwuka. *The Aro of South-Eastern Nigeria, 1650–1980: A Study of Socio-economic Formation and Transformation in Nigeria*. Ibadan: University Press, 1990.

Echeruo, Michael J. C. *A Matter of Identity: 1979 Ahiajioku Lecture*. Owerri: Culture Division, Ministry of Information, Culture, Youths and Sports, 1979.

Edeh, Emmanuel. *Towards an Igbo Metaphysics*. Chicago: Loyola Press, 1995.

Ejizu, Christopher. "Continuity and Discontinuity in Igbo Traditional Religion." In *The Gods in Retreat: Continuity and Change in African Religions*, ed. Emefie Ikenga Metuh. Enugu: Fourth Dimension, 1985.

Ezeanya, Stephen N. "The Place of the Supreme God in the Traditional Religion of the Igbo." *West African Religion* 1, nos. 1–4 (1963)

Green, Margaret M. *Igbo Village Affairs: Chiefly with Reference to the Village of Umueke Agbaja*. London: Frank Cass, 1964.

Horton, Robin. *Patterns of Thought in Africa and the West: Essays on Magic, Religion and Science*. Cambridge: Cambridge University Press, 1993.

Idowu, Bolaji E. *African Traditional Religion: A Definition*. London: SCM, 1973.

Isichei, Elizabeth. *A History of the Igbo People*. London: Macmillan, 1976.

Kalu, Ogbu. *The Embattled Gods: Christianization of Igboland, 1841–1991*. Asmara: Africa World Press, 2003.

Kalu, Ogbu. *The Embattled Gods: Chrstianization of Igboland, 1841–1991* (Asmara: Africa World Press, 2003.

Mbiti, John. *African Religions and Philosophy*. Florence: Heinemann, 1990.

Metuh, Ikenga E. *God and Man in African Religion: A Case Study of the Igbo of Nigeria*. London: Geoffrey Chapman, 1981.

Nwoga, Donatus Ibe. *The Supreme God as Stranger in Igbo Religious Thought*. Owerri: Hawk Press, 1984.

Nze, Chukwuemeka. "Pragmatism and Traditionalism in the Concept of God in African Culture," *Uche* 5 (1981):

p'Bitek, Okot. *African Religions in Western Scholarship*. Nairobi: Kenya Literature Bureau, 1970.

Shaw, Rosalind. "The Invention of 'African Traditional Religion." *Religion* 20, (1990): 339–53.

Soyinka, Wole. *Myth, Literature and the African World*. Cambridge: Cambridge University Press, 1976.

Soyinka, Wole. *Of Africa*. New Haven, CT: Yale University Press, 2012.

Tagbo, Nzeako J. U. *Omenala ndi Igbo*. Enugu: Longman, 1979.

Temples, Placide. *Bantu Philosophy*. Trans. C. King. Paris: Presence Africaine, 1959.

Ubah, C. N. "The Supreme Being, Divinities and Ancestors in Igbo Traditional Religion: Evidence from Otanchara and Otanzu." *Africa* 52 (1982).

Wiredu, Kwasi. "On Decolonising African Religions." In *The African Philosophy Reader*, ed. P. H. Coetzee and A. P. J. Roux (London: Routledge, 1998), 186–204.

Chapter 8

Discourse, Imagination, and Models of Resistance

Rereading Arrow of God

Ifi Amaduime

The[1] interest to reread Chinua Achebe's novel, *Arrow of God* (1964) follows the publication of his autobiography, *There Was a Country* (2012). What do we learn about the author's life experiences toward a better understanding of his imagination, the unraveling of the characters of this novel and the outcomes of events? The climax to unravel in Chinua Achebe's novel *Arrow of God* involves several intersecting conflicts and characters that reveal ideas about the colonial encounter, survival instincts, strategies and models of resistance, and social justice consciousness. Most important is the analyzing of these issues from indigenous thought processes and realities on the eve of colonization, since there is yet no other reality other than indigenous Igbo traditions as fictionalized in the novel. My concern here involves a deeper probing into and analysis of models of resistance through an understanding of points of rupture and the setting of a new paradigm. It is a perspective that works from within to understand and give voice to local dynamics in the encounter with change. I am therefore concerned with narrative voices and actions by all social groups, including that of the writer throughout the novel and his autobiography.

The protagonist or main character is the chief priest of an indigenous religion, based on an Igbo constructed deity, Ulu, hence Ezeulu, meaning priest of Ulu. This priest of Ulu overtakes in importance a pre-existing local priest of Idemili, called Ezidemili, which results in tension and conflicts between these two priests throughout the novel. The value or weight in importance of local thought resides in the pronouncements of these two men, together with all the titled men of Umuaro as representing the people. However, it seems that the importance of Ezeulu exceeds all others, as he refuses to call *Ili-ji*, the Feast of the New Yam, to permit the harvesting of yam at the end of the planting season that usually begins with the Feast of the Pumpkin Leaves. This refusal to open the harvest season is his strategic plan to punish the people of Umuaro for their inaction when Ezeulu was taken away and thrown in jail by the colonialists. Eze Ulu sees this inaction as his people's failure to resist the humiliation of their priest, and by extension their deity, Ulu of all Umuaro. Ezeulu punishes his people by delaying their harvesting of the essential main crop, yam. This is the deadlock over the New Yam Feast that results in widespread famine in Umuaro. But, it seems that Ulu unleashes a heavy punishment on Ezeulu himself through the death of his son Obika and Ezeulu's subsequent madness. Thus, the hero of resistance is represented as a tragic hero, while his violator, the colonial administrator Captain Winterbottom, recovers from an illness widely attributed to Ezeulu's powers and lives. Winterbottom even gets to marry his doctor, Mary Savage, as the values of the imperial presences of the colonial state and the church and school of Christian missionaries are gradually presented as the new normal against a fractured Umuaro. The novel thus speaks to changes inflicted on Igbo society by the experience of colonialism.

ULU AND THE PEOPLE

Thought processes, dialogue and arguments are contained in the narrative of a novel. The two men Ezeulu and Winterbottom are presented in the novel both as friends and antagonists. They stand for and are argued as representing more than these personal relationships; Ezeulu being the Igbo nation intruded upon and in conflict with and being colonized by an uninvited imperialist colonialism that Winterbottom symbolizes. Their ends speak to the perceived outcome of this conflict. It is therefore in this context that I would analyze the unraveling of the climatic complexities and their consequences for colonialist and post-colonialist thought, discourse and outcomes.

In the narrative, Ezeulu's deity and the other deities of Umuaro are wedged against the imperial systems surrounding Winterbottom, including government and Western medicine. While we know about Western medicine and the imperialist thought driving colonialism and its associated racism, some of the novel's narratives seem to reproduce missionary Christian and colonialist prejudices against Igbo traditional religion, the supposed heathenism. The force of the outcome of the civic assembly is also deemphasized. For example, there is the disturbing assembling of the ten notable highest-ranking titled men of Umuaro in a moment of crisis to resolve the deadlock over the

Feast of the New Yam caused by Ezeulu's refusal to call the necessary ritual for the beginning of the harvest season. Who are these people? They are said to be Umuaro itself. They also say this of themselves: "Yes, we are Umuaro."[2] They are subsequently referred to as the rulers of Umuaro.

What can we make of the dialogue that follows in the sense of understanding the forces of power in the society at the time to make better sense of the dynamics of change and models of resistance? Ezeulu no doubt is the protagonist of the novel, presented as a chief priest of Ulu, the deity that he serves, fighting colonialists and Christian missionaries. The titled elders seem to present a more civil face to the struggle through their surprisingly pragmatic and realistic approach to the deadlock. The incident of the two months of Ezeulu's imprisonment by the colonialist white man has caused a delay and he is not able to complete his monthly ritual eating of the necessary total of thirteen yams. This he needs to finish before calling the Feast of the New Yam. The novel presents many disturbing reasons why Ezeulu refuses to call the New Yam Feast other than obedience to ritual tradition and reverence for the power of Ulu to whom the Feast is dedicated. The resulting situation pitches Ezeulu against the force of Umuaro's civil society as represented by their leaders. In other words, religion as presented in the novel is counter-posed against the logic of civil society or the people of the clan.

I do think that the rulers sense this contesting or even conflicting opposition and consequently put their heads on the block. They take a risk and act assertively; they are Umuaro and order Ezeulu to go ahead against ritual regulation and finish eating the remaining two yams and call the feast. In their reasoning, the blame cannot be on Ezeulu, as they are willing and ready to take any punishment or consequences from Ulu. They send their message to Ulu through Ezeulu. At this juncture in time, history is knotted up, and whatever step the key players take decides the future direction of Umuaro, or some might see it symbolically as Igbo future. Such a serious proposition demands a close and painstaking reading of the characters and narratives. If the people have spoken, does their position serve them well? Are they in one voice with their deity? We have no other way of knowing the mind or pronouncement of Ulu except through Ezeulu, his Chief Priest, in the way that the author chooses to tell this story. Unfortunately, even with the menace of colonialism and mission Christian imperialism at their doors, Ezeulu brings back a negative answer and won't call the New Yam Feast. The consequences of this action call to mind the question of the responsibility of the writer.

Achebe has very decisive things to say at the end of the novel about the historical context in which all these struggles are taking place. He does not lightly take his storytelling responsibility, as indeed can be seen in the denseness of his narratives and the sharpness of sentences. Still, intense as the novel is, the reader also has an inquisitive and analytical mind to want to make better sense of characters and incidents and sometimes suggest or propose unintended outcomes by the author. Since Ezeulu is destroyed and Umuaro loses, one is right to ask why, going back to the narratives to trace inevitabilities or suppose different scenarios.

Colonialist and Christianity's attacks on indigenous African religions are a fact of history, even today. If the denouement of this novel involves a competition between two religions, a native one and an outsider, imperialist racist one as represented by the early missionaries, the author seems to be on the side of the outsider one. The sinister description of the temple of Ulu with human skulls and chilling cold places is troubling, including Ezeulu's actions inside there. Does he say a silent prayer? Why should the sounding of the church bell perturb a devoted Chief Priest inside his own temple? What does Ezeulu say that conveys the philosophy of Uluism or the doctrines and practices of this religion of the God of Umuaro that any Umuaro person can carry with them for assurances against any adversity? What are the ideas with which to converse or argue in exchanges with the new Christians? The tone of narrative describing both temple and Ezeulu at such a critical time for Umuaro fails to capture the narrative of the inspired eloquence of the Ezeulu in action at the center of the Pumpkin Leaves festival.

Ezeulu in running motion recites personal tales and oral traditions of boastful courage and awesome encounters in the wild. The point that I am making is that in indigenous religions where there is overlapping and integration of practices and experiences, it is important to recognize different forms of narratives and meaning. Boastful tales of masculinist valor are not necessarily where to find the deeper meaning of Igbo religious pronouncements and meaning. The outcome of both situations (the assembling of elders inside Ezeulu's house and the temple visit by Ezeulu) sets a paradigm of a lost cause rather than preparedness! The ruling elders in their pragmatism open the door to a preparedness contingency. The closing of that door means a failure to present a collective argument from civil society and Ulu in a strong thought pattern or system to carry forward, in spite of Christianity and colonization. In the end they are all knocked down one by one; all these men and their patriarchal Ulu warrior religion.

Although Ezeulu speaks of the vengeance of Ulu in reference to the suffering of the people of Umuaro due to the famine, I wonder if it is just a question of vengeance by Ulu. Indeed, there are different readings of Ezeulu that suggest madness and stubborn pride. In the deadlock over the Feast of the New Yam, some even claim his falsifying of Ulu's decision, while to others it suggests that he is just a messenger, yet to some, he is seeking revenge. His religious anguish however points to other directions with more respectful representation of indigenous religion, other than revenge or disrespectfully calling Ezeulu a fetish priest. This can be seen in the narrative that describes the isolation, loneliness and anguish suffered by Ezeulu: "Because no one came near enough to him to see his anguish—and if they had seen it, they would not have understood—they imagined that he sat in his hut gloating over the distress of Umuaro."[3] Ezeulu in ritual anguish is completely different from the suffering, but defiant Ezeulu in the white man's prison, a political situation. The tension between religion and politics is a major theme in this novel, but unfairly dealt with by the author, especially from the perspective of indigenous knowledge.

ODUCHE AND HIS MOTHER

Oduche, in whom Ezeulu places his hopes for a niche in the future, seems to be, in my view, the most disturbing of these characters. He represents a point of rupture, setting a new paradigm of undercutting traditional family trust and solidarity in two ways. One is in the attempt to kill the royal python and the negative chain of events the action brings to Ezeulu's family. This might in fact be seen as the beginning of the decline of Ezeulu. For while Ezeulu's youngest wife, Ugoye, the mother of Oduche is heartbroken and shows contrition for her son's abominable act, the Chief Priest is not privately or outwardly seen to perform any corrective ritual, being more driven by his conflict with Ezidemili. In contrast, it is Ugoye who says a simple prayer of supplication, and then feels free to proceed with her participation in the Festival of the Pumpkin Leaves.

The pragmatic reasoning used by Ezeulu to dismiss Oduche's act as personal and not a ritual crime is quite revealing:

> Every Umuaro child knows that if a man kills the python inadvertently, he must placate Idemili by arranging a funeral for the snake almost as elaborate as a man's funeral. But there was nothing in the custom of Umuaro for the man who puts the snake into a box. . . . It was the kind of offence which a man put right between himself and his personal god. And what was more the Festival of the New Pumpkin Leaves would take place in a few days. It was he, Ezeulu, who would then cleanse the six villages of this and countless other sins, before the planting season.[4]

Ezeulu absorbs all his people's wrongdoings as a divine messenger and goes to Ulu for ritual expiation and renewal.

For Ugoye, it is different:

> In previous years she would have been among the first to arrive at the market place; she would have been carefree and joyful. But this year her feet seemed to drag because of the load on her mind. She was going to pray for the cleansing

of her hut which Oduche had defiled. She was no longer one of the many, many Umuaro women taking part in a general and all-embracing rite.[5]

An attack on *Eke*, the royal python, can be read as an assault on women, for the python would belong to the women's religion under the Goddess Idemili and women's personal *Chi* deity. It is not surprising that the Christian convert Oduche gets the python from his mother's house. In Igbo history, indigenous women who remained with the traditional religion had a lot of conflicts and fights with mission Christians and colonizers.

At the festival, in the thick of events, as the festival reaches a ritual height, Ugoye says her prayer that gives an insight into the open generality and simplicity of an indigenous traditional prayer to Ulu:

> Great Ulu who kills and saves, I implore you to save my household of all defilement. If I have spoken it with my mouth or seen it with my eyes, or if I have heard it with my ears or stepped on it with my foot or if it has come through my children or my friends or kinsfolk let it follow these leaves.[6]

This is the prayer that she sends through her bunch of pumpkin leaves that she circles round her head and throws at the Chief Priest, like all the other women. This simple prayer from a simple woman shows a different face of traditional Igbo religion in the sense of an open religion of an everyday holistic life. There is neither boastfulness nor a betrayal of trust in it.

The second act of betrayal of trust by Oduche that speaks to a point of rupture, setting a new paradigm, concerns a return to the very reason why Oduche is sent to join the new religion and its mission school and the outcome of that action by Ezeulu. Ezeulu's close friend Akuebue suggests a more intriguing reading of his friend's action, posing the question of intent between Oduche being a sacrifice or a spy. Both possibilities can be deduced from the conversation between Ezeulu and Akuebue.[7] Ezeulu is portrayed as a complex and disturbing character, half-spirit and half-human, known and unknowable, capable of anything, as he boasts of himself. More noteworthy is his ability to think as a reformer toward cultural progress or cultural modernization. He cites two important reforms by both his grandfather and father to scrap the *Igbu Ichi* (facial scarification) requirement for the Ozo title, and the casting of the child of a widow as a slave. This is an important argument to support the evidence of ongoing internally generated reforms before the encounter with Christianity or British colonization. However, Ezeulu also thinks and speaks as a spirit that uses animal blood for lesser requirements and human blood for more formidable challenges.

Ezeulu privately marks the youngest son Nwafo for succession to the priesthood over and above the older sons, and sacrifices Nwafo's older brother Oduche in order to fight the challenges of the white man in the old ways of the dibia and local deities. According to Ezeulu, in one of the most dense and powerful passages in the novel, the problems of Umuaro have exceeded the need for animal and blood sacrifice. Thus, he says to Akuebue, "But sometimes even a bull does not suffice, then we must look for a human. Do you think it is the sound of the death-cry gurgling through blood that we want to hear? No, my friend, we do it because we have reached the very end of things and we know that neither a cock nor a goat nor even a bull will do. And our fathers have told us that it may even happen to an unfortunate generation that they are pushed beyond the end of things, and their back is broken and hung over a fire. When this happens, they may sacrifice their own blood."[8] He goes on to recall the sacrifice of not a stranger, but one of their own by their ancestors to make the great medicine Ulu to stop Abam.

The logic of the above passage reveals that Ezeulu is hoping for collective action, just like in the checking of the previous disturbances by the warriors of Abam, to deal with the colonialist imperialist presence. It seems that Ezeulu is thinking ahead of Akuebue who is repulsed: "Akuebue cracked his fingers and moved his head up and down. 'So, it is a sacrifice,' he muttered to himself."[9] The thinking by Ezeulu that they are now at the very end and that their back is broken is revealing and significant. Achebe narrates the bravery and courage of Umuaro in their fight and struggle against both colonialism and Christian conversion. They have been at it for a long time, being the last resisters in their province. This is also recognized by the colonial administration, especially in contemplating what to do with Ezeulu after he rejects the Warrant Chieftaincy even from prison. According to Clarke, from his reading of the colonial report, "Umuaro had put up more resistance to change than any other clan in the whole province."[10] Both the colonial administration and Christianity had experienced long periods of hostility and rejection, and were not even able to successfully set up schools or Christian missions. Things were however beginning to settle down with new schools and young missions. Clarke fearing a reversal in present successes decides to discharge and send Ezeulu home. All this means is that Umuaro is still causing some anxiety to the colonialists, suggesting that a strong collective civil action would have been effective in disrupting the colonial presence in Umuaro, or at least as an advantageous bargaining chip.

The inability to resolve the New Yam Feast deadlock causes Ezeulu to lose in both, whether sacrifice or spying. Oduche does not articulate any surprises, bafflement or disagreement with his new learning and new circle. He certainly has no discussions with his father Ezeulu about his new experiences. On the contrary, Ezeulu overhears his beloved children Nwafo and Obiageli singing a Christian song that is abusive to the royal python, but is believed to scare away the python: "Python, run! There is a Christian here."[11] Most importantly, when all seems lost and Christianity appears to be triumphing over the laws of Ulu, Ezeulu calls his son Oduche in order to reap the benefit of what had seemed a wise or clever move to send his son to spy for him. What transpires between father and son seems to me one of the saddest events and the lowest point for Ezeulu in the novel.

Why Ezeulu asks Oduche did he not report to him the plan of the Christians to "reap" the harvest of Umuaro and the sanctuary being offered "to those who wished to escape the vengeance of Ulu."[12] Achebe then narrates, "For a long time father and son looked steadily at each other in silence. When Ezeulu spoke again his tone was calm and full of grief."[13] Then Ezeulu reminds Oduche of what he was sent to do: "I called you as a father calls his son and told you to go and be my eye and ear among those people. I did not send Obika or Edogo; I did not send Nwafo, your mother's son. I called you by name and you came here—in this *obi*—and I sent you to see and hear for me."[14] Ezeulu in disappointment calls Oduche "lizard that ruined his mother's funeral."[15] This saying is also meted out to Ulu for choosing to destroy his priest Ezeulu at a dangerous time: "for in destroying his priest he had also brought disaster on himself, like the lizard in the fable who ruined his mother's funeral by his own hand."[16] Ezeulu is not the only loser; they are all losers for not continuing to act together. The derogation of the traditional religion has begun, and the seeds of new hierarches and stratifications have also been sown.

THE CIVIC ALTERNATIVE

Umuaro leaders made a grave mistake by allowing Ezeulu to go to Okperi on his own to answer Winterbottom's summons. They had suggested six important elders and a powerful dibia to accompany Ezeulu. Ezeulu rejects this idea, but it is the responsibility of the elders to know the central role played by Ezeulu and Ulu during this period of observing the moon in readiness for the harvest season. All the elders should have camped out in Government Hill, setting a group sit-in tradition for the next step strategy after the breaking of their guns. Igbo women went forward with a sit-in strategy. I think that the outcome would be different for a collective future with a sit-in preparedness scenario, for Umuaro would be able to build an internally generated argument for moving forward. By this I mean joining the forces of religion, culture, orature and oral tradition with the power and presence of civic groupings that include the youth and women in the social structure.

The image of the collective feet of the women of Umuaro stamping to dust the pumpkin leaves at the end of the Festival of the Pumpkin Leaves is a formidable one. It is one group that embraces all the women of Umuaro. There is no indication that this group was consulted over the deadlock. It is also interesting reading about his senior wife Matefi's defiance of Ezeulu, particularly her daring gesture of crossing her arms on her chest. This could translate to an attitude of arms akimbo, as if to say how dare you, or shall we say just you dare! After all, we know that "Matefi was not the kind of person another woman could tie into her lappa and carry away."[17] She gives more than she gets in insults; not just tit-for-tat with her. Here, it is a challenging departure from unquestioned narratives of domestic abuse and violence against women in other fiction, even in *Things Fall Apart*. In *Arrow of God*, brothers defend their sisters by punishing and humiliating an abusive husband. In real history, Igbo women publicly dealt with attacks on their interests. They mobilized across a vast geographical region and made war known historically as *Ogu Umunwanyi*, The Women's War of 1929, on the colonialists, forcing some important reversals of hated colonial policies.

The age-grades are also an important civic group were they not divided into different rival sets in which they seem antagonistic to each other, showing off in masculinist ways. For example, Obika is sick with fever, but does not listen to his new wife, and goes to carry the mask of his age grade that requires fitness and vigor. He dies doing so. Masculinist boastfulness seems to dominate quite a lot the Character of Obika whom Achebe describes as extremely handsome: "Obika was the handsomest young man in Umuachala and perhaps in all Umuaro. They called him Ugonachomma."[18] He also seems non-replicable: "Obika's death shook Umuaro to the roots; a man like him did not come into the world too often."[19] It is the same Obika who uses a stick to throw a disliked supposed bad dibia squatting as a cripple into the bush as if it were a worm, an action that speaks very much to pre-colonial expressions of social inequality; some might argue cruelty. Although to be seen within the context of Igbo ideals of egalitarianism, pre-colonial traditions of inequality would later feed into class expressions.

Youth are quite topical in *Arrow of God* in ways other than as a labor force in their age grades. There is the intergenerational tension of the struggle for succession that is seen in Ezeulu's conflicting relationship with his sons. It is in fact in the context of this that his friend Akuebue reads Ezeulu's action regarding Oduche. To some extent, it is also with his own difficult relationship with his own grown sons that Ezeulu judges the young left-handed colonialist intelligence officer Mr. John Clarke. Each of these youth represents a trope, standing for a different historical trajectory. Oduche is a paradigm trope for the new elite and therefore class. Mr. Clarke symbolizes imperialism and racial discrimination that have been generated through centuries of the enslavement of black people. Colonialist policies that he serves also involve wealth extortion, gender discrimination, and violence against the colonized. Colonialists whip and humiliate native grown men on trivial excuses, even handsome Obika, using the age grades for cheap or unpaid labor. In contrast, local age grades simply impose a fine for civil offenses. Most importantly, Mr. Clarke uses a structure in place to ease himself into succeeding the older sick colonial administrative head. Umuaro also needed a preparedness scenario generated through indigenous knowledge for each of these challenges to counter colonialism and for moving forward on their own terms. Nwafo is an interesting contrast to Oduche as he is groomed for succession and instinctively knows his father Ezeulu's daily routines and rituals. Could an anticipation of continuity in a preparedness scenario have been constructed in Nwafo (religion) and Edogo (art) and women and age grades (culture and civic groups) in anticipation of a strong and viable civil society?

It is interesting that it is a group of social "undesirables" and "ritual rejects" that as a class of domestic workers and clerical civil servants plays a new type of resistance role in Government Hill. Through them we also begin to get a glimpse into Igbo new formations of diasporic flexible relationships and social interactions, the beginnings of a civil society, rather than civic groups, under the network of administrations linked by the new colonial state. The servants and native African staff are the people who fill in to support Ezeulu's struggle in the absence of his fellow notables. These are the people who want Ezeulu's powers to kill the colonial boss Captain Winterbottom who had broken their guns.[20] They spread news of the presence and powers of Ezeulu, working it to a fever pitch throughout Government Hill, and visiting dibias for protective medicines. They spread false rumors of Winterbottom's death or worsening sickness, raising their rhetoric to elevate the importance of Ezeulu in their conversations, even with their bosses. The presence of this group of people in a supposed classless indigenous Igbo society also points to the presence of forms of social injustice in the pre-colonial societies. Their actions demonstrate a strong sense of ethnic pride equal to, if not greater than that of everyone else.

According to John Nwodika, "people we used to despise . . . were all now in high favour when our own people did not even know that day had broken."[21] These are the people who emphasize the importance of travel as enlightenment and a teacher of tolerance. These are also the people who speak of long-term plans to convert gains from colonial domestic servitude into self-employment in professions such as trading. They are learning the knowledge of the white man, but with a different Igbo sense. They are a different crop of youth from what we now call the working class. In pursuit of the new monetary economy, Nwodika's progression is from a village dancer to a colonial housekeeper to a self-employed tobacco trader who finds a niche in the huge new tobacco trade.

Ezeulu has a different aspiration for his son Oduche. It is in fact to be exactly like Mr. Clarke, a man with no sense in his head, but with power and

Discourse, Imagination, and Models of Resistance 163

privilege. On his return from prison, weighing all his experiences and the complex issues surrounding them, Ezeulu calls his son Oduche, and reminds him of the importance of knowing the white man's knowledge. Ezeulu says to him, "I have sent you to be my eyes there."[22] His advice to his son is to be steadfast in this quest, and not to be distracted by what people might say: "If anyone asks you why you should be sent to learn these new things tell him that a man must dance the dance prevalent in his time."[23] Once again, there is a glimpse into the complex mind of Ezeulu. He continues, "When I was in Okperi I saw a young white man who was able to write his book with the left hand. From his actions I could see that he had very little sense. But he had power; he could shout in my face; he could do what he liked. Why? Because he could write with his left hand. That is why I have called you. I want you to learn and master this man's knowledge so much that if you are suddenly woken up from sleep and asked what it is you will reply. You must learn it until you can write it with your left hand."[24] Ezeulu was deeply wounded by his experience in Okperi, and writing with the left hand, is just a manner of speech or a metaphor for other grave matters.

If Oduche is to become the root for a new elite class, it seems to me that the problems of Ezeulu do not only stem from the conflict with colonialism and Christianity, but also from the creator of his character. Achebe aids and abets in the destruction of his protagonist through the construction of a lost cause scenario by continuously undermining the Chief Priest. One gets the impression of a hierarchy of knowledge in which colonial education and Christianity are presented as superior to indigenous knowledge. The final nail driven into Ezeulu's coffin comes at the very end of the novel. Ezeulu himself in a surprise revelation sees Idemili's python as a divine messenger with quite a lot of foreboding messages in his usual half-sleep vision that he sometimes thinks a dream or nightmare. This happens during the night that his son Obika dies.

A humbled and broken man in the end, Ezeulu is presented as losing to Christianity: "many a man sent his son with a yam or two to offer to the new religion and to bring back the promised immunity. Thereafter any yam harvested in his fields was harvested in the name of the son."[25] With this conclusion, one patriarchal religion replaces another patriarchal one. The indigenously constructed patriarchal warrior Ulu religion is replaced by a foreign patriarchal Christian one. Achebe writes, "As for Ezeulu it was as though he had died."[26] There is also the finality in a lost cause: "But for Ezeulu there was no next time. Think of a man who, unlike lesser men, always goes to battle without a shield because he knows that bullets and matchet strokes will glance off his medicine-boiled skin, think of him discovering in the thick of battle that the power has suddenly, without warning, deserted him. What next time can there be? Will he say to the guns and the arrows and the matchets: *Hold! I want to return quickly to my medicine-hut and stir the pot and find out what has gone wrong; perhaps someone in my household—a child, maybe—has unwittingly violated my medicine's taboo? No.*"[27]

If according to the novel, Ezeulu and Ulu supposedly are defeated by Christianity, the powerful Goddess Idemili is not even a subtext, but a mere reference. So are numerous deities that are mentioned as left out by Nwaka in his spiteful and harsh speech. The marginalized deities with their own priests are Idemili, Eru, Udo, and Ogwugwu.[28] Ezidemili also is engaged in a resistance struggle as we glimpse through the writing of petitions against Christian insults and abuses regarding Idemili's python.[29] He in addition is engaged in a struggle against Ezeulu and Ulu's usurpation of the rights of the Goddess Idemili. He is fighting two patriarchal usurpations. The emphasis on religion in the conclusion makes it seem as if the main problem is not colonialism, but an internal structural fight for power between Ezeulu and his Chief Priest and the clan. Yet, the denial of sovereignty and the weakening of both indigenous religion and the clan by colonialism open wide the door for Christianity that in any case worked hand in hand with colonialists. Igbo people's experiences of colonization were unjust, harsh, brutal, and traumatic. The administration was always on the ready to step in "with troops for a show of force."[30]

ODUCHE AND ACHEBE

Chinua Achebe's (2012) account of his own early life journey through family and education provides an insight into the tensions between religion and politics in *Arrow of God*, and how Oduche might have developed and the outcome by comparing with the author's own experiences. In his autobiography, Achebe writes about his dichotomous personal experiences growing up with two sets of relatives, a devout Christian Igbo family and Igbo relatives in traditional religion.

Achebe's father, Isaiah Achebe, was an early Christian convert who attended St. Paul's Teachers College, Awka, and left in 1904. It shows how early some parts of Igboland came into contact with Christian missionaries. He was employed as a paid teacher and evangelist in the Anglican Mission. Achebe describes him as "a brilliant man, who deeply valued education and read a great deal—mainly the Bible and religious books, periodicals, and almanacs from the Church Mission Society."[31] Achebe writes about the successful integration of "traditional values with the education and new religion brought by the Europeans" in the experiences of his parents,"[32] and particularly their easy embrace of strangers coming into their midst. Thus, making a contrast with the antagonistic violence and racism of the whites. It was his mother and elder sister, Zinobia that initiated him into "the complicated world of Ndi Igbo"³³ We therefore know that in spite of supposed successful integration, Achebe saw himself as living between worlds. Yet these worlds have their own values, but the traditional Igbo one was considered unequal.

This initiation was through stories and songs with moral messages, "a number of wonderful stories from our ancient Igbo tradition,"³⁴ stories of *Mbe* the tortoise and his mischiefs. It is to these "mesmerized" story time experiences that Achebe attributes his later decision to become a storyteller: "Later in my literary career I traveled back to the magic of the storytelling of my youth to write my children's books: *How the Leopard Got His Claws, Chike and the River, The Drum: A Children's Story, and The Flute.*"³⁵ Stories provided a window into a magical world, but Achebe's father's library was a Eurocentric one pointing the door to another world that Achebe would encounter through church and education, to be reproduced in some of the tensions in the characters and events in *Arrow of God.*

Achebe's father's work as a teacher and catechist constitutes "the most powerful memories of my father."³⁶ Achebe describes ways in which his father encouraged his children to read: "He would often walk us through the house telling stories linked to each prized possession. It was from him that I was exposed to the magic in the mere titles of William Shakespeare's *A Midsummer Night's Dream* and to an Igbo translation of Jon Bunyan's *The Pilgrim's Progress.*"³⁷ Typical of the educational content of those days, Achebe writes, "The Bible played an important role in my education."³⁸ Passages were read out during prayers. Passages were read and memorized, and this "tradition of Christian evangelical education" also took place at Sunday school, attended by village children. Achebe describes St. Philip's Church, Ogidi as an imposing, large Gothic-style structure built on an open field on the outskirts of town, and it was "The center of our family activities."³⁹ Not only helping in its establishment, Achebe's father also helped in its construction, conducted Sunday services, translated sermons into the Igbo language, and arranged the sanctuary and vestry. Here is another major contrast to roles played by the major characters in the traditional settings of Achebe's novels, where the youth carried the bags of the elders and the *dibia*, thereby gaining knowledge in such company. In the new Christian mission system, Achebe as a boy carries his father's bag. "I remember waking up early to help out, carrying his bag for him as we set out at cock crow for the parish church."⁴⁰ There were long church sessions, lasting two hours, impassioned sermons described as "fire and brimstone sermons," plus an English rector mispronouncing Igbo words and drawing laughter. Also, there was laughter when the vector would drown down the remainder of the wine for communion. At the end of it all, there is an important admission by Achebe that his relationship with his 'heathen' relatives was carried out in secret, due to the dichotomous situation between the new Christian converts and those that they called "heathens."

This background explains the dichotomous tensions in a young man, and scholars of Achebe would find this revelation important and useful as he admits to a tension between the Christianity of his parents and he sees as "the retreating, older religion" of his ancestors. "I still had access to a number of relatives who had not converted to Christianity and were called heathens by the new converts. When my parents were not watching I would often sneak off in the evenings to visit some of these relatives.[41] We have these diehard Africans to thanks for the retentions of African traditions and knowledge, particularly the vivid capture of some of it in Achebe's work. Achebe admits that these non-converts were "very content" in their own way of life, including their religion.[42] Still, he wanted to find out why they would not convert, or in his own words, "why they refuse to become Christians, like everyone else around them."[43] Think of Ezeulu and his anxieties about the Christians that seemed more personal than his worries about the colonialists.

In his dichotomous life, one of the outside sources of indigenous Igbo traditions for Achebe was his great uncle, Udoh Osinyi, who "was able to bestride both worlds with great comfort."[44] He was an Ozo-titled man, "one of the highest titles in all of Igbo land."[45] This was the other Igbo world outside Achebe's Christian family home that is captured in his classic novels: "I was very interested in my great uncle's religion, and talking to him was an enriching experience. I wouldn't give up anything for that, including my own narrow, if you like, Christian background."[46]

Achebe now begins to describe some indigenous Igbo traditions, such as Igbo religion as non-monotheistic, but with many deities. This is a strong theme well played out in Achebe's fiction, as he puts it, "A person could be in good stead with one god and not the other—*ogwugwu* could kill a person despite an excellent relationship with *udo*."[47] Achebe sees this to constitute a major difference with Christianity and its doctrine of an almighty God. However, Achebe truthfully writes about the limitations of both his interest and his level of knowledge given his young age at the time, "As a young person that sort of complexity meant little to me. A later understanding would reveal the humility of the traditional religion with greater clarity."[48] Humility was not a characteristic that applied to Ezeulu as Chief Priest. It came to him or perhaps was forced on him when he was already a broken man. In reaction to the death of Obika and his drift into madness, Ezeulu picks up a broom and begins to sweep the compound, something unbecoming of a grown man, let alone the Chief Priest. It was a chore for children and women, and immediately is relieved of the sweeping. Humility is an interesting theme for the understanding of a religion and its philosophy but lacking in the leadership of early Christian converts and Achebe's portrayal of them in his novels.

Achebe in the familiar narrative style of his great novels compares and makes excuses for the actions of both his father and his great uncle. Africa was a continent in "disarray" and these men are movingly likened to "an orphan child" that is thrust into the barbarism of adversity and chaos. "It was not at all surprising that my father would welcome the remedy proffered by diviners and interpreters of a new word of God. But my great-uncle, a leader in his community, a moral, open-minded man, a prosperous man who had prepared such great feast when he took the *ozo* title that his people gave him a praise name for it—was he to throw all that away because some strangers from afar had said so?"[49] However, even Achebe's stoic Christian father, Isaiah Achebe seems to have mellowed in his hardened attitude toward Igbo traditional religion, especially in his relationship with his own uncle, Udoh. The conflicts brought by Christianity ate into familes and the community, dividing relatives, friends and groups.

Age, (and perhaps disillusionment), in spite of having gained a reputation as trust worthy and pious, had made his father "more openly accommodating of the old ways of doing things."[50] Achebe's analysis of himself follows, "Those two—my father and his uncle—formed the dialectic that I inherited. Udoh stood fast in what he knew, but he also left room for my father to seek other answers. The answer my father found in the Christian faith solved many problems, but by no means all."[51] He admits to benefit in his world outlook from the existing dichotomy as a young man, since it freed him from being intellectually neutral of judgment. "I was simply more interested in exploring the essence, the meaning, the worldview of both religions. By approaching the issues of tradition, culture, literature, and language of our ancient civilization in that manner, without judging but scrutinizing, a treasure trove of discovery was opened up to me."[52] Still, there were to be more periods of "oscillating faith" as Achebe grew older.[53]

There were also deeper thoughts and the questioning, according to Achebe, of "the absolutist teachings or the interpretations of religion. I struggled with the certitude of Christianity—'I am the Way, the Truth and the Life'—not its accuracy, because as a writer one understands that there should be such latitude, but the desolation, the acerbity of its meaning, the lack of options for the outsider, the other. I believe that this question has subconsciously deeply influenced my writing."[54] Achebe's outsider position is not the same as the marginalization suffered by his "outside" relatives and the indigenous practitioners of Igbo religion. Achebe's is actually in the envied marginal position of the writer, as otherness is something that many writers experience as outsiders in different ways in their locality. Some would argue that such otherness gives the writer an edge and an independent writing position and space, and not so ethnic minorities, immigrants and marginalized groups seeking rights and social justice.

Through researched into the Igbo tradition of *Mbari*, Achebe further learns about "the sophistication of Igbo phenomenological thought."[55] He emphasizes the importance of the principles of tolerance and community in the tradition of *mbari* art expression and indigenous Igbo religious thought. He again sees African tolerance and virtue in the representation of Europeans strangers in this Igbo art.[56] Villagers reproduce and celebrate the world of their experience through the this art form as well as asking for protection from their deities.[57] Achebe also admits learning lessons about indigenous Igbo traditions that would enrich his writings from his Awka maternal relatives and in-laws.

In 1958, *Things Fall Apart* was published. Achebe again gives insights into the writing of this novel, as the process enabled him to learn more about Igbo traditions and history. He was a young man at the time and was more focused on telling a story that surprisingly came to have a much wider relevance that led him to recognize the power of story. In this case, a shared historical experience of colonialism brought an interesting response by an entire class of girls' college students. This was a learning situation for Achebe. "They had a history that was similar to the story of *Things Fall Apart*—the history of colonialism. This I didn't know before. Their colonizer was Japan. So these people across the waters were able to relate to the story of dispossession in Africa. People from different parts of the world can respond to the same story if it says something to them about their own history and their own experience."[58]

Stories speak to familiar and unfamiliar experiences just as social experiences are reflected in the narrative of a story. Achebe was receiving a first-class European education, while he was researching Igbo traditions. In 1944, Achebe entered secondary school, Government College, Umuahia (GCU), at the age of fourteen. It was "a new elite boarding school established in 1929, and rapidly developing a reputation as the Eton of the East, and I fancied receiving an education akin to the royals of England!"[59] There were a few of these elite secondary schools, and according to Achebe, "we had some of the very best secondary schools in the British Empire. As a group, these schools were better endowed financially, had excellent amenities, and were staffed with first-rate teachers, custodians, instructors, cooks, and librarians."[60] There is no doubt that these institutions produced an elite group of pioneer leaders with excellent education. There also is the question of the relevance of this very British education for a newly constructed Nigerian nation. Interestingly, this is the context in which Achebe forms his position on the use of the English language as a lingua franca that has led to much debate between Achebe and other African writers who argue the use of an African language for instruction and a lingua franca in order to decolonize. Achebe clarifies his position on this issue arguing that the use of English has the power of communication and unification in a diverse country as Nigeria with more than 250 ethnic groups. "While African languages and writing should be developed, nurtured, and preserved, how else, I would wonder later, would I have been able to communicate with so many boys from different parts of the country and ethnic groups, speaking different languages, had we not been taught one language?"[61]

It might not even be due to the fact that the students spoke different languages in Achebe's secondary school, but that the dominant teachers were foreigners: "Many of our teachers at the time were alumni from Cambridge, the University of London, and other major British institutions of higher learning."[62] The missed opportunity to learn and adopt a native language as an official national language in the process of decolonization and national development remains a sore question still debated today.

Next in his educational journey, Achebe takes an entrance exam to University College, Ibadan and came first or second in the whole country.[63] At the university his voracious reading habit earned him the nickname "Dictionary."[64] Among this remarkable group with a good university education beginning were an impressive list from Achebe, with very few women: "These young men and women came from all over the country—from elite secondary schools modeled on the public schools of England."[65] At University College, Ibadan, Achebe had switched from the study of medicine to study English, History and Theology. As a consequence, he lost his scholarship, but his elder brother Augustine Achebe, an engineer who had studied in England, paid his tuition fees, a common practice in those days.[66]

In 1954, Achebe took up a job at the Nigerian Broadcasting Service (NBS), in Enugu and soon became the controller of NBS, Eastern Region.[67] Achebe's next job was as a script editor at the headquarters of the Nigerian Broadcasting Corporation (NBC), and says of the job, "A tedious job, it nevertheless honed my skill for writing realistic dialogue, a gift that I gratefully tapped into when writing my novels."[68] Under the interesting subtitle, "Discovering *Things Fall Apart*," Achebe reveals experiences at the University that would feed into his writing. Achebe had started writing and publishing short stories at the university, and was eventually editor of the campus magazine titled, *University Herald*. One of the short stories is titled, "The Old Order in Conflict with the New."[69] Thus, giving expression to the undercurrents of the tensions between the new and traditional conflicts.

With maturity and knowledge, Achebe began to question the different systems and to read more into his instructors. For example, through Parrinder, a well know scholar of African religions, Achebe was able to learn about West African religions. He writes, "Studying religion was new to me and interesting because the focus went beyond Christian theology to encompass wider scholarship—West African religions."[70] "For the first time I was able to see the systems—including my own—compared and placed side by side, which was really exciting."[71] He was gaining a higher degree of consciousness as well, acknowledging the excellence of his professors, but admitting, "they were not always the ones I needed."[72] One of his professors admitted as much that they could only teach Achebe what they knew, and not what he needed or wanted. Achebe writes, "I learned, if I may put it simply, that my story had to come from within me. Finding that inner creative spark required introspection, deep personal scrutiny, and connection, and this was not something anybody could really teach me."[73] On an important point about a professor, Achebe realized, "that despite her excellent mind and background, she was not capable of teaching across cultures, from her English culture to mine."[74] Therefore, dichotomies and binaries that he once thought advantageous come into question.

Through these painful experiences, Achebe reveals the creative writing process that yielded his classic novel: "It was in these circumstances that I was moved to put down on paper the story that became *Things Fall Apart*. I was conscripted by the story, and I was writing it at all times—whenever there was any opening. It felt like a sentence, an imprisonment of creativity."[75] Given the story content of this novel, it isn't farfetched to recall Achebe's early years and the dichotomous relationship between his pious Christian family home and the habitual secret sneaking out to visit his supposed "heathen" relatives and by extension learning about traditional Igbo life. His revelations of his creative writing process are equally interesting and involve something like a divided existence and likened to a hand having "two surfaces," yet "united in purpose but very different in tone, appearance, character, and structure. I had in essence discovered the writer's life, one that exists in the world of the pages of his or her story and then seamlessly steps into the realities of everyday life."[76]

In contrast to the empty spaces that Achebe experienced in his curriculum and the instruction of it, he seems to have had another type of satisfying learning experience with his father-in-law, and that is to do with the traditional content of this relationship. While Achebe's great-uncle Udoh Asinyi of Ogidi provides a window into traditional Igbo society and life with the insignia of his three titles, Achebe's father-in-law T. C. Okoli of Awka would be a complementary source of even deeper knowledge of Igbo worldview. The ancient town of Awka is important in Igbo history, as Achebe acknowledges, "Awka held a soft spot in my heart because it was my mother's hometown, and it was known throughout Igbo land and beyond for its skilled artisans and blacksmiths, who fashioned bronze, wood, and metal carvings of a bold haunting beauty."[77]

This connection with Awka is not only an opportunity to demonstrate his knowledge of Igbo history and art culture, but through his maternal link to his ikwunne, matrikin in Awka, Achebe also shows a matriachitarian attachment and affection for his mother each time he mentioned her. T. C. Okoli, Achebe's father-in-law, is described as "one of the most formidable Igbo men of the early twentieth century."[78] His full name was Timothy Chukwukadibia Okoli, whose father was a famous *dibia*, and "known from Arochukwu to Nri and from Onitsha to Ogoja for skills that encompassed herbal medicine, mysticism, divination, and magic."[79] All these skills are themes in *Arrow of God*, although Ezeulu seems contemptuous of *dibia* practitioners in the novel, refusing the protection the *dibia* suggested by the elders to accompany him to Okperi.

However, in his autobiography Achebe writes of this famous *dibia*, "After a lifetime in the service of the ancient medical practice, Okoli gave his son the name Chukwukadibia, which means 'God is greater than a traditional medicine man.' He encouraged his newborn son to seek a Christian life."[80] Once again, Achebe exhibits a bias or perhaps a contradiction in relation to traditional Igbo religion. I have argued elsewhere (Ifi Amadiume, "Of Kola Nuts, Taboos, Leadership, Women's Rights, and Freedom: New Challenges from Chinua Achebe's *There Was a Country: A Personal History of Biafra*," *Journal of West African History*, Vol. 1, Iss. 2 (2015): 119–146.) that Igbo proverbs on the *dibia* show that indigenously, Igbo *Chi* is higher and greater than the *dibia*, for it is *Chi* that the *dibia* serves. Also, it is *Chi* that the *Ofo* staff of blessing and justice serves. The principle of *Chi* in Igbo religion precedes Igbo encounter with Christianity. Achebe himself in a much earlier essay critiques mission Christian translation and convenient conversion of *Chi* to a unified concept of a Supreme Chukwu or Chineke to carry and convey the Christian monotheistic meaning of one God.[81] Certainly, Achebe insists on the acknowledgement of the presence of the many Gods and Spirits in Igbo religion, but seems to have difficulty with deeper indigenous knowledge of them, leaving empty spaces or showing a bias toward Christianity. As we have seen this is something that he attributes to his father and a pious Christian upbringing and Eurocentric education. But there is also the question of class, the roots of which are planted in Oduche in *Arrow of God*.

"AT THE DAWN OF A NEW ERA"[82]: ACHEBE'S UMUAHIA-IBADAN AXIS AND ITS IMPLICATIONS

On education and leadership, Achebe considers himself and his peer of pioneers as belonging to a lucky and privileged generation. Yet, in spite of the "superior" education and an elite leadership produced by Achebe's

Umuahia-Ibadan axis, things did fall apart, leading to military coups, pogrom, genocide and war. Given the superior hierarchically positioning of the new religion, the new education and the leadership that these new systems produced, it is imperative to reassess the new dawn. This is particularly in relationship to everyone else, since there are dichotomous personalities and also dichotomies at the national level that are similar to those at the local rural village level.

Achebe tries to heal his dichotomous personality through reconciliation with mission conversion as well as mission education, in spite of noting historical facts of colonialism and the transatlantic crime of enslavement. He refers again to his father who praised and supported the missionaries and the message that they preached, admitting his own support of them and the benefits the he derived from mission education. However, the crimes of that encounter remains, and Achebe writes, "But I have also learned a little more skepticism about them than my father had any need for. Does it matter, I ask myself, that centuries before European Christians sailed down to us in ships to deliver the Gospel and save us from darkness, other European Christians, also sailing in ships, delivered us to the transatlantic slave trade and unleashed darkness in our world?"[83] Does criticism of these historical wrongs and crimes matter?

It matters to criticize, deconstruct, decolonize, and link relevant past historical experiences to present issues and problems to envision a better future. This is why it is important to unpack the construction of the character of Oduche in particular in the novel. It is also just as relevant to ask questions of Achebe and the first educated elites who undertook the leadership of the new Nigerian nation.

From Achebe, one gets the impression that these first university-educated leaders very seriously took their responsibility toward building a new nation. They were a "lucky" generation. They witnessed a new era, transitions and transformations. Nigeria became "a midrange country," and "barely two decades later we were thrust into the throes of perhaps Nigeria's greatest twentieth-century moment—our elevation from a colonized country to an independent nation."[84] Achebe recognizes three generations of leadership, his granduncle Udoh Osinyi, situated in traditional Igbo history, Achebe's father, Isaiah Achebe located in the colonialist and Christian evangelist history, and Achebe's own generation, inheritors of Colonialist education and Nigeria's independence: He echoes the great rhetoric of many liberation leaders in stating, "Every generation must recognize and embrace the task it is peculiarly designed by history and by providence to perform. . . . My father's great gift to me was his love of education and his recognition that whether we look at one human family or we look at human society in general, growth can come on incrementally.[85]

Of course, we get a lot about Achebe's own generation poised as the educated intimate elite, thoroughly world class, western educated with 'excellence,' leaders and pioneers of the new Nigerian nation. In reading Achebe, with such a background, one can only imagine the frustration they must have felt with the slowness and illiteracy surrounding them and the consequent frequent accusations of mediocrity and corruption. This frustration is captured in Achebe's polemical essay, *The Trouble With Nigeria*. The verdict on "when the rain started to beat us" *(Arrow of God)* or when things went wrong with the euphoria of independence is still out, it would seem. Still the question of the indigenous library is at the center of the problems, even if hardly part of the discussion and complaint. There was a country and I had two countries, Achebe remarks with precision. Achebe makes reference to *A Man of the People* as being seen as prophetic in relation to the first coup un Nigeria but does not point to the relevance of *No Longer at Ease*. *No Longer at Ease*, a much-ignored novel about Achebe's own generation captures the inception of these problems—the inherited colonially constructed nation, the bureaucratic system, the psychological and cultural makeup of the new elite, the implied faulty top-down paradigm of leadership, and the absence of the uneducated, jobless, and unconverted rank and file, at that time constituting the bulk of the population. It is also the novel that illustrates the possible outcome of the youth character of Oduche.

Surely, there was a major problem of dichotomy in intercultural communication. What of the question of intercultural ideologically and philosophically guided inter-ethnic group solidarity that one would expect to be essential for the construction of a new nation after colonialism? One would expect such movements from the elite universities, like the Umuahia-Ibadan axis and groups emanating from this linkage and other such groups. How did these privileged leaders perceive and conceive the new national formations? What were their ideological differences, if any, that were carried forward into their various future positions? The military had weapons, but these intellectuals and the first professional unions and their leaders seem to disappear in terms of solidarity ideas as a counter-weight to military might during the early crucial years.

Igbo secession following the massacre and genocide suffered by the Igbo led to the declaration of an independent state of Biafra and resulted in the Nigeria-Biafra War of 1967–1970. For Biafrans, *The Ahiara Declaration* (June 1, 1969) that set national ideals and goals came too late in the struggle (the war ended seven months later), pointing to the individualistic and exclusive nature of the leadership. With so many experts, everything cannot be presented as a learning process. The trouble with Nigeria went beyond the problem of leadership to the question of fault lines within the learned leadership and the absence of the rank and file. After the conflict, the baffled young

Biafran Left continued to raise the question of the absence of the voices of their Nigerian counter-part during and after the war. All these people are far away from the liberation struggles elsewhere in the world, but are very much conversant with and inspired by these other struggles and their leaders in poetry, literature, political philosophy and ideas of human rights, equity and social justice.

Why is there a silence and absence of the idea, the heroic and courageous aspects of Biafra? It is really a big question out there, especially in anti-colonial resistance and post-colonialist discourse. If this is because Biafra is considered a bourgeois struggle, then let there be a debate and discourse and more literature on knowledge about Biafra. Achebe himself seems to have marked out the poet Christopher Okigbo as a romantic youth hero of Biafra who has gained international acclaim. The question of youth is also usually linked to the question of gender. On the topic of gender and Biafra, Achebe has published the book of short stories, *Girls at War*, so too has one of his Ibadan peers, Flora Nwapa and her many Biafra women's stories in *Wives at War*. Buchi Emecheta, not mentioned by Achebe, has of course written a full novel *Destination Biafra*, based on women's experiences in the Nigeria-Biafra war, particularly the theme of gruesome rape in that war.

Writers use their imagination, engaging themes and issues from the mundane to enchantments in endless possibilities. They can effectively feed progressive ideas into other more methodologically limiting disciplines for a more just society and better future. For this reason, much is usually expected of inspiring writers in topics of resistance and models of opposition to and against oppression and oppressors in all their forms.

In as much as large contemporary themes necessitate inter-disciplinary or multi-disciplinary approaches and perspectives toward broader and more holistic understanding, one cannot mistake one discipline for another. For example, literature is not political science; both disciplines might raise issues about post-colonial societies and states in Africa, but deal with these same issues in different ways. While political science and other social sciences have their theories and methods, even if developing or evolving, literature obviously has an edge due to a more unrestricted approach and a different engagement with reality. Asking more of *Arrow of God* is not intended to turn Achebe into a social scientist. It is more in the sense of a continued analysis and dialogue in the topics raised by the novel in meeting unresolved contemporary questions of progress that are raised by these same issues about culture, religion and civil society (Ulu and the people), culture, religion and gender marginalization (wives and mothers), and the presence of the youth in society and politics (age grades and sons and daughters), among other pressing issues.

Achebe writes about a unique Igbo society that idealizes egalitarianism and a democratic process of consensus through rhetoric, dialogue, and public debate, albeit fictionalized. It therefore aims at present aspirations for equity, social justice and democracy everywhere. The set-back therefore arises from the imperialistic imposition of new paradigms of hierarchy, gender and class stratification by colonization on a society already patterned on the path of egalitarianism without monarchies, monotheism and the state as developed in the West and elsewhere. This is the unique harshness and corrupting influence of colonization as experienced in real history by many Igbo societies.

CONCLUSION

The new impositions by colonialism and Christianity on Achebe's Igbo society of Umuaro present contrasting symbolisms requiring a thoughtful resolution as I have suggested—a choice between a paradigm of a lost cause or preparedness. The metaphor and symbolism of the ending for Ezeulu who is destroyed suggest a prejudice against the indigenous systems, as they contrast with that for Winterbottom who is fortified with the powers of the imperial government and Western medicine, given what they represent for post-colonialist thought and discourse. There is also the contrast between the undermining of the potential force of the power of the traditional leaders and the civic assembly and the seeming triumph of the colonial bureaucrats consisting of provincial officers and clerks. This is in spite of the fact that the natives actively present possibilities of different outcomes, as for example, the pragmatism of the ruling elders, suggesting an opening for a preparedness scenario.

The underexplored presence of the women's collective power as demonstrated in the matriarchal implications of their all-embracing public ritual at the end of the Festival of the Pumpkin Leaves also presents a contrast with the roles of the youth. Unlike Oduche who is positioned to play power musical chairs with the colonialists, Nwafo, Edogo, women and age grades constitute a possible alliance for a strong civil society in a preparedness scenario. John Nwodika and a new crop of the working class generate their own Igbo sense of enlightenment and tolerance and in practical socio-economic choices demonstrate a preparedness scenario. After all, it is the political Ezeulu who in admiration of enlightenment says, "A man must dance the dance prevalent in his time." However, the contradiction in the construction of his character means that current imperatives cloud the danger of not separating the learning of the new white man's knowledge from character development in the case of Oduche, his son. This particular father-son experience is the more reason for having a preparedness scenario.

A contrast between Ezeulu in ritual anguish and a suffering political Ezeulu presents the contrast in the tension between religion and politics if analyzed from within an indigenous knowledge system. But the author destroys his protagonist by undermining this chief priest through a lost cause scenario, as colonial education and Christianity are presented as superior to indigenous knowledge. The end result is a piling up of patriarchal usurpations on top of the marginalization of indigenous matriarchy and therefore the female gender. According to Achebe, "People from different parts of the world can respond to the same story if it says something to them about their own history and their own experience."[86] People from the related culture of a work of fiction can even have a stronger response to a story that speaks to their history and experiences. Igbo experience of colonization was unjust and traumatic; therefore, any seeming under-emphasizing of this unequal encounter presents contradictions in a narrative. Umuaro is turned on itself in an inside fight between Ulu, Ezeulu and the clan, making it seem as if colonialism is not the main offending problem.

The author's own autobiography provides insights into the tension between politics and religion in the novel, and some of the contradictions admitted by Achebe that influenced his writing. Some of these personal experiences are also reflected in the portrayal of his main characters and his narratives of Igbo encounter with the imperialism of colonialism and Christian mission imperialism. The elitist education and elitist leadership produced by what I have termed the Umuahia-Ibadan axis also raise class, gender, and leadership questions about the post-colonial nation and problems and failures that led to the Nigeria-Biafra War, resulting in Achebe's contradictory statement, "There was a country and I had two countries."

NOTES

1. The full version of this article was previously published as Amadiume, Ifi. "Discourse, Imagination and Models of Resistance: Rereading *Arrow of God*." *Igbo Studies Review*, Vol 7 (2019): 1–28.
2. Chinua Achebe, *Arrow of God*, (London: Heinemann 1964), 208.
3. Ibid., 219.
4. Ibid., 61.
5. Ibid., 68.
6. Ibid., 73.
7. Ibid., 133.
8. Ibid.
9. Ibid.
10. Ibid, 177.
11. Ibid., 205

12. Ibid., 220.
13. Ibid., 221
14. Ibid.
15. Ibid.
16. Ibid., 230.
17. Ibid., 211.
18. Ibid., 198.
19. Ibid., 228.
20. Ibid., 178.
21. Ibid., 170.
22. Ibid., 189.
23. Ibid.
24. Ibid.
25. Ibid., 230.
26. Ibid., 228.
27. Ibid., 228.
28. Ibid., 144.
29. Ibid., 214.
30. Ibid., 214.
31. Chinua Achebe, *There Was a Country: A Personal History of Biafra*, (New York: Penguin Press, 2012), 7–8.
32. Ibid., 8.
33. Ibid.
34. Ibid., 9.
35. Ibid.
36. Ibid., 10.
37. Ibid.
38. Ibid.
39. Ibid., 11.
40. Ibid.
41. Ibid
42. Ibid.
43. Ibid., 12.
44. Ibid.
45. Ibid.
46. Ibid.
47. Ibid.
48. Ibid.
49. Ibid., 13.
50. Ibid.
51. Ibid.
52. Ibid.
53. Ibid.
54. Ibid., 14.
55. Ibid.,18.

56. Ibid.
57. Ibid., 19.
58. Ibid., 39.
59. Ibid., 20.
60. Ibid.
61. Ibid., 24–25.
62. Ibid., 25.
63. Ibid., 27.
64. Ibid.
65. Ibid., 27–28.
66. Ibid., 29.
67. Ibid., 30.
68. Ibid., 33.
69. Ibid.
70. Ibid.
71. Ibid., 34.
72. Ibid.
73. Ibid.
74. Ibid.
75. Ibid., 35
76. Ibid.
77. Ibid., 31.
78. Ibid.
79. Ibid.
80. Ibid., 31–32.
81. Chinua Achebe, "Chi in Igbo Cosmology," in *Morning Yet On Creation Day*, (New York: Anchor Books, 1976), 141.
82. Achebe, *There Was a Country*, 39.
83. Ibid., 14.
84. Ibid., 39–40.
85. Ibid., 14.
86. Ibid., 39.

BIBLIOGRAPHY

Achebe, Chinua. *Arrow of God*. London: Heinemann, 1964.
Achebe, Chinua. *There Was a Country: A Personal History of Biafra*. New York: Penguin Press, 2012.
Achebe, Chinua. *Morning Yet On Creation Day*. New York: Anchor Books, 1976.

Chapter 9

The Collision of Asymmetric Civilizations

A Reading of Things Fall Apart

Ihechukwu C. Madubuike

Nine years ago, in 2008 precisely, international communities, all over the world, celebrated with aplomb the historic publication of *Things Fall Apart*.[1] That year marked its fiftieth year of existence. It was an intellectual harvest of sorts. Achebe himself was all part of it, as he journeyed from his temporary abode in the United States of America to the capital of Imo State, Owerri, to give that year's Ahiajoku Lecture. From his writings emerged a new humanism, a neo-African humanism that bestowed dignity, honor and gravitas to the black race and hastened the death of colonialism. He was consistently rated among the first one hundred such intellectuals in the world of his time. Sickness did not allow Achebe to fully enjoy the later part of his life. Yet he avoided the existential ideology of nihilism. He could not therefore, endorse the darkness and total void inherent in verses such as the following lines penned by Thomas Hardy:

> That . . . be not told of my death
> Or made to grieve on account of me
> And that I be not buried in consecrated ground.[2]

It is evident that Achebe could not have been in any hearty accord with the above thoughts of perjorism. But every author has his reason for writing and has every right to espouse a point of view or views. I came in contact with Thomas Hardy's work as a student of English and French literatures in 1963–1965 at the then–Advanced Teachers Training College, now Alvan Ikoku

College of Education, Owerri. I came across the name again fortuitously when I thumbed through Fredrick Forsyth's *The Dogs of War,*[3] his third novel, written after the Biafran war, and published in 1974. Thomas Hardy, from the poem earlier, had expressed a wish, a poetic wish, if you like. But poetry is not reality. The author, it would appear, would not give a damn if nothing were heard of him after he has passed on. Yet his novels and poems, would inevitably assure that he remains immortal. And so, however we look at it, a good work of art can justify itself by not only being therapeutic, but also by representing man's attempt at fighting death.

Hardy's poem differed exponentially from one, which I penned down a couple of years ago. It was simply a poetic exercise, but foregrounded on observed, nay, on observable reality. It is titled Epitaph 1: a poem in my second volume of poetry *Die Oh Death (Or the Musings of a Split Conscience & Other Poems).*[4]

> REGARD this marble trunk
> With some kind eyes, a grateful sigh
> A benevolent word. Some comforting glance
> Hide not your emotion for long
> Suppress not the truth in shame
> Confess the virtues that made the difference
> Opened doors. Mentored youths . . .
> Do not deride the effort nor scorn the vision
> That spawned a myth of a greater tomorrow.

In this poem, the mood is different, the tone is measured; the expectation tentative. The cultural setting is also different. It denotes a different world view.

Hardy was not only a poet of despair and disappointment; he was a great exponent of human cataclysm. His works are birthed in fatalism. Many of Achebe's characters (Okonkwo Unoka, Ezeulu, Obi Okonkwo) are conflict characters (and we shall show this later in the essay) that are preys to adverse conditions in their milieu. But Achebe handles their weaknesses with unparalleled compassion and understanding. Unlike in Thomas Hardy's works, the theme of death is not an obsession but a natural consequence of living, something that happens as a result of the tragic flaw in the character of the protagonist. We follow this flaw as the narration unfolds. Achebe did not write to conform to a literary theory, like the existentialists of Hardy's time did.

For Achebe art is a celebration of life, not of death. Igbo culture abhors the theory of a return to nothingness when our brief existence here on earth is over. His vision of life is one of hope and of determination, of struggles and conquests. Achebe's own life exemplified this. Despite his physical disability caused by a near fatal motor accident, he continued to lead a productive life churning out essays, lectures and books that challenged some accepted orthodoxies, activated debates in intellectual and political milieus and added value to universal episteme. He never abdicated or gave up as a result of this contre temps. Achebe essentialized the Igbo spirit of *Onye kwe chi ya ekwe.* That spirit is what has kept NdiIgbo on the upbeat of a life of continuous struggle and competition, of triumph and celebrations, of not standing at one place to watch the masquerade.

It is no wonder that in his first novel, Achebe recreates and captures the essential values embedded in the Igbo Weltanschauung to demystify the source of imperialism. *Things Fall Apart* is a novel of change, and it is only apposite to show how that novel literally "changed" the world when a pristine Igbo society came into contact with a western alien culture to spawn a countervailing ideology of values, cultures and civilizations.

The colonial experience thematically pervades and dominates Achebe's writings. It could easily be termed the leitmotif of his works, the one theme that defines his writings and novels. He explored it to the fullest in his literary works, that is his novels, short stories, poems and essays in various forms. But it is Achebe's artistry and craftsmanship that make his works literary, that define their esthetic values and make them enjoyable; it raises these works beyond the mundane and the merely documentary.

In *Things Fall Apart,* Achebe shows how the themes of Power, Ideology and Conflict undergird the differences between two worlds and necessarily led to a conflict of ideas and values that resulted in the overthrow of a culture of relative peace and internal stability. *Things Fall Apart* specifically challenges the racist assumptions inherent in the imperial thought system and the prejudices that litter its literature and defined the works of its promoters, such as Joyce Cary, a British colonial officer, Joseph Conrad, and Rudyard Kipling, the metropolitan poet of imperialism. *In Things Fall Apart*, Achebe challenges imperialist thoughts about Africa, using the Igbo society as a template. Through it he posits a countervailing ideology and presents an authentic traditional worldview. The novel is above all a narration of the conflict between two worldviews; a veritable saga of how might, that is power can be made to seem right.

SITUATING THE SUBJECT MATTER

I shall quote some sections of the book, which advance our discourse and help to unfold the tragic nature of the colonial experience.

> We have brought a peaceful administration to your people so that you may be happy. If any man ill-treats you we shall come to your rescue. But we will not

allow you to ill-treat others. We have a court of law where we judge cases and administer justice just as it is done in my own country under a great queen.[5]

It is not our custom to fight for our gods, said one of them. Let us not presume to do so now. If a man kills the sacred python in the secrecy of his hut, the matter is between him and the god. We did not see it. If we put ourselves between the god and his victim we may receive blows intended for the offender. When a man blasphemes, what do we do? Do we go and stop his mouth? No. We put our fingers into our ears to stop us hearing. That is a wise action—.[6]

He turned again to the missionary. "You can stay with us if you like our ways. You can worship your own gods. It is good that a man should worship the gods and the spirits of his fathers. Go back to your house so that you may not be hurt. Our anger is great but we have held it down so that we can talk to you."[7]

These three nuggets represent some of the dramatic moments in *Things Fall Apart* and help to illuminate the thought processes that under gird its central theme. They, among several similar others, define the ideological templates of two cultures which came into conflict at the tail end of the nineteenth century. We shall analyze briefly each of these extractions and see how they advance the narrative and define the subject of this discussion, which are *Power, Ideology and Conflict in Things Fall Apart* that is the collision of two cultures.

DEFINITION OF TERMS

Power

Power, the ability to control events or people, is pervasive in the novel so much so that it can be read as a discourse on power from the point of view of its victim. It is a different reading from a novel like *The Heart of Darkness*,[8] which is also written as a narrative on power but from the point of view of the colonizer. Achebe did not leave the issue of power on the intellectual level. The novel is not a theory on power. Power in the novel is practical as it relates to events that happened to a particular people: its conquest by coercion and force. It shows the method of control and the instruments of domination, information flow and other variables of power. These are fully delineated in a subtle and overt style. All parties in the novel have and exercise power even though their strengths are relative and unequal, showing the balance of power. The social divisions in Umuofia are also a function of power: the noble or titled men, *the Ndichies*, the women and *the efulefus*—the lazy and the poor—show how power relations work to construct societal norms and functions. Power can be seen as the various forms of constraint on human activities and its exercise is common to all human beings and institutions. This exercise is evil or unjust, beneficent or humane. The novel clearly shows that all injustice and evil against humanity involve the exercise of power.

Ideology

The attitudes or ideas that determine or define a people's worldview and how they behave are presented in a dialectical manner. The novel can be read as a conflict between two world views, two different ways of behaviour that could not yield to a synthesis. When, for instance, the *Egwugwu* of Umuofia invites the white man to stay it was a conditional invitation on specific terms: "if you like our ways," but the white man obviously had other ideas which he was bent on imposing. It is this uncompromising stance that led to the exercise of power and therefore to conflict.

Conflict

Conflict is a situation or state of disagreement between individuals, groups, communities or countries. There is a conflict of ideas, where there is a disagreement between one set of ideas against another set of ideas. These are construed as ideological conflicts. Imposition of alien cultures, mores or values leads to conflicts. So also, is imposition of authority, influence or leadership by those in power as this intensifies struggles to assert positions.

Failure to resolve conflicts could lead to personal loss or group tragedy or both, as is the case *in Things Fall Apart*. Indeed, we live in a world that has failed to resolve conflicts. Thus, our various societies and communities continue to be victims of all forms of repression, totalitarianism and domination. As we can see in the novel, every conflict situation engenders a response that may be negative or positive. Conflict is emotive because it arouses passions, challenges values, fundamental rights, and even sometimes, our humanity. All the extracts at the beginning of this essay collapse within the above definitions and elaborations. They foreground the narrative structure and add depths to the scope and nature of the dramatic tension in the novel. It is therefore apposite to look a little more closely at them in an effort to further elucidate the central theme of *Things Fall Apart* as well as the other sub themes therein. The three are thematically, structurally and artistically interwoven to provide a novel of intense density and rigorous clarity.

The first extract deals with power. It is indeed a statement of raw power by the district commissioner. That type of power is still in display in our modern Nigeria. It is at the same time a display of insensitivity, ignorance, and arrogance, harbingers of conflict and confrontation and the bedrock of imperialism. The strategy to dehumanize, and colonize at all costs was the bane of the new dispensation. In the process the Church became complicit and a willing tool in the hands of the colonizer. It was not a free moral agent with a strong root in what would normally pass as an independent, self-respecting Christian organization. Indeed, the Bible was used to support all sorts of abuses, including family and societal disintegration: "Blessed is he who forsakes his father and his mother" for my sake. Those that hear my words are my father and mother, the Reverend Kaima had enthused at the news that Nwoye, the effeminate son of the principal character, Okonkwo Unoka, had joined the Church.

Reverend Kiaga's preachment was a literal translation and application of a section of the New testament injunction in order to proselytize but it denotes at the same time the beginning of the collision of two power structures in one community, an invidious aggregation of power variants, imperialists and Christianity alike, that pitched a totalitarian, capitalist force, against a communalistic, traditional ethos.

At that stage, evangelization had become synonymous with colonization and western civilization. The messianic doctrine was intertwined with the colonization principle, a programme of assertion of power, control and cultural supremacy. Yet the tenets of Christian ideology are clearly incompatible with imposition of consent or the raw use of naked power. They are at variance with the mind of Jesus Christ and his teaching. You only have to read closely the gospel of Saint Mathew and that of Saint Luke, chapters 9 and 10 respectively to see the point of departure. Rather than a message of conversion by peace and persuasion what is displayed in the novel is a programme of coercion, intimidation and military force. No love was shown, no compassion displayed, two of the most critical qualities emphasized by Christ in his evangelization mission. In their place is a witchcraft mentality whose effect is the value reduction of the positive gifts the Church brought with it at the beginning of the twentieth century. The boss mentality, the arrogance of power, inevitably led to conflict and confrontation. It left a permanent scar and hurt. And we are still hurting as a result of the misplacement of values that matter.

The second quotation calls to mind the *laissez-faire* principle of freedom of action. It was an eighteen-century terminology of Free Trade Economists. But in our context, it is a principle wrapped in eschatological overtones and double entendre. It is a religious ideology of non-interference by mortals in the affairs of gods or deities. Whereas today, it can be interpreted as a mood of apathy or indifference, if not cowardice (as indeed Okonkwo saw it), it was, nonetheless, a strongly held view that the gods could fight for themselves. (When a similar episode took place in Umuofia, the alleged killer of the sacred python, Okoli died before anybody could do anything and it was interpreted as a proof that the gods could still fight for themselves). Mbanta's dilemma was that nobody had ever knowingly killed the sacred python and there was no antecedent. Yet it was wrong to indulge the killer. If those who accidentally killed the python were asked for atonement, those who killed it knowingly deserve severer punishment. Ostracization of a people with powerful allies in a now plural society was bound to be counter-productive. The incident polarized the society and showed the rupture caused by the conflict of two religious beliefs. It was also a patent demonstration that Mbanta was losing its moorings and was drifting apart. It was also another example of Church duplicity in the colonization process.

The third extract is not only a demonstration of political correctness and realism but also a lesson in cultural diplomacy and progressivism from a society that was described as barbaric and without culture. It is in tandem with the Igbo spirit of accommodation and tolerance encapsulated in the proverb *Egbe belu, ugo belu, nke si ibe ya ebele, nku kwaa ya* (Let the kite perch and let the eagle perch, if any says the other should not perch let its wing break).

In this episode, Ajofia, one of the ancestral masquerades, which dispensed justice in the land, was addressing the Reverend Smith, a missionary, in a subdued or controlled anger. This exponent of Umuofia way of life was already prepared to come to terms with the new civilization and to enter into a dialogue with its representative. But the latter, notoriously insensitive and narrow-minded, refused. By so doing, he lost the chance of avoiding an unnecessary clash of cultures that would have promoted harmonious living, enriched civilizations and advanced the concept of pluralism. Pluralism is the coming together of a society made up of two different cultural and religious groups in order to give peace a chance. It has been argued that it was this inherent and natural disposition of the pristine Umuofia culture to accommodate change that led to its breakdown. By advocating pluralism or its concept, the African society of Umuofia was ahead of its time by several years.

BACKGROUND

Achebe admitted that he wrote *Things Fall Apart* in response to the colonial situation in Africa, and particularly in response to *Mr. Johnson*, a novel set in colonial Africa by Joyce Cary. He regretted that admission for it popularized the novel of Cary. *Mr. Johnson*, an eponymous novel is a quixotic narrative about a Nigerian character called Johnson. The novel is set in colonial Nigeria. Through it, Joyce Cary, a British colonial servant, paints an unsavory picture of Africa, its people and its environment, leaving a canvass of barbarians without any iota of culture or civilization according to his euro-centric understanding of these concepts.

Mr. Johnson conveys flavors of traditional Africa in the 1930s when colonization had taken root in Nigeria, long after the amalgamation in 1914. Achebe's *Things Fall Apart*, on the other hand, reflects a traditional society at the end of the 1800s, at the beginning of the colonial expedition and Christianity's inroad into the East of Nigeria. One would hardly believe he is reading about the same people and culture, given that Okonkwo and Johnson are both Nigerians. One of the hallmarks of Achebe in all of his writings is his impartial and objective portrayal of situations. His realism is set against the propaganda and project of colonial apologists.

Another racist literature of the period that caught the attention of Chinua Achebe and influenced his writing is Joseph Conrad's *Heart of Darkness*. Achebe was enraged by the kind of treatment Conrad gave to Africans in his novel. Says the author of *Things Fall Apart:*

> Look at the way this man handles Africans. Do you recognize humanity there? People will tell you he was opposed to imperialism. But it is not enough to say I'm opposed to imperialism. Or, I'm opposed to these people—these poor people—being treated like this. Especially since he goes on straight away to call them "dogs standing on their hind legs." That kind of thing. Animal imagery throughout. He didn't see anything wrong with it. So we must live in different worlds. Until these two worlds come together we will have a lot of trouble.[9]

Without *Mr. Johnson* of Joyce Cary, and perhaps without the *Heart of Darkness* of Joseph Conrad, two racist novels written at the beginning of the last century, *Things Fall Apart* probably would not have seen the light of the day.

Racist propaganda in the form of novels gave impetus to a literary sensibility and dynamics that led to the production of one of the best novels written since after the Second World War. *Things Fall Apart* is thus the paradoxical literary response to an existential condition that combines a personal tragedy and a group loss, a reflex of power, ideology and conflict, fundamentals encapsulated in *two mutually antagonistic world views*. Through it, the author engaged himself in the search for existential meaning as well as cultural relevance. The novel had a small beginning but like Okonkwo its principal character, its reputation has spread like a harmattan fire.

What was the traditional environment like before the "shock" intrusion of the "alien" worldview into the fictive Igbo society of Umuofia? There are several anthropological, historical and missionary accounts of the Igbo society before the advent of full blown colonialism. Insights are also provided by accounts of the people themselves through the oral tradition, the passage of knowledge and information from one generation to another through the oral medium.

There is also a literary view. This view is what Achebe undertook in both *Things Fall Apart* and *Arrow of God*, two of his best novels to my mind. The most important view, however, is the account of the people about themselves. Every other account can be rendered suspect because it is tainted by propaganda. Achebe did not set out to achieve immortality. Immortality came to him through his works. He set out to educate those who thought they had a lien on knowledge. Here is where Achebe and *Things Fall Apart* come in. He says in the interview with Jerome Brooks, "*Things Fall Apart* is a kind of a fundamental story of my condition that demanded to be heard, to retell the story of my encounter with Europe in a way acceptable to me."[10]

The District officers in *Things Fall Apart*, the anthropologists and missionaries that paved the way for him and his likes, all colluded to validate white supremacist views on almost all their writings. Information gathered by these anthropologists and missionaries were used by the colonial administrators not only to divide the communities but also to control them. Thus, a people that had no idea of the word chief, had *warrant chiefs* imposed on them. Colonial messengers assumed powers disproportional to their roles.

Chinua Achebe realized quite early "that the story we had to tell could not be told for us by anyone else no matter how well gifted or well intentioned." *Things Fall Apart* is an attempt to repair some of the damages done by earlier colonial storytellers about Africa and Africans by an indigenous master storyteller. Through it he sets out an agenda for reclaiming Africa's past cultural heritage and its glory:

> It is my business as a writer to teach that boy that there is nothing disgraceful about the African weather, that the palm-tree is a fit subject for poetry. Here then is an adequate revolution for me to espouse—to help my society regain belief in itself and put away the complexes of the years of denigration and self-abasement.[11]

Umuofia people lived a well-ordered life based on a democratic system. It provided opportunity for all to realize their dreams within the law, which was drawn from the wisdom of the elders and their ancestors and their religion. As imperfect as it was, it recognized the fundamental rights of the individual to participate unhindered in the affairs of the community as prescribed by its ethos. It was an ordered society far from tarzanism and the Robinhoods Nature, the seasons and the gods defined the activities of the people: yam festivals, holiday periods, religious observances, title taking ceremonies, marriages and burial events, naming ceremonies, sport festivals characterized mainly by wrestling matches, were some of the defining attributes of a coherent society, a civilization that preceded the advent of the colonizer.

In this set up, children were brought up to meet set objectives of the community according to prescribed, even if unwritten codes. Adults were expected to live by the rules of the community or get sanctioned; the judgment process was unambiguous. Special masquerades (*Egwugwus*) representing ancestral spirits performed the judicial function. Women knew their roles, which again, fit into the total objectives of a traditional set up. The oral tradition and storytelling flourished and were accepted as important channels for recording history, transmitting values and educating the young. Uncommon incidents like the arrival of the locusts were celebrated with excitement. The stories of the Sky and the Earth and the Mosquito and the Ear do not only enhance narrative meanings but also illustrate the didactic angle. Apprenticeship and on the job training were part of the traditional education system. Okonkwo made his wealth through sharecropping. Wars were infrequent and when engaged on, it was not for frivolous reasons, but took place after observing due diligence and process. Peace terms were religiously kept.

Pristine cultures all over the world have their obverse sides and the Umuofia way of life was no exception. Twins were ignorantly thrown away, war prisoners were dedicated to gods, set apart or even killed, or denied certain rights. The sacred and the profane are all weaved together to portray a society that worked. A *Time magazine* critic, Richard Lacayo, was right when he observed that:

> Instead of being treated as onlookers to the arrival of the colonial power, either passive or menacing, here the Africans are at the centre stage, capable all the while of nobility but also of cruelty, wisdom and bewilderment. By the time the British colonial administration arrives towards the end of the book to dismiss the natives as savages, we knew how profoundly mistaken that word is.[12]

We shall in due course consider the implications of this dismissive appraisal in the contextual dynamics of the relativity of all cultures. Before that, however, we shall examine some of the engaging themes that characterize this great novel and see how they further illuminate the narrative.

POWER AND THE COLONIAL EXPERIENCE

Power or politics is the dominant ideology in *Things Fall Apart*. Colonialism is nothing else if not the use of power or misuse of it for the imposition of a dominant culture or way of life on others. The discreet or open use of power by those who wield it, its aggregation in the manipulation of issues of a nascent administration is more anecdotal than analytical in the novel. At a substructural level, Umuofia itself demonstrates the invidious use of power when dealing with its erring neighbours as in the threat of war against one of their neighbors who had killed one of their own and had to avert war by offering a virgin and Ikemefuna to Umuofia. The invidious use of power also manifests in the killing of Ikemefuna and in the ironic banishment of Okonkwo into exile. Umuofia goes to war only when provoked. When atonements were made, they remained at peace with their neighbours. It's only the powerful that can command these conditions.

The missionaries had a different idea about the use of power. It was for domination and control and they did it without looking back. Even at the family level, Okonkwo displayed some dismal use of power or authority, almost without restraint.

In the conflicts that ensued at the different structures of engagements in the novel, power became openly and brutally used in the effort to subdue the nine villages of Umuofia by the white missionaries and their colonial collaborators. At the end it was clear that the missionaries had the upper hand because their instruments of coercion were superior. The various anecdotes in the novel, the killing of the sacred python, the imprisonment of the elders of Umuofia, the burning down of the church, the unmasking of the *Egwugwu*, the death of Okonkwo by suicide—all are graphically painted, especially in the second and third parts of the novel. They demonstrate the pattern of power that led to the wrenching experience that is called colonization.

COLONIALIZATION AND EVANGELIZATION: THE UNHOLY PACT

The destruction of Abame reminds one of the wars in Iraq or present-day Syria where towns and cities are reduced to dust and rubbles with hardly any prisoners taken. The destruction of this small village took place on a market day when every able person went to the market. According to the narrative, captured as an eyewitness account, everybody, "except the old and the sick that were at home" was killed. Literarily the village seized to exist. What a better example of genocide can there be! It is not unlike what happens when Fulani herdsmen attack villages or settlements that oppose their grazing culture and nomadic lifestyle.

In Mbanta, the village of Okonkwo's mother, where he was in exile because he had inadvertently killed a kinsman, the missionaries recorded an enormous success. They were able to win many converts, including Nwoye, Okonkwo's estranged son. They also succeeded to build a Church in a forbidden place (*Ajofia*) and thereby established a permanent presence in the village. Rationalization through debate and shifting of blames, rather than outright cowardice and fear of war, prevented Mbanta from engaging in a full-scale war with the missionaries and their converts. Mbanta reasoned that the gods could defend themselves (a fundamental error of religious rationalization); the converts were their kit and kin and killing them amounts to committing evil—*nso ani*, and the punishment for this is the banishment of the offender (this again derives from a fundamentalist religious world view); and the converts were *efulefus*—the undesirable elements in the society, and their conversion was seen as a good riddance.

The Church grew because of these rationalizations and especially because its message of peace appealed to people like Nwoye, Okonkwo's effeminate son. It welcomed the rejected in the community—*the ohus*, or outcasts as well as the parents of twins. In collusion with the colonial administration, it set up a court where it tried and punished the people according to foreign laws. But in Mbanta were thinkers, idle debaters and onlookers. They were also men of action who had their own strategy of containment and punishment for recalcitrant elements of the society. The provocation and aggravation by the converts came to a head with the alleged killing of the sacred or royal python, the most revered animal in Mbanta. This last act in particular, a sacrilege, was the breaking point of their *cool*, and they decided to ostracize the converts. But the tragedy caused by the new religion and dispensation did not go unnoticed by the sensitive and discerning among the elders of Mbanta. The overall effect of the new dispensation on the people was that they could no longer speak with one voice.

In Umuofia, the situation was not different for the church had also recorded many converts and grown in size and strength. It built schools and hospitals. With the schools it bewitched and mesmerized the soul; with the hospitals it cures and soothes the physical and psychological bruises. It was thus able to attract to its fold not only the lowly in birth and status but also some titled men. A man like Akunna, a well-respected and intelligent person, had sent his son to the white man's school, his opposition to Christianity notwithstanding.

The white man also introduced a new administration: it built a court, a prison yard and a new system of dispensing justice, subjecting the natives under laws that were foreign to them. Erstwhile men of importance had their heads shaved. To crown the humiliation, they were beaten with rods by the "*Efulefus*" of yesterday in the service of foreign conquerors. These were the court messengers or *kotmas*, in the local vocabulary, arrogant and high handed as well as corrupt. They manipulated cases in favour of those who gave them money.

In effect the church and the colonial administrators governed without understanding the customs of the people, not that it would have mattered, given their supremacist cultural posturing and evangelical ecumenism. But the tragedy for the communities was that the white man succeeded in dividing the people because of a conflict of values and ideologies. Power, politics, and conflicting ideologies combined to produce the personal and group tragedies that led to the melt down in Umuofia. The reflective and cerebral Obierika succinctly verbalized the tragedy: "Now he has won our brothers, and we can no longer act like one. He has put a knife on the things that held us together and we have fallen apart."[13]

The tension between the Christian religion and traditional culture and values was the result of a combination of ecclesiastical arrogance, insensitivity, administrative high-handedness and manipulations. It was the product of an unholy and unexpected pact. The Christian religion was expected to operate from a higher moral ground. It did not. It gave the impression that white people—the missionaries and the colonizers—were psychopaths, probably more ignorant than those they pretended to have come to civilize. Compare the polite, humane behaviour of the leader of the Egwugwu cult towards Mr. Smith, the missionary, when he tried to stop the band from destroying his church.

You can stay with us if you like our ways. You can worship your own god. It is good that a man should worship the gods and spirits of his fathers. Go back to your house so that you may not be hurt. Our anger is great but we have held it down so that we can talk to you.[14]

Note the cordiality and civility, the tolerance and spirit of accommodation exhibited by a culture that is supposed to be inferior. Also note the invitation to dialogue. This is practical religion with social conscience, the offspring of a humane culture. Yet it was this tolerance that led to the downfall of Umuofia civilization.

The essence of this discourse is to create understanding, to narrow the gap between traditional religion and Christianity, but the Church in Umuofia started on the wrong foot. Instead of standing firm for freedom and social justice, for compromise and tolerance it sauntered along with colonial misrule and closed its eyes to the numerous abuses committed by the district commissioner and deepened resentment. It acquiesced to oppression and exploitation and narrowed the constituency of Jesus Christ, whom it proclaimed its leader. It promoted a corrupted vision of Christianity through its involvement in the politics of colonization. As the novel reveals, "the missionary often went to see his brother white man. There was nothing strange in that." That is to say that the collusion and collaboration between the Church and the Colonizer did not escape the notice of the villagers. Since then there has not been a détente of conflict and tension between tradition and modernity.

Chapter 9

CHARACTERS OF CONFLICT, IDEOLOGY, AND POWER

There is a whole lot of character mix and opposites in *Things Fall Apart* that advance the story line and sharpen the focus of our essay. The principal ones are the protagonist Okonkwo Unoka, his father, Unoka, his son, Nwoye, his daughter Ezinma, his friend Obierika and the missionaries, Reverends Brown and Smith. The District Commissioner is a character type without a name. He is the symbol of all that is negative in colonial administration. All these characters come alive as conflict characters, embodying distinct ethos and values. Some act as foils to others.

Okonkwo is presented as the opposite of his father. He is ambitious, industrious, fearless and wealthy and possesses all the manly attributes sanctioned by his community. Unoka on the other hand is lazy, laid back, indolent and poor. He is soft, while Okonkwo is strong and stoic, even though he displays softness when it is a matter that concerns Ezinma, the daughter. The values of both men never met as they were constantly in conflict. These physical and ethical differences became the burning fuel that drove Okonkwo's action plan and determined his way of life: "And so Okonkwo was ruled by one passion: to hate everything that his father loved. One of those things was gentleness and another was idleness." Unoka's gentleness was replaced with toughness; his laziness with hard work; so that by the age of eighteen years, Okonkwo was already" one of the greatest men of his time." This was no mean achievement, considering the competitive nature and robust individualism of the Umuofia society, glimpses of which we see in the Igbo society of today.

This philosophy of life and outlook put him in conflict with the new values espoused by the new dispensation represented especially by conflict-inducing Christianity. The meek and the weak would never inherit the earth was the countertheology of Okonkwo and those who thought like him. To the end Umuofia would have kept faith with their philosophy as captured by this powerful speech by the acclaimed and celebrated orator of Umuofia, Okika, a great man and one of the six leaders of Umuofia who had been imprisoned by the white man despite the defection of some of the members of the clan.

It is evident that the conflict was not only between Okonkwo and members of his family or between him and his community, but between the clan and the alien dispensation. In *Things Fall Apart* individual conflict was used also to sharpen community conflicts and push them to a point of no return. Okonkwo killed the messenger who came to stop the clan meeting and thereafter-committed suicide. Umuofia did not raise a finger to defend him. They could not fight.

Nwoye, Okonkwo's first son, ironically, is one of those who have joined the stranger. Nwoye resembles more of his grandfather Unoka than his father,

Okonkwo. Father and son never saw things from the same point of view. The presence of Ikemefuna seemed to have turned the behaviour around but not substantially. Nwoye was simply too "effeminate" to meet the father's expectations. The arrival of the missionaries provided the opportunity to permanently separate father and son and exacerbated the conflict of personalities. It also exacerbated the angst of Okonkwo against the new dispensation.

Ezinma was presented as *the alter ego* of the father, Okonkwo even though she is a woman. Subtle and bristling with confidence she is Okonkwo's favourite child because of her "masculine qualities: she is bold, precocious and is the only one in the family who could contradict Okonkwo. Okonkwo, who does not like to display emotions openly, does so when it comes to Ezinma. She remained a conflict personality until her *Iyi-uwa*—the spirit of Ogbanje—was effectively destroyed.

Mr. Brown, the missionary is presented as a considerate person with an open mind. His approach, especially his occasional visits to and discussions with the elders of the community won him many converts. The Reverend Smith who replaced him, on the other hand, was brash, and frontal in his approach. He danced a furious step and the drum beat accordingly. Soon after his arrival, his overzealous converts breached the law of the clan by killing the sacred python and started an open confrontation with the community. The district commissioner was scornful of the values and way of life of the people. He was vengeful and manipulative, the archetype of the colonial master for whom everything traditional was reprehensible and must be crushed.

Obierika was a faithful friend of Okonkwo Unoka. A successful man in his own right he thought about things before acting. Cerebral, cool and calculating he, unlike his friend, was able to come to terms with the new dispensation and the challenges it imposed upon the community by looking at the situation realistically. He was a man of wisdom.

OKONKWO AS A CONFLICT CHARACTER

Okonkwo is the personification of character conflict. He is also the hero of the novel and therefore deserves some special mention in the overview of our topic. The conflict is induced by fear, *the fear of failure*. Some critics think that anger is the dominant trait. Anger against what? I ask. Anger is manifested only because of fear, the fear to be taught weak, not anger to be a failure. Failure leads to frustration and frustration could lead to unnecessary anger, and to the so-called "righteous anger." It is the fear to be seen as a failure like his father. Fear can lead to creative possibilities; anger to senseless destruction or madness. Remember that Okonkwo abhorred his father because he was a failure, because he was weak, a trait he saw in his son,

Nwoye. Fear and anger are the products of internal conflict, disequilibrium between opposing or contending forces of powerful passions. A number of Okonkwo's outbursts and actions derive from this internal conflict. "I will not have a son who cannot hold his head in the gathering of the clan. I would sooner strangle him with my own hands. And if you stand staring at me like that . . . Amadiora will break your head for you."[15] Okonkwo broke the custom of his people when he beat one of his wives, Nwonye's mother, during the Week of Peace and was duly punished for his insensitivity. Says Achebe: "Okonkwo was not the man to stop beating somebody half-way through, not even for fear of a goddess." Fear, like anger, is a consuming passion.

There is also the banana tree incident during the New Yam Festival when Okonkwo's second wife cut a few leaves off the tree to wrap some food items: "Without further argument Okonkwo gave her a sound beating and left her and her daughter weeping." And as if this was not enough Okonkwo shot at his wife for daring to scoff at his shooting ability. Luckily, he missed his target. It was out of fear, not anger, that Okonkwo killed Ikemefuna: "He [Okonkwo] heard Ikemefuna cry: my father, they have killed me," as he ran towards him. Dazed with fear, Okonkwo drew his market and cut him down. He was afraid of being thought weak."[16]

Okonkwo could not draw a boundary between the dictates of bravery (manliness) and the nature of circumspection. He had what many would call "one-track mind." Consideration of alternatives is anathema. For him, a man is a person who does not display fear, who does not display weakness, for fear is weakness. Fear is for women not for men who are men. To kill Ikemefuna was a show of manliness. Besides, he cannot stand failure, personified by his father, for "Whenever the thought of his father's weakness and failure troubled him, he expelled it by thinking about his own strength and success."[17] Okonkwo remained faithful to his vision of manliness to the end. If Umuofia would not fight, he would fight. He was brought up on the menu of bravery and manliness and all his life has been defined by this. A brave man, a commander-in-chief of his people's army for that matter, would not allow his head to be taken in any war by the enemy. He commits suicide and ends a life driven by fear and show of strength. By taking his own life Okonkwo denied the district commissioner and his agents the satisfaction of humiliating him, of killing him, possibly by hanging. Thus, even in death Okonkwo was still a victor. He must be smiling with satisfaction at the agents of imperialism for beating them at their own game, for not being subjected to their dehumanization tactics and cruelties. In the spirit world of the ancestors where he now lives, he must be weeping with *Ogwugwu, Idemili, Agballa*, and other ancestral spirits at the dismantling of a people's way of life and at the decay of their culture and heritage.

Personally, I like Okonkwo, his excesses notwithstanding. I like his passion, his focus, his determination to succeed where his father and others had failed, his desire to be the champion of his people's way of life, his rise from rags to riches. I admire people who have principles and are ready to die for their beliefs, people who are committed. Okonkwo was committed on the side of tradition. He died defending what he believed in. If tradition had won the battle against change, Okonkwo would have been given a post-humous award for gallantry. Achebe used Okonkwo to show that tradition has its own respect and dignity. In climes where suicide is regarded as a form of bravery and sacrifice for higher ideals Okonkwo's body would have been lifted high with pomp, drum beating and pageantry. But Okonkwo's life is nothing but a heavy irony, the stuff with which tragedy is made.

CHI AND THE DYNAMICS OF INDIVIDUAL RESPONSIBILITY

Things Fall Apart could be described as an existentialist novel in terms of modern ideology, even though Achebe did not set out to write an existentialist novel or espouse the theory a la Kierkegaard or Jean-Paul Sartre. We have already discussed the difference between him and Thomas Hardy in this respect. The conflict between the individual and his *chi* or personal god, which places the individual on his own terms, is existentialist. The ideology lays emphasis on the role of the individual vis-à-vis the choices before him. When failure confronted Okonkwo he was accused by his detractors of having challenged his *chi*, but when fortune smiles at him it was construed to be as a result of a benevolent god. Both of these interpretations were seriously challenged in the novel, which insists that the individual is the architect of his own fortune or misfortune. Unoka, Okonkwo's indigent father had gone to the Oracle of the Hills and the Caves to find out why he always had miserable harvests:

> "Hold your peace" screamed the priestess . . . You have offended neither the gods nor your fathers. And when a man is at peace with his gods and his ancestors, his harvest will be good or bad according to the strength of his arm. You, Unoka, are known in all the clan for the weakness of your matchet and your hoe. When your neighbours go out with their axe to cut down virgin forests, you sow your yams on exhausted farms that take no labour to clear. They cross seven rivers to make their farms; you stay at home and offer sacrifices to a reluctant soil. Go home and work like a man.[18]

On the other hand, Okonkwo was a successful man by all standards. His success was attributed to his industry and hard work. Remember he made his wealth through sharecropping, a very slow process of possessing yams and owning barns of them. A benevolent *chi* had not cracked his proverbial kernel for him as some of his detractors had alleged:

> But it was not really true that a benevolent spirit had cracked Okonkwo's palm-kernels for him. He had cracked them himself. Anyone who knew his grim struggle against poverty and misfortune could not say he had been lucky. If ever a man deserved his success, that man was Okonkwo. At an early age he had achieved fame as the greatest wrestler in all the land. That was not luck. At the most one could say that his chi or personal god was good.[19]

In effect it was the individual who determines his own fortune, not his *chi*. This contradicts the notion that it is *chi,* the personal god that enhances or limits individual responsibility. Okonkwo did not fail or succeed because his *chi* said yes or no. He succeeded because he worked hard, confronted poverty squarely and was at all times focused. His personal god responded to these attributes and said yes—you are on the right path. His community also sanctioned these attributes "that when a man says yes his chi says yes also."[20] Some existentialists believe that man is a Prometheus, the sole architect of his own fortune and spurns the idea of either a benevolent creator or a malevolent one. Nietche believed that it is our nature that dictates some of our choices. Kierkegaard has faith in an omniscient Creator who imposes some limits on our free will. The Igbo, notoriously religious, believes ideally in the notion of a Supreme creator (*Chukwu*) who through a fragment of himself in individual lives, *chi* or personal god, helps those who help themselves. In this highly individualized society with a very strong labor or work ethics nobody will pity you because you think your *chi* is not favorably disposed to you. That also accounts for the fact that before the coming of the white man there were hardly any beggars in the society.

Yet there were no unresolved theological conflicts between the individual and his *chi* such as were perceived in the theology of the early existentialists. Any such conflict was removed through appropriate reproaches and religious cleansings. Religious obligations were both personal and communal, for the sin of one could affect the entire society. Thus, when Okonkwo broke the sacredness of the Peace of Week by beating his wife and committing *nso ani*, the social implications of his action was unequivocally brought home to him through the intervention of the priest of the earth goddess, Ezeani who admonished him with the following words: "Take away your kola nut. I shall not eat in the house of a man who has no respect for our gods and ancestor."[21] The concept of *chi* derives from a philosophical, economic, social, and political rationalization with a religious overtone. Existence is without meaning, without the daily and careful observance of the ethical norms that derive from this concept. The concept of *chi,* interwoven with the religious beliefs of the people interfaced with the concept of predestination and of *Ogbanje.* The latter is a phenomenon of life, explainable only when put in the context of the worldview of the people.

An *ogbanje* is a person destined to die early, who not only physically dies but who mysteriously re-enters the womb of the mother to be re-born, and until is "arrested," continues the transition between life and death. Ezinne the lovely daughter of Okonkwo is an *ogbanje*. She is a source of both existential worry and religious anxiety for her parents and the community. Both sources are linked to the concept of *chi,* for as we have explained, the concept does not take away personal responsibility from an individual. The saying is that if a person says yes, his *chi* will also say yes is relevant. It was Ezinne who put a stop to these worries, by taking her parents and the traditional healer, through what looked like a merry-go round in the neighborhood, to a spot where *her iyi-uwa*—her link with the underworld—was buried. It was after the ritual following this lifesaving exercise that her mystical tie with death was severed and the certainty of normal living assured. This is one example of how an individual can transcend his destiny.

Choice is inherent in the concept of *chi*. The individual always has a choice; and it is through his choice that he defines himself. Action through choice determines how far an individual can get on in life. *Chi* is the projection of one's self into the realms of possibilities. The individual can project himself into greatness or into nothingness (nihilism). The Igbo acknowledges the presence of this personal God, a fragment of the Superior Being (*Chi-Ukwu),* sometimes represented figuratively by *his Ikenga* and maintains a harmonious relationship with him as all good believers do. But he also knows that his success in life does not simply depend on a ritual existence based on routine sacrifices and obedience to his *chi,* but on activities that are fore grounded on the ethics and ethos of his people, activities that the community must sanction as worthy and befitting.

The Umuofia community of *Things Fall Apart* lays stress on individualism, freedom and choice. They have no kings or princes, but noble men who achieve that status by recognized and demonstrable feats of greatness. Okonkwo demonstrated existential angst by his efforts to rise above the circumscribed lot at birth. His life is thus defined by this angst, this anxiety and existential worry. In the existential theology, Okonkwo's set back, rather than being a cause for despair should cause him to continue the Sisyphean struggle against the forces that keep him down, for in that lies his essence as a human being. This is the base of the theory of the absurd *a la Camus*, where existence precedes the essence. But the Umuofia philosophy of life is theocentric because the cosmos and universe are under the control of *Chineke*—God the creator, the author of all things. This philosophy contains the message of indestructibility of human life through the cult of the ancestors, whose spirits never die but continue to influence the course of human actions and activities. Hence the primacy of ancestral worship in Igbo culture of the time.

It was Thomas Hardy; the English novelist who authored *Far From the Madding Crowd,* who said that *character is fate*. Okonkwo's Chi does not limit his character; it embraces his fate (destiny). The point is that *chi* alone is not enough to define an individual or determine what he is or can become. Hence the idea of destiny or *akaraka* in Igbo philosophy. Some of the traits that dominate Okonkwo's character, for instance, fear or dread, freedom, individualism and commitment, are issues that characterized the early twentieth century philosophical movement known as existentialism. While this ideology remains a non-cohesive philosophical theory even in the literature of the western world, traits of it abound in this great novel, which is steeped in African phenomenology.

KNOWLEDGE AND THE DECOLONIZING PROCESS

It was John Locke who defined *knowledge* as the perception of the agreement or disagreement of two ideas. According to Plato, however, for there to be knowledge a statement must be *justified, true,* and *believed.* For him, knowledge is "justified true belief." Writing a novel in our context falls within the process of knowledge acquisition, transfer, management, and retention. Writing has since been accepted as one of the most permanent forms of knowledge transfer. It was the world's commonest form of retaining knowledge—facts and information—before the revolution of information technology and the age of the videos and the cassettes. However, retaining and propagating knowledge through writing has also a draw back since it can be used to spread false information and propaganda in a more permanent form and in a very quick way. That was one of the reasons early Egyptians were skeptical about the written word.

The story had it that the acclaimed inventor of what is now western form of writing, Mr. Theuth, while presenting his invention (writing) to King Thamus said that his new invention would improve both the wisdom and memory of the Egyptians. The skeptical King argued, however, that the written word would rather afflict the Egyptians with fake knowledge, especially from foreign sources and could also make them mentally lazy as they would no longer be able to mentally retain large quantities of knowledge.

Things Fall Apart was written to reduce propaganda and track the truth. Falsehood not countered can easily pass for truth, says an Igbo adage. That explains why, despite the apparent merit in King Thamus argument, Achebe had to use the written medium (rather than the oral tradition familiar to the people of Umuofia) to counter the falsification of knowledge and facts about his people. For as the Igbo proverb has it: *an unusual ailment requires an unusual treatment*. Besides, writing is the culture of the powerful.

Joyce Cary and Conrad's views of Africa and the African society are propaganda. They derive from a consciousness that encouraged enslavement and conflict. The explorations of Marlowe and Kurtz provided the justification for the colonization of Africa. A whole political process began with this reading of the *Heart of Darkness*, for it conveyed the impression that Africa was a virgin of inhumans waiting for exploitation, if necessary, by rape. For Achebe it was necessary to proffer a different point of view, a countervailing knowledge to counter this erroneous impression. Here again, the theory of Nkari (the syndrome of the powerful) and the concept of "the single story" are evoked and are at play.

Things Fall Apart is thus a strategic response to the myth of a continent of barbarians without culture. This response is done with epistemic authority:

> The worst thing that can happen to any people is the loss of their dignity and self-respect. The writer's duty is to help them regain it by showing them in human terms what happened to them, what they lost. There is a saying in Igbo that a man who can't tell where the rain began to beat him cannot know where he dried his body. The writer can tell the people where the rain began to beat them.[22]

Achebe lives no one in doubt that an alternative knowledge is a beneficent capital through which the liberation of the mind from the prejudices of the past can be achieved. This alternative knowledge is also necessary to win Africa's many battles for development and progress. The relevance of this truism cannot be, must not be lost to the present generation of the Igbo people.

In order to be able to do this, Achebe posits that we must begin to build blocks of knowledge that support our own view of life and pull-down orthodoxies and gospels that hold us down. A people's knowledge of themselves and account of their life is their most important resource for development and defense. They therefore need to control it. They need to continuously research into it and propagate its values so that other body of knowledge does not eclipse it. This accounts for the difference between dominant cultures and weak ones, between civilizations that have survived and the ones that have failed. Strong civilizations develop mechanisms for sustenance and renewal and for the control of other cultures and peoples.

Knowledge is power. This is the primary ideology in Achebe's first novel and *the raison d'etre* for its being. In this regard it is important we rediscover the traditional techniques of inquiry, curiosity, scholarship and storytelling. For knowledge is what is known in a particular field, either through experience or education. This rediscovery and expertise even through the cognitive process will reveal the fundamentals that make the stories we tell our own. That is the way also to develop and present an authentic countervailing point of view. Some of these narrative artifacts are masterly used in *Things Fall Apart* and that's what makes it a classic, one of the best of all times.

It is worth noting also that colonialism, which is also a major theme of *Things Fall Apart*, is a disjunctive venture. You could be its subject without being part of it; it has an alienating imperative and ideology. Umuofia is subdued, sequestered and segregated by a system, which, because it could not assimilate their culture, left them with the opportunity to continue to think differently and also act differently.

Alienation creates resentment, leads to tension and tension leads to the development of a critical consciousness necessary for reformation of beliefs and re-appraisal of structures and situations. Things fell apart not only because white missionaries and their colonial agents brought commotion and destruction to the community in Umuofia leading to psychological and cultural shocks. Things failed apart in the racist ideological camp because there was a new story being told in a different way, a story that was also enabling people to see the other side of the coin, a story based on a different worldview. Because of this new story as it were, because of this new knowledge, old beliefs began to crumble. That is why *Things Fall Apart* has also been described as "a novel of great power that turns the world upside down." The implication has been awesome. Says Achebe:

> There is that great proverb—that until the lions have their own historians, the history of the hunt will always glorify the hunter. Once I realized that I had to be a writer; I had to be that historian. It's not one man's job. It's not one person's job. But it is something we have to do, so that the story of the hunt will also reflect the agony, the travails, the bravery, even of the lions.[23]

Is there a hint of the negritude ideology here, the valorization of black virtues and values, which are also human virtues, the narration of the black man's story and exposition of his worldviews by blacks themselves? The lion must tell his story and not simply wait, hoping or believing that his activities alone will reflect his bravery. The lizard, which jumped from the iroko tree, said that if nobody would praise him for his feat he would praise himself lest his detractors think he sustained pains in his neck, as a result of which he is shaking his head up and down. *Things Fall Apart* did not only portray a valid African culture, its strength and beauty; it also showed its flaws and weaknesses.

Knowledge is an intellectual capital. Its acquisition, management, and organization are important and must be tied to the development and liberating process in Africa. We must encourage knowledge sharing among Africans in all fields. As a teacher, Achebe is not simply interested in theoretical web spinning; he is an inclusive writer who interprets human actions and experiences. He has a coterie of followers all over Africa, indeed, all over the world inspired by *Things Fall Apart* in which the issue of objective knowledge and its resource utilization have been seriously discussed and raised to a rational level.

Still, Achebe did not leave epistemic discourse at the purely intellectual level. He put it at the service of the political and social conditions of the people because of the urgency of what must be done to liberate Africa from the wrenching experience of colonialism. His is not an abstract ideology, *a la Hegel*, content to rationalize the opposition between subject and object, after which the opposition dissolves into a nebulous synthesis. *Things Fall Apart* posits a more radical reading and appreciation. The division of the novel into parts symbolizes the division of the old and the new—of two different worldviews that are opposed, but in which one, the African by its nature is more accommodating. He lives no one in doubt that as long as colonialism continues to blame the victims, as long as the West refuses to recognize the inherent humanity and validity in Africa's way of life, and apologize for the hurt done so long will tension continue to define the relationship between the two cultures, the hunter and the hunted.

CONFLICT AND COMPROMISE

The idea of conflict is as old as creation itself. It is an existential condition; it is at the heart of all beliefs and characterizes the struggles between good and bad; it is at the base of our moral values, of all our values. *Things Fall Apart* is a narrative of an individual and of Umuofia, but it also tells the story of power relations in the world; it is about the drama of existence which posits that human existence is one long drama of conflict, of struggles, of our will against other wills—individual will, group will, systemic will, metaphysical will; it is a clash of wills, of forces or powers—what some theorists have termed ideology of conflicts—in which there must be a resolution—a leviathan world in which only the fittest survive. The weak, in this type of world, can only survive through acquiescence, and if he has the strength, through compromise.

Conflict is not only a literary theme; it is a daily phenomenon. The colonial experience is a conflict-driven experience whose impact is ever lasting. Indeed, the dramatic power of the novel derives from the pressure and tension of daily existence and from the colonial experience. *Things Fall Apart* is mute as far as the solution to the conflict is concerned, but there is no doubting where Achebe's mind points to—harmony through compromise. The tragic end of Okonkwo, which leaves hurt in the minds of his admirers, is not a solution. The group loss by the clan of Umuofia deepens resentment. The situation leads to individual and group cynicism, and its unsavory moral and political consequences. Achebe took up these issues in his other novels. The colonial administrator could write all the history books celebrating its "civilizing" exploits in Africa and elsewhere but that would be from his point of view and as far as his limited vision can accommodate. The Africans have told their own story through their *griot in Things Fall Apart* and since then things are no longer what they used to be or seemed.

NOTES

1. Chinua Achebe, *Things Fall Apart* (New York: Anchor Books, 1994).
2. Thomas Hardy, "The Mayor of Casterbridge," https://www.fulltextarchive.com/page/The-Mayor-of-Casterbridge-by-Thomas-Hardy2/
3. Fredrick Forsyth, *The Dogs of War* (Penguin Publishing Group, 1974).
4. Ihechukwu Madubuike, *Die Oh Death (Or the Musings of a Split Conscience & Other poems)* (CITY: Apex Books Limited, 2010).
5. Achebe *Things Fall Apart*, 137.
6. Achebe, *Things Fall Apart*, 113
7. Achebe, *Things Fall Apart*, 134
8. Joseph Conrad, *Heart of Darkness*, (New York: W. W. Norton & Company; 5th edition, 2016).
9. *The Paris Review Interviews, III: The Indispensable Collection of Literary Wisdom* (The Paris Review Interviews (Picador; First edition (October 28, 2008), 254.
10. Chinua Achebe interviewed by Jerome Brooks, https://viennachinuaachebe.wordpress.com/2013/11/10/chinua-achebe-interviewed-by-jerome-brooks/#:~:text=Things%20Fall%20Apart%20is%20a,a%20way%20acceptable%20to%20me.&text=So%20I%20don't%20resent,I%20don't%20really%20know.
11. The Novelist as Teacher, http://mrhuman.weebly.com/uploads/2/1/5/1/21516316/thenovelistasteacher.pdf
12. Richard Lacayo *Things Fall Apart, Time Magazine*, https://entertainment.time.com/2005/10/16/all-time-100-novels/slide/things-fall-apart-1959-by-chinua-achebe/.
13. Achebe, *Things Fall Apart*, 176.

14. Achebe, *Things Fall Apart*, 190.
15. Achebe, *Things Fall Apart*, 33.
16. Achebe, *Things Fall Apart*, 61.
17. Achebe, *Things Fall Apart*, 66.
18. Achebe, *Things Fall Apart*, 17.
19. Achebe, *Things Fall Apart*, 27.
20. Ibid.
21. Achebe, *Things Fall Apart*, 30.
22. Robert Baah, "*Things Fall Apart*: Chinua Achebe and the Voice of Wisdom," https://spu.edu/depts/uc/response/fall99/fall.html#:~:text=For%20Achebe%2C%20%22the%20worst%20thing,very%20high%20for%20African%20writers.
23. Chinua Achebe, "The Danger of Not Having Your Own Stories," http://shaulaevans.com/chinua-achebe-the-danger-of-not-having-your-own-stories/

BIBLIOGRAPHY

Achebe, Chinua. *Things Fall Apart*. New York: Penguin Books, 1994.
Conrad, Joseph. *Heart of Darkness*. W. W. Norton & Company; 5th edition, 2016.
Forsyth, Fredrick. *The Dogs of War.* Penguin Publishing Group, 1974.
Hardy, Thomas. Quotes. https://www.goodreads.com/quotes/7402333-that-elizabeth-jane-farfrae-be-not-told-of-my-death-or
Madubuike, Ihechukwu. *Die Oh Death (Or the Musings of a Split Conscience & Other poems)* Apex Books Limited, 2010.

Chapter 10

(Re)Memorising Igbo Traditions in Achebe's *Arrow of God*
A Psychoanalytical Study

Linda Jummai Mustafa

Born Albert Chinualumogu Achebe on November 16, 1930, Achebe is rather more referred to as the "Father of modern African literature." His prowess in Igbo proverbs pitches his works against great dramatic dialogues from the famous William Shakespeare's *Julius Cesare*, his masterly presentation of the Igbo culture to counter Western claims that Africans had no culture, culminated to his becoming one of the major proponents of postcolonial epistemologies and his audacity to tell the truth through fictitious characters single him out as a master storyteller. Despite his demise in 2013, his works lives on while presenting him as a living icon to the world. It is against this backdrop that this study approaches Achebe's fictional work, *Arrow of God* using Trauma-Memory, a sub theory embedded in Freud's psychoanalysis. The discourse combines trauma and rememory as an epistemology put forward to advance a proper understanding of trauma experiences by Africans and in this case, Achebe's concerns on the didactic traumatic experiences of the Igbos as they slowly lose their culture to British traditions. In so doing, the adoption of Trauma-Memory will bring to the fore Achebe's narcissist resolve to decipher the dilemma of Ezeulu, the Chief priest and other characters who are caught in a struggle to keep their customs as they battle colonialist invasion through the enforcement of Christianity, a religion alien to the worship of the sacred python god. Equally significant, is the fact that this paper interrogates whether Achebe embraces an intellectual ambivalence of rememorizing trauma in order to assert a definite Igbo identity that cannot be fragmented by colonialist exploitative ideals.

In reading Achebe's *Arrow of God*, Charles Nnolim argues that the more one seem to read Achebe's works, "the harder it is not to come to the conclusion that the forces of change are the Fates, the Nemesis that must forcefully tame the stubborn individual."[1] Again, Blaise Machila contends that Ezeulu is an ambiguous and complex character.[2] G. D. Killam expresses the following about Ezeulu:

> Ezeulu, the protagonist is compelled to defend his unique position as a priest of Ulu, the most powerful of the village deities against, on the one hand, reactionary forces within the tribe and, on the other, against European Culture and religion.[3]

And David Caroll argues that Ezeulu is "half black, half white"—a medium between the spirit world and the human world.[4]

But Simon Gikandi reads *Arrow of God* as the conflict between two ideologies: "The conflicts in Umuaro are not a rivalry between two gods Ulu and Idemili but actually a struggle between two conflicting ideological interests and authorities represented by Nwaka and Ezeulu" (1987).[5] This view can be deciphered in Ezeulu's refusal to become the "white man's chief" because he sees himself as the arrow of god who is especially chosen to preserve Igbo customs, traditions and beliefs. Thus, with this particular act, Ezeulu acts as an epitome of identity for the Igbo people.

According to Urama Nwachukwu, "Achebe successfully explore the theme of tragedy in *Arrow of God* through a vision of complexities inherent in Igbo society."[6] Nwachukwu further explained that the power tussle that revolves around Ezeulu, the major protagonist, eventually reduces such a great man to a "mad man sweeping his floor." Similarly, Donatus Nwoga in his *Literature and Modern West African Culture* calls Ezeulu "the ultimate existential defeat because he lived on crazed."[7] Ngozi Ulogu's psychoanalytic study also afford the academic community an inquest into the anxiety and repression Ezeulu feels in concealing his fears about his diminishing powers in the presence of colonial invasion. According to Ulogu, Ezeulu "ponders over his limited powers as a priest. He has since repressed this fact and secretly wishes for an opportunity to play out his authority. He desires to be more than a watchman for Ulu."[8]

From Nnolim's perspective of change as a force to softening an unyielding individual who tenaciously clings to his past, to Ulogu's psychoanalytical view of Ezeulu's anxiety of what would be the fate of the Igbo people as a result of ideological clash of the Igbos and the white colonialist lords; this study seeks to bring to the fore, Ezeulu's trauma of holding on to Igbo traditions and culture despite an overpowering force of change as a result of colonialist condemnation of the ways of the Igbo people. It is this study's aim to reveal Ezeulu's application of trauma-memory as a means of not being scathed even though he had to submit to the overwhelming force of colonial invasion.

THE IGBO-WORLD PHILOSOPHY/VIEW

In the maiden Ahiajoku Lecture Series started in 1979, which was enacted to celebrate the Igbo people, Micheal Echeruo declared the Igbo people as a "headstrong" and "ambitious" people. He further stated that these two words better qualify the Igbo people's character and is the source of their strength and disaster they face. [9] Echeruo went on to cite Achebe's *Arrow of God* in which Ezeulu the Chief Priest exhibited such character in a handshake with some visitors as described thus: "he tensed his arm and put all his power to the grip, being unprepared for it, they winced and recoiled with pain."[10] This daring strength which Ezeulu exudes when he shakes his visitors can be said to be a behaviour which Echeruo proposes can be used to trace the cult of individual daring in past Igbo history such that the Igbo psyche can be understood as one which is stubborn but resolute and humane.

With valour comes the wish to have unlimited power and this need of a man to single-handedly wield much power is what led to the doom of Ezeulu as he (Ezeulu) refuses to declare the day of the New Yam festival. This drastic decision to avenge his (Ezeulu) public disgrace becomes the traumatic conflict that accelerates the acceptance of Christianity by a desperate people who were told by Jaja Goodcountry to bring not only one yam but as many as they could to the Christian god in order for them to be able to successfully harvest their yams.[11] Echeruo therefore insists that the Igbo identity should be re-established as a means for eradicating tyrannical maladies which emanates from the Igbo people being slaves to Igbo culture, the community and other people. This view to re-establish the Igbo identity may have encouraged Chikezie Uchendu in the 1995 Ahiajoku Lecture to explain the Igbo world view as a means of understanding the Igbo man, his ideology, his family structure or network and his deep connection to his community.

Uchendu summarises the Igbo worldview in seven propositions which he lists as: "first the Igbo world integrates the living and the dead as necessary communication channels where the world of man and the world of spirits are in a synchronic relationship.[12] The second is that the Igbo word demands a cosmological balance that must be sustained at all times, thirdly, the Igbo world is conceived in market terms, fourthly, status seeking in the Igbo society is cyclical and a never ending-quest, the fifth Igbo world view is that individuals must "live a transparent life." Living a secret life from *ezi na ulo/* and from kins and social groups can be deemed as sorcery, anti-society and disorder while the sixth Igbo world view is that an individual is held responsible for his wrong doings and because the society is spoilt by one man, then divination may be consulted to look into a man's reincarnate lives to avoid disasters. The seventh and final world view is that the Igbos live in a world of constant change and can easily adapt to it or simply exist the world by suicide if a person refuses to live a communal life.

Uchendu went on to explain that an Igbo man would rather commit suicide to gain freedom, liberty and human dignity in order to escape inhuman conditions such as slavery and in the process gain "family respect" for their descendants. And this view, largely comes to mind when an Igbo man decides to do something that he conceives to be utterly for the good of himself and his community. Again, in the same vein, Donatus Nwoga in the 1984 Ahiajoku Lecture, quotes James Horton, an Igbo receptive in Sierra Leone when he said, "The Igbo cannot be driven to an act but with kindness they could be made to do anything, even to deny themselves of their comforts. They would not as a rule, allow anyone to act the superior over them, nor sway their conscience"[13] An example of this instance can be read in Achebe's *Arrow of God* when Ezeulu refuses to declare a date for the new yam festival and dares anyone to challenge his decision.[14]

To establish a corporate identity is therefore paramount in sustaining the Igbo world view. Nwoga surmise that because of blood ties, the brotherliness of the Igbo people outside their homes may have encouraged outsiders to want to destroy their loyalty to their culture, home, and identity hence the trauma they encounter as they try to be indestructible is transmitted through family tie from generation to generation. From Olaudah Equiano's (an Igbo ex-slave) explicit narrative of the gruesome life of a slave as far back as 1789 to the Nigerian civil war against Biafra in 1969, the Igbo people's main concern therefore is to assert their uniqueness and identity. Echeruo stresses the fact that for centuries the Igbo people have been slaves to other cultures, and communities when the Igbos as a proud people are supposed to learn from history and resolve to be themselves. This view maybe what Achebe preaches in *Arrow of God* when he makes Ezeulu to traumatise greatly at colonial degradation of the customs of Umuaro through his son, Oduche who locked up the sacred python in a box in an attempt to kill it.[15]

THE METHODOLOGICAL APPROACHES

The methodological approach for this paper is based on interpreting and analysing Chinua Achebe's *Arrow of God*. This chapter applies psychoanalytical postulations of the trauma theory, beginning from Sigmund Freud down to recent postulators of the theory such as Cathy Caruth, Judith Herman,

Roger Luckhurst, and Michael Rothberg. Views on the trauma theory arising from such theorists as Cathy Caruth, Michelle Brown, Carl Lacan, Roger Luckhurst and others is incorporated into the analysis. The application of these varied concepts of the trauma theory will elicit an objective inquest into the psychological implications of trauma and the eventual effects of an individual's fall to trauma in a community that also suffers from trauma. The new and recent concept of trauma-memory is discussed as an enabling theory best suited for analysing Africans and Africans in diaspora's struggle with traumatic experiences. The postulation of the duo of Linda Mustafa and Joshua Usman is thus discussed and applied as a discourse that best resolves traumatic experiences of Africans even though their identities may be scathed as in the case of Ezeulu in the text of study. Finally, textual analysis of *Arrow of God* is juxtaposed with critical discussions of trauma as it affects the Igbo tradition and the eventual change that causes a tumultuous relocation of loyalty by the people of Umuaro.

THEORETICAL CONCEPTION OF TRAUMA AND TRAUMA-MEMORY

Michelle Brown opines that "trauma" refers to the experience of surviving a life-threatening incident, which creates the sense of having missed the event. The traumatic moment is a lapse between the life-threatening event, which occurs before the ego is prepared to handle such unexpected and disturbing stimuli, and its recognition of the injury. To be traumatized therefore, is to be doubly haunted by two realities: that of the violent event and that of not fully knowing that violence. "Trauma," then, is a psychic lapse between the traumatic event and the potential for knowledge.[16] Cathy Caruth characterizes this lapse as "the breach of the mind's experience of time, self, and the world."[17] But Jacques Derrida conceptualizes it differently, in terms of the temporal or as an existence in time that is "out of joint."[18] An inquest into Fanon Franz's discussion of Lacan's concept of trauma, reveals that the black man learns [is traumatized] to see himself in terms that differentiate *him* from *whiteness*. Fanon agrees with this statement when he surmise that the colonized Antillean's ideal sense of self is framed in terms of having "no color" prior to encountering his blackness when he meets a white person and begins to idealize whiteness.[19]

This brings us to the problematic debate of using psychoanalytic theory to analyse a book by an African. Not unlike other Western knowledge systems, although most often masquerading as dispassionate "science," psychoanalysis itself is merely another discourse that has been shaped by the specific cultural and historical contexts within which it is produced and which, in turn, helps to shape culture and history.²⁰ Psychoanalysis has therefore been criticized as "ethnocentric" by those who question the "usefulness of applying a method developed in one culture to the study of another."²¹ Again, Roger Luckhurst's *The Trauma Question*, published in 2008, presented an overview of the theory's inherent inconsistencies and contradictions, concluding that it had serious limitations for literary studies. Luckhurst went on to explain that for a theory (in this case the trauma theory) to be positively viable it must:

> [a concept] succeeds through its heterogeneity rather than its purity . . . a successful statement can be measured by how many links or associations it makes, not only within the rigours of its own discipline but far beyond it, too, as it loops through different knowledges, institutions, practices, social, political and cultural forums.²²

Because of the issue of psychoanalysis being an ethnocentric epistemology, and that it cannot fully meet the psychological needs of Africans and Africans in the diaspora, the duo of Mustafa and Usman in their article titled "Trauma, Rememory and Trauma-Memory: The African Experience" opine that with the combination of Freud's postulation of the trauma theory and Morrison's rememory, Africans are best situated to overcome trauma in order to adequately trace their sufferings without necessarily being overwhelmed by past trauma.²³ They went on to indicate that Trauma-memory ensures that the black race can "reconstruct painful pasts without instigating a psychological breakdown."²⁴ This line of thought is in line with Uzoma Esonwanne when in her reading of *Nervous Conditions,* she argues that investigating psychoanalysis and African literature concurrently can help us identify heretofore unexplored desires represented in the literature that precipitate and address the colonized individual's repressed identity, a nervous condition that Simon Gikandi calls "Crises of the Soul."²⁵

Michael Rothberg argues that one way in which trauma narratives detail a past denied or repressed is through what he calls traumatic realism which he explains to exhibit the following:

> is marked by the survival of extremity into everyday world and is dedicated to mapping the complex temporal and spatial patterns by which the absence of the real, a real absence, makes itself felt in the familiar plenitude of reality.²⁶

Such a form of realism strives to represent accurately the unknowable traumatic past while also maintaining an awareness of the ideological constructions of realism. As such, Rothberg claims, "traumatic realism is an attempt not to reflect the traumatic event mimetically but to produce it as an object of knowledge and to transform its readers so that they are forced to acknowledge their relationship to posttraumatic culture."[27]

Rothberg's claims of remembering past trauma as a means to being in touch with reality fits the claims of Mustafa and Usman when in their findings they surmise that when Africans indulge in trauma-memory, they "create an alternate sense of reality for those who remember their tragic past."[28] They equally state that one of the features of trauma-memory is the fact that the theory allows sufferers of trauma the allowance to be able to identify past events that are threatening as well as enabling Africans to be empowered such that in their pains, they can reconstruct subjective histories told by the oppressive white colonialist. [29]

Furthermore, Mustafa and Usman insist that Freud's trauma theory may not be suitable for Africans because it "elicits pain and a conscious will to re-enact the traumatic incidence over and over again without a possible healing." But when trauma theory is fused with rememory Mustafa and Usman believe that:

> [with] the combination of trauma and rememory as a means of overcoming past pains, the sufferer is empowered to trace lapses of the past without getting consumed by locating troubled memories; he/she is also equally protected from other possible psychological manipulations.[30]

The fact that the black race suffered slavery, colonialism, and neo-colonialism perpetrated on them by whites, makes Freud's position on traumatic memories inadequate for Africans to locate past traumas in order to be healed. Hence with the study of the corporeality of the uncanny side by side with rememory, there could be a total trace of mnemic symbol which gives voice to the indelible real.[31]

In conclusion, the use of trauma-memory to analyse traumatized characters in African literature, enables a more objective inquest into the psyche of Africans during and after their traumatic encounter. Since trauma according to Erikson emanates from both "*a constellation of life experiences*" and "a discrete happening," from "a *persisting condition*" and "an acute event,"[32] then trauma-memory invigorates a remembrance of the past such that traumatized Africans can reconstruct their histories without a psychological breakdown. With trauma-memory therefore Africans are empowered to adopt defence mechanisms that ensures healing from past traumatic events.

REMEMORIZING IGBO TRADITIONS AND THE COLONIALIST'S FORCE OF CHANGE IN *ARROW OF GOD*

As earlier stated, the Igbo world view integrates the individual with the community, in a way which locates an individual to be bounded by a ritualistic urgency to seek the greater good for his community. With his immense power as the Chief Priest, Ezeulu searches his subconscious to locate his identity as a Chief Priest who is assigned to intercede on behalf of his people and as he rememorizes his supernatural responsibilities to the community, he sees that he is bounded by the Igbo world view to serve his people with humility: "His power was no more than the power of a child over a goat that was said to be his."[33] But the trauma Ezeulu goes through when he is locked up by Winterbottom changes him into a bitter man who divorces himself from the world of spirits, and with his human reasoning, he refuses to name the day for the new yam festival and dares anyone in Umuaro to challenge his stance.[34] However, as Ezeulu rememorizes his dilemma, he does not become depressed, instead, his ego is challenged by the knowledge that he wields more power than an average man of Umuaro.

Achebe's knowledge of the symbolic interactions between man and spirits/ancestors takes precedence in his works. Again and again, Achebe directs readers' attention to the fact that the Igbo identity is embedded in a strict religious code that demands absolute loyalty and dedication to the gods of the land. However, the incredible rapid spread of Christianity among the Igbo people disrupts the communion with the gods of the land hence the outbreak of war between the people of Umuaro and Okperi is inevitable. The people of Umuaro, proud and unwilling to find out and accept the wishes of the gods, decide that war is the only way to put an end to the land disputes between them and as missionaries enter inwards into Igbo communities choosing to stay in communities that accommodates them, they provoke hostilities among Igbo communities by uprooting Igbo customs and replacing them with their own laws, thus creating flourishing trade for those who accept Christianity, while they disband old commercial centres, establishing schools only in communities that accept the colonialist's religion.

The new way of life that does not respect the established Igbo customs causes great pains to the people of the East and Ezeulu who is the Chief priest of Ulu is especially traumatized. Ezeulu, being overwhelmed by the religion, power, wisdom, and ways of the white man, remembers the prophesy of the oracles and instead of being weary of the white man's encroachment, he sends his son, Oduche. But Echeruo summit that an Igbo man is stubborn but humane. This characteristic of stubbornness, manifests in Ezeulu's resolve to send his son to join the white man's religion against the disapproval of his people. Unknown to his community, the Igbo worldview of status seeking and being a cyclical thing, is the catalyst that spurs Ezeulu to seek knowledge of the white man's religion as a means of holding on to the chieftaincy of his land if eventually all his traditional powers are stripped off.

Ezeulu's uncertainty at ensuring that the highest status of the land is not bequeathed to someone outside his bloodline, pitches him against his people. Although traumatized, Ezeulu rememorizes his fears and creates an alternate reality of a life influenced by the white man's ways as he prepares for priestly duties through his son, Oduche. Contrary to other people's opinion and allegation of his alliance with Winterbottom, Ezeulu searches his inner conscience to locate his trauma of slowly losing his grip of the authenticity of Ulu. Because he engages his subconscious to locate his stance within the world of the spirits and that of the physical, he becomes aware of a disconnect between his linage and the Ulu god hence his disappointment of having sent his son, Oduche to learn the white man's way. Ezeulu explains his traumatic recognition of the white man's way of worshiping his god here: "the new religion was like a leper."[35]

Even his rejection of the offer of installing him [Ezeulu] as a warrant officer, is actually from a deeper inquest by Ezeulu to "trace his lapses" of having sacrificed his son to the white man's religion. In his pain of having no upper hand over the infiltration of white colonialists in the affairs of his people, Ezeulu rejects the offer of a warrant chieftaincy to the utter amazement of both the white colonial administrators and the people of Umuaro.[36] Ezeulu's rejection, situates him closer to his people and customs because he assumes an identity or personality that is not scathe by his anxiety at losing his authority to white colonialist lords. Instead, Ezeulu creates an identity that sets him apart from the rest of the people. To Ezeulu, the ability to overcome being deeply worried by alien infiltration of his customs and authority as the Chief Priest of Ulu is based on the fact that the Igbo world is always changing and his defiance to go along with the new way of life may be fatal to his descendants' worship of Ulu and to avoid this, he has to be strong physically and psychologically to pave new ways for his children to be able to continue the worship of the Ulu god.

According to the principles of Trauma-memory, one is invigorated by the trauma of the past to recreate history and as such avoid psychological implications. This is what Ezeulu engages in as he creates an identity which he unconsciously applies to distort his trauma of being drawn into the new ways of the white man. In the guardroom, Ezeulu rememorizes how he had warned his people against claiming lands that was not theirs:

> For years he had been warning Umuaro not to allow a few jealous men lead them into the bush. But they had stopped both ears with fingers. They had gone on taking one dangerous step after another and now they have gone too far. They had taken away too much for the owner to notice ... Let the white man detain him not for one day but one year so that his deity not seeing him in his place would ask Umuaro questions.[37]

In this state of self-pity, even though he is traumatised, Ezeulu gets ready for a fight with the people of Umuaro because of their disobedience to him as a Chief Priest and also to the Ulu god. According to the Igbo world view there must be a cosmological balance between the land of the living and that of the dead. In Ezeulu's incarceration, this relationship is cut off and normal communication with the Ulu god ceases. Ezeulu's absence from the presence of Ulu is drastic and dire with unforeseen consequences and as the new moon is welcomed by all, Ezeulu is incapable of doing the same and he is greatly troubled, as indicated in the following:

> The first time Ezeulu heard the children's voices his heart flew out. Although he had expected it, when it did come he was not ready. His mind had momentarily forgotten. But he recovered almost at once. Yes, his deity must now be asking: 'Where is he?' and soon Umuaro will have to explain.[38]

For having allowed the removal of the Chief Priest from his duties, the people of Umuaro must be held responsible especially since the Igbo ontology of "all for one/one for many" is embedded in the consciousness of every Igbo man and equally highlighted in *Arrow of God*. His stance therefore of having to avenge the wrong done to the Ulu god projects him more as a person who is endowed by the spirits to confront ordinary men who refuse to hold on to their identity and responsibility. His biological nature therefore predisposes him to be constricted by his fragility of being filled with the secret love and desire for revenge and also being spiritually strong to appease the gods through punishing the people of Umuaro, hence he is shaped by the need to institute cosmological balance without being engulfed by his fears of the wrath of Ulu. His rejection of the white man's chieftaincy title situates him as an authority that can deny the white man's power and hold over the Igbo people. In this way, Ezeulu becomes the first headstrong Igbo man who dares the white man and at the same time creates a new history of being the first to be a man with an irrevocable Igbo identity of being a dignify Igbo man.

According to Fanon, the Black man is traumatized when he is confronted with whiteness. This is the case with John Nwodika, Ezeulu, and even all the Igbos in close proximity with the white men in their midst. For instance, John Nwodika is scorned for being the white man's cook (a job considered to be a woman's). He sees himself being demeaned in relation to "whiteness," so he gives his reason why he does the demeaning job for the white man:

> I know that some people at home have been spreading the story that I cook for the white man. Your brother does not see even the smoke from his fire; I just put things in order in his house. You know the white man is not like us; if he puts this plate here he will be angry if you have it there. So I go round every day and see that everything is in its right place. But I can tell you that I do not aim to die a servant.[39]

From his statement, Nwodika's son is frustrated about his supposedly demeaning job but because he rememorizes his trauma, he is able to overcome his shame and looks towards a positive future where he will be a tobacco trader as soon as he collects enough money to start up his business. This shows that John does not deny his trauma of "having no color" yet he does get healed from this psychological situation by consciously locating his identity over all other identities that is assumed on him by others (i.e., both the white man's perception of him as a mere native help and his people's conception of him being less than a man).

Again, Ezeulu feels insulted by Clarke's intention to make him a Chief of the British administration. To him there can be no job so insulting like doing duties for the white man when he is actually more than that. His trauma transcends from his identity as a supernatural being, who cannot be a slave to the white man. Ezeulu therefore is repressed by the white man's earthly favour of institutionalising a human puppet with no power, when all along he is a god being in a cyclical circle of unimaginable supernatural powers. His outbursts, "Tell the white man that Ezeulu will not be anybody's chief, except Ulu,"[40] confirms is sense of trauma in relation to having no color. But he faces his trauma by being self-confident, bold, and determined to hold on to his beliefs, custom and the Igbo traditions as observed in his determined stance: "Ezeulu himself was full of satisfaction at the way things had gone. He had settled his little score with the white man and could forget him for the moment."[41] This victory according to trauma-memory is the situation where an African has power and is empowered to reconstruct his subjectiveness.[42] Ezeulu did not just refused the powerful white man by being merely an antagonist to colonial encroachment, he exercised his rememory of subjective effects of the white word and used it as his launching pad to break away from a looming threat of the trauma of losing his past, identity and history.

From the Igbo worldview, Ezeulu's trauma goes beyond his fight with the white man while he was incarcerated. According to trauma-memory, there is a participation of the public in private traumatic experience.[43] This is also obtainable in Igbo societies hence the entire populace of Umuaro see Ezeulu's betrayal of his people during the land dispute between Okperi and Umuaro as an act that takes the chief priest from his *ezi na ulo* or his kith and kins. In acting against the general position of his people, Ezeulu is considered a traitor and a "sorcerer" who according to the Igbo philosophy must be ostracised. And by the time he refuses to declare the new yam festival, Ezeulu and his entire family members suffer public rebuttals: "Almost overnight Ezeulu had become something of a public enemy in the eyes of all and, as was to be expected, his entire family shared in his guilt."[44] Yet, the trauma Ezeulu and his family go through for holding the community to ransom, cements his resolve to continue the fight between him and his community insisting that "the punishment was not for now alone but for all time. It would afflict Umuaro like an *angulu-aro* disease."[45] The collected memories of his sojourn in the white man's den should not be his alone, but that of him and the community. His action of seeking redress from communal humiliation enables him to start the process of healing rather than rememorizing his hurt alone and then being psychologically knocked down.

But Ezeulu meets a tragic end for not eating the yam at the right time. Does this mean that his revenge to make everyone suffer his abandonment by his people at the hands of the white man finally led to his downfall and psychological breakdown when he his confronted with the death of his son Obika? To this study the answer is no. Ezeulu dementia is as a result of his discontinued reliance on rememorizing his past and present such that he remains unscathed. With the knowledge of the Igbo philosophy of life, Ezeulu's consciousness recedes back to a view of the world as a marketplace (uwa bu ahia). This Igbo worldview posits that problems are negotiable. By haggling with spirits or ancestral bodies in a marketplace where both the living and the dead do business, a troubled person can demand a better life in his reincarnation.[46] During the battle between Ezeulu and the people of Umuaro, Ezeulu dreams of impending doom but he does nothing, meaning he does not bargain with his ancestors to prevent a calamity that may affect him greatly as can be deciphered in the following:

> That night Ezeulu saw in a dream a big assembly of Umuaro elders, the same people he had spoken a few days earlier. But instead of himself it was his grandfather who rose up to speak to them. They refused to listen. They shouted together: He shall not speak; we will not listen to him . . . Then the people seized the Chief Priest who had changed from Ezeulu's grandfather to himself and began to push him from one group to another. Some spat on his face and called him the priest of a dead god.[47]

Because Ezeulu did not bargain with his dead grandfather, he becomes predispose to being possessed by evil spirits. The cyclic interaction, therefore, between the dead, the gods and the physical man is not completed because of Ezeulu's reluctance to bargain his way out of trouble. Eventually, he ends up losing the protection of the Ulu god as well as losing his mind.

Ezeulu's "marketplace" is short circuited because he imbibes a conscience of not being prepared to experience and overcome trauma.[48] Angry, bitter, and vengeful, Ezeulu decides to frustrate the people of Umauro by not declaring a date for the new yam festival. Even though he knows that as a supernatural being and a true Igbo man he is supposed to make decisions for the good of his people, Ezeulu however discards reason for pride and went on to delay harvest and the yam festival such that the whole community undergo a period of hunger, and uncertainty. Despite being begged by the elders of Umauro to plead to Ulu on behalf of his people, Ezeulu is adamant and does not agree with Nnanyelugo who cautions that change should be uppermost in Ezeulu's mind,[49] Ezeulu has already made up his mind to hold to ransom, the collective memories of his people as a means of building his own myth of resistance and in the process he overrides one of the Igbo worldview which states that change is an adaptation which every Igbo man must be ready to do.

Ezeulu is frustrated not because he held on to Ulu, but because he used the Ulu god for a personal vendetta, the death of his son and his final dementia distorts his consciousness to the extent that he has no relationship with his community. Hence, he suffers his trauma alone as a result of rememorizing his self and community in the reality instead of an alternate reality as trauma-memory encourages. Therefore, when Ezeulu in his trauma asked himself the reasons why he is abandoned by Ulu and what was his offence[50] he detaches himself for a possible denial and dismemory of his trauma which would have helped him absorbed the shock of losing Obika.

CONCLUSION

It is apt to say that Ezeulu's refusal to go with the era of change is what made him fall victim to a tragic end, but this paper sees Ezeulu as a winner despite losing his cognitive reasoning when he learns of the death of his son, Obika. First, Ezeulu is the first Igbo man to refuse the white man's offer of making him a chief in the colonialist government, an offer many would have accepted. Instead of betraying his clan's men by accepting a subjugating and oppressing colonialist government that would eventually invade his entire village, Ezeulu boldly rejects being reduced to a mare man when he is actually a supernatural being who is empowered by his ancestors and the spirits of the land-a virtue more powerful than the white man's arsenal. Secondly, in his ego to deal with the whole village for seeing him as a betrayal, Ezeulu holds the public responsible for his disgraceful incarceration and in the process both the public and private trauma he experiences during this time shaped his past and his present such that he is able to create a new history that is not subjugated by the white man's oppressive ideals. Thirdly, Ezeulu's apprehension of a fatal end at the hands of white colonialist rulers if his people do not embrace the white man, projected him more as the only person who understood change. He had fully prepared for change by sending Oduche to the Christian faith to be his "ears and eyes" but this is done as a form of espionage and in time when the situation is right, Ezeulu would use the knowledge of the white man's god to constitute a rebellion and uproot the offending oppressive colonialist and his religion.

Again, it is interesting that this study observes that the psychological breakdown of Ezeulu is synonymous with the slow eradication of a communal hold to Igbo tradition, customs, and beliefs. This can be seen in the anxiousness of the elders who in their quest to see that the new yam festival is carried out, they decide to do whatsoever is required for them to usher in the yam festival. The elders of the land lost their faith, trust, and confidence in the Ulu god when Ezeulu and Ulu refuses to conform to their wishes. Because the Igbo man is open to change, many therefore looked for a god that is willing to receive not just one tuber of yam but as much as they could bring without delay. So instead of waiting patiently for the Ulu god to resolve the battle between the people of Ulu and Ezeulu's ego, the people become fixated on this problem as Freud's concept of trauma posits and instead of disremembering their trauma in order to achieve healing from communal disunity, they desecrated the land by buying and eating foreign yams bought from neighboring towns hence the stage is set for a tragic end of the proliferation of Igbo customs and tradition.

NOTES

1. Charles Nnolim, "Technique and meaning in Achebe's *Arrow of God*: Approaches to the African novel* (Lagos: Malthouse, 2010): 159.
2. Blaise N. Machila, "Ambiguity in Achebe's *Arrow of God*," *Kunapipi*, 3 (1) (1981), Accessed on November 19, 2019. http://ro.uow.edu.au/kunappipi/vol3/issl/14
3. See G. D. Killam, *The Writings of Chinua Achebe* (London: Heinemann Education Press, 1987).
4. David Caroll, *Chinua Achebe: Novelist, Poet, Critic* (London: Palmgrave Macmillan, 1980, 1990): 87.
5. Gikandi explains here the encroachment of colonialist ideology as the deciding factor between Nwaka's rhetorical praises of Idemili over Ezeulu's conservative submission to Ulu and at the same time Ezeulu's reluctance to fight against Christianity. Simon Gikandi, *Reading the African Novel* (London: Heinemann Educational Books, 1987).

6. Urama Evelyn Nwachukwu, "Psychoanalytical Theory and Contending Personalities and Forces in Achebe's *Arrow of God*," *IDOSR Journal of Humanities and Social Sciences* 3(1) (2018): 86–101.

7. Nwoga, Donatus I. *Literature and Modern West African Culture*. (Benin City: Ethiope Publishing Corporation, 1978): 27.

8. Ngozi Dora Ulogu, "Anxiety and Repression: A Psychoanalytical Study of Ezeulu," *Okike: An African Journal of New Writing*, No. 52 (2014): 294.

9. Micheal Eheruo, "Ahamefula: A Matter of Identity." *Ahiajoku Lecture Series*, (1979). ahiajoku.igbonet.com/1979/ (Accessed 25 April 2020).

10. Chinua Achebe, *Arrow of God* (Ibadan: Heinemann Ltd, 1970).

11. Ibid., 216.

12. Chikezie Uchendu, "Ezi Na Ulo: The Extended Family in Igbo Civilization." *Ahiajoku Lecture Series*, (1995)ahiajoku.igbonet.com/1995/ (Accessed 25 April 2020).

13. Donatus Nwoga. "Nka Na Nzere: The Focus of Igbo Worldview" *Ahiajoku Lecture Series*, (1984). ahiajoku.igbonet.com/1984/ (Accessed 25 April 2020).

14. Achebe, *Arrow of God*, 205.

15. Ibid., 44.

16. See Michelle Lynn Brown, "Screams Somehow Echoing: Trauma and Testimony in Anglophone Literature," unpublished thesis. (2008): 2–19.

17. Cathy Caruth, *Unclaimed Experience: Trauma, Narrative and History*, (Baltimore: Johns Hopkins University Press, 1996), 4.

18. Jacques Derrida, *Specters of Marx: The State of the Debt, the Work of Mourning, and the New International*, trans. Peggy Kamuf (London: Routledge, 1994), 18.

19. Fanon discusses Lacan's theory of the mirror stage in *Black Skin, White Masks*. Frantz Fanon, *Black Skin, White Masks*, trans. Charles Lam Markmann (New York: Grove, 1967). Lacan, Jacques. *Ecrits: The First Complete Edition in English*, trans. Bruce Fink, Héloïse Fink, and Russell Grigg (New York: Norton, 1996).

20. See Sigmund, Freud, *The Standard Edition of the Complete Works of Sigmund Freud.* (London: Hogarth, 1961)

21. Cornell Drucilla, *Transformations: Recollective Imagination and Sexual Dzference.* (New York: Routledge, 1993): 170.

22. Roger Luckhurst, *The Trauma Question.* (London: Routledge, 2008): 14

23. Mustafa and Usman explain that Freud's trauma theory does not suggest a solution to ending the pains of trauma, rather, it encourages a re-enacting of traumatic events without a possible healing. Hence for Africans, a combination of Morrison's rememory which encourages an inquest into the past in order to locate a traumatic history for possible realigning with the present, ensures healing and at the same time initiates a proper build-up of the scathed psyche of a trauma victim. See Mustafa, L. J., and Usman J. "Trauma, Rememory and Trauma-Memory: The African Experience," *FUDMA Journal of Arts* Vol. 3, No. 1 (2019): 147–158.

24. Linda Mustafa and Joshua Usman, "Trauma, Rememory and Trauma-Memory: The African Experience." *FUDMA Journal of Arts Vol.3, No.1* (2019): 155.

25. Uzoma Esonwanne, "The 'Crisis of the Soul': Psychoanalysis and African Literature," *Research in African Literatures* 38.2 (2007): 140–42. Simon Gikandi,

"Chinua Achebe and the Invention of African Literature," *Things Fall Apart*, by Chinua Achebe (Oxford: Heinemann, 1996) ix–xvii.

26. Michael Rothberg, *Traumatic Realism: The Demands of Holocaust Representation*. (Minneapolis: U of Minnesota Press, 2000), 140.

27. Michael Rothberg. *Traumatic Realism: The Demands of Holocaust Representation*. (Minneapolis: U of Minnesota Press, 2000): 140.

28. L. J. Mustafa and J. Usman "Trauma, Rememory and Trauma-Memory: The African Experience." *FUDMA Journal of Arts Vol. 3, No. 1* (2019): 156.

29. In merging trauma and rememory to make up an enabling theory for proper psychological analysis of Africans, Africans in diaspora and their works/histories, eighteen viable features of trauma-memory was observed as reasons why the theory best suits the African traumatic experience of slavery, colonialism and neo-colonialism.

30. According to Morrison's rememory, trauma victims do not suffer alone but Freud's trauma theory sees the individual as the sole recipient of traumatic experience hence he or she will have to heal by himself or herself but Morrison opine that the public and community also shares in individual trauma. See also Mustafa and Usman,156.

31. See Freud and Breuer's discussion on Hysteria. (1957).

32. Kai Erikson "Notes on Trauma and Community," in *Explorations in Memory*, ed. Cathy Caruth (Baltimore and London: The John Hopkins University Press 1995): 185.

33. Achebe, *Arrow of God*, 3.

34. Ibid.

35. Ibid., 42.

36. Ibid., 175.

37. Ibid., 174.

38. Ibid., 163.

39. Ibid., 170.

40. Ibid., 175

41. Ibid., 175.

42. See "Trauma, Rememory and Trauma-Memory: The African Experience," *FUDMA Journal of Arts* Vol. 3, No. 1 (2019): 156.

43. Mustafa and Usman, "Trauma, Rememory," 29

44. Achebe, *Arrow of God*, 211.

45. Achebe, *Arrow of God*, 219.

46. Biko Agozino and Ike Anyanike "Imu Ahia: Traditional Igbo Business School and Global Commerce Culture" *Dialectical Anthropology 31*, no. 1/3 (2007): 235–52. http://www.jstor.org/stable/29790780 (Accessed 28 February 2020).

47. Achebe, *Arrow of God*, 159.

48. See L. J. Mustafa and J. Usman "Trauma, Rememory and Trauma-Memory: The African Experience." *FUDMA Journal of Arts Vol. 3, No. 1* (2019): 157

49. Achebe, *Arrow of God*, 209.

50. Achebe, *Arrow of God*, 229.

BIBLIOGRAPHY

Achebe, Chinua. *Arrow of God.* London: Heinemann, 1964.
Agozino, Biko, and Ike, Anyanire. "Imu Ahia: Traditional Igbo Business School and Global Commerce Culture." *Dialectical Anthropology 31*, no. 1/3 (2007): 235–52. http://www.jstor.org/stable/29790780.
Breuer, Josef, and Sigmund, Freud. *Studies On Hysteria (1893–1895).* In James Stracey. Edited and Translated. New York: Basic Books, 1957.
Brown, Michelle Lynn. "Screams Somehow Echoing: Trauma and Testimony in Anglophone Literature" (PhD diss., University of Maryland, 2008), 2–19.
Caruth, Cathy. *Unclaimed Experience: Trauma, Narrative and History.* Baltimore: Johns Hopkins University Press, 1996, 4.
Derrida, Jacques. *Specters of Marx: The State of the Debt, the Work of Mourning, and the New International*, trans. Peggy Kamuf. London: Routledge, 1994, 18.
Drucilla, Cornell. *Transformations: Recollective Imagination and Sexual Dzference.* New York: Routledge, 1993,170.
Eheruo, Michael. "Ahamefula: A Matter of Identity." *Ahiajoku Lecture Series*, (1979) ahiajoku.igbonet.com/1979/ (Accessed April 25, 2020).
Esonwane, Uzoma. "The 'Crisis of the Soul': Psychoanalysis and African Literature," *Research in African Literatures* 38.2, 2007, 140–42.
Frantz, Fanon. *Black Skin, White Masks*, trans. Charles Lam Markmann. New York: Grove, 1967, 196.
Gikandi, Simon. "Chinua Achebe and the Invention of African Literature," *Things Fall Apart*, by Chinua Achebe. Oxford: Heinemann, 1996, ix–xvii.
———. "Chinua Achebe and the Post-colonial Esthetics: Writing, Identity, and National Formation." *Studies in 20th Century Literature*. Vol. 15: Iss. 1, Article 4. 1991, https://doi.org/10.4148/2334-4415.1263
———. *Reading the African Novel.* London: Heinemann Educational Books, 1987.
Jacques, Lacan. *Ecrits: The First Complete Edition in English*, trans. Bruce Fink, Héloïse Fink, and Russell Grigg. New York: Norton, 1996.
Kai, Erikson. "Notes on Trauma and Community," in *Explorations in Memory*, edited by Cathy Caruth. Baltimore: John Hopkins University Press, 1995.
Killam, G. D. *The Writings of Chinua Achebe.* London: Heinemann Education Press, 1987.
Luckhurst, Roger. *The Trauma Question.* London: Routledge, 2008,14.
Machila Blaise. "Ambiguity in Achebe's Arrow *of God*," *Kunapipi*, 3, No.1(1981), http://ro.uow.edu.au/kunappipi/vol3/issl/14 (Accessed on November 19, 2019).
Mustafa, Linda J, and Usman Joshua. "Trauma, Rememory and Trauma-Memory: The African Experience." *FUDMA Journal of Arts* Vol. 3, No. 1, 2019, 147–158.
Nnolim, Charles. "Technique and meaning in Achebe's *Arrow of God*," in *Approaches to the African novel*. Lagos: Malthouse, 2010.
Nwoga, Donatus. "Nka Na Nzere: The Focus of Igbo Worldview" *Ahiajoku Lecture Series,* (1984). ahiajoku.igbonet.com/1984/ (Accessed April 25, 2020)
Nwoga, Donatus I. *Literature and Modern West African Culture.* (Benin City: Ethiope Publishing Corporation, 1978.

Rothberg, Michael. *Traumatic Realism: The Demands of Holocaust Representation.* Minneapolis: University of Minnesota Press, 2000.

Sigmund, Freud, *The Standard Edition of the Complete Works of Sigmund Freud.* London: Hogarth, 1961.

Uchendu, Chikezie. "Ezi Na Ulo: The Extended Family in Igbo Civilization." *Ahiajoku Lecture Series*, (1995) ahiajoku.igbonet.com/1995/ (Accessed April 25, 2020).

Ulogu, Ngozi Dora. "Anxiety and Repression: A Psychoanalytical Study of Ezeulu." *Okike: An African Journal of New Writing*, No. 52 (2014), 294.

Urama, Nwachukwu Evelyn. "Psychoanalytical Theory and Contending Personalities and Forces in Achebe's *Arrow of God.*" *IDOSR Journal of Humanities and Social Sciences* 3(1), 2018, 86–101.

PART III

Achebe, History, and the National Question

Chapter 11

Telling Africa's Story
Chinua Achebe and the Power of Narratives

Chijioke Azuawusiefe

> *Until Lions learn to write their own history, the tale of the hunt will always glorify the hunter.*[1]

The Igbo have a myth in which humans sent Dog to Chukwu, the Big God, to request that the dead be permitted to return to life. The dog dawdled on the way, but Toad, who had eavesdropped on the message, reached Chukwu first. Wanting to punish humans, Toad reversed the message and informed Chukwu instead that humans did not wish to return to life after death. Novelist and acclaimed father of modern African literature Chinua Achebe draws a fundamental message from this myth: One cannot rely on someone else to tell one's story, otherwise the story could be garbled and misrepresented.[2] This essay's opening proverb above encapsulates that inherent wisdom. Throughout the six decades of Achebe's writing career which produced an impressive oeuvre, among them five novels and numerous critical essays,[3] Achebe strove to reclaim and assert Africa's agency to (re)construct its history and take charge of its own narratives.[4] His first novel, *Things Fall Apart*,[5] for instance, does not only tell the African story from the inside, it also challenges the arrogance of the West which arrogated to itself the right to speak for Africa and by so doing denied its history.[6] The power, then, to tell Africa's story informs the power to assert Africa's culture and identity in the face of their many denials by the Other.

This paper explores Achebe's commitment to constructing Africa-centered narratives that deploy Africa's own voices and stories. It demonstrates how Achebe's pursuit bears out the power of narratives to create histories and ideologies. The paper argues that Achebe's use of storytelling as a mechanism for reconstructing African narratives and thereby affirming Africa's histories, cultures, and identities derives from an understanding which locates the power to control discourse in a group's capability to create acceptable "truth" and "knowledge." Rooting Achebe within Edward Said's and Stuart Hall's contestations of representation as a constructed reality, the paper first positions Achebe as a storyteller and, afterwards, presents a critique of Achebe's approach to re-centering Africa's narrative through stories as well as looks at storytelling in Africa beyond Achebe. For its purposes, the essay uses "storyteller" to refer to African scholars and writers.

WHY NARRATIVES? ACHEBE AND THE CONSTRUCTION OF MEANING

The opening epigraph of this essay speaks to the importance of narrative to the construction of history and ideology as well as of the power of discourse in generating knowledge. In articulating the importance of taking charge of one's narrative, it captures the Orwellian mindset: "who controls the past controls the future; who controls the present controls the past."[7] Edward Said's[8] brilliant critique of essentialism bears out the veracity of that statement when Said argues that within cultures, representation, not truth, is what gets circulated and exchanged. Focusing on how the Orient is "translated into activity,"[9] Said points out the strategic role of narrative for countering the essentialist view of the "Other" embedded in representations. Thus, narration, as a key strategy for representation, counters the "official" view of the colonized as ahistorical and primitive. It becomes an "indispensable agent of history" in the hands of anti and post-colonial storytellers for returning history to their people.[10] This understanding underlines Achebe's approach to storytelling, for according to him, it is the storyteller that saves the day. The storyteller not only constructs a people by creating their history, he or she also creates the memory that sustains the survivors and gives purpose to their surviving.[11]

Representation then becomes an exchange between language and the act of meaning making. Stuart Hall points out that representation "connects meaning and language to culture."[12] Meanings float, so a representational practice is an act of fixing floating meanings by privileging preferred meanings.[13] In other words, context gives meaning to texts; "they do not carry meaning or 'signify' on their own."[14] Michel Foucault articulates this process of meaning-construction as discourse, and attributes to it knowledge and power.[15] In every society, Foucault argues, "the production of discourse is at once controlled, selected, organized and redistributed according to a certain number of procedures."[16] There are multiple explanations to every reality in the world; but few of them predominate. Whichever explanation that emerges victorious in the end, often with institutional and political support, becomes "knowledge," and therefore the dominant and controlling "truth." Achebe understood the power of agents within cultures to construct basic discourses of representation through narratives. His understanding informed his rejection of the ideological realities constructed for Africa in history, realities that must be countered with alternative pro-African narratives, he insisted.

ACHEBE, THE STORYTELLER, AND THE IMPORTANCE OF NARRATIVES

When Europe encountered the West-constructed Africa of "mute ancestral spirits,"[17] through such writings of early Greek historians like Herodotus (484–425 BCE), philosophers like David Hume, Immanuel Kant, and Georg Hegel as well as later colonial explorers, it proceeded to negate and deny Africa's humanity and history through a series of historical and epistemic violence.[18] Africa has since offered multiple epistemological responses, like Negritude, pan-Africanism, cultural nationalism, decolonization, post-colonialism, and so on, as ways of countering those denials. Achebe's disappointment with the absurd representations of Africa and Africans particularly in Joyce Cary's *Mister Johnson* and Joseph Conrad's *Heart of Darkness*, for instance, filled him, as a student in colonial Nigeria, with "the desire to initiate a discourse of resistance and to re-present Africans [in ways] other than they have been presented in colonialist discourse."[19] Hence, the young Achebe reasoned that if outsiders with no inside knowledge of Africa could get away with their ignorant descriptions of Africa and Africans, he was perhaps obligated to offer a more informed narrative.[20]

Thus he set out to tell his stories so as to let his African readers know that "their past was not one long night of savagery from which the first European acting on God's behalf delivered them."[21] Africa was not Conrad's heart of darkness wherein Africans lived a primitive, language-less existence. Hence, Achebe insisted on the value of narrative to humanize a people. He remained emphatic in demanding that one has to, as a necessity, accept Africans as people rather than as oddities that require curious attention.[22] But over and above that, one has to listen to them and to their preferences. One should, in the least, be respectful enough to listen to Africans tell their human stories. In *Things Fall Apart,* for instance, a work that has come to represent the most authoritative voice in the representations of pre-colonial Igbo society, Achebe invites the reader to listen from the outset by contextualizing the protagonist within the ozo chieftaincy title-taking among the Igbo as well as the consequent demand for industry and reward for hard work that the title occasions.

The novel opens with the narrator declaring: "Okonkwo was well known throughout the nine villages and even beyond. His fame rested on solid personal achievements."[23] The reader immediately situates the character within a specific context of diligence, accomplishment, and communal as well as regional renown. Achebe tells the reader that Okonkwo dreaded being like his father, Unoka. He was actually ashamed of him, so he worked very hard not to be like his father, who had died in poverty due to his own inability to work his farm like "a man" should in his society. Unoka did not only die in debt, he also died without taking any title. It is worth noting, even if briefly, the patriarchal biases present in those opening lines. Unoka is called a woman who does not farm like a man—a statement indicative of the second place position of women in the culture, even though storytellers and scholars like Flora Nwapa, Ifi Amadiume, Obioma Nnaemeka, and Akachi Ezeigbo have contested such representations of women in traditional Igbo society.[24] Nevertheless, Okonkwo will later bemoan the fact that Ezinne his daughter and favorite child was not born a boy.

Understanding women then as weak and inferior to men, Okonkwo was not in the least proud of his father. Fortunately for him, as Achebe goes ahead to point out, "among these people a man was judged according to his worth and not according to the worth of his father."[25] Hence, Okonkwo worked very hard not to be like his father. At a young age he became renowned as one of the greatest men of his time, having established himself as a wealthy farmer and the greatest wrestler in the nine villages of Umuofia. But more than these two accomplishments, Okonkwo's biggest achievement was taking two titles early in life. Achebe remarks that even though age was respected among Okonkwo's people, "achievement was revered."[26] In keeping with the elders' wisdom, then, that if a child washed his hands he could eat with kings, Okonkwo was fit to dine with kings since he had washed his hands.[27]

Among the Igbo, the ozo chieftaincy title may be the one surest way of earning one's seat at the table with kings and elders. Joining the esteemed rank of its membership motivated and drove Okonkwo. However, Achebe does not only idolize ozo and what it represents, he also lets the reader know how the socio-economic realities within the rapidly changing colonial Igbo society affected that revered institution. In a conversation between Okonkwo and his friend, Obierika, Achebe sets forth one of the earliest concerns about its depreciating value on the eve of Umuofia's contact with colonization and Christianity. The two friends bemoan the fact that the young men of Umuofia are destroying the community's palm trees with their inexperience in tapping the trees' sap for wine. Due to the elevated status that their ozo titles bestow men like Okonkwo and Obierika, "the law of the land" forbids them from climbing palm trees to tap the sap. But even as Obierika points out that Umuofia's neighboring communities do not have such a law, the two friends agree that it is good that Umuofia holds ozo in high esteem, for in villages like Abame and Aninta, ozo has become so worthless that "every beggar takes it."[28] Obierika adds that to further devalue ozo in those villages, "every man wears the thread of title on his ankle, and does not lose it even if he steals."[29] Okonkwo agrees with his friend. "They have indeed soiled the name of *ozo*," he adds.[30]

The dialogue referenced above signals changing times. It reminisces a glorious era that is threatened with dilution, a devaluation of cherished tradition. But it also speaks of a persisting tradition in the midst of this threatening reordering of reality. Okonkwo's concern here appears to center on the financial worth of the most cherished status-conferring position in his community. He and his friend agree that its value is most preserved by ensuring that only those who distinguished themselves by a dint of hard work (evident in their wealth) could access it. However, the conversation equally reveals an impending danger. Abame and Aninta have already welcomed the Christian missionaries to their communities and the boundaries of their respective cultures are gradually beginning to be redrawn on the basis of those encounters. The devaluation Okonkwo fears finally rides into Umuofia with the Christian missionaries on the heels of their colonialist compatriots. The Christianization of his own people constituted the biggest challenge not only to Umuofia but also to the Igbo way of life in general.

By introducing the reader thus to the life and world of Okonkwo, Achebe invites the reader to pay attention to some of the important factors and forces that will drive and affect both Okonkwo and that world later in the story. By *listening*, Achebe seems to be reminding his reader, the Other learns about Africa. Ironically, this Achebe's approach has a biblical ring to it, for faith comes through hearing and what is heard comes from spoken words.[31] To hear the spoken words, Achebe insists, the Other has to listen.

Storytelling, as a result, possesses for Achebe a more fundamental, deeper meaning of asserting Africa's history and culture before its encounter with Europe.[32] This deeper pedagogical value, Achebe insists, engages the storyteller to radically re-orientate contemporary cultural discourse, to re-position the mind on the realities and truths it has been conditioned to ignore.[33] Hence, the writer, as a storyteller, is implicated in the deconstruction and reconstruction of a culture and cultural mindset without which a people cannot free itself from any form of domination. One hears in this desire to liberate the African mind from colonial complex echoes of Frantz Fanon's popular insistence that a people's liberation is "that material keystone which makes the building of culture possible."[34]

Simon Gikandi rightly contends that Achebe's central position in the history of African literature lies in his ability to engage storytelling as "a new way of reorganizing African cultures," particularly at the critical moment of transition from colonial to national independence as well as in "proposing an alternative world beyond the realities imprisoned in colonial and postcolonial relations of power."[35] In seeking, then, to write a new African identity, Achebe must interrogate the colonial ideologies, historical claims and theories of Africa. He engaged his task in earnest, examining not only the conditions under which African knowledge could be produced but also the problematics of such knowledge. *Things Fall Apart* grapples with the questions of where, why, and when the Other began to seize the initiative to organize the African society and culture. From such an interrogation exercise emerges a new order of knowledge that de-centers the colonial discourse and evokes an alternative space of representation.[36]

The sense of mission in Achebe's narratives, no doubt, produces some narrative anxiety. On the one hand, African storytellers find themselves between the self-consciousness of a mission to re-write Africa and produce an adequate cultural representation and on the other hand, they encounter the disquietude of employing colonial forms and languages in the realization of this mission. Achebe resolved this uneasiness with a finality that borders on fatality: "history has forced [a colonial language] down our throats,"[37] he writes, and "there is no other choice. I have been given this language and I intend to use it."[38] The actualities of communicating with foreign languages are the African reality, but it is the duty of the African storyteller to leverage this reality to his/her advantage in projecting the re-centered African narrative to a global audience. Nevertheless, not everyone among Achebe's contemporaries, as will be shown in the next section, was comfortable with this resolution.

WHO WRITES FOR AFRICA?: A CRITIQUE OF ACHEBE

In his essay on "African Modes of Self-writing," in which he addresses deep and important questions on the crafting of identity and the self in postcolonial Africa, Achille Mbembe, articulates identity as multi-processes of meaning making.[39] African identity exists in plurality[40] and as such should be spoken of through a plurality/multiplicity of narratives in an attempt at recovering the African agency. In writing African narratives, Africans revise and revert colonial narratives in which, according to Valentin-Yves Mudimbe, African worlds have been set up as "realities for knowledge"; for even in the postcolonial context, "Africans themselves read, challenge, rewrite these discourses as a way of explicating and defining their culture, history, and being."[41]

Unlike Achebe, Kenyan novelist Ngugi wa'Thiong'o championed for decades the telling of Africa's stories in the African indigenous languages.[42] For wa'Thiong'o, language carries culture and thus loses some strength when deployed in narratives of different cultures. Echoing Fanon, he argues that the storytellers of postcolonial Africa remain connected to their revolutionary struggles for liberation from neocolonialism by telling their stories in their indigenous voices. In using colonial languages, wa'Thiong'o maintains, storytellers accede their power to the oppressor and limit their ability to engage and portray African cultures and histories effectively. Whereas one acknowledges the value in wa'Thiong'o's point, it is worth noting that what he considered strength limited his audience reach and forced him later on in his writing career to translate his own works, originally written in Kikuyu, into English.

wa'Thiong'o's misgivings notwithstanding, while acknowledging that writing in the colonial language comes with serious utility setbacks and creates cultural tension for the storyteller, Achebe insists that, of necessity, the mission of the storyteller, part of which is "to encourage the creation of an African identity,"[43] justifies the employment of the colonial language in the construction of this identity. That colonial language, however, has to evolve and be deployed in such a way that it "carries the weight of my African experience," Achebe maintains.[44] He illustrates the point of ensuring that the colonial language "speaks" Africa in the hands of the African storyteller with a quote from his third novel, *Arrow of God*, offering an insight into his use of English. In the novel, the Chief Priest explains to his sons the necessity for him to send one of them to the white man's church:

> I want one of my sons to join these people and be my eyes there. If there is nothing in it you will come back. But if there is something there you will bring home my share. The world is like a Mask, dancing. If you want to see it well you do not stand in one place. My spirit tells me that those who do not befriend the white man today will be saying *had we known* tomorrow.[45]

Achebe acknowledges that he could have rendered the above paragraph differently. He could have written, for instance: "I am sending you as my representative among these people—just to be on the safe side in case the new religion develops. One has to move with the times or else one is left behind. I have a hunch that those who fail to come to terms with the white man may well regret their lack of foresight."[46] This alternative rendition, of course, communicates the same message but with a completely different tone that does not do justice to Achebe's appropriation of the colonial language to speak for Africa. "The material is the same," Achebe notes, "but the form of the one is in *character* and the other is not."[47]

Achebe, no doubt, scores a huge success with his localization of the colonial languages for his own purposes. In her reading of Achebe's "The African Writer and the English Language" essay, for instance, Toni Morrison recalls the great impact Achebe's work had on her life and her writing through his unique way of employing the colonial language in narrating African experiences in *Things Fall Apart*.[48] Morrison notes that Achebe's approach is all about language and which language one chooses to write in.[49] Whichever language the African storyteller settles for determines what gaze to adopt as well as the subject and the object of the gaze, particularly in the context of Morrison's post-slavery America that denigrated Black language as "something not just ungrammatical but almost incomprehensible."[50]

Ironically, Achebe, whose sole aim for writing was to reconstruct such a bastardized image of Africa that Morrison decries, once criticized Negritude for its sentimental clinging to Africa's past. He declared his unequivocal distaste for slogans and then asserted: "I don't think, for example, that 'negritude' has any meaning whatsoever . . . I can't understand why a large number of African writers, notably those who write in French, have such a nostalgia for the past."[51] The dismissal smacks of double standard, without doubt; but to be sure, Achebe's Africa was not perfect. According to him, traditional African societies had their communal happiness, art and poetry as well as a cruel side.[52] However, to those who blame African writers for romanticizing Africa's past, Achebe argues that the romanticization was Africa's response to Europe's "irreverence and arrogance"[53] in denying that past in the first place. Africans only reached back into their pristine past to retrieve their cultural histories and practices in order to show to those who denied the existence of such histories.

AFRICA'S STORYTELLERS BEYOND ACHEBE

Within the first decade of its publication, *Things Fall Apart* established itself "as a big factor in the formation of a young West African's picture of his [or her] past, and of his [or her] relation to it."[54] It was adopted as a textbook for English classes for high schools and universities across Africa and beyond. In a 1967 interview, Achebe expressed satisfaction at the difference his works and those of his contemporaries were making, particularly in schools, with regards to providing alternative narratives that speak to the realities of Africa's younger generation.[55] What, however, no one could have foreseen at the time was the far-reaching transformational impact *Things Fall Apart* would have on later generations of peoples of African descent and how they would perceive and frame their identities as Africans. Achebe's singular determination to tell the African story from a distinctively African point of view has ensured that generations of writers after him who found their voices from his writings have continued to empower the African with their writings. One of such Achebe's literary descendants, Chimamanda Ngozi Adichie, found her writing voice and, for the first time, characters who looked like her, in *Things Fall Apart*.[56]

Adichie, whose first novel, *Purple Hibiscus*, opens with a subtle tribute to Achebe ("Things started to fall apart at home when . . .".[57]), follows Achebe's trail of centering stories at the very heart of African civilization and culture.[58] Teasing out the multiple overlapping stories of postcolonial cultural domination and power play, Adichie, in "The Danger of a Single Story," recounts how she found her authentic cultural voice and warns of the danger of not allowing a multiplicity of stories to be told.[59] She insightfully locates the exercise of power at the root of telling a single story, emphasizing that it is impossible to talk about the single story without talking about power. Using "nkali," an Igbo noun that loosely translates as "to be greater than another" to illustrate this power structure, Adichie brilliantly points out, "power is the ability not just to tell a single story of a person, but to make it the definitive story about that person."[60]

Like economic and political words, Adichie rightly argues, "stories too are defined by the principle of nkali. How they are told, who tells them, when, and how many stories are told are dependent on power."[61] And when a people is represented in a particular way over and over again, they inevitably become that representation in the eyes and minds of the audience. Foucault's location of discourse at the center of meaning-construction and its inherent knowledge-power dynamics immediately bears out Adichie's argument.[62] Single story creates stereotypes, and the problem with stereotypes, Adichie continues, "is not that they are untrue, but that they are incomplete. They make one story become the only story."[63] The often-unacknowledged consequence of such stereotypes is that such a single story has the power to continue to rob Africa of its humanity, history and culture.

Like Adichie, the younger generations of African writers inspired by Achebe such as Okey Ndibe, Chika Unigwe, and Adaobi Tricia Nwaubani,[64] have also taken up the mantle of ensuring that the African story is told in multiple voices. Nwaubani, however, laments the restrictions African writers face. In order to get published and reach a wider global audience, she remarks, the African storytellers are forced to tell only the stories that their Western readers allow them to tell and what the publishers in New York and London are willing to present to the world.[65] Unfortunately, faced with this challenge, many contemporary African storytellers, desiring a space on the world stage, further the stereotypes of a continent riddled with corruption, bad governance, war, genocide, violence against women and the girl child, child soldier, and human trafficking. Western publishers ensure that the re-telling of these stereotypes of brutality and depravity determine the success of the contemporary African storyteller on the West-dominated global publishing stage. Gayatri Spivak's "colonialism of capital"[66] speaks true of this context. The post-colonial mode of production excludes certain voices in the narrative-creating enterprise due to capital. This reality reflects the nature of Africa's literary agency in the world today, an agency of self-recovery entangled in global ideological (geo)politics.

That entanglement happens on multiple fronts and the World Wide Web is one front (although Western capitalism still controls its infrastructure) that opens up the space and levels the ground for a multiplicity of voices and stories. The Internet together with the accessibility of its ancillary blogosphere and social media not only guarantees a platform for the African storyteller to be heard across the world, it also makes self-publishing ever more possible and accessible. It enables young African writers to bypass the gate-keeping structures that the West-owned publishing houses and their editors use to regulate African voices. America-based Nigerian literary critic Ikhide Ikheloa, for instance, remains consistent in his assertion that the most incisive contemporary African writings happen on the Internet. He applauds the young and often unacknowledged writers who continue to creatively center African literature and African voices in the digital space where they unapologetically "do not feel the need to italicize ugali or egusi."[67]

A number of these writers tell their African stories from their bases in the diaspora. The emergence and growing number, since the late twentieth century, of the new African diaspora,[68] for instance, means that Africa's stories can no longer continue to be told without Africa's diaspora voices.[69] These voices will sustain Africa's narratives within the twenty-first century global community of stories. While these voices counter and deconstruct the stereotypical aid narratives about Africa, they do not gullibly embrace the counter-narratives of Africa's hope and progress. Often their relentless scrutiny of such narratives pitches them against the State in Africa, raising the perennial question of "who has the right/power to speak for Africa?"[70] Unfortunately, political elements within continental Africa continue to delegitimize the new diaspora, accusing it of "always talking about corruption and poor governance as if that were the only story in Africa."[71] But the task of telling Africa's stories also involves exposing the ills that stop Africa from performing to its full capacity. Besides, given the new diaspora's annual remittance to Africa now in excess of $50 billion US dollars,[72] the new diaspora insists on its legitimacy to tell its own stories of Africa and its right to demand accountability through these stories. It adds its voice to the voices that today continually challenge the impunities on the continent that give traction to the single story of a corrupt and unthinking Africa.

CONCLUSION

The value of storytelling bears out on how realities and histories are constructed through narratives as well as how ideology is produced through language. Achebe's conviction, evident in his corpus, maintains that the role of the African storyteller is the validation of the African culture and identity denied by colonial historiography. As Achebe himself consistently asserted: "African people did not hear of culture for the first time from Europeans . . . their societies were not mindless but frequently had a philosophy of great depth and value and beauty . . . they had poetry and, above all, they had dignity."[73] In insisting that Africa's history be rewritten as a way of recovering it from the colonial tradition, Achebe demands the collapsing of the terms history and story. In Africa's story is contained its history, a history denied it by the West, but a history which Achebe and many African storytellers like him continue to invoke its narration as they evolve new traditions and construct new identities for Africa's engagement with itself and with the Other.

NOTES

1. African proverb. Proverbs constitute an essential element of Africa's oral tradition. They are full of wisdom and are employed by the elders to construct guiding worldviews as well as the ethos for their communities. Achebe notes about proverbs among his people in *Things Fall Apart*: "Among the Igbo the art of conversation is regarded very highly, and proverbs are the palm-oil with which words are eaten" (New York: Anchor Books, 1994, 7).

2. Chinua Achebe, "Language and the Destiny of Man," in *Morning Yet on Creation Day* (London: Anchor Press, 1976), 47–59.

3. See Achebe's works in bibliography.

4. Ruth Franklin, "After Empire: Chinua Achebe and the Great African Novel," *The New Yorker*, May 26, 2008, https://www.newyorker.com/magazine/2008/05/26/after-empire.

5. Chinua Achebe, *Things Fall Apart* (London: Heinemann, 1958). The novel, considered the most widely read book in modern African literature, has been translated into more than fifty languages, with over twenty million copies sold. See also "Things Fall Apart: A Novel by Chinua Achebe," *Penguin Random House*, accessed November 10, 2018. https://www.penguinrandomhouse.com/books/565351/things-fall-apart-by-chinua-achebe/9780385474542/.

6. See G. W. F. Hegel's *The Philosophy of History*, trans. J. H. Clarke (New York: Dover, 1956), which declared Africa incapable of history and the development of morality, religions, and political constitution.

7. George Orwell, *1984* (New York: New American Library, 1961), 204.

8. Edward Said, *Orientalism* (New York: Vintage, 1979).

9. Edward Said, 240.

10. Simon Gikandi, *Reading Chinua Achebe: Language and Ideology in Fiction* (Nairobi: Heinemann Kenya, 1991), 4.

11. Bill Moyers, "Interview with Chinua Achebe" in *A World of Ideas*, ed. B. S. Flowers (New York: Doubleday, 1989), 337.

12. Stuart Hall, *Representation: Cultural Representations and Signifying Practices* (London: Sage, 1997), 15.

13. Ibid., 228.

14. Ibid., 232.

15. Michel Foucault, *Archeology of Knowledge and the Discourse on Language*, trans. A. M. Sheridan (New York: Pantheon Books, 1972).

16. Ibid., 216.

17. Abioseh Nicol, "The Meaning of Africa," 1964, accessed November 10, 2018, https://afrilingual.wordpress.com/2011/08/18/the-meaning-of-africa---abioseh-nicol/.

18. Herodotus wrote, for instance, in *The Histories* (440 BCE) that Africa was inhabited by "wild men and women and many other creatures the existence of which cannot be denied." Kant, in *Observations on the Feelings of The Beautiful and Sublime* (1764), insisted that "Negroes of Africa" were incapable of excelling in art, science, or any other praiseworthy endeavor. In his infamous footnote in "Of Characters" in his *Essays, Moral, Political, and Literary* (1758), Hume maintained that blacks were naturally inferior to whites. See Footnote 6 above for Hegel's denial of Africa's capacity for history and the development of morality, religions, and political constitution.

19. Gikandi, 24.

20. Lewis Nkosi and Wole Soyinka, "Conversation with Chinua Achebe, 1963" in *Conversations with Chinua Achebe*, ed. Bernth Lindfors (Jackson: University of Mississippi, 1979), 13.

21. Chinua Achebe, "Africa and Her Writers," in *Hopes and Impediments: Selected Essays 1965–1987* (New York: Anchor Books Doubleday, 1988), 45.

22. Bill Moyers, "Interview with Chinua Achebe," in *A World of Ideas*, edited by Betty Sue Flowers, 333–44 (New York: Doubleday, 1989). Emphasis added.

23. Chinua Achebe, *Things Fall Apart,* in Everyman's Library edition, *The African Trilogy: Things Fall Apart, No Longer at Ease, Arrow of God* (New York: Alfred A. Knopf, 2010), 5.

24. See Flora Nwapa, "Women and Creative Writing in Africa, in *Sisterhood: Feminism Power—From Africa to the Diaspora*, ed. Obioma Nnaemeka (Asmara and Trenton, N.J.: Africa World Press, 1998), 89–99; Ifi Amadiume, *African Matriarchal Foundations: The Igbo Case* (London: Karnak House, 1987), *Male Daughters, Female Husbands: Gender and Sex in an African Society,* 2nd ed. (London: Zed, 2015 [1987]); Obioma Nnaemeka, "Nego-Feminism: Theorizing, Practicing and

Pruning Africa's Way," *SIGNIS: Journal of Women in Culture and Society* 29, 1 no. 2 (Winter 2004): 359–385; Akachi Adimora Ezeigbo, *Gender Issues in Nigeria: A Feminist Perspective* (Lagos: Vista Books, 1996), *Snail-Sense Feminism: Building on an Indigenous Model* (Lagos: University of Lagos monograph Series, 2012, no. 17).

25. Achebe, 2019, 8.
26. Ibid.
27. Ibid.
28. Achebe, 2010, 50.
29. Ibid.
30. Ibid.
31. Romans 10:17.
32. Donatus Ibe Nwoga, "Interview with Chinua Achebe," in *African Writers Talking*, eds. Dennis Duerden and Cosmo Pieterse (London: Heinemann, 1972), 7.
33. Ibid.
34. Frantz Fanon, *The Wretched of the Earth*, trans. Constance Farrington (New York: Grove Press, 1968), 233.
35. Gikandi, 3.
36. See Gikandi, 4–5. See also Bernth Lindfors, ed., *Conversations with Chinua Achebe* (Jackson: University of Mississippi, 1979), ix–xiii.
37. Chinua Achebe, "The African Writer and the English Language," in *Morning Yet on Creation Day* (London: Anchor Press, 1976), 97.
38. Ibid., 102.
39. Achille Mbembe, "African Modes of Self-writing," *Public Culture* 14, no.1 (2002), 239–273.
40. See Wole Soyinka, *The Burden of Memory, the Muse of Forgiveness* (Oxford: Oxford University Press, 1998).
41. Valentin-Yves Mudimbe, *The Invention of Africa: Gnosis, Philosophy, and the Order of Knowledge* (Indianapolis: Indiana University Press, 1998), xi.
42. Ngugi wa Thiong'o, *Decolonizing the Mind: The Politics of Language in African Literature* (London: Heinemann, 1986).
43. Kwame Anthony Appiah, John Ryle, and D. A. N. Jones, "Interview with Chinua Achebe," *Times Literary Supplement*, February 26, 1982.
44. Achebe, "The African Writer and the English Language," 103.
45. *Arrow of God*.
46. Achebe, "The African Writer and the English Language," 103.
47. Ibid.
48. Toni Morrison, "Toni Morrison Reads 'English and the African Writer' by Chinua Achebe," *PEN America*, August 7, 2008, https://pen.org/multimedia/toni-morrison-reads-english-and-the-african-writer-by-chinua-achebe/
49. Ibid.
50. Ibid. One hears here echoes of Conrad's description of Africans in *Heart of Darkness*.
51. Judith E. McDowell, "An Interview with Chinua Achebe," *Afrique* 27 (1963), 41.
52. Nkosi and Soyinka, "Conversation with Chinua Achebe, 1963."

53. Bernth Lindfors, Ian Munro, Richard Priebe, and Reinhardt Sander, "Interview with Chinua Achebe, 1969" in *Conversations with Chinua Achebe*, ed. Bernth Lindfors (Jackson: University of Mississippi, 1979), 29.

54. *Times Literary Supplement*, "Things Fall Apart," (London: News UK, 1965).

55. Tony Hall, "Chinua Achebe: I Had to Write on the Chaos I Foresaw, 1967" in *Conversations with Chinua Achebe*, ed. Bernth Lindfors (Jackson: University of Mississippi, 1979), 19.

56. Chimamanda Ngozi Adichie, "The Danger of a Single Story," *TED Global*, 2009, accessed November 11, 2018, https://www.ted.com/talks/chimamanda_adichie_the_danger_of_a_single_story/transcript?language=en

57. Chimamanda Ngozi Adichie, *Purple Hibiscus* (London: Harper Perennial, 2005), 3.

58. See Jonathan Cott, "Chinua Achebe: At the Crossroads," *Parabola: The Magazine of Myth and Tradition* 6, no. 2 (1981), 30–39. See also Chris Searle, "Achebe and the Bruised Heart of Africa," *Wasafiri* 7, no. 14 12–16.

59. Adichie, "The Danger of a Single Story," 2009.

60. Ibid.

61. Ibid.

62. Foucault, *Archeology of Knowledge and the Discourse on Language*, 1972.

63. Adichie, "The Danger of a Single Story," 2009.

64. See Okey Ndibe, *Never Look an American in the Eye* (New York: Soho, 2016), *Arrows of Rain* (New York: Soho, 2000/2015), *Foreign Gods, Inc.* (New York: Soho, 2014); Chika Unigwe, *On Black Sisters' Street* (London: Vintage Books, 2009); Adaobi Tricia Nwaubani, *I Do Not Come to You by Chance* (New York: Hyperion, 2009).

65. Adaobi Tricia Nwaubani, "African Books for Western Eyes," *The New York Times* Online (2014), accessed November 11, 2018, https://www.nytimes.com/2014/11/30/opinion/sunday/african-books-for-western-eyes.html.

66. Spivak, "Can the Subaltern Speak?" 2010.

67. Ikhide R. Ikheloa, "Of African Literature and the Language and the Politics of the Stories," *Jalada* (2015), accessed November 14, 2018, https://jaladaafrica.org/2015/09/15/of-african-literature-and-the-language-and-the-politics-of-the-stories-by-ikhide-r-ikheloa/

68. These are mainly Africans who left the continent as a result of the 1980s economic downturn.

69. Pius Adesanmi, "Africa's New Story Won't be Told Without its Diaspora," *CNN* Online (2014), accessed November 11, 2018, https://www.cnn.com/2014/12/05/world/africa/facing-forward-with-africas-stories/index.html.

70. See Gayatri C. Spivak, "Can the Subaltern Speak?" in *Can the Subaltern Speak?: Reflections on the History of an Idea*, ed. Rosalind C, Morris (New York: Columbia University Press, 2010), 22–78.

71. Adesanmi, "Africa's New Story Won't be Told Without its Diaspora," 2014.

72. World Bank, "Migration and Remittances: Recent Developments and Outlook," (April 2018), accessed November 14, 2018, http://documents.

worldbank.org/curated/en/805161524552566695/pdf/125632-WP-PUBLIC-MigrationandDevelopmentBrief.pdf

73. Chinua Achebe, "The Role of the Writer in the New Nation," in *African Writers on African Writing*, ed. G. D. Killam (London: Heinemann, 1973), 8.

BIBLIOGRAPHY

Achebe, Chinua. *Things Fall Apart*. London: Heinemann. 1958.
Achebe, Chinua. "The Role of the Writer in the New Nation." In *African Writers on African Writing*, edited by G. D. Killam, 7–13. London: Heinemann. 1973.
Achebe, Chinua. *Arrow of God*. New York: Doubleday. 1974
Achebe, Chinua. *Morning Yet on Creation Day*. London: Anchor Press. 1976.
Achebe, Chinua. *The Trouble with Nigeria*. Enugu: Fourth Dimension. 1983.
Achebe, Chinua. *Anthills of Savannah*. London: Heinemann. 1987
Achebe, Chinua. *Hopes and Impediment: Selected Essays 1965–1987*. New York: Anchor Books Doubleday. 1988.
Achebe, Chinua. *Things Fall Apart*. In Everyman's Library edition, *The African Trilogy: Things Fall Apart, No Longer at Ease, Arrow of God*. New York: Alfred A. Knopf. 2010 [1958].
Adesanmi, Pius. "Africa's New Story Won't be Told Without its Diaspora." 2014b. http://www.cnn.com/2014/12/05/world/africa/facing-forward-with-africas-stories/
Adichie, Chimamanda Ngozi. *Purple Hibiscus*. New York: Anchor. 2004.
Adichie, Chimamanda Ngozi. "The Danger of a Single Story." TEDGlobal. 2009. http://www.ted.com/talks/chimamanda_adichie_the_danger_of_a_single_story?language=en
Amadiume, Ifi. *African Matriarchal Foundations: The Igbo Case*. London: Karnak House. 1987.
Amadiume, Ifi. *Male daughters, female husbands: Gender and sex in an African society*. 2nd ed. London: Zed. 2015 [1987].
Appiah, Kwame A., John Ryle, and D. A. N. Jones. "Interview with Chinua Achebe." *Times Literary Supplement*. 1982.
Cott, Jonathan. "Chinua Achebe: At the Crossroads." *Parabola: The Magazine of Myth and Tradition* 6, no. 2 (1981): 30–39.
Duerden, Dennis and Cosmo Pieterse, eds. "Interview with Donatus Nwoga." In *African Writers Talking*. London: Heinemann. 1972.
Ezeigbo, Akachi Adimora. *Gender Issues in Nigeria: A Feminist Perspective*. Lagos: Vista Books. 1996.
Ezeigbo, Akachi. *Snail-Sense Feminism: Building on an Indigenous Model*. Lagos: University of Lagos monograph Series, no. 17. 2012.
Fanon, Franz. *The Wretched of the Earth*. Translated by Constance Farrington. New York: Grove Press. 1968.
Foucault, Michel. *Archeology of Knowledge and the Discourse on Language*. Translated by A. M. Sheridan Smith. New York: Pantheon Books. 1972.

Franklin, Ruth. After Empire: Chinua Achebe and the Great African Novel. 2008. Retrieved from http://www.newyorker.com/magazine/2008/05/26/after-empire

Gikandi, Simon. *Reading Chinua Achebe: Language and Ideology in Fiction*. Nairobi: Heinemann Kenya. 1991.

Hall, Stuart. "Introduction." In *Representation: Cultural Representations and Signifying Practices*, edited by Stuart Hall, 1–12. London: Sage Publications. 1997

Hall, Tony. "Chinua Achebe: I Had to Write on the Chaos I Foresaw." In *Conversations with Chinua Achebe*, edited by Bernth Lindfors, 1997, 18–26. Jackson: University Press of Mississippi, 1967.

Lindfors, Bernth, ed. *Conversations with Chinua Achebe*. Jackson: University Press of Mississippi. 1997.

Lindfors, Bernth, Ian Munro, Richard Priebe, and Reinhard Sander, eds. *Palaver: Interviews with Five African Writers in Texas*. Austin: University of Texas Press. 1969.

Mbembe, Achille. "African Modes of Self-writing." *Public Culture*, vol. 14, no. 1. (2002):239–273.

McDowell, Judith E. "An Interview with Chinua Achebe." *Afrique*, vol. 27 (1963):41–42.

Morrison, Toni. "Tony Morrison Reads 'English and the African Writer' by Chinua Achebe." n.d. http://www.pen.org/book/toni-morrison-reads-english-and-the-african-writer-by-chinua-achebe

Moyers, Bill. "Interview with Chinua Achebe." In *A World of Ideas*, edited by Betty Sue Flowers, 333–44. New York: Doubleday, 1989.

Mudimbe, Valentine-Yves. *The Invention of African: Gnosis, Philosophy, and the Order of Knowledge*. Indianapolis: Indiana University Press. 1998.

Nicol, Abioseh. The Meaning of Africa. 1964.https://afrilingual.wordpress.com/2011/08/18/the-meaning-of-africa---abioseh-nicol/

Nkosi, Lewis and Wole Soyinka. "Conversation with Chinua Achebe." In *Conversations with Chinua Achebe*, edited by Bernth Lindfors, 1997, 11–17. Jackson: University Press of Mississippi. 1963

Nnaemeka, Obioma. "Nego-Feminism: Theorizing, Practicing and Pruning Africa's Way." *SIGNS: Journal of Women in Culture and Society* 29, 1 no. 2 (Winter 2004.): 359–385.

Nwapa Flora. "Women and Creative Writing in Africa. In *Sisterhood: Feminism Power—From Africa to the Diaspora*, edited by Obioma Nnaemeka, 89–99. Asmara and Trenton, N.J.: Africa World Press. 1998.

Nwaubani, Adaobi T. "African Books for Western Eyes." 2014. http://www.nytimes.com/2014/11/30/opinion/sunday/african-books-for-western-eyes.html?_r=4

Said, Edward. *Orientalism*. New York: Vintage. 1979.

Searle, Chris. "Achebe and the Bruised Heart of Africa." *Wasafiri*, 7, no. 14: 12–16 (1991). DOI:10.1080/02690059108574245.

Soyinka, Wole. *The Burden of Memory, the Muse of Forgiveness*. Oxford: Oxford University Press. 1998.

Spivak, Gayatri C. "Can the Subaltern Speak?" In *Can the Subaltern Speak?: Reflections on the History of an Idea*, edited by Rosalind C. Morris, 22–78. New York: Columbia University Press. 2010.
Times Literary Supplement. *Things Fall Apart*. London: News UK. 1965.
wa Thiong'o, Ngugi. *Decolonizing the Mind: The Politics of Language in African Literature*. London: Heinemann, 1986.

Chapter 12

Narrativizing History

Chinua Achebe and the Politics of Interpretation

Anwesha Das

The question of narrative in historiography is central to debates in the field of historical theory. What role does narrative play in depicting the "real"? How effective is the use of narrative in describing objects of study and explaining structures and processes to represent the past? This chapter takes into account Hayden White's concept of the narrative in history—in his essay "The Question of Narrative in Contemporary Historical Theory"—and examines Chinua Achebe's use of a fictional narrative to represent the history of Igboland in his novel *Things Fall Apart*.

What is the significance of narrative in historical writings? Does narrative contribute to knowledge, or is it merely a medium to represent history? Does narrative bring in an ideological perspective to a historical event? How does narrative justify or not justify history as science? As a literary critic, I have no intention of arguing the *usefulness* of narrative in historiography. I use these questions in order to examine Achebe's representation of human past in his novel *Things Fall Apart*.

Things Fall Apart is set in "the period between 1850–1900—that is, the period just prior to and after the arrival of white men in this part of West Africa,"[1] in the two Igbo villages, Umuofia and Mbanta. Achebe reclaims the past of Igbo people by providing a picture of indigenous culture and traditions from the point of view of an *insider*. One gets to know the Igbo society as a democratic and egalitarian one, as expressed in the proverb: *Igbo enwe eze*, that is, Igbos do not have kings. Professor Cyril Agodi Onwumechili sheds light on independent village government, councils and assemblies that used to meet periodically in pre-colonial Nigeria, to decide on matters of pressing concern to villages. The significant aspect of these meetings was that: "Every man could and did have his say on all matters under discussion. Nobody had any special privilege because of ancestry."[2] Community was ascribed a significant role. Communities were divided according to "age grades."[3] Each age had its own duties and responsibilities. Even though community held an important part of Igbo life, at the same time, individual achievements also shared an equal place of importance in Igbo society. In the novel, Achebe shows how the coming together of the society in the New Yam Festival and the rituals give the picture of a close-knit community, while the wrestling match on the second day of the festival is a means for the display of individual physical might. The novel itself opens with an emphasis on individual achievements, and a link is immediately established with the honor personal accomplishments bring to the community: "Okonkwo was well known throughout nine villages and even beyond. His fame rested on solid personal achievements. As a young man of eighteen he had brought honor to his village by throwing Amalinze . . . the great wrestler."[4] Achebe revisions precolonial Igbo history by not merely depicting the cultural beliefs and practices of Igbo people but also establishing the African village as a civilization based on a structured communitarian principle where social order plays a significant role. He emphasizes the importance attributed to community in Igbo society in order to bring out the democratic nature of the societal structure; as he writes:

> The Igbo postulate an unprecedented uniqueness for the individual by making him or her the sole creation and purpose of a unique god-agent, *chi*. And yet . . . this unsurpassed individuality [is balanced] by setting limits . . . The first limit is the democratic one which subordinates the person to the group [or community] in practical, social matters. And the other is a moral taboo on excess which sets a limit to personal ambition . . .[5]

Okonkwo's attempts to act against the community and its customs lead to his downfall. The title holders in Igbo society, such as Okonkwo here, have traditional roles and responsibilities, and they "function like standing committees of the village assembly."[6] They implement important decision-making changes in society, determine general policies, handle abominations, take economic decisions, to name a few. To fall from that stature of respect and honor by committing suicide, Okonkwo falters in upholding his community ideals and beliefs. The "segmentary structure" of Igbo government prevents it from raising groups of people as armies against a penetrating body of colonial rule and governmental control. The subtle way of recognizing the community to stand up against any imposing force fails to establish its foothold in the face of colonial imposition, leading to Okonkwo's unsuccessful attempt to fight against the White administration. As Professor Onwumechili writes:

> Igbo traditional government could not raise large armies because of its segmentary structure. On account of that the Igbo developed pacifist tendencies. In place of empire building through military might, they sought other subtle ways of promoting affiliations and common action by larger groups of communities and peoples.[7]

Language is another important aspect of concern in resisting colonial rule. Igbo is a spoken language where symbols play important role in communication. Such a symbolic way of communication makes intercultural communication quite difficult, especially when the other culture is heavily dependent on the written word. Language here depicts the Igbo worldview, and an imposition of a European language uproots Igbo people of their traditional ways of life, belief-systems and myths. Professor Donatus I. Nwoga emphasizes the significance of language in preserving the Igbo worldview, as he writes that: "A language . . . carries within its vocabulary, its structures and its contexts . . . [It is] the embodiment of a people's world view."[8] Achebe's use of oral story-telling narrative pattern—as an *insider*—brings out the indigenous culture of Igbo people. Orality is an important aspect of Igbo society, apart from the communal unity that they share. Proverbs and anecdotes in everyday speech form essential elements of Igbo culture, and oral story-telling practices within the family play significant role in imparting values to children. In the precolonial period, it has been the only form of preserving native culture. Achebe embeds orality as a part of the text in a way that becomes part of his narrative style. He does not historicize the practice of oral traditions but incorporates orality in the pattern of narrative development.

At the backdrop of the onset of colonial rule and the Scramble for Africa in the nineteenth century, the novel stands as a repertoire of human past in depicting "how a traditional Igbo lifestyle was disrupted by the advent of colonialism, together with the Igbos' own internal processes of change and development."[9] Achebe introduces the readers to the coming of White men in Umuofia through second person narration. Okonkwo comes to know about the destruction caused by White men in Umuofia from Obierika: "The three white men and a very large number of other men surrounded the market . . . And they began to shoot. Everybody was killed, except the old and the sick who were at home and a handful of men and women . . ."[10] Thereafter he is reported about the building of the Church, and finally about his son Nwoye's conversion to Christianity. Christianity has made its inroads, captivating young men like Nwoye by propagating the presence of one God and the gospel. Nwoye gets attracted toward the "poetry of the new religion."[11] The outcasts or *osu* have become the first converts, and "Igbo egalitarianism has been challenged and surpassed."[12]

In his representation of human past, Achebe questions the very basis of the White man's religious beliefs. Okonkwo, after listening to the White man's words about Christianity and Jesus Christ, says: "'You told us with your own mouth that there was only one god. Now you talk about his son. He must have a wife, then.' The crowd agreed."[13] Achebe "writes back" against the colonial discourse of dehumanizing African cultures. He addresses the dilemmas of resisting not only alien forces but also fellowmen who have accepted the new religion as a way of life:

> "Does the white man understand our custom about our land?" [Okonkwo] "How can he when he does not even speak our tongue? But he says that our customs are bad; and our own brothers who have taken up his religion also that our customs are bad. How do you think we can fight when our own brothers have turned against us?" [Obierika][14]

Okonkwo—unlike Obierika—fails to realize the deeper impact of White culture on Igbo society. He voices his protest by killing the White man's messenger, ultimately acting against the customs of his own land by hanging himself. He demeans himself in the eyes of his community by committing suicide which is considered a sin in Igbo culture. The narrative historicizes local ways of life and the importance of individuality in Igbo culture, as well as establishes the value of a communitarian way of life. The society accepts certain changes in order to go on. The community adapts to Christianity and holds the society from falling apart: "the novel's title has a misleading finality because Umuofia, rejecting Okonkwo's counsel of a war of resistance which would have meant total obliteration, does not fall apart: it changes in order to go on."[15] Okonkwo's difficulty to accept the change can be very well explained by what Professor Michael J. C. Echeruo calls "A Matter of Identity." In his lecture with the same title, Echeruo explains how brutal life was for the Igbo in the nineteenth century. "Traditionally hard-working, the Igbo man found the chaos of the changing world around him both seductive and disorienting,"[16] as was the case with Okonkwo. On the one hand, he was worried about the harvest of the yam, while on the other hand, he was disoriented with his own son's conversion to Christianity. His character represents the anxiety and chaos during the period of time dealt with by Achebe. Achebe's text historicizes the social and religious concerns which worked a long way in generating a series of dilemmas among Igbo people, before they succumbed to the religious privileges offered by Christianity.

Things Fall Apart does not merely act as a medium of representation of human past. It brings an ideological perspective to the inroad of colonial rule in Africa. The author highlights an alternative image of African cultures as a response to the dehumanized representation of Africans by James Joyce in *The Heart of Darkness* and Joyce Cary in *Mister Johnson*.[17] He is "writing back" in protest to the Eurocentric image of Africa. His attempt at re-writing history by re-imagining the past represents the "past—with all its imperfections—[which] was not one long night of savagery from which the first Europeans acting on Gods' behalf delivered them."[18] His revision of the past is "not a mere recitation of facts, but a revolutionary act with meaning for the present. *Things Fall Apart* was both written and received by its readers as such an act."[19] In his re-writing of the past, Achebe's positionality as an *insider* (or an *outsider*?) is often a subject of question. Is he adopting an ethnographic voice, or is he writing as a historian of Igbo culture? Is the reference to the Commissioner's book in the novel, a reference to Achebe's own book? The closing lines of the novel represents an ethnographic approach, and the question of an *insider/outsider* becomes a subject of prime importance:

> The story of this man who had killed a messenger and hanged himself would make interesting reading. One could write almost a whole chapter on him. Perhaps not a whole chapter but a reasonable paragraph, at any rate. There was so much else to include, and one must be firm in cutting out details. He had already chosen the title of the book, after much thought: *The Pacification of the Primitive Tribes of the Lower Niger*.[20]

Okonkwo's life story and the intricacies of Igbo cultural practices, beliefs, and customs get reduced to the term *Primitive Tribes*. The white gaze—against which Achebe intends to write—becomes pronounced in these lines. So, is Achebe taking the role of a kind of "native anthropologist" in representing the culture of Umuofia? Is his voice as an *insider* giving an ethnographic account, or is he a detached historian of Igboland? The debate of *Things Fall Apart* being an ethnographic account or a historical one is not the focus of this chapter, and therefore I do not intend to argue on this line of thought. But the questions I ask here attempt to examine *Things Fall Apart* as a narrative representing the history of precolonial Igbo culture. The author acts as a historian of Igboland, rather than providing an ethnographic account. His use of fictional narrative to reclaim the history of Igbo culture reflects in his vivid portrayal of Igbo beliefs, lifestyle, cultural practices and social structure of Umuofia (as has been discussed in the previous paragraphs). The intriguing question that arises in this context is: How effectively can a fictional narrative represent Igbo history?

The narrative mode of representation of history is a subject of intense debate among historians. Hayden White distinguishes between "historical" and "fictional" writings in his essay "The Question of Narrative in

Contemporary Historical Theory," and addresses the question of authenticity. He takes into account traditional historical theory, Anglo-American analytical philosophers, structuralists and post-structuralists, and puts forth his argument that narrative history is something other than a scientific account. However, that is not adequate reason to reject it the "'truth-value."[21] If historical processes are represented with coherence "in the 'literary' or 'poetic' endowment of modern, secularized cultures, this is no reason to rule them out as *merely* imaginary constructions. To do so would entail the denial that literature and poetry have anything valid to teach us about 'reality.'"[22] He argues that historical discourse and literary discourse differs in subject-matter—one being "real" and the other "imaginary—and not in form. But that should not be a matter of concern as "the systems of knowledge production" for both generate from the historical experience of people, as he writes: "In the historical narrative, experiences distilled into fiction as *typifications* are subjected to the test of their capacity to endow "real" events with meaning."[23] The "allegorical" nature of a historical narrative does not mean that it deals with false beliefs and experiences. What it does is to use "imaginary" events to endow deeper meaning to "real" happenings related to human past. The language plays a significant role here, and to miss out the allegorical element would lead to a loss of a more nuanced representation of past experiences and history. White emphasizes this allegorical nature of a historical narrative and claims that: "A narrative account is always a figurative account, an allegory."[24] He further states that:

> In any event, the dual conviction that, on the one hand, truth must be represented in literal statements of fact and, on the other, that explanation must conform to the scientific model or its commonsensical counterpart, has led most analysts to ignore the specifically "Literary" aspect of historical narrative and therewith whatever "truth" it may convey in figurative terms.[25]

He draws references from Ricoeur's notion of historiography and writes how history writings contribute towards developing a plot which symbolically represent the past. Narrative, then, is considered more as a "mode of representation" rather than "a vehicle for conveying information."[26] The existing records that hold significance in historiography are also of importance in reclaiming history through narrative accounts. Narrative constitutes a sense of ambiguity which is evident in the writing of history too. White considers narrative as a "mode of discourse, a manner of speaking," which can be used to "represent "real" events, as in "historical narrative," and the result of this would be a "kind of discourse with specific linguistic, grammatical, and rhetorical features, that is, 'narrative historiography.'"[27] The element of imagination in a narrative does not necessarily relate to a false portrayal of the past.

An imaginary account of something "real" holds the same significance as an objective literal way of writing because the content of the discourse remains the same. It is only the mode of representation that varies, and that cannot question the authenticity of the subject represented. White very clearly states that: "One can produce an imaginary discourse about real events that may not be less 'true' for being 'imaginary.' It all depends upon how one construes the function of the faculty of imagination in human nature."[28]

It can—therefore—be said that a fictional narrative as that of Achebe's *Things Fall Apart* can very well be considered as a history of Igbo past because the author makes every attempt to reclaim the history. Achebe claims—in his own words—that he wants to teach his readers "that their past—with all its imperfections—was not one long night of savagery from which the first Europeans acting on God's behalf, delivered them."[29] His historical novel is more of a chronicle revisiting the past. The past is build up with intricate plot development making it an important part of the present. Sofia Samatar rightly points out that, "Writing history is not a mere recitation of facts, but a revolutionary act with meaning for the present,"[30] as is very well evident in Achebe's handling of history in *Things Fall Apart*. The fall of the pre-colonial society of Umuofia—symbolized by the fall of Okonkwo—makes a statement on the colonial project that had attained great success in Igboland by defiling Igbo gods and cultural beliefs. The introduction of an alien religion and the forced building of Churches bring a chaotic change in the societal pattern of Igbo community, whereby the "structure of their world crumbles in the face of a radically different ideology."[31] Order leads to disorder, only to reinstate order by an alien group. This interplay of order and disorder results in Okonkwo committing an abomination toward the land, by hanging himself. The new order, imposing a racist ideology, is very well apparent in the closing lines of the novel. The story of Okonkwo and Umuofia turns into the story of the *Primitive Tribes of the Lower Niger*.

Achebe uses history to make strong statements about the violence of establishing colonial rule in Africa. History is not simply revisiting the past from an objective point of view. History is infused with stories, claims, impulses, viewpoints that speak to contemporary perspectives in interesting ways. The use of narrative in writing that story holds significance in the revision of the history of a culture, a society, that had experienced obliteration under the auspices of the colonial rule. Achebe uses his narrative also to highlight how language played a predominant role in accelerating the colonial imposition on Igbo people. The languages Igbo and English have neither cultural background nor linguistic patterns similar to each other. Translation leading to distortion of opinions, beliefs and thoughts have acted as an influential factor in creating miscommunication. The conversations between Okonkwo and Captain Winterbottom explicates the failure in understanding each other's point of view, due to such disparity of linguistic systems. Professor Nwoga addresses the issue of "language and worldview" in his lecture, and emphasizes on the disparity that results from translation:

> The Igbo *nna m ukwu* translates to "master" and one knows that whereas the Igbo expression carries implications of fatherhood, the English equivalent speaks of the slave and owner situation . . . These translation problems have certainly led to some of the distortions that have existed in the interpretation of Igbo cultural patterns.[32]

Achebe uses his text as a space where history, translation, language, play significant roles in developing the story line. As Samatar rightfully says: "The story of Okonkwo's life and death, viewed not as a recitation but as 'a unique experience with the past,' emerges less as a defense of a specific culture than a many-voiced commentary on the rise of global modernity."[33]

It is not merely a narrative of the pre-colonial era, or that of the colonial past, not a mere reclaiming of postcolonial identity, or a revision of history; *Things Fall Apart* as a narrative history experiments with its form to position itself as a revolutionary text in world history. The narrative fabric re-envisions history in meaningful ways. The use of imagination as a narrative device connects the narrator and the readers in significant ways. Thus, White:

> In the historical narrative [as in *Things Fall Apart*] the systems of meaning-production peculiar to a culture or society are tested against the capacity of any set of "real" events to yield to such systems . . . [There is] no reason to rule them out as *merely* imaginary constructions. To do so would entail the denial that literature and poetry have anything valid to teach us about "reality."[34]

NOTES

1. G. D. Killam, *The Writings of Chinua Achebe* (London: Heinemann, 1977), 13.
2. Cyril Agodi Onwumechili, "Igbo Enwe Eze: The Igbo Have No Kings" (Ahiajoku Lecture, Igbonet: The Igbo Network, November 2000).
3. Onwumechili, "Igbo Enwe Eze: The Igbo Have No Kings."
4. Chinua Achebe, *Things Fall Apart* (Delhi: Surjeet Publications, 2007), 3.
5. Chinua Achebe, "The Writer and His Community," in *Hopes and Impediments: Selected Essays 1965–1987* (Oxford: Heinemann, 1988), 59.
6. Onwumechili, "Igbo Enwe Eze: The Igbo Have No Kings."
7. Onwumechili, "Igbo Enwe Eze: The Igbo Have No Kings."
8. Donatus I. Nwoga, "Nka Na Nzere: The Focus of Igbo Worldview" (Ahiajoku Lecture, Igbonet: The Igbo Network, 1984).
9. Nahem Yousaf, *Chinua Achebe* (New Delhi: Atlantic, 2010), 35.
10. Achebe, *Things Fall Apart*, 144.

11. Achebe, *Things Fall Apart*, 151.
12. David Carroll, *Chinua Achebe: Novelist, Poet, Critic* (Houndmills: Macmillan Press, 1990), 53.
13. Achebe, *Things Fall Apart*, 151.
14. Achebe, *Things Fall Apart*, 183.
15. Derek Wright, "Things Standing Together: A Retrospect on *Things Fall Apart*," in *In Celebration of Chinua Achebe*, ed. Kirsten Holst Petersen and Anna Rutherford, Special Issue on *Kunapipi* 12, no. 2 (1990): 81.
16. Michael J. C. Echeruo, "A Matter of Identity" (Ahiajoku Lecture, Igbonet: The Igbo Network, 1979).
17. Kwaku Larbi Korang, "Making a Post-Eurocentric Humanity: Tragedy, Realism and *Things Fall Apart*," *Research in African Literatures* 42, no. 2 (2011): 2.
18. Chinua Achebe, "The Novelist as Teacher," in *Hopes and Impediments: Selected Essays 1965–1987* (Oxford: Heinemann, 1988): 45.
19. Sofia Samatar, "Charting the Constellation: Past and Present in *Things Fall Apart*," *Research in African Literatures* 42, no. 2 (2011): 62.
20. Achebe, *Things Fall Apart*, 215.
21. Hayden White, "The Question of Narrative in Contemporary Historical Theory," *History and Theory* 23, no. 1 (1984): 21.
22. Ibid.
23. Ibid.
24. Ibid., 24.
25. Ibid., 25.
26. Ibid., 29.
27. Ibid., 32.
28. Ibid., 33.
29. Achebe, "The Novelist as Teacher," 45.
30. Samatar, 62.
31. Samatar, 63.
32. Donatus I. Nwoga, "Nka Na Nzere: The Focus of Igbo Worldview" (Ahiajoku Lecture, Igbonet: The Igbo Network, 1984).
33. Samatar, 70.
34. White, "The Question of Narrative," 21.

BIBLIOGRAPHY

Achebe, Chinua. "The Novelist as Teacher." In *Hopes and Impediments: Selected Essays 1965–1987*, 40–46. Oxford: Heinemann, 1988.

Achebe, Chinua. "The Writer and His Community." In *Hopes and Impediments: Selected Essays 1965–1987*, 47–61. Oxford: Heinemann, 1988.

Achebe, Chinua. *Things Fall Apart*. Delhi: Surjeet Publications, 2007.

Carroll, David. *Chinua Achebe: Novelist, Poet, Critic*. Houndmills: Macmillan Press, 1990.

Echeruo, Michael J. C. "A Matter of Identity." Ahiajoku Lecture, Igbonet: The Igbo Network, 1979.

Killam, G. D. *The Writings of Chinua Achebe*. London, Heinemann, 1977.

Korang, Kwaku Larbi. "Making a Post-Eurocentric Humanity: Tragedy, Realism and *Things Fall Apart*." *Research in African Literatures* 42, no. 2 (2011): 1–29.

Nwoga, Donatus I. "Nka Na Nzere: The Focus of Igbo Worldview." Ahiajoku Lecture, Igbonet: The Igbo Network, 1984.

Onwumechili, Cyril Agodi. "Igbo Enwe Eze: The Igbo have No Kings." Ahiajoku Lecture, Igbonet: The Igbo Network, November 2000.

Samatar, Sofia. "Charting the Constellation: Past and Present in *Things Fall Apart*." *Research in African Literatures* 42, no. 2 (2011): 60–71.

White, Hayden. "The Question of Narrative in Contemporary Historical Theory." *History and Theory* 23, no. 1 (1984): 1–33.

Wright, Derek. "Things Standing Together: A Retrospect on *Things Fall Apart*." In *In Celebration of Chinua Achebe*, edited by Kirsten Holst Petersen and Anna Rutherford, 76–82. Special Issue on *Kunapipi* 12, no. 2, 1990.

Yousaf, Nahem. *Chinua Achebe*. New Delhi: Atlantic, 2010.

Chapter 13

Achebeism and the Nigerian Leadership Problem

Ada Uzoamaka Azodo

The abolition of corruption and nepotism alone will not fully solve the Nigerian leadership problem, as some people believe. This paper will advance new ideas and visions on leadership by personal example and public responsibility as panacea for the Nigerian leadership problem. Employing Chinua Achebe's parlance in *The Trouble with Nigeria*, his 1984 pamphlet on the Nigerian political, social and economic instability, the problem is the failure, inability and unwillingness of Nigerian leaders to govern responsibly or be good role models for future generations. Whereas current views blame past colonial history and contemporary endemic corruption and nepotism, this paper interrogates the quality of great leaders, the place of language, worldview, beliefs, moods and emotions in leadership, and the benefits of such self-awareness at the inceptive and transformative stages of leadership. The goal is to foster the foundation for leadership authenticity, while increasing the ability, capacity and competence of present and future leaders.

During the First Republic before the Nigeria-Biafra war and the Second Republic after the war, Nigerians would glibly place the cause of the country's social, political and economic woes at the door step of leadership inadequacy, prompting many a commentator to liken the situation to Westerners eternally lamenting the weather, with resignation, without serious thought to their banter, because everything is out of their control and there is nothing they can do about it. So, Nigerians believe that corrupt, greedy, selfish and authoritarian public servants are the norm. By harboring such cynicism, they do no less than promote nepotism, inequity, injustice, lack of vision and foresight, and there is nothing that anyone can do about it. In the currency of the very present situation, the dire nature of the situation remains the belief that nothing and nobody can change the status quo. It is the realization of the helplessness of Nigerians in the face of leadership failure in their country that prompted the eminent writer Chinua Achebe, widely known as the father of the African novel, to depart from his habit of fiction writing to pen his political science tract, *The Trouble with Nigeria*.

The Trouble with Nigeria, explores the Nigeria leadership question and the need for change, ending with the belief that it is possible to have better leadership in Nigeria for the greater good of the common majority. In the same vein, this article challenges the resignation and assumption of the ordinary citizen that the Nigerian situation is hopeless, and the tacit complicity of those with power and influence that believe that the best that one can do is join them, since one cannot beat those leaders who have gone before them. They believe in scheming for their survival and that of those closely related to them by blood or friendship, rather than putting strategies in place to work through set objectives with vision towards anticipated goals and outcomes for all Nigerians. Erroneously, leaders upon leaders without much critical thinking have come to believe that the best thing to do is to save themselves first and save their families and friends. Nepotism has become thereby the order of the day.

This essay suggests a culture of educational reform that can put in place good and visionary citizens able and willing to lead, through coaching, training, and formation. The task of founding good leaders will require leaders and their followers alike to turn leadership in Nigeria upwards. To that end, a few pertinent questions come to mind. What does leadership connote? Who is a leader? What are the leadership problems of Nigeria? What are the challenges facing the nation and its leaders? What solutions could bring about sound and modern-day leadership amidst Nigerian linguistic, cultural, religious, social and economic diversities and complexities? What is needed to create a sustainable social, economic, and political structure in the rest of the twenty-first century Nigeria? Theoretically, Chinua Achebe's *The Trouble with Nigeria* will light our path towards ideological leadership in Nigeria.

THEORETICAL FRAMEWORK: CHINUA ACHEBE'S *THE TROUBLE WITH NIGERIA*

The trouble with Nigeria is simply and squarely a failure of leadership. There is nothing basically wrong with the Nigerian character. There is nothing wrong with the Nigerian land or climate or water or air or anything else. The Nigerian problem is the unwillingness or inability of its leaders to rise to the responsibility, and to the challenge of personal example which are the hallmarks of true leadership.[1]

Africa is poor not because the world has denied the continent the market and financial means to compete; far from it. It has not been because of aid per se. Nor is African poverty solely a consequence of poor infrastructure or trade access, or because the necessary development and technical expertise is unavailable internationally. Why then has the continent lagged behind other developing areas when its people work hard and the continent is blessed with abundant natural resources? The main reason why Africa's people are poor is because their leaders have made this choice.[2]

In the introductory excerpt above from *The Trouble with Nigeria*, Achebe looks seriously at the leadership question in Nigeria, summarizes the "trouble" with Nigeria in six keywords and phrases: failure of leadership, unwillingness or inability of its leaders, their lack of responsibility, the challenge of personal example, and the hallmarks of true leadership. The odd sixty-seven pages of the pamphlet that make up the ten chapters of *The Trouble with Nigeria* are Achebe's desperate attempt to see leadership culture in Nigeria change. The titles of the chapters speak eloquently of the problems: Where the Problem Lies; Tribalism; False Image of Ourselves; Leadership, Nigerian Style; Patriotism; Social Injustice and the Cult of Mediocrity; Indiscipline; Corruption; The Igbo Problem, and The Example of Aminu Kano. Each chapter builds on the one preceding it, culminating in the qualities of a good and strong leader willing and able to take the people to the shores of contentment, stability and prosperity. Thus, the leadership question is the hinge on which hangs all the other ills of Nigeria and will become the reason for its turn-around as well, if only the nation and the citizens would work together towards the common goal of true leadership through good government.

HARD QUESTIONS ON LEADERSHIP

First, what does leadership entail? Leadership is defined by many people in many different ways, but all agree that leadership is not merely management of structures and systems. A leader can come along equipped readably with the requisite traits for leadership. Then, leadership can also be learned as a process. According to an article on "The Art and Science of Leadership,"[3] the people follow their leader when they discover his or her acute intelligence, height, fluency and articulate skills in the use of language, among other traits. With leadership as a learned process, however, a two-way interaction between the leader and his or her followers can be observed.[4] The personal qualities of the leader that contribute in large part to success in leadership are knowledge, people skill, trust, conviction, and goodness. They are attributes that form the leader's personality trait, which trait compels followers to tow the paved path with almost blind passion. Thereafter, a leader proceeds through personal example to influence his or her people to work through a shared set of objectives that would lead to envisioned goals and outcomes. In other words, if need be, the leader is not remiss to soil his hands, but would join the people to get the work done. In order to continue to carry the people along, to meet their perceived aspirations and needs, the leader can learn, change and transform self along the way. Because needs and aspirations change with the passage of time, the leader needs to continue to change, in order to continue to meet the perceived aspirations and needs of the people.[5] Above all, a leader is prepared to lay down his or her life in pursuit of the well-being of the people. It is a truism that leaders rise from their people, their history, their structures and institutions, and fall with them. To believe that good leaders will fall from heaven would be pushing eccentricity, even romanticism, too far, as Ibrahim Bello-Kano has mooted in a newspaper article, "Achebe: A non-romantic View."[6]

Second, how and why has leadership failed in Nigeria? We learn from *The Trouble with Nigeria* that the leaders and the people are not always united and looking towards a common goal, through discovering and rooting out the bad eggs engaged in corrupt practices in public and private lives. On the contrary, the state apparatus seems to condone the iniquity of the average Nigerian, who would take recourse to ethnic identification and rivalry to get ahead, when they should be flaunting merit and qualifications for jobs, school admissions, scholarships, and so on. And nepotism at the individual and state levels also extends to the national level, causing many a Nigerian to bestow loyalty to state alone, rather than to the nation. If a given citizen is not allowed to engage in patriotic duties in a state that he or she calls home, albeit not an indigene of that state, how would one be patriotic towards the nation? Achebe defines a patriot as he or she who does things that show his love and deep caring for his country and fellow citizens. He or she craves the happiness and wellbeing of the entire people, demands the highest standards in all walks of life and rebukes those who downgrade the country and its people. He or she does all these without degenerating to "superiority, despair and cynicism."[7] Achebe thinks patriotism will be possible with Nigerians and their leaders, when they begin to look in one direction with a goal for social justice and a public policy of fairness to all in true equality.[8] Then, Achebe concludes that to achieve a robust national life, leadership should eschew selfishness, courageously avoid the ills of corruption and abhor those that condone corruption.[9] Indeed, Achebe maintains that leaders should be above board, in order to set good example for the followers to emulate. Corrupt practices and laziness thrive because the leaders who should call them have soiled hands.

To help the country to turn around requires working hard on leadership, not hoping in an imaginary redemption from out of space. Achebe calls on Nigerians to eschew the "cargo mentality" of downtrodden people that believe that someday without their input they will be delivered from their sufferings.[10] Social justice, fair treatment, and merit denied at the individual, state and national levels lead to the cult of mediocrity, compromise, ineffectiveness, and inefficiency and waste, because they condone sex and gender discrimination, corruption and ethnic rivalry, and religious and political bigotry. To maintain peace and stability in the land, one needs to establish social programs and justice without which everyone is grabbing and not waiting for their turn that may never come.[11] When citizens forego discipline, it is each person to his or her own whims and caprices, which could lead to lawlessness and crime on a large scale.[12] It is worse when leaders are also undisciplined, for lawlessness trickles down to the ordinary citizens from the top. When the leader lacks discipline, says Achebe, it is a "fatal threat to society." Such a leader seizes the legislative and executive powers, turns into a terrible role model for the powerless citizens. Under a *"climate of indiscipline"* so created, the nation is on the brink of extreme anger that could lead to insurrection and rebellion.[13]

Clearly, states Achebe, Nigerian leadership is yet to see men or women who possess intellectual rigor and who have applied the same to work out an ideology before getting into the seat of leadership. What Nigeria has had, the eminent thinker continues, are leaders that arrive with no serious thoughts about how to move the country forward. On the contrary, they implant materialistic values and the love of money at the expense of more enduring human values of justice, goodness, fairness, and honesty. This wrong strategy has led to most of the "troubles with Nigeria."[14]

NIGERIAN LEADERSHIP PROBLEM

In spite of conventional opinion Nigeria has been less than fortunate in its leadership. A basic element of this misfortune is the seminal absence of intellectual rigour in the political thought of our founding fathers—a tendency to pious materialistic woolliness and self-centered pedestrianism.[15]

Chinua Achebe states that the leadership problem in Nigeria stems from past and present history. It is the problem of the legacy of the Founding Fathers of the nation and their wrongful guiding concepts, coupled with the demeaning and degrading British colonization of Nigeria, which have allowed them and their descendants to manipulate the social organism to serve their selfish ends before catering to the ordinary citizen. Hence, the lack of meaningful and selfless leadership ideology of the founding fathers and the history of the British colonization of Nigeria are illaudable legacies. How to engender peace and justice, enduring measures and structures in the country, virtues that cannot be trampled upon by the greedy and the irresponsible with impunity is the million naira question that Achebe asks in *The Trouble with Nigeria*.

It is important, therefore, to note that the problem is not the absence of concepts and ideologies, but the leaders' selfish intent and focus on self and family and friends. According to James Booth,[16] Dr. Azikiwe,[17] and Chief Awolowo's[18] biographies are poor in thought, are materialistic and lacking in selfless service, when compared to the stronger ideological expressions seen in the informal works of other such key African leaders as Kenya's Thomas Mboya and his *Harambee*, Tanzania's Julius Nyerere and his *Ujamaa*, and Ghana's Kwame Nkrumah and his *Nkrumaism*. Harambee, a form of African Socialism, similar to Ujamaa and Nkrumaism, advocate the virtues of communalism, where members of the society do projects to make life better for the entire community. The Nigerian examples pale from lack of good articulation and focus of the philosophies before these other African ideologies.

Dr. Nnamdi Azikiwe espouses some very important concepts on leadership in his book, *Ideology for Nigeria: Capitalism, Socialism or Welfarism?*[19] Rhetorically, this book blends the best of capitalism, socialism and welfarism, what Agbafor Igwe has called an *eclectic pragmatism* that "accommodates the fact that man is selfish and altruistic, rational and irrational, individualistic and communalistic."[20] Elsewhere, Ada Uzoamaka Azodo has noted as well that "the philosophy of eclectic pragmatism takes into account the complex and contradictory social, religious, economic and political landscapes of Nigeria, in order to achieve a certain desired set of goals."[21] But, the real question, Azodo adds, remains whose goals are to be served. Would it be the goal of the individual, the nation or the leaders? According to *The Trouble with Nigeria*, the Fathers of the Nation put their own personal materialistic legs forward first before thinking of the nation. Achebe warns that history will hold the leaders and the entire nation accountable for bad stewardship and waste of its prodigious endowment by Providence.[22] Instead of good stewardship, Nigeria has presided over vast losses of billions from the nation's coffers. The country has missed opportunities that could have launched it into the rank of developed countries of the world. Again, history will blame Nigerian for the lost opportunity, Achebe warns, during the twentieth century and also now in the twenty-first century."[23]

Therefore, Achebeism on leadership is not the Aminu Kano type[24] "voluntarism [. . .] even a form of messianic thinking" based on "flawed logic" for whom only will and morality constitutes the driving forces of the leader, as Ibrahim Bello-Kano has noted. Bello-Kano states that Achebe doubts the blind attention to the virtues of faith, unity, and goodness that many a Nigerian worships, without deep thoughts on the complexities and contradictions inherent in the makeup of Nigeria. Nigerian leaders, he continues, have had blind adherence to the inviolability of the inherited national structure entrusted by the colonial past, which have done nothing but derail the Nigerian political machine both in the First Republic and the Second Republic. The citizenry is not exempt either, for they are unable or unwilling to ask "searching questions" of the past and the post-independence leaders, thanks to their gross cynicism. They fail to demand service, thereby robbing the nation of the virtues of justice, honesty, truth, and fair play at every instance, as a concept and in practice.

Indeed, Achebe insists that enduring values and virtues of honesty, truth, and justice, legacies of the Founding Fathers of the nation, should prevail over the concepts of unity and faith, which are hard to define and which can easily be manipulated by corrupt leaders and their cynical and collaborative citizenry.[25] At the root of social injustice and the cult of mediocrity and compromise are ethnic loyalty or tribalism and sexism. Meritocracy is yet to become an attitude of mind in Nigeria, because mediocrity thrives galore. It is the nation that suffers, when the aggrieved citizen consistently sidelined, maligned or bypassed so that less competent persons with grandfathers or connections can be hired for work, he or she cannot or refuses to function efficiently. Then, the pertinent question to ask is "what is the purpose of government," if it is not to ensure peace, justice and stability in the country?[26] Achebe sees that peace and social justice are intertwined like two sides of a coin. Like two parts, he reiterates, they are also inter-related, for the entire nation needs peace and stability to function, as well as justice to ensure social, economic and political stability.[27]

There is the possibility of a violent revolution, if the leaders do not take heed to serve the ordinary citizenry that far outnumber the elite."[28] Achebe cites Mallam Aminu Kano as an example of a good leader, who was famous for promoting a culture of change. He was also a progressive with modernist views that was in favor of education and total political emancipation of women, and a promoter of democracy to make life easier for the downtrodden. Alan Feinstein adds that Aminu Kano was an exemplary leader that was not a mere "head of state," (he could have been one), given that he lived for the people rather than for himself.[29] The responsibility for reformulating and transforming leadership in Nigeria sits on the shoulders of the elite, Achebe continues, helped by the ordinary citizens who must ask questions without fear, and who must treat the answers they get with skepticism.[30] After all, it is society that helps to create the kind of leader one gets, a leader free from institutional and structural pressures of past and contemporary history or the lack thereof.

THE CHALLENGES OF NIGERIAN LEADERSHIP

If we were to add all these "invisible" emoluments to the salary (of the politicians) there would be no word in the dictionary adequate to describe the institutionalized robbery of the common people of Nigeria by their public "servants." Now, this is not a new phenomenon; it certainly was not created by the post-military civilian administration. It might even be called one of the legacies of colonialism. If so we have had more than two decades to correct it; we have failed to do so but rather chosen to multiply the evil ten-fold. We have no excuse whatsoever.[31]

The original challenge of leadership in Nigeria is the continuation of business as usual, even after the dastardly Nigeria-Biafra war with its enormous toll on human lives (over two million Nigerians dead on both sides of the battle line), destruction of infrastructure and values, and the list continues. It is not only that the first generation of Nigerian leaders were lacking in foresight to eschew colonial corruption, which allowed these latter to rob the nation's coffers to pay themselves, the new leaders emulated the old, on many occasions becoming worse; the earlier leaders failed to entrench worthy ideologies to carry the nation. Now, since after the civil war, the new crop of youth has allowed the old rangers to come back and continue the same self-serving attitude towards leadership. The youth who should have taken the reins of society to carve out a promising future for the people are arid of meaningful thoughts, not to mention the strategies to execute them. They are lacking in ability to question their leaders on what they promise to bring in their service to the nation. On the contrary, anxious to make immediate and cheap headway, the youth mystify the past for their selfish benefits. As a result, the lessons of the nation's past instability and the war are not learned. Hence, the country's yesteryears' problems, namely, corruption, nepotism, injustice, lip service and mediocrity are still here, Achebe sums up the problem with Nigeria.

In sum, the challenge of the new Millennium is to find a new crop of politicians, youthful leaders with a new kind of guiding philosophy, who would not be "revivalists of a bankrupt and totally unusable tradition of political maneuvering, tribal expediency and consummate selfishness."[32] There is hope for the future, concludes Achebe, for all the electorate needs to do is have the courage to ask questions that must be asked, and to move towards a new vision for future generations to come.

THE SOLUTIONS TO NIGERIAN LEADERSHIP PROBLEM

The importance to society of people like Aminu Kano and Mahatma Gandhi is not that every politician can become like them, for that would be an impossible and totally unrealistic expectation. But the monumental fact which they underscore and which no one can ignore again after they have walked among us is this: Gandhi was real; Aminu Kano was real. They were not angels in heaven; they were human like the rest of us, in India and Nigeria. Therefore, after their example, no one who reduces the high purpose of politics which they exemplified down to a swinish scramble can hope to do so without bringing a terrible judgment on himself. Nigeria cannot be the same again because Aminu Kano lived here.[33]

Achebe affirms that a new kind of politics of peace and fairness is needed. But how does one get beyond the unworkable past and present, in order to prepare for the future? Achebe advises the nation to hold up good and legendary national leaders as heroes for the youth to emulate. No doubt, Nigeria fifty years after the civil war is still wallowing in social, economic, and political ills. Nigerians are not proud of the unflattering national reputation for corruption, injustice and inequities. They would like to see a change at the personal, state and national levels. They know it can be done, but are still in search of how to do it. They are also aware that it will take a lot of time. The ills have been long with the society and cannot realistically vanish overnight. Sordid experiences have ruffled feathers both before the First Republic and after the Second Republic. Still, many Nigerians believe that the Nigerian conglomerate can metamorphose into a viable nation, with one voice and one destiny, as opposed to the current divergent viewpoints and focus. The grassroots Zikist Movement with which Nnamdi Azikiwe exerted a positive energy ended colonial rule in Nigeria. Today, Nigeria's nationalist aspirations have changed, given past history and present-day challenges and perspectives. Hence, a new politics of fair play and peace is needed, an all-encompassing ideology to get Nigeria and Nigerians to the next level.

First, Nigerians must seek leaders with integrity and moral probity, whom Achebe has called "saintly" leaders, leaders who eschew self-centeredness, refuse half-measures, compromises and corruption. They are the stuff of which revolutionaries are made. They are elected by the people or have risen from them, and so have shared experiences of nation-building, of 'being in this together,' and a sense of common destiny. They govern by example and encourage the citizenry to be aware of themselves, their needs and everyone else's needs, and above all to ask searching questions when their expectations are not being met. This kind of political leader-follower relationship can only lead to better economic destiny of shared vision, not dependence.

First, indeed, this is part and parcel of the traditional African communal vision; I am my brother's keeper and sister's keeper, what Southern Africans call "Ubuntu," and Zimbabweans "Unhu," a social philosophy of personhood according to which nobody in the community is well until everybody is well.[34] Certainly, Nigerians can look up and revive one of the traditional communal virtues that could hold the nation together and help it to stop the current waste in human and material wealth, energy, and drive. Potential intellectual ability is daily being diverted to unsavory ends, like kidnapping, armed robbery and embezzlement in paid offices. If Nigerians understand that in society one's fate is bound up with that of others in it—one is simply as wealthy or poor as his or her people, and the rich is rich because the poor is poor—then it makes sense to see that the most worthy thoughts on nation-building should go to asking oneself what one can do to help the next person one meets along life's highway. If the rich keep all their wealth to themselves and do not share with the poor, then the natural flow of wealth is thwarted; an anomaly would have occurred. A just society, therefore, is one where the people understand their innate obligations and responsibilities to do good acts and be kind in judgement and generosity towards the other without being policed. One may give it whatever name one likes, but the basic tenet of human life is that one is a social animal.[35]

Second, the proposed change of leadership culture is possible despite its complexity and the Nigerian realities. Sakah S. Mahmud in "Mallam Aminu Kano and the politics of Change in Nigeria," pays a tribute to the late illustrious leader,[36] saying that a reconditioning of the attitude of mind will be needed, with emphasis on discipline, where the majority views to do well and abide by the laws of the land will drown out the minority voices. In other words, a reversal of the present situation should take place, so that the silent minority is no longer drowned out by the majority grabbers of the wealth of local governments, states and the nation.

There is also a need of a national consciousness, pride and patriotism that does not pay lip-service to whoever wants to hear it, but rather a deeply felt belonging that transcends ethnic loyalty, language and worldview. Promoting inter-ethnic marriage among the youth at the highest national platform, with members of the Youth Service Corps, for example, could help to temper, if not completely abolish, "tribal" loyalties and discrimination. Thereafter, respect for and enforcement of the rule of law in all facets of life in local and state governments to ensure social justice, fair play, peace, stability, efficiency, and effectiveness of all could become the order of the day.

Third, leaders would then become shining examples for their followers to emulate. Chinua Achebe has not lost hope. If only the nation's leaders would pick up courage, eschew corruption and condemn it in their administrations, true leadership would arrive in Nigeria.[37] Leaders will then understand that as Presidents the essence of political office is service to the people, self-sacrifice in service, if need be, because they are on a sacred mission. Recall that the South African model leader, Nelson Mandela, while facing a possible death judgement at the 1951 Rivonia Trial for treasonable felony said the following:

> During my lifetime I have dedicated myself to the struggle of the African people. I have fought against white domination, and I have fought against black domination. I have cherished the ideal of a democratic and free society in which all persons live together in harmony and with equal opportunities. It is an ideal which I hope to live for and to achieve. But, if needs be, it is an ideal for which I am prepared to die.[38]

LEADERSHIP TRAINING INITIATIVES IN NIGERIA TODAY

If we have learned nothing else from Chinua Achebe it is that to be educated is to develop the questioning habit, to be skeptical of easy promises and to use past experiences creatively.[39] Leaders need education to raise the level of awareness of the average citizen to modern political, social, and economic values.[40] Indeed, many like-minded people have founded leadership institutions that are shining examples not tied to religion or particular ministries in Nigeria. They demonstrate the fact that many Nigerians are willing to go the extra mile to safeguard the nation's future. There is the Institute of Management, Leadership and Productivity Development with a few educational centers focused on inculcating integrity in the youth, according to its Deputy Registrar, Mr. David Imhonopi.[41] There is also the premier institution in Africa, the Nigeria Leadership Institute based in Jos, Abuja, and London, solely established for training of model leaders in all walks of life to lead Africa to development.[42] The Institute hopes to train leaders with ability to deliver change and understand the problems of Africa and how to solve them. These are emerging leaders that will be transformational, service-oriented, reformists, game-changing, selfless, and exemplary. Then, there is the Africa Leadership Initiative (ALI), also known as The Aspen Institute. Fellows there are highly successful, entrepreneurial individuals from business, government and civil society. They participate in four seminars modeled on the Aspen Institute's successful Henry Crown Fellowship Program: The Challenge of Leadership, The Aspen Seminar—In Search of the Good Society, Leadership in an Era of Globalization, and The Promise of Leadership. They are also required to carry-out a project of their own design and passion for the betterment of their societies. The projects seek a tangible demonstration of the Fellows' commitment to community service in a leadership capacity, and encourage Fellows to expand their leadership abilities while making a contribution. Importantly, the projects are expected to serve as values-based leadership in action.[43] It would appear that all that is needed to solve the Nigerian leadership problem now is to see to the integrity of the institutes to abide by the rules and regulations that would produce the best public servants based on African traditions, first and foremost, as well as others that are worthy of emulation, like the French whose public servants go through the *École nationale d'administration* (*ÉNA*),[44] to ensure they have competent and morally sensitive leaders. And, with that report on the leadership training initiatives in Nigeria, we have come full circle in this study on Achebeism and the Nigerian Leadership Question.

CONCLUSION

We have borrowed theoretical light from Chinua Achebe's political science tract, *The Trouble with Nigeria*, and have noted the writer's optimism of a bright future for Nigeria against all odds. As he opined in a *New York Times* 2011 essay, "Nigeria's Promise, Africa's Hope," the Nigerian leadership problem will be solved in stages that include nurturing and strengthening the nation's democratic institutions to ensure free and fair elections, a free press, a strong social justice system, checks and balances, and laws against corruption. Then, the leaders having eschewed corruption must gain new awareness of themselves as the servants of the people. "It is from this kind of environment that a leader, humbled by the trust placed upon him by the people, will emerge," Achebe then concludes, "willing to use the power given to him for the good of the people."[45]

NOTES

1. Chinua Achebe, The Trouble with Nigeria (Enugu: Fourth Dimension Publishing Co.; Revised ed. 2000), 1.

2. Greg Mills, "Economic growth does not demand a secret formula" back cover of Why Africa Is Poor, (Penguin Random House South Africa, 2013).

3. "The Art and Science of Leadership," Big Dog and Little Dog's Performance Juxtaposition, accessed June 6, 2021, http://knowledgejump.com/leader/leader.html.

4. A. G. Jago, "Leadership: Perspectives in Theory and Research," Management Science, 28(3), (1982): 315–336; G. Northhouse, Leadership Theory and Practice. (3rd ed.) (Thousand Oaks, CA: Sage Publications, 2007), 5.

5. A. G. Jago, "Leadership: Perspectives in Theory and Research," *Management Science*, 28 (3), (1982): 82.

6. *Nigerian Vanguard*, April 3, 2013.

7. Achebe, *The Trouble*, 15–16.

8. Ibid., 16.

9. Ibid., 17.

10. Ibid., 9–11.

11. Ibid., 24.

12. Ibid., 27.

13. Ibid., 32.

14. Ibid., 11–13.

15. Ibid., 11.

16. James Booth, *Writers and Politics in Nigeria* (London: Hooder and Stoughton, 1981), 49.

17. Booth, *Writers and Politics in Nigeria*, quotes Dr. Nnamdi Azikiwe as saying: "That henceforth I shall utilize my earned income to secure my enjoyment of a high standard of living and also to give a helping hand to the needy," 49.

18. Booth, *Writers and Politics in Nigeria*. James Booth also quotes Chief Obafemi Awolowo as having said: "I was going to make myself formidable intellectually, morally invulnerable, to make all the money that is possible for a man with my brains and brawn to make in Nigeria" (198), 49.

19. Nnamdi Azikiwe's book, *Ideology for Nigeria: Capitalism, Socialism or Welfarism?* (Lagos: Macmillan, 1980): x.

20. Agbafor Igwe, *Zik, the Philosopher of our Time*, (Enugu: Fourth Dimension Press, 1982), 8.

21. Ada Uzoamaka Azodo, "Nigerian Women in Search of Identity: Converging Feminism and Pragmatism," in *Emerging Perspectives on Flora Nwapa: Critical and Theoretical Essays*. Marie Umeh, ed. (Trenton: African World Press, 1997), 244.

22. Achebe, *The Trouble with Nigeria*, 2.

23. Ibid., 3.

24. Ibrahim Bello-Kano, "Chinua Achebe: A Non-Romantic View" (*Vanguard*, April 3, 2013). Ibrahim Bello-Kano, Archived July 10, 2013, at Archive.today, *Pambazuka News*, Issue 624, 3 (April 2013).

25. Achebe, *The Trouble*, 13.

26. Ibid., 24.

27. Ibid.

28. Ibid., 25.

29. Alan Feinstein, *African Revolutionary: The Life and Times of Nigeria's Aminu Kano* (New York: Quadrangle, 1987), ix. See also: Sakah S. Mahmud "Mallam Aminu Kano and the Politics of Change in Nigeria," *Africa Today*, Vol. 35, No. 1; *Black Consciousness in South Africa* (1st Quarter, 1988): 57–60.

30. Achebe, *The Trouble*, 53.

31. Ibid., 23.

32. Ibid., 60.

33. Ibid., 63.

34. Ada Uzoamaka Azodo, "A Zimbabwean Ethic of Humanity: Tsitsi Dangarembga's *The Book of Not* and the *Unhu* Philosophy of Personhood," in Ernest N. Emenyonu, *African Literature Today*, Vol. 27 (2010): 117–129.

35. *Transition*, No. 8, March 1963.

36. *Africa Today*, Vol. 35, No. 1; Black Consciousness in South Africa (1st Quarter, 1988): 57–60.

37. Achebe, *The Trouble*, 43.

38. *Nelson Mandela: A Hero's Journey, 1918–2013*. New York: Time Home Entertainment Inc. / Time Books, 2013. 59–60. See also: "Nelson Mandela: A Hero's Journey, 1918–2013," *Time Special Commemorative Edition*, 2013, New York: Time Books.

39. Achebe. *The Trouble with Nigeria*, 53.

40. Achebe, *The Trouble with Nigeria*, 53. "Our (the Nation's) inaction and cynical action, opines Achebe, are a serious betrayal of our education, of our historic mission and of succeeding generations who will have no future unless we save it now for them."

41. Olufemi Ayotebi, *Nigerian Punch Newspaper,* accessed September 1, 2019, https://punchng.com/

42. "Training Tomorrow's Leaders," accessed June 6, 2021, https://nigerialeadershipinstitute.com/.

43. "ALI is a collaborative effort of seven partner organizations in Africa and the United States—Infotech Investments (Tanzania), The Aspen Institute (United States), CETA Construction Services (Mozambique), the Databank Foundation (Ghana), LEAP Africa (Nigeria), The Letsema Foundation (South Africa), and TechnoServe (Africa and United States)—to foster values-based, action-oriented leadership in Africa. There are currently some 216 African fellows from all of the countries above including Kenya, Uganda, and Rwanda plus forty-five Nigerian leadership fellows in the Diaspora. The ALI is the result of Aspen Institute Executive Vice President Peter Reiling's Henry Crown Fellows community leadership project: "Mobilizing young [African] business leaders . . . to take more responsibility for the society in which they live and work. ALI was designed to capture the energy, the talent and the resolve of an emerging generation of leaders in Africa—leaders who have already realized a certain level of success—and to inspire them to move from success to significance by engaging in the foremost challenges of their countries and their times with support and confidence." See, "African Leadership Initiative," The Aspen Global Leadership Network, accessed September 1, 2019, https://www.bing.com/search?q=aspen+institute+leadership+program+africa+leadership+initiative&FORM=AWRE.

44. "École nationale d'administration," accessed June 6, 2021. https://en.wikipedia.org/wiki/%C3%89cole_nationale_d%27administration

45. "Achebe," *New York Times*, January 15, 2019, accessed September 1, 2019, https://www.nytimes.com/2011/01/16/opinion/16achebe.html.

BIBLIOGRAPHY

Jago, A. G. Leadership: Perspectives in Theory and Research. *Management Science*, 28 (3), (1982): 315–336.

Achebe, Chinua. *The Trouble with Nigeria.* Enugu: Fourth Dimension Publishing, 1983.

Azikiwe, Nnamdi. *Ideology for Nigeria: Capitalism, Socialism or Welfarism?* 1980.

Azodo, Ada Uzoamaka. "A Zimbabwean Ethic of Humanity: Tsitsi Dangarembga's *The Book of Not* and the *Unhu* Philosophy of Personhood." In Ernest N. Emenyonu, *African Literature Today*, Vol. 27 (2010): 117–129.

Azodo, Ada Uzoamaka. "Nigerian Women in Search of Identity: Converging Feminism and Pragmatism." In: *Emerging Perspectives on Flora Nwapa: Critical and Theoretical Essays.* Marie Umeh, ed. Trenton: African World Press, 1997: 241–259.

Booth, James. *Writers and Politics in Nigeria.* London: Hooder and Stoughton, 1981.

Feinstein, Alan. *African Revolutionary: The Life and Times of Nigeria's Aminu Kano.* Lynne Rienner Pub; Revised, Subsequent edition, 1987.

Ibrahim, Bello-Kano. "Chinua Achebe: A Non-Romantic View" (*Vanguard*, April 3, 2013).

Igwe, Agbafor. *Zik, the Philosopher of our Time.* Enugu: Fourth Dimension Publishing, 1982.

Mahmud, Sakah S. "Mallam Aminu Kano and the Politics of Change in Nigeria." *Africa Today*, Vol. 35, No. 1; *Black Consciousness in South Africa* (1st Quarter, 1988): 57–60.

Mills, Greg. *Why Africa Is Poor.* South Africa: Penguin Global, 2010.

Time, *Nelson Mandela: A Hero's Journey, 1918–2013*. New York: Time Home Entertainment Inc. / Time Books, 2013. 59–60.

Chapter 14

Chinua Achebe as a Voice of Reason on the Nigerian Crisis

A Historical Look at the Larger Picture

Odigwe A. Nwaokocha

> *Does it ever worry us that history which neither personal wealth nor power can pre-empt will pass terrible judgment on us, pronounce anathema on our names when we have accomplished our betrayal and passed on? We have lost the twentieth century; are we bent on seeing that our children also lose the twenty-first? God forbid!*[1]

That is Chinualumogu Albert, son of Achebe (known to the world and history simply as Chinua Achebe), at perhaps at his creative and critical best. The question he poses here is for every Nigerian, more particularly the parasitic elite class, who seem to have lost every sense of decency and history. It is a haunting question which he answered in the negative because an affirmation represents doom. However, it remains unresolved and its huge shadows continue to cast a bigger shade on the Nigerian state and society. The above quotation is set against the background of six decades of failure as a nation-state in virtually all indices of modern development. Nigeria has become the model of what it means to be a failure as a country, most of her wounds being self-inflicted. Her rendezvous with exceptionally bungling and pathetically naive and corrupt regimes explains the crushing misrule and near palpable poverty in the country despite some obvious advantages nature had conferred on her. Though a crassly mismanaged entity, Nigeria has given the world some exceptional talents. Chinua was one of them. Chinua Achebe has emerged as one of Africa's greatest literary icons. However, his contribution to African studies and knowledge generally goes beyond the field of literature. He has been quite influential with his writings on the troubles threatening to bring Nigeria to her knees as the Nigerian crisis has received his attention. While a lot has been written on his contributions to Igbo, Nigerian, African and global literature, his works on the continuing Nigerian crisis have been largely ignored in scholarly circles. This work is an attempt to highlight his works on the Nigerian crisis that is looking increasingly intractable. The study exclusively employs secondary sources in its analysis and extensively x-rays all manner of literature on the chosen subject. The work proceeds that Achebe's total contribution to human studies can only be fully understood if his contributions to fields outside literature are studied. The work argues that his comments on the Nigerian crises both in his fictional pieces and pseudo-historical writings highlighted epochal issues that need our attention and further analysis. It goes further to place his works within the historical epochs in which they are situated. Beyond that, the study highlights Achebe's works, comments, and actions on the Nigerian crises; places them within historical perspectives and evaluates their importance to the larger understanding of the Nigerian crisis. The study concludes with the position that the iconic Chinua Achebe and his works can never be fully understood and appreciated without his breathtaking writings and positions outside the literary field, particularly those dealing with the Nigerian crisis.

HISTORICAL PERSPECTIVES ON THE ACHEBE NOVELS AND OTHER WRITINGS

It will be impossible to understand Chinua Achebe's contribution to the debate on the crisis that has continuously buffeted the Nigerian state and society without an attempt to locate his major novels within some historical milieu. In a way, Achebe's three major novels appear rooted in history. In essence, they are works of historical fiction. These novels form a continuous stream of a story steeped in history. In this light, they all qualify to be classified as historical fiction. When their storylines and general themes are placed side-by-side with the solid facts of certain aspects of Nigeria's history, a deep reflection reveals a lot that can only be historical. Each of the novels sheds fictional lights on different epochs of Nigerian history from the pre-colonial period to 1966. His first novel, *Things Fall Apart* (published in 1958), is located within the traditional setting of a typical Igbo village just before and during the early days of colonial rule. *Arrow of God* (published in 1960) is set in the same village environment about a quarter of a century later. This time, Christian missions and colonial rule were already entrenched. In *No Longer at Ease* (published in 1966), a picture of an educated Nigerian elite is the focus just years before independence from Britain. *A Man of the People* stretches the story of the new Nigerian nation and her political dynamics in a riveting political sketch that culminated in a military overthrow of democratic rule. In a way, they all represent a narrative of the Nigerian story with lessons to be learned along the way. In a telling comment, Bernth Lindfors says: "Achebe's novels read like chapters in a biography of his people and his nation since the white man."[2]

But why was Chinua Achebe so interested in telling the Nigerian story. Perhaps his background and the forces that shaped him and his times can come to the rescue. He was born on November 6, 1930, in the Eastern Nigerian town of Ogidi in present-day Anambra State and joined his ancestors on March 21, 2013, in Boston, Massachusetts in the United States of America. Between that fateful day he was born and when he exited the planet earth, a lot was packed into his charmed and eventful life. His life was shaped by the traditional values of his Igbo people, within whose cultural milieu he spent his formative years and was conditioned also by the then-new Western European cultural values with Christianity as a major weapon. The latter represented a major assault on the former. It was the destiny of children born at the time he was born that they came to have imprints from both ends, particularly if they were sent to the new Western-styled schools promoted by Christian missionaries and the colonial government or interacted closely with the new Christian religion. Chinua Achebe's life was particularly shaped by two opposing cultural values as he grew up within an Igbo society that insisted on her traditional values being left intact against the rampaging weight of a new religion, as his father was a convert to Christianity and fraternized closely with European Christian missionaries as a catechist of the Anglican Communion. He struggled not to get lost in the labyrinth created by two opposing civilizations. After his primary education, he proceeded to the elitist smart academy fashioned after the British public school system funded by the colonial government at Umuahia, known as Government College, Umuahia, where he received a peerless secondary education between 1944 and 1947. He proceeded to the University College, Ibadan (now the University of Ibadan), where he studied English Literature graduating in 1953. His sojourns at Umuahia and Ibadan equipped him with powerful tools with which he interpreted his experiences and knowledge with which he awed the world. After Ibadan, he combined his job as a staff of the Nigerian Broadcasting Corporation with active writing, producing three very impactful novels, between 1958 and 1966. Chinua Achebe flowered early. At the age of thirty-five in 1966, he was already Director of External Broadcasting at Voice of Nigeria. In a way, the fame he acquired was built "on solid personal achievements."

Until 1990, Achebe lived mostly in Nigeria. In that year, however, an auto accident that left him paralyzed from the waist down forced him to relocate to the U.S.A. For the rest of his life, he would be confined to a wheelchair. That seemingly disadvantaged position never dulled his activism on behalf of society. For the last twenty-three years of his life, he spread the shadow of his mighty intellectual influence on the human audience. In the words of Sonala Olumhense, "He cast his considerable wisdom far wide, and at the foot of that chair, a worldwide horde of admirers came to hear him say whatever he wished."[3] He left his mark on the sands of time. The world will continue to discuss his contributions because he left humanity with so much that is authentic and original.

Essentially, Achebe was a literary giant, whose interests eventually transcended many boundaries as he deployed his considerable writing skills to promote the interests of Africa, his Igbo race, and Nigeria. When his writings are historicized, it is revealed that he started out promoting the general interests of Africa against the Eurocentric view that Africans had no past worthy of mention. That was until 1966. The tragic events that occurred that year in Nigeria, particularly the waves of the killings of Nigerians suspected to be of Igbo extraction in the North and West of Nigeria—which contributed largely to the Nigeria-Biafra war (1967–1970)—produced a revulsion in Chinua Achebe that propelled him away from producing his great novels and deep story-telling, into a heavy, genuine, and radical engagement with pan-Nigerian affairs. Taking off with his disenchantment with and condemnation of the Nigerian system that allowed the repeated massacre of Nigerian citizens in 1966 and beyond, he never really shied away from speaking up and putting his critical views into writing after that. Beyond his teaching at the University of Nigeria, Nsukka, and several universities in the U.S.A., this activism can be said to have dominated Chinua Achebe's life after the events leading up to the Nigeria-Biafra war, the war itself and afterward. As we shall see, that period, a continuation of the earlier years dedicated to story-telling and fictional thoughts, was a life well-spent with conviction in the service of his Nigerian community and humanity at large.

ACHEBE: THE WRITER AS A PATRIOT, TEACHER, AND SOCIAL ACTIVIST

It will not be out of place to say that China Achebe's zeal for the well-being of his community propelled his commitment to popular freedom and general enfranchisement. He was very much aware of his role as a writer and the additional burden that confers on him: the added duty of being a patriot. It is difficult to decipher which came first in his thoughts. It will appear that both duties re-enforced each other. It is, therefore, easy to understand why in the words of Ugumanim Bassey Obo, "He selflessly deployed his overwhelming talents and skills as a writer for the betterment of his country."[4] Because Africa needs redemption from the many forces assailing her, Chinua Achebe believes that "An artist in Africa cannot avoid that involvement . . . If you're an African, the world is upside down. We can't conceal our dissatisfaction . . . It is impossible to be neutral."[5] A lot of what Chinua Achebe did all through his eventful life was out of his philosophy that a writer must carry the added yoke of living up to the full meaning of what it means to be a patriot, teacher, and social activist: a voice for the voiceless; the one who speaks when all are silent in the face of tyranny, injustice, and oppression; the conscience of a society in disarray. According to Jean-Paul Sartre, "Whether he is an essayist, a pamphleteer, a satirist, or a novelist, whether he speaks only of individual passions or whether he attacks the social order, the writer, a free man addressing free men, has a single subject—freedom."[6] Arising from his conception of who a writer should be and what the writer must be, Achebe once told an interviewer that "An artist, in my understanding of the word, should side with the people against the Emperor that oppresses his or her people."[7] The writer can do this by helping create awareness about the happenings in society and informing to help enrich understanding of issues.[8] The social role of the writer is socially in tandem with Muhammad Ahmad Mahjub, who asked "what would be the value of literature if it does not assist the people on revolution and change in life and in thought and in awakening the minds and propelling it on to the currents of progress and development."[9] The intellectual is a creative force due to his or her fundamental tendency to differ and proffer solutions to societal tribulations. These set of people are seen as troublesome by oppressors because they ask critical and seemingly embarrassing questions that are often swept under the carpet and tackle conventions.[10] To the writer Najib Mahfuz, writing is a means of liberation.[11]

So, the writer, as an intellectual, is a freedom fighter of some sort. The role of the writer as a combatant and social builder is so beautifully captured in the words of Arthur Nwankwo:

> In a very definite sense, writing is more of a mission than a profession. This is so because first and foremost the writer is an individual, a concrete human being who has a vision, and who intends to reconstruct society, both literally and figuratively, along an envisioned line of action. Thus, a writer's first and primary task is to procreate humanity, using the published material as a tool. This task centers around the writer's immediate geo-physical and social surroundings as well as the history or evolution of those surroundings.[12]

The writer's task is quite daunting, therefore, on account of his/her vocation and the associated burdens. The writer has to necessarily make a conscious choice of taking ideological and philosophical positions. This has prompted a researcher into asking:

> But how can Nigerian writers help solve the socio-political, economic, and security crisis in which the nation is stuck? Should they occupy the position of passive witnesses or take up active roles through the medium of writing in order to effect change? Should they tell the truth and be damned or tell lies and be done for?[13]

As a patriot and a determined loyalist to the cause of his beloved community, Chinua Achebe saw it as a duty to continuously use the medium at his disposal to draw attention to the many avoidable missteps and negative developments in Nigeria only capable of producing and multiplying poverty, ignorance, underdevelopment, and chaos. In the words of Charles E. Nnolim, Achebe was "a politically committed writer because of his concern for the fate or destiny of the Igbos in particular and Nigerians and Africans in general in their collective encounter with Europe."[14] His deep concern with the post-colonial nation-state drove him to the magnitude of the plethora of challenges of different hues confronting Nigeria, which has lost her self-respect and is verging on becoming a failed state. This, according to Chinua Achebe, is the worst thing that can happen to any nation.[15]

ACHEBE'S LAMENTATIONS ON THE ETHNIC CONUNDRUM IN NIGERIA

Nigerian history has been marked, marred, defined, defied, and even defiled by the challenge of managing and manipulating Nigeria's ethnic plurality. It has traveled along the lines of Nigerian history and got progressively worse along the dreadful line. Nigeria's challenge with the negative currents of ethnicity, popularly known as tribalism in many Nigerian circles, manifests in very many ways and will seem to have affected many facets of her national life and brought Nigeria to her knees. It was already rearing its ugly head in pre-independence Nigeria and seems to have been a topical issue among those who cared about the future of Nigeria. An excerpt from a speech delivered by a Nigerian politician—who appeared to have underestimated its potential for multiplication—in 1959 is instructive at this juncture: "The truth is that the days of principalities and provincialisms are gone. To continue to play on the fear of tribes and families and hamlets is to ignore immense expanse of Nigeria's destiny in the scheme of the world."[16] Chinua Achebe was quite aware of the major drawback ethnocentrism represents in Nigeria's national life and never shied away from rallying against it and condemning it as a major bane to national cohesion and development despite half-hearted measures by the establishment—through constitutional safeguards—to limits its influence. He lamented the damaging impact of ethnocentrism on Nigeria's attempt at nation-building and insisted that efforts at stopping its cancerous spread have been mostly dishonest. He asserted that:

> A Nigerian . . . graduate seeking employment in the public service, a businessman tendering for a contact, a citizen applying for a passport . . . or seeking access to any of the hundred thousand avenues controlled by the state, will sooner or later fill out a form which requires him to confess his tribe.[17]

Chinua Achebe located the virulent trends of ethnic plurality in Nigeria to prejudice, a mental attitude that targets those considered to be outsiders or strangers and cautions that "no modern state can lend its support to such prejudice without undermining its own progress and civilization."[18] His warning is important as prejudice has the tendency to disunite and spread group hatred, which ultimately militates against group cohesion, a necessary ingredient in national advancement. It assumes a critical position when we bring to the fore Margaret Peil's position that once acquired, prejudice is difficult to unlearn.[19] Since prejudice appears to be one of the factors that rule the waves and determines who gets what and who becomes what, does it mean Nigeria is stuck in a bottomless pit? We may never know. However, its stultifying consequences continue to drag Nigeria down and promote a cult of mediocrity that does the country no good. According to Achebe, ethnocentrism damages social morality by advancing mediocrity and forcing a general decline in societal morale with all its inherent disadvantages and attendant consequences.[20] The cult of mediocrity that ethnocentrism has thrown up to run Nigeria has ensured that Nigeria has consistently put square pegs in round holes and expects to have firm foundations. She plants mangoes and expects to harvest apples. She goes to battles with her second and third eleven and expects to be competitive against teams employing their very best and fully prepared for battle.

The bane of the Nigerian system and why modern development has continued to elude her is that some narrow-minded Nigerians who think they are benefiting from the sick order are opposed to a merit-based system. They, however, fail to realize that denial of basic social justice to those who deserve places based on merit does not just hurt the denied individual but the entire society. It was one of Achebe's firm beliefs that each time narrow-mindedness ignores merit, as it does so often in Nigeria, citizens and the nation itself become victims.[21] The kernel of the issue here is that favoritism and discrimination based on ethnic considerations do not promote social justice. Its consequences are legion for the Nigerian society. Many beneficiaries of this flawed order are happy it enables them access to loot public funds and abuse their positions with impunity without pausing to think about the larger ramifications of their actions for society.

Among the many issues of ethnocentrism and its fallout in Nigeria, Achebe was particularly interested in the case of his own Igbo group and the Nigerian state and society. This cold yet hot relationship produced the 1966 three-waves of Igbo killing that dragged Nigeria to war between 1967 and 1970. He alleges that Nigerians of other ethnic groups seem united in their dislike of the Igbo.[22]

Harsh as his claim that Nigerians of other ethnic groups take exception to the Igbo group, facts that seem to objectify that appear littered all over the pages of Nigerian history. The high-point of it will appear to be the Nigeria-Biafra war fought essentially between the Igbo and the rest of Nigeria. Subsequent discriminatory practices geared toward constraining Igbo progress within the Nigerian space represent a voiceless but powerful announcement that the war is still very much on. The Igbo seem to be paying a stiff price for being overtly enterprising and materially successful. This has made many of them quite visible and some high level of showmanship, being highly individualistic as republican-bred folks. According to him, this kind of insensitivity, invites resentment and odium.[23] This has created an Igbo challenge for many Nigerians of other ethnic stocks. Given that state of affairs, Achebe did not spare his Igbo kinsmen of harsh criticism for being bashful and noisy in celebrating their successes to the utter consternation of people from other groups. He asked them to show more wisdom and diplomacy in their public displays.[24]

ACHEBE ON THE NIGERIAN ELITE AND FAILURE OF LEADERSHIP

Chinua Achebe believed that part of the challenge preventing Nigeria from reaching her full potentials is the challenge of leadership and corruption. At different points of his life, he carpeted the Nigerian elite class, the leadership, and people for what Nigeria has turned out to be. In the first place, he is firm in his belief that Nigeria has been prodigiously blessed by nature with abundant natural resources and a strong pool of humans that can be transformed into a strong human capital and that all that is lacking for her to be transformed into a successful entity is viable leadership. According to him, the elite factor is an indispensable element of leadership. And leadership itself is indispensable to any association of human beings desirous of achieving whatever goals it set for itself. When such an association is engaged in a difficult undertaking or is in pursuit of a risky objective such as nation-building, the need for competent leadership becomes particularly urgent.[25]

The importance he attaches to the fundamental position of leadership in nation-building is reflected in the opening sentence of his *The Trouble with Nigeria* when he declared that "The trouble with Nigeria is simply and squarely a failure of leadership."[26]

Even while commenting on the complementary role of followership in the developmental process, the kernel of his focus remained the centrality of leadership. In his opinion:

> we need not spend too long on the argument for pre-eminence of followers. It is enough to say that no human enterprise has flourished on the basis of the following leading the leaders. The cliché that people get the leadership they deserve is a useful exaggeration-useful because it reminds the general populace of the need for vigilance in selecting their leaders (where they have the chance to do so), and for keeping them under constant surveillance.[27]

It will appear that in bringing the Nigerian citizenry up and heaping some blame on them for the Nigerian quagmire, Achebe did not quite appreciate the inner linings of Nigerian history. The advent of military adventurers in power, their activities therein, and the activities of the civilian neophytes who succeeded them produced a large chunk of citizens who are perpetually asleep to their responsibilities as members of an ailing society. They have run down all social institutions capable of challenging evil or staying focused on the great questions of the day. No institution was spared in this evil enterprise, including the civil service, the schools, and even academic subjects capable of conferring some enlightenment on the citizenry. The result is a society of zombies masquerading as citizens but bereft of all that the concept connotes. All sectors capable of engaging society critically and asking why things are the way they are were labeled dangerous and so, unnecessary for the good health of the nation. As Pius Adesanmi put it:

> When you plan to turn the largest political union of black people on the face of the earth into the most embarrassing open sore of the black race; when you plan to turn Africa's most populous country into a continental example of how not to run a country; when you plan to loot on such a scale as to make . . . your own appointed anti-corruption czar declare in exasperation that the scale of looting by Nigeria's political leaders is a "symptom of mental illness"; when you are planning to loot on that uninterrupted scale . . . since the 1980s, the first thing

you need to do is manufacture a followership incapable of critically challenging you or one that would applaud and hail your actions, especially if there is the occasional trickle down from the table of the bacchanals you organize at their expense.[28]

As demonstrated above, the Nigerian leadership-followership conundrum is deep, complex, and not easily explainable. It is difficult to explain which failure produced the other. They seem to sharpen and re-enforce each other. However, the primacy of the head places more of the weighty blame on leadership. In weighing into the debate that predates Nigeria's independence in 1960, Achebe demonstrated his patriotic zeal for the country of his birth. He demonstrated a strong nationalistic spirit. It should be noted that as far back as 1959, Dr. Abyssinia Nwafor-Orizu had raised the issue of the kind of leadership an independent Nigeria would need to move forward. In a speech titled "The Leadership We Want" delivered at the National Hall, Aba, he enumerated the qualities of the kind of leadership Nigeria desired. In an excerpt from the speech, the Nnewi-born prince crowed: "No nation can really exist until those who lead have grown so loyal as to forget themselves and forfeit a good deal of pseudo-liberties in the service of the nation."[29] In other words, Nwafor-Orizu espoused the hope that Nigeria should have serious-minded patriots and visionaries in leadership positions. Did Nwafor Orizu express his hope against a background of an emerging national leadership that lacked people of vision? Perhaps another opinion from a Nigerian pre-independence writer may be of help. Writing in April 1959, Jasper Oji said: "If our politics has no vision, we perish. If we perish, our children will mourn our perdition and live in shame of their fathers who could not make history."[30]

It is safe to say at this juncture that lack of visionary leadership was a national challenge even as the modern Nigerian state was emerging from the womb of time. It has become a stronger demon now. It has stalled many positive things from happening to Nigeria. It was one of the ills Achebe never ceased talking about until he breathed his last. He remained consistent in his condemnation of bad leadership in Nigeria. He was a practical drum-major for all that was right for Nigeria to be placed on the path of growth and rallied against opportunists who applauded, and acquiesced, with evil if they gained some advantages from its fall-out. At a point, he complained that:

There will always be some people whose personal selfish interests are, in the short term at least, well served by the mismanagement and social iniquities. Naturally, they will be extremely loud in their adulation of the country and its system and will be anxious to pass themselves off as patriots and to vilify those who disagree with them as trouble-makers or even traitors. But doomed is the nation that permits such people to define patriotism for it.[31]

The large cult of minions who support evil in Nigeria has continued to enlarge further because leadership failure in Nigeria has somewhat become an accepted integral part of the Nigerian story. Achebe has historicized how the negative progressive growth of the evil has imposed itself on Nigerian society. To him:

> The First Republic produced political leaders in all regions who were not perfect, but compared to those that came after them they now appear almost "saint-like"—they were well educated, grounded politicians who may have embodied a flawed vision or outlook for the country (in my opinion); but at least had one. Following a series of crises that culminated in the bloody Nigeria-Biafra war, Nigeria found itself in the hands of military officers with very little vision for the nation or understanding of the modern world. A period of great decline and decadence set in, and continues to this day. The civilian leadership of the Second Republic continued almost blindly the mistakes of their predecessors. At a point in our history, the scale of corruption and ineptitude had increased exponentially, fuelled by the abundance of petro-dollars. By the time the Third Republic arrived, we found ourselves in the grip of former military dictators turned 'democrats' with the same old mindset but now donning civilian clothes. So, Nigeria following the First Republic has been ruled by the same cult of mediocrity—a deeply corrupt cabal—for at least forty years, recycling themselves in different guises and incarnations. They have then deeply corrupted the local business elites who are in turn often pawns of foreign business interests.[32]

The challenge of leadership and the worsening crisis it presented Nigeria with remains a huge mountain that demanded dismantling, a task only patriots could dare. In Achebe's patriotic zeal and in his bid to situate the challenges confronting Nigeria within some perspectives, he raised the question of who a patriot is against the background of many charlatans and upstarts laying claim to patriotism. In his words, a patriot "is not even a person who shouts or swears or sings his love for his country . . . A true patriot will always demand the highest standards of his country and accept nothing but the best for and from people."[33]

With this logical conviction at the back of his mind, it is easy to understand Achebe's position that the unpatriotic, self-serving, parasitic and clueless Nigerian ruling class who masquerade as patriots is responsible for bringing Nigeria to her knees. Starting from the bloody ethno-regional crisis of 1966 that dragged Nigeria to war with itself, Achebe never stopped placing the blame on the Nigerian elite class for the parlous state of affairs in Nigeria. Commenting on the hunting and mass killings of Igbo people in three waves of attacks in 1966 that partly led to the Nigeria-Biafra war between 1967 and 1970, he put his feelings, in a way akin to mourning Nigeria, into the following words:

> As we reached the brink of the full-blown war it became clear to me that the chaos enveloping all of us was due to the incompetence of the Nigerian political ruling class. They clearly had a poor grasp of history ... My feeling towards Nigeria was one of profound disappointment not only because mobs were hunting down and killing innocent civilians ... but because the federal government sat by and let it happen.[34]

This position mirrored an avoidable national catastrophe. Ineptitude and mediocrity prompted by power games had unleashed an entire nation against a section of it. Achebe's position was a product of his frustration arising not just from the attitude of the ruling class but also the ordinary people to the fate that befell a section of the Nigerian community. The fact that the Igbo group was abandoned as other Nigerian groups strutted about as if all was well and the Igbo were the problem of Nigeria and their own worst enemy, pained him beyond the marrow. Perhaps the following observation by a foreigner who visited Nigeria in 1966 will throw more light on the fact that the Igbo were abandoned by other Nigerians:

> Visiting Nigeria in November 1966, I was conscious of the extreme gulf between the attitude towards the massacres in the East and in the rest of Nigeria. It was astonishing how many people, not only in Kano and Kaduna but in Ibadan and Lagos merely commented that while it is very sad, "the Ibos had it coming to them", and that despite evidence that the massacres were planned by political groups for political ends, they were somehow, "God's will".[35]

The fact that the Igbo predicament was considered isolated and not seen as a national challenge even when it was dragging Nigeria to pieces spoke volumes about the disposition of Nigeria's elites. This lackadaisical attitude to a major threat facing a segment of the Nigerian society was very much lamented by Chinua Achebe in the following lines when someone advised him to relocate from his house in Lagos because Nigerian military troops were looking for him:

> I was not a criminal, I had done nothing. Eventually, I did leave and sought refuge in a friend's house with my family. Yet for about a week I still did not believe—I simply thought that things had temporarily gone out of hand—it would be all right. After a week I decided to send my family home, and as we were doing this the people were jeering and saying, "Let them (the Ibos) go, food would be cheaper in Lagos." We expected to hear something from the intellectuals, from our friends. Rather what we heard was "Oh they had it coming to them or something to that effect ... That kind of experience is too powerful; to me, it is something I could not possibly forget.[36]

Chinua Achebe was never the type of character to keep mute in the face of tyranny. He felt perturbed at what was happening to the new nation of Nigeria. He voted with his feet and joined the movement to secure all Igbo and Eastern Nigerian lives against the rampaging larger Nigerian population egged on by the government that did nothing to protect Nigerian lives. That movement led to Biafra, where he emerged as a roving ambassador of the new state of Biafra that rose from the defiant spirit of his Igbo people. He refused to abandon his people at their greatest hour of need. As a patriot and patron of righteous causes, he gave leadership and a voice to his people's lamentations at a time of great travails.

It is Chinua Achebe's belief and view that Nigeria's travails have arisen because of the quality of leadership and the cult of mediocrity that it consequently built around itself. He also believed that if Nigeria is to be spared future crises and escape from the clutches of underdevelopment, she must be armed with the right leadership capable of answering the greatest questions of the day as they unfold. He prescribed what he termed "servant leaders." In his words:

> When I talked about the need for a servant leader, I have emphasized a well-prepared individual—educationally, morally, and otherwise—who wants to serve (in the deepest sense of the word); someone who sees the ascendancy to leadership as an anointment by the people and who holds the work to be highly important, if not sacred. I know that is asking for a lot, but that really should be our goal. If we aim for that, what we get may not be so bad after all. That elusive great Nigerian leader that can transcend our handicaps—corruption, ethnic bigotry, the celebration of mediocrity, indiscipline, etc will only come when we make the process of electing leaders—through free and fair elections in a democracy—as flawless as possible, improving on each exercise as we evolve as a nation. Once we have the right kind of leaders in place—the true choices of the people—then, I believe, it will be possible to solidify all the freedoms we crave as a people—freedom of the press, assembly, expressions, etc. Within this democratic environment, the three tiers of government filled with servant leaders chosen by the people can pass laws that will put in place checks and balances the nation desperately needs to curb corruption.[37]

Achebe was baffled that with all it has done to bring Nigeria on her knees, the obviously clueless and self-serving Nigerian elite class appears incapable of understanding the workings of historical forces feels neither shame nor remorse, and struts about as though it had built up the best possible place on planet earth. He took the Nigerian elite class to the cleaners for their indiscipline and corruption, which they display brazenly at every turn in an ostentatious exhibition of their importance. He captured Nigeria as an unlucky place to have such a ruling class when he declared:

Unlucky is the country where indiscipline is seen by ordinary people as the prerogative of the high and mighty ... I don't know of any other country where you can find such brazen insensitivity and arrogant selfishness among those who lay claim to leadership.[38]

CHINUA ACHEBE ON CORRUPTION IN NIGERIA

Corruption and all the negative baggage it carries with it have become an albatross on the neck of Nigeria. It has permeated every facet of Nigeria's national life. Its growing manifestations and unedifying possibilities are simply sickening and frightening. According to Moses E. Ochonu, "Nigerians are right to agonize over corruption. It is the single most important reason their country is comatose and lacks the capacity to fulfill even the most modest niceties of government. It is the reason for many preventable deaths and sufferings."[39] While locating the myriad of challenges confronting Nigeria as a modern nation-state principally on the failure of leadership, Chinua Achebe also acknowledged that a sub-plot of the failure apparent in the Nigerian system is due to the problem of corruption and its various ramifications. Somehow, he tied up the challenge of corruption with the disappointment of leadership. Concerning the scourge of corruption facing Nigeria, he took a swipe at the collective Nigerian society. According to him:

> At this point in Nigeria's history ... we can no longer absolve ourselves of the responsibility for our present condition. Corruption is endemic because we have had a complete failure of leadership in Nigeria that has made corruption easy and profitable. It will be controlled when Nigerians put in place checks and balances that will make corruption "inconvenient"—with appropriate jail sentences and penalties to punish those that steal from the state.[40]

Stealing from the state under many guises has become a phenomenon. It was minimal at independence but eventually grew to become a big challenge to national development. In his general concern about the growing scope of corruption among the ruling elite, Achebe was unsparing of the ruling class in his condemnation of a plague that will simply not go away. His perspective on the huge financial resources Providence has blessed Nigeria with is that it would have been enough to launch Nigeria into the top league of developed countries. His comments on how Nigeria misused an opportunity that would have given her a place in the sun represents a sad commentary on the waywardness of the Nigerian elite. He accused them of flagrant corruption and wastefulness.[41]

Achebe further added that the Nigerian elite class is primitive in its accumulation of riches without a care in the world for the generality of Nigerians and how their actions affect the very fabric of the society. He dwelt on the disruptive influence of corruption on society. According to him:

> The real explosive potential of social injustice in Nigeria does not reside in the narrow jostling among the elite but in the gargantuan disparity of privilege they have created between their tiny class and the vast multitudes of ordinary Nigerians.[42]

Arising from the depth of corruption; how well organized it is; its capacity to multiply and have a serious effect on the Nigerian society and what that may mean in the long run; Chinua Achebe classified Nigeria as ailing and warned that corruption, which had reached the terminal phase will kill her if Nigerians keep treating the ailment as light.[43]

ACHEBE'S DISENCHANTMENT WITH NIGERIA

The many faults of the Nigerian system have nauseated and flustered Achebe to the extent that by the 1980s he had begun to question and mock many things Nigerian. For instance, he queried and mocked the concept of Nigerian "greatness." He was baffled and scoffed at the idea that a country that could not pull her people out of poverty nor run basic institutions of state successfully could delude itself into believing that she was "great." On that score, he was very harsh in the words he chose to describe the Nigerian situation when he dismissed Nigeria as "one of the most disorderly nations in the world."[44]

Chinua Achebe's disappointment with Nigeria and disillusionment with what Nigeria turned out to be after promising so much took him to a level where he was at odds with the "Unity and Faith" tag on the Nigerian coat of arms and as the directive principles of Nigerianism. He mocked both principles as they seem based on not serving the general good, and so, questionable. According to him, "Unity can only be as good as the purpose for which it is desired . . . faith is as good as the object on which it reposes."[45]

One needs no rigorous research to state that Chinua Achebe was utterly disenchanted with Nigeria. It is important that this has a history that we can possibly locate in his disappointment with what became of his Nigeria from July 1966 onward. Rather than diminish, this disappointment grew as Achebe grew older. As pointed out elsewhere in this work, the catastrophic events that produced the Nigeria-Biafra war and the terrible consequences of the war, including the fact that no lessons appeared to have been learned from those terrible episodes, propelled him to a place of no return: an optimist about the

Nigerian project. Beyond his criticisms of the failed Nigerian system and its huge consequences for the toiling mass of the Nigerian people, his actions concerning national honors conferred on him by the Nigerian state demonstrated his deep frustration and anger with the sorry state of affairs in Nigeria. In 2004 and 2011, Chinua Achebe rejected the Nigerian state award of the Commander of the Federal Republic (CFR). He did so out of his patriotic duty to the Nigerian people reeling from pain inflicted on them by bad governance and who have had to battle socio-economic strangulation. It needs to be noted that Achebe had accepted awards bestowed on him by the Nigerian state between 1961 and 1999. In 1979, he had accepted the Nigerian National Order of Merit and the Order of the Federal Republic (OFR). In 1999, he also agreed to be conferred with Nigerian National Creativity Award. His rejection of the other awards by the Nigerian government in 2004 and 2011 will seem to have been his own way of saying "enough is enough" to the incompetent managers of the Nigerian project that had been run aground by greed, nepotism, and corruption. It has a ring of history to it and can only be located in his long-suffering history of pain and hope regarding the Nigerian enterprise. That singular action spoke in a million decibels without words and sounds.

CONCLUSION

It is easy to see Chinua Achebe's involvement with the Nigerian project and his tirades against it was a product of genuine concern for the health of the country. His commitment to the ideal of good leadership looms supreme in his hierarchy of what Nigeria urgently needs to climb out of the woods. His concern for the good of his community saw him transform as a writer of different genres all through his life. However, he never forgot the centrality of the people and their freedom in his engagement. He started as a writer of prose fiction with historical anecdotes as his pillars. That produced the great novels that announced him to the world in his youth. The astonishing circumstances of Nigerian history soon forced him away from his great fictional stories. The historical occurrences that produced the Nigeria-Biafra war filled him with a disappointment hard to capture in words. Before his death, that disappointment seems to have turned to anger as reflected in his rejection of Nigeria's national honors on two occasions. It is fundamental to point out here that the disappointment Chinua Achebe expressed about the Nigerian project attracted some condemnation to him from a section of the Nigerian community. In his appraisal of his last book, *There was a Country: A Personal History of Biafra*, Minabere Ibelema charged that "Achebe's Igbo-centric rhetoric is undermining Nigeria."[46] Another commentator on the same book opined that he "seemed to share a by and large self-inflicted persecution complex of his Igbo kith and kin."⁴⁷

Much as we all may not have agreed with his idea and opinions, Chinua Achebe was a pitcher for the welfare of his people. Just as he attacked colonizers and colonization for denigrating Africa and Africans, he turned on post-colonial African elites for their misrule, corruption, and for lacking in a sense history and needed diligence for the sake of uplifting the teeming population of Africans left in the lurch. Harsh as his criticisms of Nigeria may appear, Achebe was neither a nihilist nor a misanthrope. He was rather an idealist, who proceeded from the real facts around him instead of dwelling in unscientific optimism. The profundity of Achebe's talent and influence is not in doubt. *Things Fall Apart*, his first novel, was his *magnum opus* while he signed off with *There Was a Country: A Personal History of the of Biafra*, which was his attempt at putting down his recollections of a war that has become a watershed in Nigerian history.

NOTES

1. Chinua Achebe, *The Trouble With Nigeria* (London: Heinemann, 1984), 3.
2. Bernth Lindfors, "The Palm-oil with Which Words Are Eaten," in C. L. Innes and Bernth Lindfors (Eds), *Critical Perspectives on Chinua Achebe* (London: Heinemann, 1979), 48.
3. Sonala Olumhense, "Chinua Achebe, "Chinua Achebe: Larger in Death." Available at www. saharareporters.com. Accessed on October 10, 2019.
4. Ugumanim Bassey Obo, "China Achebe and the Nigerian Predicament: A Tribute to a Patriot," *Global Journal of Interdisciplinary Studies*, 3 (5), 2014, 55.
5. Chinua Achebe as quoted in Charles Trueheart, "Chinua Achebe Politics of Art," *The Washinton Post*, February 16, 1988. Available at www.the washintonpost.com. Accessed on October 30, 2019.
6. Jean-Paul Sartre as cited in Adele L. Jinadu, *Fanon: In Search of the African Revolution* (Enugu: Fourth Dimension Publishing Company, 1980), 136.
7. Scott Baldauf, "Chinua Achebe on Corruption and Hope in Nigeria," Chinua Achebe's interview with *The Christian Science Monitor*, March 22, 2013, 5. Available at www.csmonitor.com/World/Africa/2013/0322/Chinua-Achebe. Accessed on September 12, 2019.
8. G. Lamming, *Social Role of Writers* (Paris: United Nations Educational, Scientific and Cultural Organization, 1968), 2–4.
9. Kahar Wahab Sarumi, "Who Will Save Nigeria?: On Writing and the Writer's Role in Securing the Nation," IOSR Journal of Humanities and Social Sciences, 19 (6) VII, 2014, 42.
10. Edward Said, "Representations of the Intellectual," *The 1993 Reith Lectures* (New York: Pantheon Books), 11.
11. Najib Mahfuz, *As-sukkariyyah* (Cairo: Maktabat Misr, 1959), 91.

12. Arthur Nwankwo, *Before I Die* (Enugu: Fourth Dimension Publishing Company, 1989), 177.
13. Sarumi, 42.
14. Charles E. Nnolim, "Chinua Achebe: A re-Assessment," *TYDSKRIF VIR LETTERKUNDE*, 48 (1), 2011, 42.
15. Chinua Achebe, "The Role of the Writer in a New Nation," in G. D. Killam, (ed.) African Writers on African Writing (London: Heinemann, 1973), 7–13.
16. Abbysinia Nwafor-Orizu, "The Leadership We Want." *Eastern States Express* (Nigeria), February 24, 1959, 1.
17. Chinua Achebe, *The Trouble With Nigeria* (London: Heinemann, 1983), 6.
18. Ibid., 7.
19. Margaret Peil, *Consensus and Conflict in African Societies: An Introduction to Sociology* (London: Longman, 1977), 116.
20. Achebe, *The Trouble With Nigeria*, 19.
21. Ibid., 22.
22. Ibid., 45.
23. Ibid., 46.
24. Ibid., 46–48.
25. Chinua Achebe, "The Leadership Crisis in Nigerian Politics," *Daily Sun* (Nigeria), January 10, 2010, 49.
26. Achebe, *The Trouble With Nigeria*, 1.
27. Achebe, "The Leadership Crisis in Nigerian Politics," 56 and 49.
28. Pius Adesanmi, "Nigerian Netizens and the Man with the Palm Oil Bling Bling." Available at www.saharareporters.com. Accessed on October 2, 2019.
29. Abbysinia Nwafor-Orizu, "The Leadership We Want," *Eastern States Express* (Nigeria), March 3, 1959, 2.
30. Jasper Oji, *Eastern States Express* (Nigeria), April 3, 1959, 3.
31. Chinua Achebe as cited in Aladesanmi, *Op cit.*
32. Ibid., 3–4.
33. Chinua Achebe, *The Trouble With Nigeria* (Enugu: Fourth Dimension Publishers, 1983), 15–16.
34. Chinua Achebe, *There Was a Country*, 68–71.
35. Kaye Whiteman, "Enugu: The Psychology of Secession" in S. K. Panther-Bricks, Ed., *Prelude to the Civil War*, (London: Athlone Press, 1970), 116
36. Quoted in John de St. Jorre, *The Nigerian Civil War* (London: Hodder and Stoughton, 1972), 101.
37. Scott Baldauf, "Chinua Achebe on Corruption and Hope in Nigeria," Chinua Achebe's interview with *The Christian Science Monitor*, March 22, 2013, 4. Available at www.csmonitor.com/World/Africa/2013/0322/Chinua-Achebe. Accessed on September 12, 2019.
38. Achebe, *The Trouble With Nigeria*, 33–34.
39. Moses E. Ochonu, "The Other Problems of Corruption" (mimeograph).
40. Scott Baldauf, "Chinua Achebe on Corruption and Hope in Nigeria."
41. Achebe, *The Trouble With Nigeria*, 2.
42. Ibid., 22.

43. Ibid., 38.
44. Ibid., 9–10.
45. Ibid., 12–13.
46. Minabere Ibelema, "Achebe and the Biafran Religion," *Sunday Punch*, October 4, 2012.
47. Mohammed Haruna, "Achebe: Africa's Best," *The Nation*, March 27, 2013.

BIBLIOGRAPHY

Achebe, Chinua. "The Leadership Crisis in Nigerian Politics." *Daily Sun* (Nigeria), January 10, 2010, 49.

Achebe, Chinua. "The Role of the Writer in a New Nation." in G. D. Killam, (ed.) *African Writers on African Writing*. London: Heinemann, 1973, 7–13.

Achebe, Chinua. *The Trouble With Nigeria*. Enugu: Fourth Dimension Publishers, 1983.

Adesanmi, Pius. "Nigerian Netizens and the Man with the Palm Oil Bling Bling." Available at www.saharareporters.com. Accessed on October 2, 2019.

Baldauf, Scott. "Chinua Achebe on Corruption and Hope in Nigeria," Chinua Achebe's interview with *The Christian Science Monitor*, March 22, 2013, 5. Available at www.csmonitor.com/World/Africa/2013/0322/Chinua-Achebe. Accessed on September 12, 2019.

Haruna, Mohammed. "Achebe: Africa's Best." *The Nation*, March 27, 2013.

Ibelema, Minabere. Achebe and the Biafran Religion," *Sunday Punch*, October 4, 2012.

Jinadu, Adele L. *Fanon: In Search of the African Revolution*. Enugu: Fourth Dimension Publishing Company, 1980.

Lamming, G. *Social Role of Writers* (Paris: United Nations Educational, Scientific and Cultural Organization, 1968), 2–4.

Lindfors, Bernth. "The Palm-oil with Which Words Are Eaten." In C. L. Innes and Bernth Lindfors (eds.), *Critical Perspectives on Chinua Achebe*. London: Heinemann, 1979.

Mahfuz, Najib. *As-sukkariyyah*. Cairo: Maktabat Misr, 1959.

Nnolim, Charles E. "Chinua Achebe: A Re-Assessment," *TYDSKRIF VIR LETTERKUNDE*, 48 (1), 2011.

Nwafor-Orizu, Abbysinia. "The Leadership We Want." *Eastern States Express* (Nigeria), February 24, 1959, 1.

Nwankwo, Arthur. *Before I Die*. Enugu: Fourth Dimension Publishing Company, 1989.

Obo, Ugumanim Bassey. "China Achebe and the Nigerian Predicament: A Tribute to a Patriot." *Global Journal of Interdisciplinary Studies*, 3 (5), (2014): 53–57.

Olumhense, Sonala. "Chinua Achebe, "Chinua Achebe: Larger in Death." Available at www.saharareporters.com. Accessed on October 10, 2019.

Peil, Margaret *Consensus and Conflict in African Societies: An Introduction to Sociology*. London: Longman, 1977.

Said, Edward. "Representations of the Intellectual." *The 1993 Reith Lectures*. New York: Pantheon Books.

Sarumi, Kahar Wahab. "Who Will Save Nigeria?: On Writing and the Writer's Role in Securing the Nation," *IOSR Journal of Humanities and Social Sciences*, 19 (6) VII, (2014): 39–44.

Trueheart, Charles. "Chinua Achebe Politics of Art." *The Washinton Post*, February 16, 1988. Available at www.thewashintonpost.com. Accessed on October 30, 2019.

Whiteman, Kaye. "Enugu: The Psychology of Secession." in S. K. Panther-Bricks, Ed., *Prelude to the Civil War*. London: Athlone Press, 1970.

Chapter 15

Chinua Achebe and the National Question

Bernard Steiner Ifekwe

This chapter examines Chinua Achebe's perspectives on the national question in Nigeria through the prism of his fictional works. The founding fathers of Nigeria adopted a federal system in order to assuage the fear and suspicion of all ethnic groups in the country. Hardly had this constitutional provision become operative did the same leaders undertook some unconstitutional acts that perpetuated dissensions and fissures in the polity. There were several cases of electoral violence, corruption, nepotism, human rights violations, among others, which provoked much vitriolic debate on the national question, particularly the role of the government in the dispensation of justice and national cohesion. These problems accentuated military interventions, civil war, and perennial conflicts prompting a prominent imaginative writer such as Chinua Achebe to explore these problems in his novels, poems, and essays. Achebe, thus, submits that the leadership question since 1960 compromised and created a nation in perpetual conflict against itself. Consequently, this essay has deepened our understanding of the interplay between fact and fiction in historical narrations.

The spate of crisis in Nigeria had been quite mind boggling and provoking an avalanche of debates and opinions, from well-meaning citizens, and friends who had, on different fora, questioned the crass leadership programmes in post-colonial Nigeria. Such programmes, in most cases, had promoted the culture of impunity, dictatorship, ethnicity, and mediocrity within a country primed as the giant of Africa.[1]

The leadership factor, according to Achebe, had undermined Nigeria's growth, in all ramifications, and was at the core of the national question.[2] This situation, however, had created a country, in civil and military administrative settings, a country where there was "no tomorrow"[3] due to policy summersaults and overt emasculation of many ethnic nationals. The Nigerian political elite dominated and controlled by the Northerners, with support from many Southern surrogates, had plunged the country in unending conflict since 1960. From this perspective, the national question, based on equity, devolution of power, ethnic harmony, and respect for human rights had remained at the country's front burner, through several conferences. From the British-controlled constitutional conferences within the colonial era, the core of the political elites, particularly Nnamdi Azikiwe, Ahmadu Bello, and Obafemi Awolowo, as leaders with disparate views, could not find a common ground to address multiple differences within the nation.[4] The post-colonial conferences, namely the 1966 Yakubu Gowon's ad hoc conference, the 1994 Sani Abacha's constitutional conference, the 2003 Olusegun Obasanjo's political Reform programme, and the 2014 Goodluck Jonathan's conferences were parts of the major landmarks towards the national question.

This debate on the national question was not solely within the province of Nigerian governments and their lackeys only. Other critical stakeholders including literary icons, of Chinua Achebe's era, initiated the debate through fictional and other related works, couching their debates with imaginary characters in their works to reflect the political and historical saga in Nigeria. In an essay entitled "The Truth of Fiction," Chinua Achebe advances the importance of art to historical realities:

> Art is man's constant effort to create for himself a different order of reality from that which is given to him; an aspiration to provide himself with a second handle on existence *through his imagination*. The great virtue of literary fiction is that it is able by engaging our imagination to lead us to . . . locate again the line between the heroic and the cowardly when it seems most shadowy and elusive, and it does this by forcing us to encounter the heroic and the cowardly in our own psyche.
>
> How often do we hear people say, "Oh I don't have the time to read novels" implying that fiction is frivolous? They would generally add—lest you consider them illiterate—that they read histories or biographies, which they presume to be more appropriate to serious—minded adults. The life of the imagination is a vital element of our total nature. If we starve it or pollute it the quality of our life is depressed or soiled.[5]

The italicized phrase, *through his imagination*, extracted from this Achebe's statement, replicates a writer's pursuit of historical events, through imaginary situations. From this perspective, Nigeria had remained a country, even in colonial settings, to set a self-destructive agenda where primordial interests, corruption, and leadership squabbles would dominate national affairs. In such delicate situations, Achebe's works have adorned "opposition" status by expressing national discourse in a manner other political elite in opposition in the country would fear to tread.

Against this background, the thesis of this essay is that Achebe's stance on events in Nigeria through his novels, essays, and poems, exemplify his personal contributions to the national question.

CHINUA ACHEBE AND GRAFT IN NIGERIA

Graft was a phenomenon that dominated Chinua Achebe's writings as he focused on its implications within Nigeria's First and Second Republics. Graft contributed much to instability in the polity, when development programmes of successive governments remained ineffective through wanton looting of the public treasury by the leaders.

Democracy was bequeathed to Nigeria by the British. It was expected to implant transparency in governance, political stability, and economic development in post-colonial Nigeria. The fundamental focus of regionalism, political party formation, and electoral practices, were not well formulated by the British within this period. The major Nigerian political elites, and supporters, exploited these differences for personal and regional gains. Nigeria, however, became unstable, and caved in to military intervention in January 1966.

Chinua Achebe's imaginative writings have focused on the Nigerian road to nation building since his formative years as a student at the Government College, Umuahia, and the University College, Ibadan. The cosmopolitan nature of these two cities probably shaped Achebe's perspectives on the national question for the intermingling of cultures, which related to ethnic and religious conglomerations provided fundamental issues in his writings. His description of electoral campaigns, corruption, and government activities at the federal and regional levels, revealed an intimate grasp of their implications to nation building.[6]

There were three major political parties that dominated Achebe's discourses. They were: The National Council of Nigeria and the Cameroons (NCNC), led by Nnamdi Azikiwe; the Northern People's Congress (NPC), led by Ahmadu Bello, and the Action Group (AG), led by Obafemi Awolowo. The material conditions of these political elites determined the nature and directions of their administrations while in power. Politics for them, as events unfolded, was an avenue for personal enrichment and party patronage because many of these party members and active financiers had become the emerging petty bourgeoisie and represented foreign interests in the country. Consequently, legislative functions, party activities, and contract awards, stipulated certain percentage from government revenue to be reserved for such members. From these perspectives, corruption festered in Nigeria.[7]

Corruption was an anathema to Nigeria's growth to nationhood. Through systemic looting of the national wealth by the politicians, it "stigmatized the image of the government, weakened its credibility and reduced the effectiveness of the development programmes and policies which so far have been formulated."[8] Chinua Achebe's views on these malaises were propagated in the activities of major protagonists in his novels such as Obi Okonkwo, in *No Longer at Ease* (1994), Odili Samalu, Maxwell Kumalo, and others in *A Man of the People* (1988).

After his graduation from the University, Achebe joined the services of Radio Nigeria, Lagos, where he learned about the graft in the polity. Setting his narratives in these two novels, he adjudged the government as one which reveled in profligacy, and insensitive to democratic norms which included good governance. Achebe's reproach against graft exemplifies his craft in using imaginative literature to explore Nigeria's social history, using fictitious characters in place of political actors to comment or criticize the prevalent nature of corruption in the country.

Against this background, when Achebe raised his anger through the actions of Obi Okonkwo, the civil servant, Odili Samalu and Maxwell Kumalo, proponents of Marxist ideology in the polity, he saw in his characters, as emerging bureaucratic and political neophytes who were against the malaise festering the country and were poised to challenge them frontally but lacked the clout to resist them. Though their appearance to curtail corruption through exemplary leadership or personal commitment showed a new breed of leadership in the country, their rhetoric and actions could not overwhelm the status quo at the helm of Nigeria's affairs.

Obi Okonkwo, with his austere religious upbringing during his formative years in Umuofia his village, and university educational background in Britain, replicated a man as an anti-graft crusader in Nigeria on his return. While in Lagos, the capital city of Nigeria, he observed that almost every segment of society there was infested with corruption. In his thoughts to reclaim Nigeria from moral decadence, he exclaims thus: "What an Augean Stable!."[9] Corruption was something he thought Nigeria should cure in order to develop but the strategy to do so was elusive because the post-colonial government lacked the will to do so. Then Okonkwo asks himself:

> Where does one begin? With the masses? Educate the masses? Not a chance there it would take centuries. A handful of men at the top. Or even a man with a vision—an enlightened dictator. People are scared of the word nowadays. But what kind of democracy can exist side by side with so much corruption and ignorance.[10]

Obi Okonkwo represented a segment of the new breed of Nigerian citizens who were disturbed by the magnitude of corruption in the country. Nigeria's leaders in the First Republic promoted graft as a state policy and reward system. In such situations, both the political leaders and supporters were guilty of promoting it. According to D. A. Briggs and K. S. Bolanta:

> Politics in Africa . . . is sometimes hard to keep clean merely because people are moving from one set of values to another. In no other area of life is this better illustrated than in the whole issue of ethnic solidarity and kingship obligations. Pressures are exerted on an African official or politician to remind him of those who share his ultimate social womb. Parents from his area or from his clan enquire on how best the well-placed African politician, or even academic, might help his kinsmen to gain access to a job or to scholarship.[11]

In this despairing situation, Nigeria bled morally, economically, and socially. Many people holding privileged positions saw graft as a way of making breakthrough in life. Under such precarious situations, Obi Okonkwo, unable to contain insatiable desires, however, succumbed to corruption and became a victim of its unquantifiable proportion and was jailed. His anti-corruption crusade, however, ended in disaster.[12] Achebe, however, to a large extent, bemoaned Obi Okonkwo's fate as an active young man inclined to social renaissance but found himself on the wrong side of a story of moral rectitude but could not complete his campaign.

With the fall of Obi Okonkwo, Achebe elevated other characters in another novel mainly political neophytes to continue the campaign against graft. Composed of fresh graduates from the universities, they saw themselves as new Nigerians on a rescue mission. These young politicians notably Odili Samalu and Maxwell Kumalo, formed their own political party called the Common People's Convention (CPC) in order to challenge the status quo represented by Achebe's character, M. A. Nanga and his party, the People's Organization Party (POP) who had dominated party politics in the country.[13]

The CPC was a Marxist party of a sort, which in its study of post-colonial politics discovered the existence of two Nigerians: one represented by corrupt politicians of Nanga's hue, and two: represented by Samalu and his ilk, mainly traders, workers and peasants. The country was primed as the giant of Africa, with abundant wealth, but poverty was rife everywhere. In this state of affairs, Odili Samalu, on a visit to M. A. Nanga's house, to study the status of these two Nigerians was bewildered by the opulence he saw there. In his reminicenses during the visit, Odili Samalu said:

> The first thing critics tell you about our ministers' official residences is that each has seven bedrooms and seven bathrooms, one for every day of the week. All I can say is that on that first night there was no room in my mind for criticism. I

was simply hypnotized by the luxury of the great suite assigned to me. When I lay down in the double bed that seemed to ride on a cushion of air, and switched on that reading lamp and saw all the beautiful furniture anew from the lying position and looked beyond the door to the gleaming bathroom and the towels as large as *lappa* I had to confess that if I were at that moment made a minister I would be most anxious to remain one forever. And maybe I should have thanked God that I wasn't. We ignore man's basic nature if we say, as some critics do, that because a man like Nanga has risen overnight from poverty and insignificance to his present opulence he could be persuaded without much trouble to give it up again and return to his original state.[14]

Odili Samalu's stand, from the above perspectives, represents a new nation in a state of flux because post-colonial leaders reveled in affluence while the citizens wallowed in poverty. Odili's interactions with members of his political group after the Nanga visit, and interactions with other foreigners perturbed by these state of affairs, revealed the identities of many Nigerian politicians with questionable assets in the country. Many of them fronted for many multilateral institutions for commissions,[15] which prompted many Nigerian citizens to hear "of scandalous deals in high places-sometime involving sums of money" which they "didn't believe existed in the country"[16] in the first place. In this state of despair, the emergence of Odili's Common People's Convention (CPC), in Achebe's novel, *A Man of the People,* was ostensibly, an alternative route to grassroot mobilization and electoral victory for a radical change. The CPC, in this context, was akin to the Socialist Workers and Farmers Party (SWAFP), launched in post-colonial Nigeria by Tunji Otegbeye, Wahab Goodluck, S. U. Bassey, and others, to seek alternative routes to combat crass leadership.[17]

The confrontation between the Nigerian political elite, along political and ideological divides, provoked much consternation in the country during the 1964 General Elections. Achebe, in his imagination, implicitly drew the curtain for the fall of the First Republic with a military coup as a result of multifarious problems in the country. When his imagination drew him to such a treasonable act, prior to the actual January 1966 debacle, Achebe, to a large extent used the power of imagination to foretell a major event in the country.[18] However, on January 15, 1966, a coup took place, and its leader, Chukwuma Nzeogwu, in his broadcast, cast aspersions on graft, lampooning Nigerian post-colonial leaders as "our enemies . . . political profiters . . . the men in high and low places that seek bribes and demand 10 percent"[19] while Nigeria bled perpetually.

The power of imagination in actual historical events dominated much of Achebe's discourse in *A Man of People*. When published, Africa had witnessed unconstitutional acts towards regime change in Egypt and Guinea and gradually began to spread to other countries. Consequently, the fulcrum of Achebe's creativity particularly on the dictatorial tendencies of the First Republic leadership, compelled him to narrate about a country-wide celebration following the ousting of the government where M. A. Nanga had served as a Minister even before the actual military intervention occurred. In that novel, Achebe writes:

> Overnight everyone began to shake their heads at the excesses of the last regime, at its graft, oppression and corrupt government: newspapers, the radio, the hitherto silent intellectuals and civil servants—everybody said what a terrible lot; and it became public opinion the next morning and these were the same people that only the other day had owned a thousand names of adulation, whom praise-singers followed with song and talking-drum wherever they went.[20]

The importance of *A Man of the People* on Achebe's stand on national question is noteworthy. The aforementioned novel was launched in Lagos on January 14, 1966, amidst the political turmoil in the country. Achebe's friend, and ally in the literary circles, John Pepper Clark, who had read an advance copy of the novel, prior to the launching exclaimed: "Chinua, I *know* you are a prophet. Everything in this book has happened except a military coup."[21] On January 15, 1966, a day later, the first military coup swept away the First Republic. Many Nigerians, particularly from the South, jubilated after the coup while their Northern counterparts remained sullen as having lost prominent politicians and military personnel in the putsch. As John de St. Jorre, observes:

> The coup was greeted by a wild outburst of rejoicing in the southern half of the country ... in Lagos and other major Southern towns there were popular demonstrations expressing support for Ironsi's military government. The press, the most outspoken and ebullient in Africa, indulged itself in an orgy of invention and high spirits. One of the best headlines of all, in West African Pidgin English, ran: "Bribery is dead. Corruption is not there."[22]

Against this background, the Aguiyi-Ironsi military administration the successor to the ousted regime, instituted many enquiries aimed at the recovery of stolen properties. Startling revelations on the activities of some politicians, civil servants and bureaucrats during the First Republic were revealed from their reports. In assessing the reports, Mokwugo Okoye writes:

> Several ministers raised magnificent private palaces and industrial complexes rivaling those in Europe; one of them, C. D. Akran (subsequently jailed by the military regime) had £125,000 in raw cash when the Army searched his house on January 30, 1966 and a bank account of £2.6million as was revealed during a

court case in 1967, while Dr. K. O. Mbadiwe erected a "People's Palace" complete with swimming—pool and all the latest in luxury furniture at an estimated cost of £ 750,000. One Regional Premier, Chief D. C. Osadebay, netted over £92,000 in his bank account after 30 months in office in addition to £101,000 in real estate properties; and several official investigations revealed a similar state of affairs in many walks of life, including the public corporations and the civil service, so that minor clerks on £400 a year were able to show saving accounts of up to £6,000 in less than six years, one £1,800 a year corporation official saved £42,000 in six years; one ex-minister was found guilty in court in receiving a bribe of £7,500 and a car from one contractor, and many good-time girls and contact-men were able to amass assets worth tens of thousands of pounds in the first five years of independence.[23]

From the above revelations, one can appreciate Chinua Achebe's description of graft in Nigeria, as "an Augean Stable"[24] because in Greek mythology, Hercules was instructed to clean the stable of Augeas, King of Elis, with a herd of three thousand oxen, for the stalls remained unclean for thirty years. With remarkable efforts involving the extraordinary use of Rivers Alpheus and Peneus, Hercules cleaned that stable in one day, and brought an end to its stench.[25] Consequently, in the Nigerian context, corruption was an Augean Stable. Attempts to stamp it out in Nigeria, from the military regimes of Murtala Muhammad and Muhammadu Buhari had failed because corruption remained defiant. Under President Olusegun Obasanjo's administration (1999–2007), he set up two anti-corruption agencies, namely, the Independent Corrupt Practices and Other Related Offences Commission (ICPC) in 2000, and the Economic and Financial Crimes Commission (EFCC), in 2002,[26] to handle the menace, but corruption had "grown bold and ravenous," in Achebe's views ever since.[27] Through President Shehu Shagari's regime in the Second Republic (1979–1983), when the country plunged into recession as a result of the plundering of the economy by the political class, Achebe remained defiant in his campaign, stressing among others, that the festering sore of corruption, was attributed to failures of Nigerian leadership.[28] From these perspectives, Achebe's fictional works have driven home to their importance to political, social and historical discourses in post-colonial Nigeria.

CHINUA ACHEBE AND POLITICAL EVENTS IN NIGERIA

Chinua Achebe's perspectives on the national question in this section will address three major political events in Nigeria. First, his views on the First Republic particularly on two major events: the 1962 proposal by the Federal Government (for a National Government and the Preventive Detention Act.

Secondly, the 1964 General Election crises. Thirdly, the 2003 Constitutional Crisis in Anambra State on the attempted removal from office of Governor Chris Ngige.

The above related events, which spanned several years from each other, caught Achebe's attention in his literary discourses. The Federal and Regional governments opposed each other on fundamental state policies which undermined the parliamentary democracy inherited from the British during the First Republic. Their clashes brought much tension in the country. They further encouraged debates among scholars, publicists, journalists, trade unionists, and others, who addressed the crises in order to sustain the fledgling democracy. These events coincided with the rise of Chinua Achebe as a novelist. In retrospect, Achebe writes that:

> It is clear to me that an African creative writer who tries to avoid the big social and political issues of contemporary Africa will end up being completely irrelevant—like that absurd man in the proverb who leaves his burning house to pursue a rat fleeing from the flames. If an artist is anything he is a human being with heightened sensivities; he must beware of the faintest nuances of injustice in human relations. The African writer cannot therefore be unaware of, or indifferent to, the monumental injustice which his people suffer.[29]

When independence was won, the Parliamentary system of government bequeathed by the departing British came under severe strain. Two major political parties, the Northern People's Congress (NPC), and the National Convention of Nigerian Citizens (NCNC), formed an alliance and controlled the Federal Government. The opposition party, the Action Group (AG), was led by Obafemi Awolowo. Awolowo's astute political action at the Federal Parliament, though quite constitutional, caused the infraction between him and the Federal Government. Prime Minister Abubakar Tafawa Balewa, in an attempt to curtail the opposition, proposed to abolish it and install a national government. Further, the same prime minister had proposed the enactment of a Preventive Detention Act, in order to stifle human rights in the country as further proof of his penchant to dictatorship.[30]

In a forum, Prime Minister Balewa defended his position on the proposed Preventive Detention Act thus:

> I should mention a very controversial matter which was discussed at the all-party conference, also at the meeting of the prime minister and premiers at Jos, that is the question of what people call a preventive detention act. As far back as 1957, I thought—and I said it at the time—that the Nigerian constitution was too rigid. It did not give the government the opportunity to deal with very difficult situations, short of declaring an emergency. We cannot deal with groups of individuals who engage in subversion. We cannot stop and we cannot

forestall people who are planning evil. That was why . . . we should find some means by which the government should be empowered, through this parliament, to curtail the liberty of a Nigerian citizen. We cannot hold anybody for more than twenty-four hours—that is the criminal code. We are well aware that people are being trained for subversion abroad. Should we allow a small group of people to disturb the peace? The sad thing about the whole issue is that it is not Nigerian brains, it is outside brains which are organizing all these things in this country, that is the sad thing about it. Nigerians who are traitors to their country, and Nigerians with ambition who want to disturb the peace of their country, must be severely dealt with.[31]

Nigeria being a country with multiplicity of political views, ideologies, and platforms must be respected despite divergent opinions of others, many analysts stated. There was much apprehension in Nigeria in the First Republic, in the proposed Bill by the Prime Minister because it was a recourse to dictatorship. Thus, it provoked a country-wide opposition and demonstration to it.[32] In Achebe's world, such opposition was demonstrated by his protagonist, Odili Samalu, a graduate from a Nigerian University, who had observed these political shenanigans, and joined politics to bring fresh ideas into the polity.

Odili Samalu berated Nigerian post-colonial leaders as mediocre, whom he called "hardly ever the best," for their divisive politics, party patronage and corruption.[33] For instance, M. A. Nanga the protagonist in Achebe's novel and the Minister of Culture, had, before venturing into politics, being a mere primary school teacher barely affording his daily needs. His foray into politics, and astronomical rise in his party hierarchy opened doors for him for property acquisition and insatiable desire for cars and women. In their euphoria to dominate in the affairs of the state, Nigerian politicians, the likes of M. A. Nanga, called on all citizens, despite their harsh policies which had instilled austerity and hunger, to speak "with one voice"—that is, to reject opposition in parliamentary democracy, clamoring that "any more dissent and argument would subvert and bring down the whole house"[34] that is Nigeria. Their clarion call was buffeted by developments in the polity.

In 1964, Nigeria was set for the first post-colonial general elections. There was realignment of political parties between the NPC, NCNC, and AG. From such political groups, two were hurriedly created namely: the Nigerian National Alliance (NNA), and the United Progressive Grand Alliance (UPGA). By this time, Chinua Achebe was the Director of External Service of Radio Nigeria, Lagos, from where he witnessed these unconstitutional acts prior to the election. The 1964 General Election, when it took place under such a political arrangement was dominated by electoral malpractices, intimidation of voters and violence. At first, the UPGA called for a boycott which the NNA rejected. At the end, the NNA won. When UPGA contested their opponent's victory, the nation degenerated into electoral violence.[35]

Chinua Achebe captured these political developments in his novel, *A Man of the People.* M. A. Nanga, desperately craving for power in that dispensation, attacked his political opponents, Odili Samalu and Max Kumalo, with political thugs. Nanga's political grouping called Nanga Youth Vanguard or Nangavanga, for short, confronted his opponents with dangerous weapons at campaigns and election days and had them defeated. At the end of this electoral farce, according to Achebe:

> The Prime Minister . . . appointed Chief Nanga and the rest of the old Cabinet back to office and announced over the radio he intended to govern and stamp out subversion and thuggery without quarter or mercy. He assured foreign investors that their money was safe in the country, that his government stood "as firm as the rock of Gibraltar" by its open-door economic policy. "This country," he said, "has never been more united or more stable than it is today."[36]

Many years after this event, Achebe, once again, tackled an overt display of naked power, by the federal government, under President Olusegun Obasanjo's regime in 2003. In Anambra State, the governor, Chris Ngige, was harassed by the police, and bungled out of office on the pretext that he had resigned. However, the true state of affairs, was that the said governor had had a running battle with his political mentor, Chris Uba, on the composition of the State Executive Council which was skewed in favour of his godfather. When the Governor refused to rubberstamp this proposed cabinet, his travails with the police began. This crisis between Governor Ngige and Chris Uba raised the political barometer high in the country and questioned the ability of the federal government under President Obasanjo to handle a treasonable act by a political gladiator such as Chris Uba. Consequently, the crisis was seen as another "coup" orchestrated under another democratic system.[37]

In 2004, during the announcement of that year's honors' list by the Federal Government, Chinua Achebe was conferred with the award of the Commander of the Federal Republic (CFR) which he rejected on account of the attempted removal of Governor Ngige from office.[38] In a letter to President Obasanjo rejecting the award, Achebe writes:

> I write this letter with a very heavy heart. For some time now, I have watched events in Nigeria with alarm and dismay. I have watched particularly the chaos in my own state of Anambra where a small clique of renegades openly boasting its connections in high places, seems determined to turn my homeland into a bankrupt and lawless fiefdom.[39]

Against this background, Achebe's perspectives on Nigerian democracy demonstrated a writer with acute sense of history and political commitment. From his novel, *A Man of the People*, press statements and letters, Achebe demonstrates the importance of fictional works to historical narratives.

CHINUA ACHEBE'S "ENLIGHTENED DICTATOR" AND THE NATIONAL QUESTION

Chinua Achebe's thoughts on the national question focused mainly on the search for a meaningful and desirable leadership for Nigeria. He had discovered, much to his chagrin, that an alternative to the crass and corrupt leadership in Nigeria shortly after independence was the enthronement of what he calls an "enlightened dictator."[40] Though not clearly defined by the author in character and disposition, it was, however, a desideratum made to curb the social, political and economic malaise momentarily.

Obi Okonkwo, Achebe's protagonist in the novel, *No Longer at Ease* reflects the author's thoughts on the nature of this "enlightened dictator." Okonkwo had returned to Nigeria after his studies in the United Kingdom and discovered that Nigeria was in a flux due to rampant corruption.

In his thoughts on these ugly spectacles, Obi Okonkwo's lamentations run thus: "What an Augean Stable!" In furtherance to its elimination, Obi Okonkwo asks himself:

> Where does one begin? With the masses? Educate the masses? Not a chance there. It would take centuries. A handful of men at the top or even one man with vision—an enlightened dictator. People are scared of the word nowadays. But what kind of democracy can exist side by side with so much corruption and ignorance?[41]

The above comments represent Chinua Achebe's thoughts on matters of national importance. By advocating for an "enlightened dictator," in the polity, these thoughts exemplified that corruption had weighed heavily in his mind and he expressed his desires for a change in leadership at the end of *A Man of the People*. On January 15, 1966, a military coup took place in Nigeria, which replaced the political elites of the First Republic. However, this "enlightened dictator" in Achebe's parlance became a full-blown dictator later in the country with no scruples to human rights and clear-cut vision to governance. Nigeria, thereafter, wallowed from one military regime to the other, and had, in recent years, had a hangover of their retired personnel who had recycled themselves to retain power under new democratic dispensations. From the multiplicity of military turned politician syndrome, it appears that in Achebe's thinking, that the trajectory of Nigerian leadership could be resolved in a whiff of a gunshot had failed. Ostensibly alarmed by military atrocities over the years, Achebe changed his mind on the desirability of an "enlightened dictator" as an alternative for a sustained campaign against them in the country. In another novel, entitled *Anthills of the Savannah* (1988), Achebe catalogued these military atrocities by using Sam, his fictitious military leader, as a composite of various Nigeria's military dictators, whom he describes as "medieval monarchs"[42] towards ostentatious display of power in the country much to the detriment of the populace.

Under this dispensation Achebe observes, the military in Nigerian politics had failed to provide credible leadership. After many years in power, Nigeria had remained poor under their watch and corruption had remained unabated. When Achebe captures Sam's profile in that novel, he examines the culture of their self-induced solidarity visits by paid agents who thronged to the seat of power to ask them to transmute from military dictatorship to civilian leadership just for the allure of power.[43] Achebe further demonstrates cases of human rights violations in Nigeria such as harassment of defenseless civilians, incarceration and killing of students and journalists, banning of media houses, among others.[44] In this scenario, Achebe's laments thus:

> The prime failure of this government began also to take a clearer meaning [on Nigerians]. It can't be the massive corruption though its scale and pervasiveness are truly intolerable; it isn't the subservience to foreign manipulation, degrading as it is, it isn't even the second-class, hand-me-down capitalism, ludicrous and doomed; nor is it the damnable shooting of railway-workers and demonstrating students and the destruction and banning thereafter of independent unions and cooperatives. It is the failure of our rulers to re-establish vital inner links with the poor and dispossessed of this country, with the bruised heart that throbs painfully at the core of the nation's being.[45]

From the above perspectives, the military in a nutshell, had left the nation in severe crises. When the civil war was fought between 1967 and 1970, the citizens of Biafra at war with the rest of the federation were nearly annihilated in a Federal Military Government (FMG) policy of "One Nigeria." The Igbo were starved by the Federal Government and also strafed by their invading armed forces and forced to unnecessary flight when their towns and villages crumbled by their advance. In his war memoirs entitled, *There Was a Country: A Personal History of Biafra* (2012), Chinua Achebe accused the Yakubu Gowon-led Federal Government of genocidal acts against the Igbo. His reasons being that:

> At the end of the thirty-month war Biafra was a vast smoldering rubble. The head count at the war was perhaps three million dead, which was approximately

20 percent of the entire population. This high proportion was mostly children. The cost in human lives made it one of the bloodiest civil wars in human history.[46]

The above analysis on Achebe's "enlightened dictator," is quite significant for revealing his thoughts on periods of emergency in the country. By trying to seek an alternative route to Nigeria's fledgling democracy, he opted for a variant, though unconstitutional in practice which he presumed would resolve the lingering crises in the nation. Achebe's "enlightened dictator" transformed to full-blown dictatorship and plunged the country to deepening crises ever since then. From the fulcrums of messiah ship in the Nigerian political spectrum, the military lost its bearing and became a major discourse in the national question. Chinua Achebe's *Anthills of the Savannah* and *There Was a Country: A Personal History of Biafra* were pointers to the debate.

CONCLUSION

This essay has interrogated Chinua Achebe's views on the national question. As a Nigerian scholar, his position on the devolution of power, good governance, social engineering, among others, had dominated much of his literary output. From different epochs in Nigerian history, his opinion on the national question had remained germane to the present realities.

From his foray into public service, which spanned several years and until his death, Chinua Achebe would be remembered for being a fearless crusader for equity and good governance in Nigeria. Through his imaginative thoughts, he created many characters in his works to replicate real situations in the country. From this perspective, Achebe's contributions to the relationship between fact and fiction in Nigerian historical narratives had accorded him a notable place in Nigerian social and political history.

NOTES

1. For details, see Karl Maier, *This House has Fallen: Nigeria in Crisis,* (London: Penguin Books, 2000); Agwuncha Arthur Nwankwo, *Terminus: Power, Hegemony and End game Doctrine*, (Enugu: Fourth Dimension Publishing Company, 1998); Tekena N. Tamuno, *Stakeholders at War in Nigeria: From Lord Lugard to President Goodluck Jonathan, Volumes 1 and 2,* (Ibadan: Stirling-Horden Publishers, 2012); Joseph Nanven Garba, *Fractured History: Elite Shifts and Policy Changes in Nigeria* (Princeton: A Sungai Book, 1995); Chinua Achebe, *The Trouble with Nigeria* (Enugu: Fourth Dimension Publishers, 1983); Billy Dudley, *An Introduction to Nigerian Government and Politics;* (London: The Macmillan Press, 1982); Larry Diamond, A.

Kirk-Greene, Oyeleye Oyediran (eds), *Transition without End: Nigerian Politics and Civil Society under Babangida* (Ibadan: Vantage Publishers, 1997).

2. See Achebe, *The Trouble with Nigeria*, 1–3; Chinua Achebe, *The Education of a British Protected Child: Essays* (New York: Alfred K. Knopf, 2009), 138–149.

3. Maier, *This House Has Fallen*, xviii.

4. See Michael Crowder, *The Story of Nigeria* (London: Faber and Faber, 1978), 188–258; Kole Omotoso, *Just Before Dawn* (Ibadan: Spectrum, 1988), 114–150; Yusufu Bala Usman and George Amale Kwanashie, (eds) *Inside Nigerian History, 1950–1970: Events, Issues and Sources* (Ibadan: The Presidential Panel on Nigeria Since Independence History Project, 1995), 20–25.

5. Chinua Achebe, *Hopes and Impediments: Selected Essays* (New York: Anchor Books, 1990), 139, 146–147.

6. See Ezenwa-Ohaeto, *Chinua Achebe: A Biography,* (Ibadan: Heineman, 1999), 21–50; Chinua Achebe, *A Man of the People,* (London: Heinemann, 1988), 17–74.

7. For details of these developments, see Achebe, *The Trouble with Nigeria*, 11–13; Segun Osoba, "The Nigerian Power Elite, 1952–65," in *African Social Studies: A Radical Reader;* (eds), Peter C. W. Gutkind and Peter Waterman, (London: Heinemann, 1981), 368–382; James Booth, *Writers and Politics in Nigeria,* (London: Hodder and Stoughton, 1981), 49–50; D. A. Briggs and K. S., Bolanta, "The Issue of Corruption," in *The Politics of the Second Republic* (ed) T. A. Imobighe (Kuru: National Institute For Policy and Strategic Studies, 1992), 567–614.

8. Briggs and Bolanta, "The Issue of Corruption," 568.

9. Achebe, *A Man of the People*, 50.

10. Ibid.

11. Briggs and Bolanta, "The Issue of Corruption," 569.

12. See Chinua Achebe, *No Longer at Ease* (New York: Anchor Books, 1994), 97–194.

13. Ibid., 3–72.

14. Ibid., 36–37.

15. Ibid., 99–100.

16. Ibid., 39.

17. For details, see Tunji Otegbeye, *The Turbulent Decade* (Apapa: The Times Press, 1999), 168–244.

18. See Achebe, *A Man of the People*, 148.

19. Cited in S. K. Panter-Brick (ed) *Nigerian Politics and Military Rule: Prelude to the Civil War* (London: University of London Press, 1971), 185.

20. See Achebe, *A Man of the People*, 148.

21. Ohaeto, *Chinua Achebe*, 109. The italicized word is in the original.

22. See John de St. Jorre, *The Nigerian Civil War* (London: Hodder and Stoughton, 1979), 42.

23. Mokwugo Okoye, *The Growth of Nations* (Enugu: Fourth Dimension Publishers, 1978), 56.

24. See Achebe, *No Longer at Ease*, 50.

25. For details, see Thomas Bulfinch, *The Age of Fable or the Stories of Gods and Heroes* (New York: Thomas Y. Cromwell Company Publishers, 1913), 144–150.

26. For details, see Bernard Steiner Ifekwe, "The Press on President Olusegun Obasanjo's War on Corruption in Nigeria's Fourth Republic, 1999–2007: A Historical Analysis," in *The Fourth Republic in Nigeria: Politics, Elections and Civil Society*, (eds), Terhemba Wuam, Boumo Ezonbi, and Changwak Emmanuel Jonah, (London: Bahite and Dalila Publishers, 2017), 27–39; Bernard Steiner Ifekwe, "Systemic Leadership Failures in Fostering Corruption and Human Rights Violations in Nigeria, 1999–2007: A Historical Analysis," *Kaduna Journal of Historical Studies, Volume 9, Number, 2017*, A Publication of the Department of History, Kaduna State University, Kaduna, Nigeria.

27. See Achebe, *The Trouble with Nigeria*, 42.

28. See Chinua Achebe, "The Duty and Involvement of the African Writer," in *The African Reader: Independent Africa*, (eds) Wilfred Cartey and Martin Kilson, (New York: Vintage Books, 1970), 162–163.

29. For details of these proposals, see Wogu Ananaba, *The Trade Union Movement in Nigeria* (Benin City: Ethiope Publishing Corporation, 1969), 232–236.

30. Cited in Trevor Clark, *A Right Honourable Gentleman: The Life and Times of Alhaji Sir Abubakar Tafawa Balewa*, (Zaria: Hudahuda Publishing Company, 1991), 600.

31. Cited in Trevor Clark, *A Right Honourable Gentleman: The Life and Times of Athaji Sir Abubakar Tafawa Balewa*, (Zaria: Hudahuda Publishing Company, 1991), 600.

32. See A. A. Amakiri, *The Left in Nigerian Politics*, (Lagos: Amkra Books, 1997), 41–64; Obafemi Awolowo, *Adventures in Power Book One: My March Through Prison*, (Lagos: Macmillan Nigeria Publishers, 1985), 126; Obafemi Awolowo, *Adventures in Power, Book Two: The Travails of Democracy and the Rule of Law*, (Ibadan: Evans Brothers, 1987), 53–83.

33. Achebe, *A Man of the People*, 37.

34. Ibid.

35. Ohaeto, *Chinua Achebe*, 104.

36. See Achebe, *A Man of the People*, 143.

37. For details, see Adegbenro Adebanjo, "A Godfather's Red Card," *Tell*, Lagos, July 21, 2003, 19–23.

38. See Bamidele Johnson, "No Longer at Ease," *The News*, Volume 23, no. 17, Lagos, November 1, 2004, 14–18.

39. Ibid., 16.

40. See Achebe, *No Longer at Ease*, 50.

41. Ibid.

42. Chinua Achebe, *Anthills of the Savannah*, (London: Heinemann, 1988), 74.

43. Ibid., 126–128.

44. Ibid., 13–97; 173–223.

45. Ibid., 141.

46. See Chinua Achebe, *There Was A Country: A Personal History of Biafra*, (London: Penguin Books, 2012), 257.

Index

Abuja, 263
Achebeism, 11, 49, 51, 253, 258, 264
Adesanmi, Pius, 277
Adichie, Chimamanda Ngozi, 233
Afigbo, Adiele, E., 97
Africa Leadership Institute, 269
African cosmology, 64
African culture, 2–4, 7, 11, 37–38, 57–58, 69, 141, 201, 230–231, 235, 247
African diaspora, 45, 115, 209–210, 234
African nationalists, 9, 134, 140–141
African Philosophy, 63, 74.
African Traditional Religion, 9, 24, 141
Agbala, 39–40, 61, 63, 65, 67, 79, 101
Ahiajoku, 59, 62, 179, 207–208
Ahiara Declaration, 173–174
ana/ala, 26, 61, 119, 137, 145–146, 190, 186
Arochukwu, 33, 134. 138–139, 142, 171
Awolowo, Obafemi, Chief, 258, 290–291, 297
Azia, 144, 145
Azikiwe, Nnamdi, 258, 290–291, 267
Azodo, Ada Uzoamaka, 258

Basden, G. T., 123
Bello, Ahmadu, 290–291
Bello-Kano, Ibrahim, 256, 258

Booker, Keith, 38
Booth, James, 258
Brown, Michelle, 209

capitalism, 234, 258, 264, 301
Caruth, Cathy, 209
Cary, Joyce, 57, 181–182, 185–186, 227, 247
Cesaire, Aime, 58
chi, 9, 26–34, 65–66, 109, 132, 139–122
Chineke, 26–28, 139, 145, 149–150, 177, 204
Christian apologists, 140, 146
Christianity, 9, 65, 126, 135, 141, 156, 158–159, 163–164, 166–167, 171, 175–176, 184, 186, 191–192, 205, 212, 217, 228, 245–246, 271
Clarke, J. H., 159, 161–162, 215
colonial apologists, 186
colonialism, 2–3, 5, 7, 58, 92, 126, 154–155, 159, 162–164, 168–170, 172–176, 178–179, 181, 186–187, 200–201, 211, 228, 231, 234, 245, 260, 266
colonization, 10, 116 153, 156, 158, 164, 169, 175–176, 184–185, 191, 199–200, 227–228, 257, 285
Conrad, Joseph, 3, 57, 181, 186, 199, 227

corruption, 12, 173, 233–234, 253, 255, 257, 260–264, 276–277, 279, 281–282–285, 289, 291–293, 294, 296, 300–301
cosmogonic narration, 7, 37, 39, 40, 52
Culler, Jonathan, 60

Damas, Leon-Gontran, 58
decolonization, 169, 227
Derrida, Jacques, 209
Diop, David, 58

Echeruo, Michael, J.C., 61, 64, 212–213, 252
École normale d'administration, 264

Economic and Financial Crimes Commission, 296
ethnicity, 5, 11, 274, 289
ethnocentrism, 2, 275–276
ethno-text, 7, 37, 39, 44, 45, 50, 52
Eurocentric, 3, 40, 57–58, 165, 171, 247, 272
Eurocentrism, 58
Eyong, Charles Takoyoh, 111

Feinstein, Alan, 259
folklore, 5, 38, 43–44, 48–51, 142, 144
Foucault, Michael, 226–227, 233

Gandhi, Mahatma, 261-2
Ghana, 37, 41, 258
Ghanaian people, 39
Gikandi, Simon, 2–3, 50, 206, 210, 230
Gorjestani, Nicolas, 112
Government College, Umuahia, 168, 271, 291

Harambee, 258
Hardy, Thomas, 179–180, 195, 198
Hoppers, Odora, 113, 118, 126
Hume, David, 21–22, 227

Ibadan, *See* University College and University of Ibadan, 271

Ibelema, Minabere, 284
ideology, 4, 10, 38, 40, 76–77, 116, 179, 181–184, 186, 188, 192, 195, 198, 200–201, 213, 226, 235, 249, 257–258, 261, 292
Igbo cosmology, 9, 24, 33, 83, 96–97, 106, 118, 133–137, 141
Igwe, Agbafor, 258
Ikenga, 24–27, 97–98, 104, 107, 203
Ikhide Ikheloa, 234
Imhonopi, David, 263
imperialism, 6, 10, 58, 155, 161, 176, 181, 184, 186, 194
Independent Corrupt Practices and Other Related Offences Commission, 302
indigenous knowledge, 8–9, 111–113, 116, 118, 126, 157, 162–163, 171, 176
Institute of Management, Leadership and Productivity Development, 263
Izevbaye, Dan, 93

Jeffreys, M.D.W., 97
Jos, 267, 297

Kalu, Anthonia, 120–121
Kano, Aminu, Mallam 255, 258–259, 261–262
Kant, Immanuel, 23, 227
Kerr, James, 92
Killam, G. D., 5, 37–38, 206
King, V.E., 57
Korieh, Chima, J., 123
Kwasi Wiredu, 140

Lacan, Carl, 209
leadership, 8, 10–11, 43–44, 76, 85–86, 93, 96, 102, 104–105, 112–115, 119, 172, 177–179, 182, 189, 259–266, 268–270, 282–285, 287–288, 290, 295–296, 298, 300–302, 306–307
Leonard, Major A.G., 95
Levy-Bruhl, Lucien, 31
London, 169, 233, 263

Luckhurst, Roger, 209

magical realism, 7, 41, 52
Mahfuz, Najib, 273
Mahjub, Muhammad Ahmad, 273
Mahmud, Sakah S., 262
Mandela, Nelson, 263
Mbembe, Achille 230
Mbiti, John, 140
Mboya, Thomas, 258
McLaren, Joseph 73–74
mediocrity, 259–260, 279
memory, 9, 50, 85, 198, 205, 207, 209–211, 213, 215, 217, 226
meritocracy, 259
monotheism, 9, 134, 147–148, 180
Morrison, Toni, 210, 232
Muller, Max, 94
Mutiso, G. C., 91

Negritude, 58, 200, 227, 232
nepotism, 12, 253–254, 256, 260, 284, 289
Ngugi wa 'Thiong'o, 1, 37, 58, 231
Nigeria Leadership Institute, 263
Nigeria-Biafra War, 173–174, 176, 253, 260, 272, 276, 279, 283–284
Nigerian Broadcasting Corporation, 169
Njoku, F.O.C., 74
Nkrumah, Kwame, 258
Nkrumaism, 258
Nwafor-Orizu, Abbysinia, 278
Nwankwo, Arthur, 273
Nwaubani, Adaobi Tricia, 233
Nwoga, Donatus, I., 60, 62–63, 134, 137–139, 143, 206, 208, 245, 250
Nyerere, Julius, 258

Obo, Ugumanim Bassey, 273
Ochonu, Moses, E., 282
Ogidi, 134–135, 146, 165, 170, 271
oha, 8, 26, 74–87
Ojaide, Tanure, 57, 126
Oji, Jasper, 278
Okafor, Clement, 1–2, 12

Okot p'Bitek, 134
okpala, 5, 96
Okpala, Jude, 6
Onwuanibe, Richard C., 60
oracle, 27, 39–40, 62–63, 65, 102, 138–139, 195, 212
Osei-Nyame, Kwadwo, 120
Osuagwu, Chidi 76
Ottenberg, Simon, 98–99, 138
Ozo, 96, 158, 166–167, 228–229

Parrinder, Geoffrey, 141
patriarchal, 61–63, 79, 121, 156, 163–164, 228
patriot, 262, 272–274, 278–279, 281
patriotism, 258, 262–263, 278–279
Priestess 39–40, 61, 63, 65, 101, 195

Radcliffe Brown, A. R., 95
revolution, 48, 187, 189, 259, 273
Rivonia Trial, 263
Rothberg, Michael, 209

Said, Edward, 226
Sawant, Datta, 4
Senghor, L. S., 58, 141
socialism, 258.
South Africa, 263
Soyinka, Wole, 37, 58, 135, 152
Stock, A, G., 6
symbols 7, 57, 60–61, 63–64, 67, 69–70, 245

Tanzania, 141, 258
The Aspen Institute, 263
totems 7, 61, 67
trauma, 9, 82, 211, 213–223
tribalism, 255, 259, 274

Ubuntu, 262
Ujamaa, 258
Umuahia, *See* Government College, 168, 271, 291
Unhu, *See* Philosophy, 262

University College, Ibadan, 169, 271, 291
University of Ibadan, 271, 309

voluntarism, 258

wa Thiongo, Ngugi, 1, 37, 58, 60, 231
Walsh, William, 93

Welfarism, 258
White, Hayden, 11, 243
Wolfensohn, James D., 126

Youth Service Corps, 262

Zikist Movement, 261
Zimbabwe, 141, 262

About the Contributors

Ifi Amadiume is a tenured full professor at Dartmouth College, where she has taught both in the Department of Religion and the African and African American Studies Program. She is also a writer and an award-winning poet of many books. Professor Amadiume is the author of several books and articles, including the influential *Male Daughters, Female Husbands* (1988) that won the Choice Outstanding Academic Book of the Year award in 1989.

Ada Uzoamaka Azodo, educator, literary and cultural critic, scholar, feminist theorist (Di-feminism), recipient of the Marquis Who's Who V.I.P. Albert Nelson Marquis Lifetime Achievement Award, teaches African, African American and African Diaspora Studies, and is currently affiliated with the College of Arts and Sciences, Indiana University Northwest, USA.

Chijioke Azuawusiefe is a lecturer in the Department of Communication Studies at the Catholic Institute of West Africa, Port Harcourt, Nigeria. He earned his PhD from the University of Pennsylvania, Philadelphia. His research focuses on the interplay of media, religion, and culture in local and transnational contexts, especially of Africa and African Diaspora, with emphasis on Nollywood, the cinema of Nigeria. He has published articles in peer-reviewed scholarly journals like *Cross Currents* and *Igbo Studies Review*.

Anwesha Das, PhD, is a critical writer interested in interdisciplinary research with focus on postcolonial and neocolonial issues, history and literature of Africa and Africa-India interrelated concerns. Her doctoral dissertation focuses on recent developments in postcolonial theory. She explored the concept of "postcolonial soliloquies" and addressed the politics of cross-cultural encounters in reading the West African novelist Thomas Obinkaram Echewa. Presently, she is working on political theory with focus on Fred Dallmayr and Hans Koechler. She has published articles in international journals of repute, such as *Research in African Literatures, Igbo Studies Review*, and so on. She is a member of African Studies Association, Igbo Studies Association and MELUS/MELOW.

Alassane Abdoulaye Dia, PhD, is a Senegalese scholar. He is assistant professor of English at the Université Virtuelle du Senegal. He is the author of a range of research articles on African and African American literatures. He is also the author of *The Voice of the Tradition in the African Novel: Chinua Achebe's Artistic Use of Orature in Things Fall Apart and Anthills of the Savannah*, a literary criticism on Achebe's works.

Nureni Oyewole Fadare, PhD, teaches aspects of African literature in English in the Department of English Language and Linguistics, Sokoto State University, Sokoto. His areas of interest are, postcolonial literature, migrancy, gender discourse, ecocriticism and literary theory. His articles have appeared in some Nigerian and international journals.

Bernard Steiner Ifekwe, PhD, graduated from the Department of History, University of Calabar, Nigeria, specializing in social and political history. He is a senior lecturer in history, University of Uyo, Nigeria. His contributions on African labor history; Jamaican cultural history; the careers of Bob Marley, Peter Tosh, and Malcolm X; and Rastafarianism have been widely acclaimed.

Chima J. Korieh is director of the Africana Studies program at Marquette University. Dr. Korieh's research and teaching focuses on social and economic change in colonial Africa. His most recent book is *Nigeria and World War: Empire, Colonialism and Global Conflict* (2020).

Ihechukwu Madubuike is the director of the Igbo Renaissance Center at Gregory University, Uturu.

Linda Jummai Mustafa is a PhD candidate at the University of Ilorin. She teaches English and literature-in-English at Ibrahim Babangida Badamasi University Lapai, Niger State. A teacher, journalist, novelist, poet and designer, Mustafa has served in other public functions. She rose to be the acting director of the School of Preliminary Studies, IBB University, New-Bussa campus. her interests are in gender studies, commonwealth literature and contemporary African writing.

N. Tony Nwaezeigwe, is a senior research fellow at Institute of African Studies, University of Nigeria, Nsukka, Nigeria.

Ijeoma C. Nwajiaku, PhD, obtained a doctoral degree from the University of Ibadan, Nigeria. Her scholarly research interests span the fields of African literature, diaspora studies, contemporary Nigerian female fiction and gender studies. She teaches English and African literature in the Languages Department of Federal Polytechnic, Oko, Nigeria. She is also a member of the editorial board of a number of academic journals including the *Igbo Studies Review* (ISR) USA; *Mbari*, USA; *Nigerian Studies Review*; *International Journal of General Research and Development* (IJOGERD); and the *International Journal of the Arts and Sciences* (IJOTAS).

Boniface Enyeribe Nwigwe is a lecturer in the Department of Philosophy, University of Port Harcourt, Nigeria. His areas of specialization are philosophy, sociology and comparative linguistics, history and philosophy of science, epistemology environmental ethics, metaphysics contemporary philosophy, and philosophy of language. His publications include *Temporal Logic, Omniscience, and Human Freedom: Perspectives in Analytic Philosophy* (1991) and *Naming and Being: A Philosophical Investigation on Names and Objects with Special Reference to Igbo Anthroponyms* (2001).

Odigwe A. Nwaokocha, PhD, is senior lecturer at the Department of History and International Studies, University of Benin, Nigeria. He earned his doctorate degree in history from the University of Ibadan, Nigeria, researches on the history of modern Nigeria and is particularly interested in how ethno-regional tensions have shaped modern Nigerian history. He has articles in numerous learned journals as well as chapters in books. He was the secretary-general of the Historical Society of Nigeria from 2014 to 2018.

www.ingramcontent.com/pod-product-compliance
Lightning Source LLC
Chambersburg PA
CBHW021346300426
44114CB00012B/1097